Love me for who I am

01

VOLUME
ONE

CONTENTS

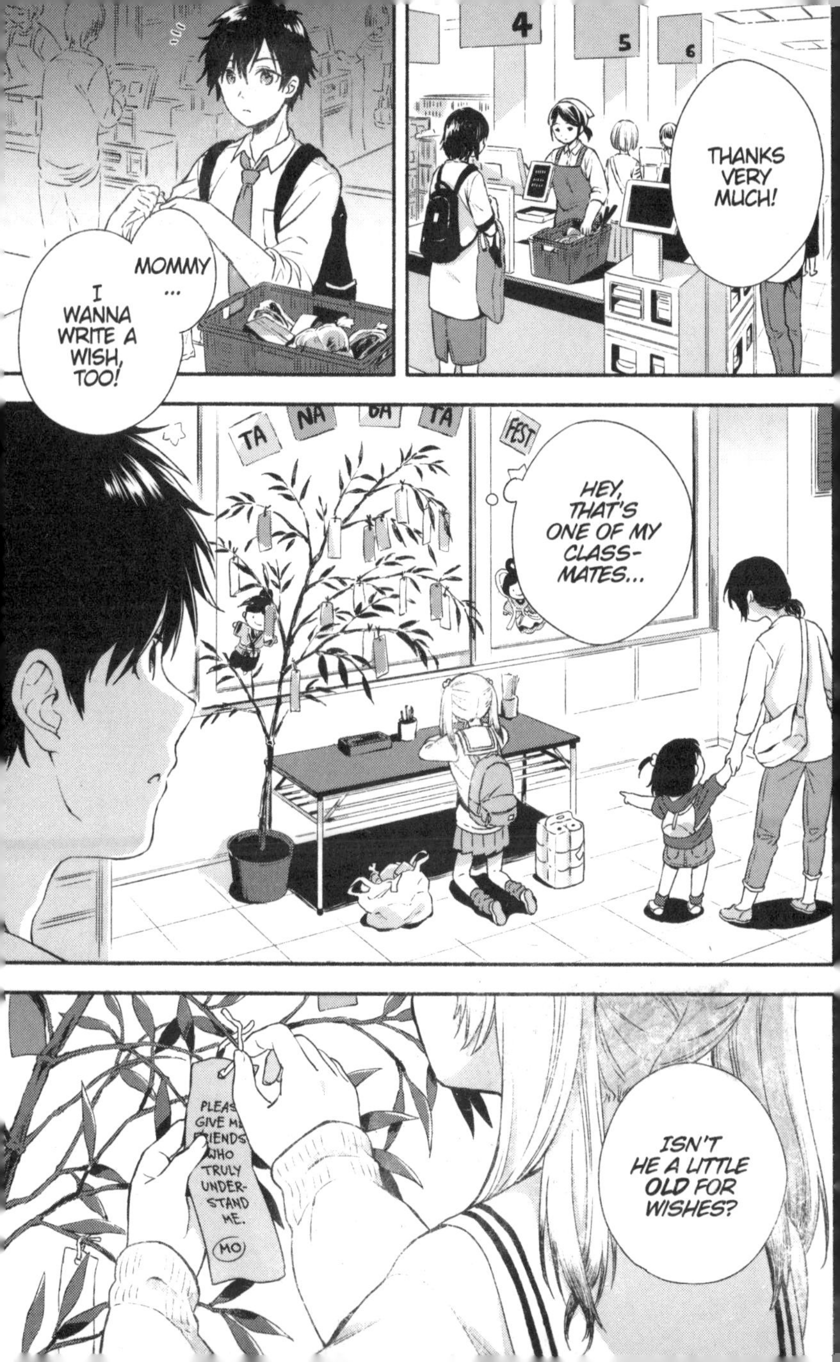
THANKS VERY MUCH!
MOMMY...
I WANNA WRITE A WISH, TOO!
TA NA BA TA FEST
HEY, THAT'S ONE OF MY CLASS-MATES...
PLEAS GIVE M RIENDS WHO TRULY UNDER-STAND ME.
MO
ISN'T HE A LITTLE OLD FOR WISHES?

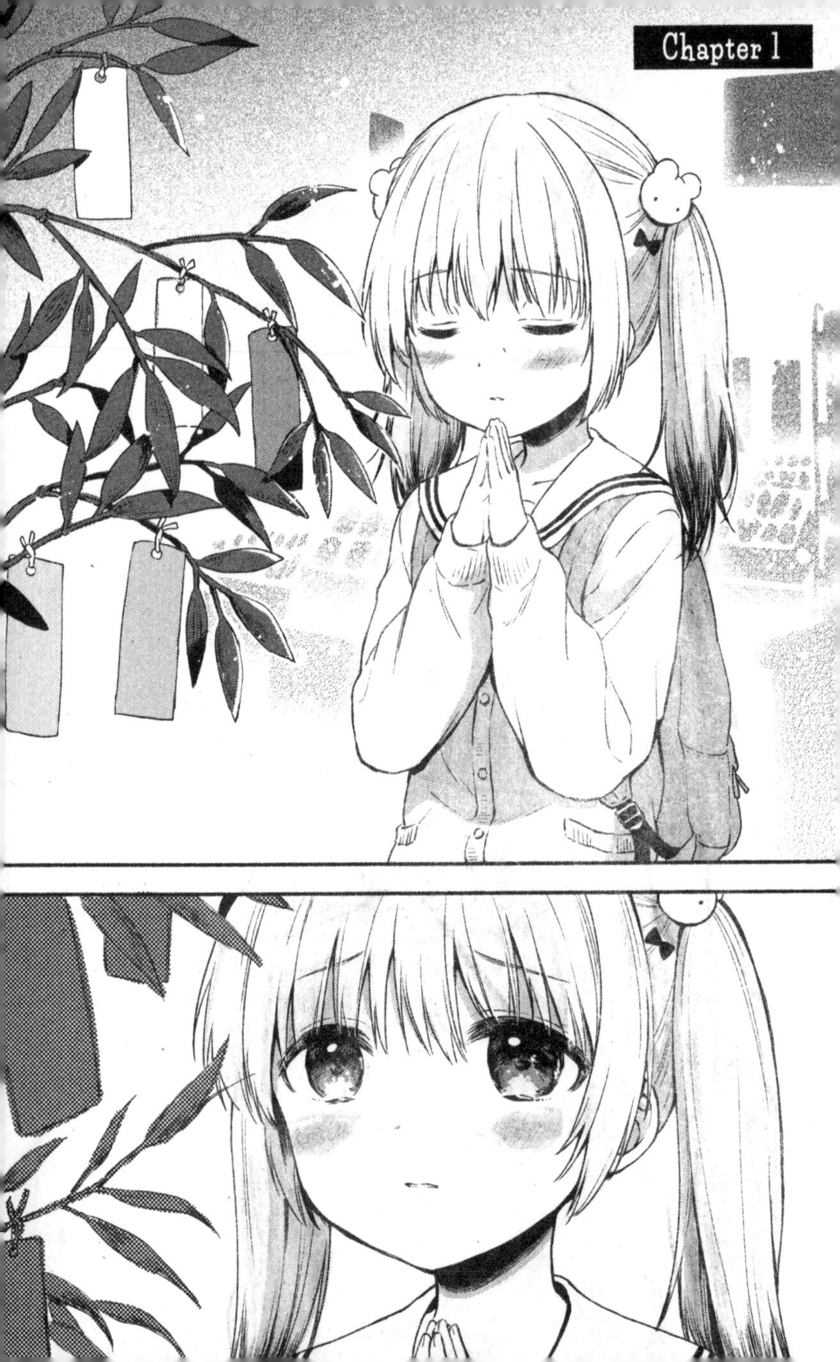
Chapter 1

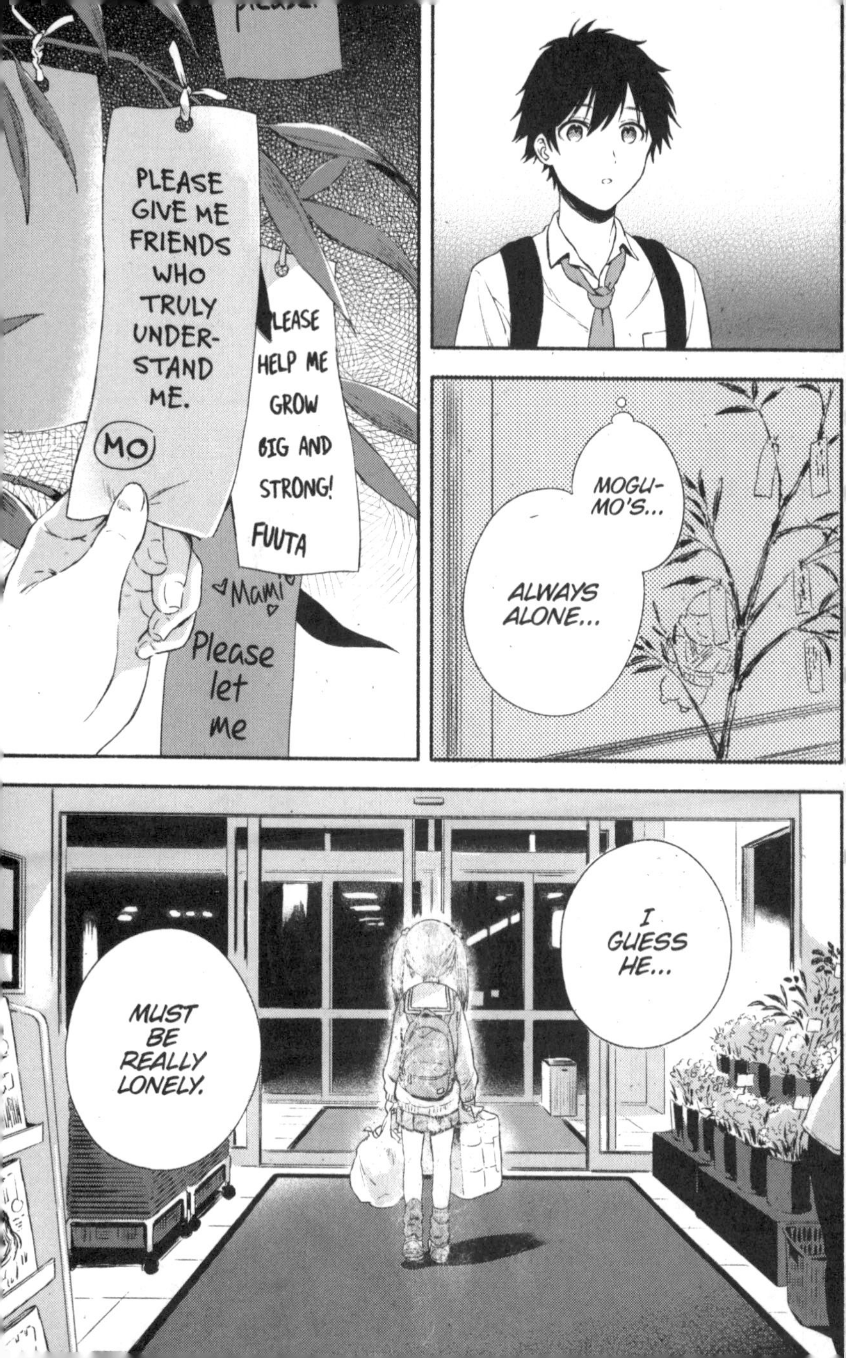
MOGU-MO'S...
ALWAYS ALONE...
PLEASE GIVE ME FRIENDS WHO TRULY UNDER-STAND ME.
MO
PLEASE HELP ME GROW BIG AND STRONG!
FUUTA
Mami
Please let me
I GUESS HE...
MUST BE REALLY LONELY.

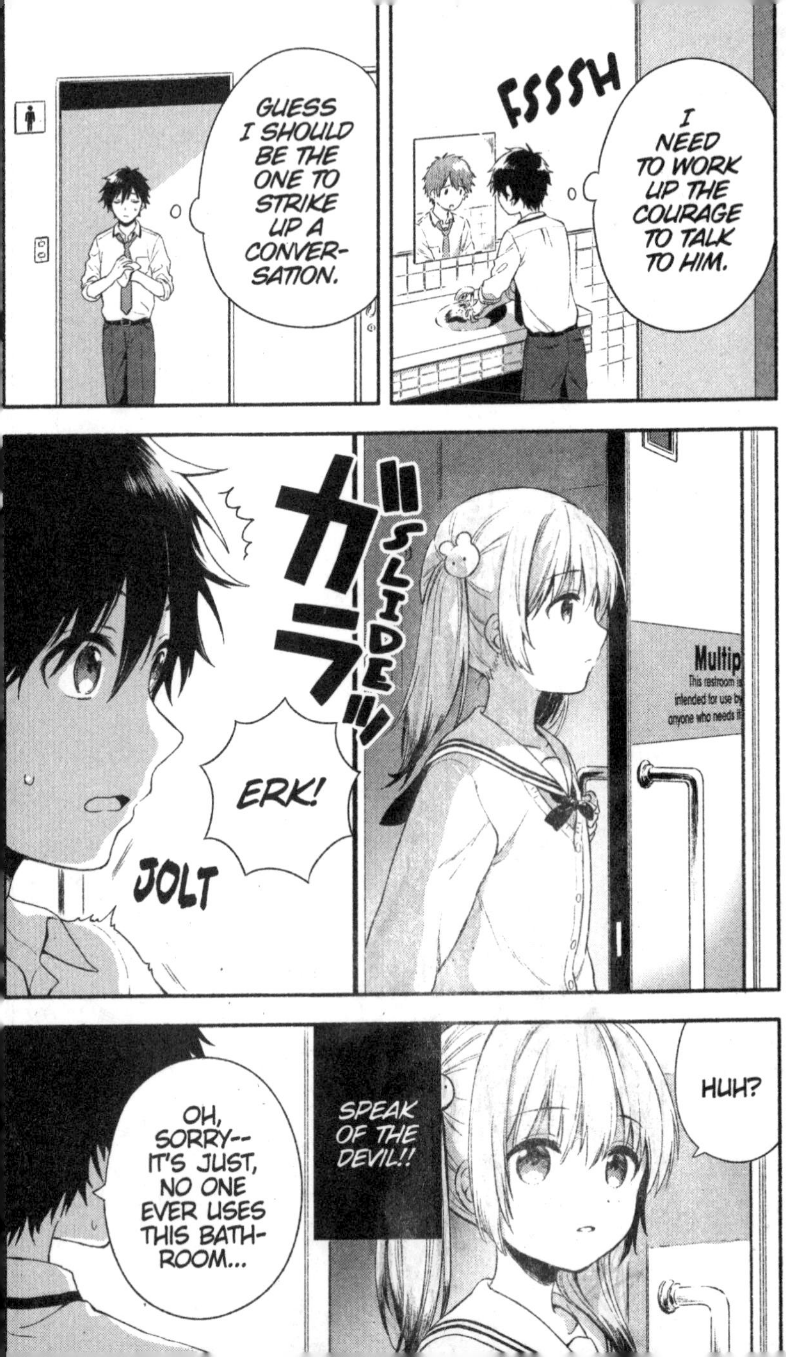
FSSSH
I NEED TO WORK UP THE COURAGE TO TALK TO HIM.
GUESS I SHOULD BE THE ONE TO STRIKE UP A CONVER-SATION.
ガラッ
SLIDE
Multip
This restroom is intended for use by anyone who needs it
ERK!
JOLT
HUH?
SPEAK OF THE DEVIL!!
OH, SORRY-- IT'S JUST, NO ONE EVER USES THIS BATH-ROOM...

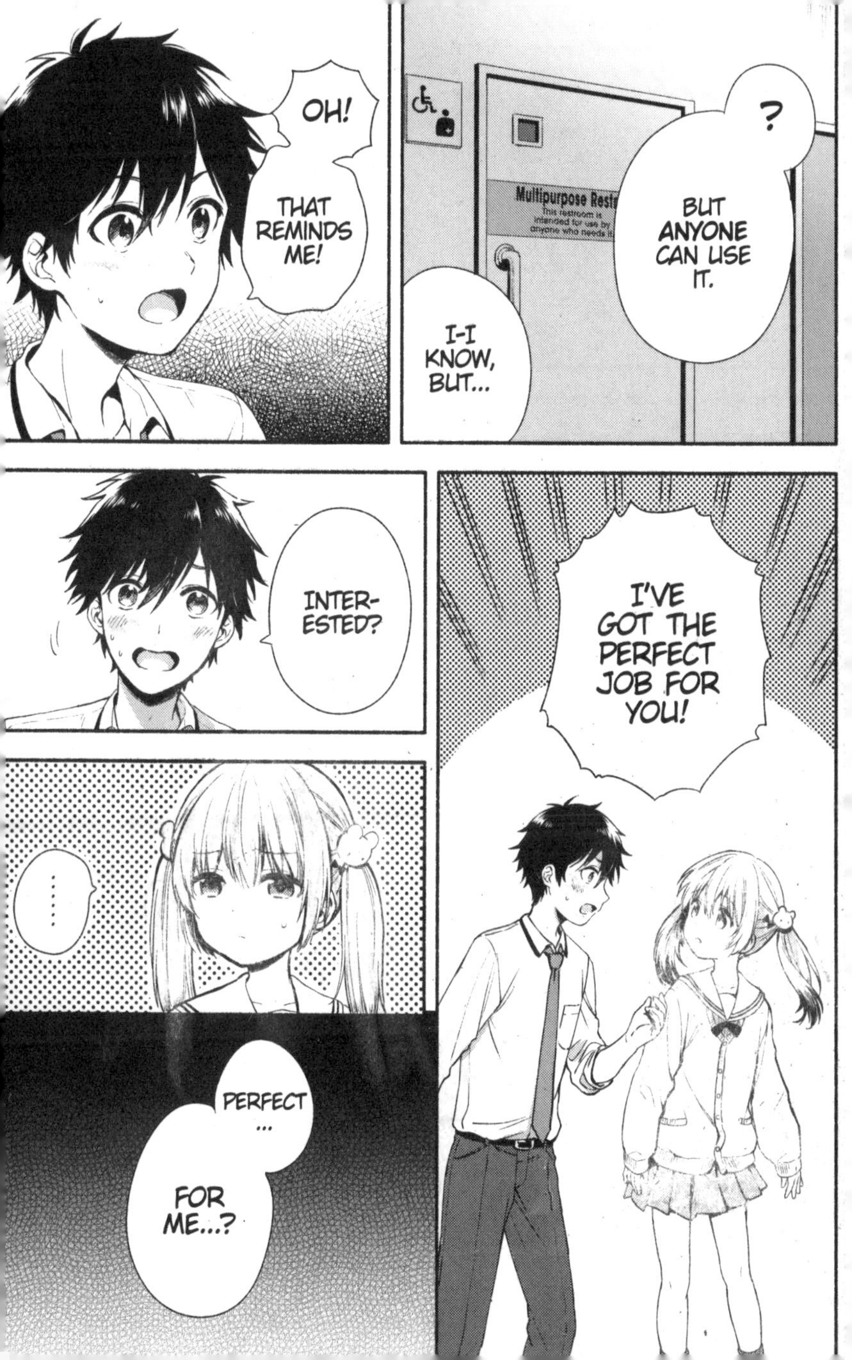
?
Multipurpose Rest
This restroom is intended for use by anyone who needs it.
BUT ANYONE CAN USE IT.
I-I KNOW, BUT...
OH!
THAT REMINDS ME!
I'VE GOT THE PERFECT JOB FOR YOU!
INTERESTED?
......
PERFECT...
FOR ME...?

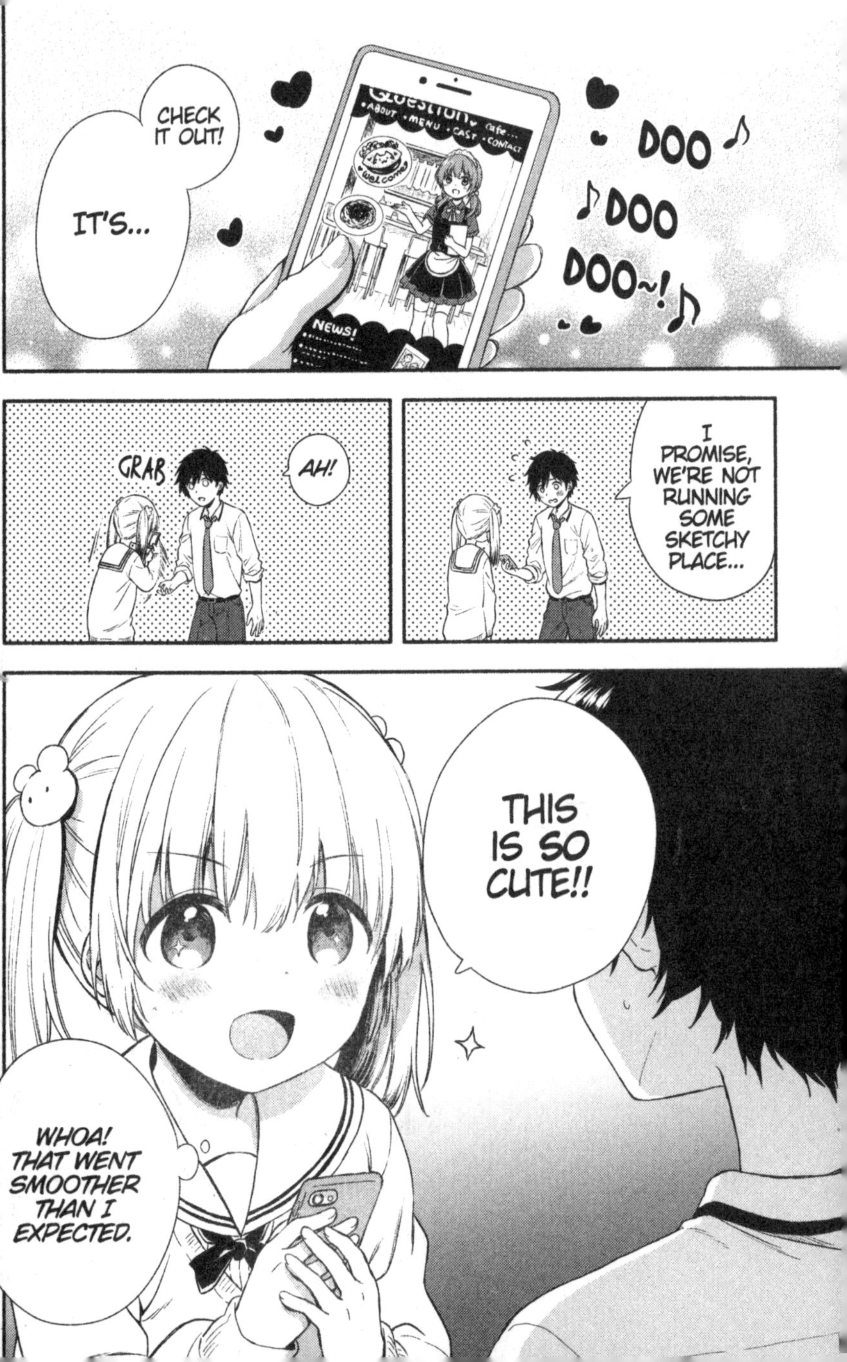
DOO ♪ ♪ DOO DOO~! ♪
CHECK IT OUT!
IT'S...
•ABOUT •MENU •CAST •CONTACT
welcome
NEWS!
I PROMISE, WE'RE NOT RUNNING SOME SKETCHY PLACE...
AH!
GRAB
THIS IS SO CUTE!!
WHOA! THAT WENT SMOOTHER THAN I EXPECTED.

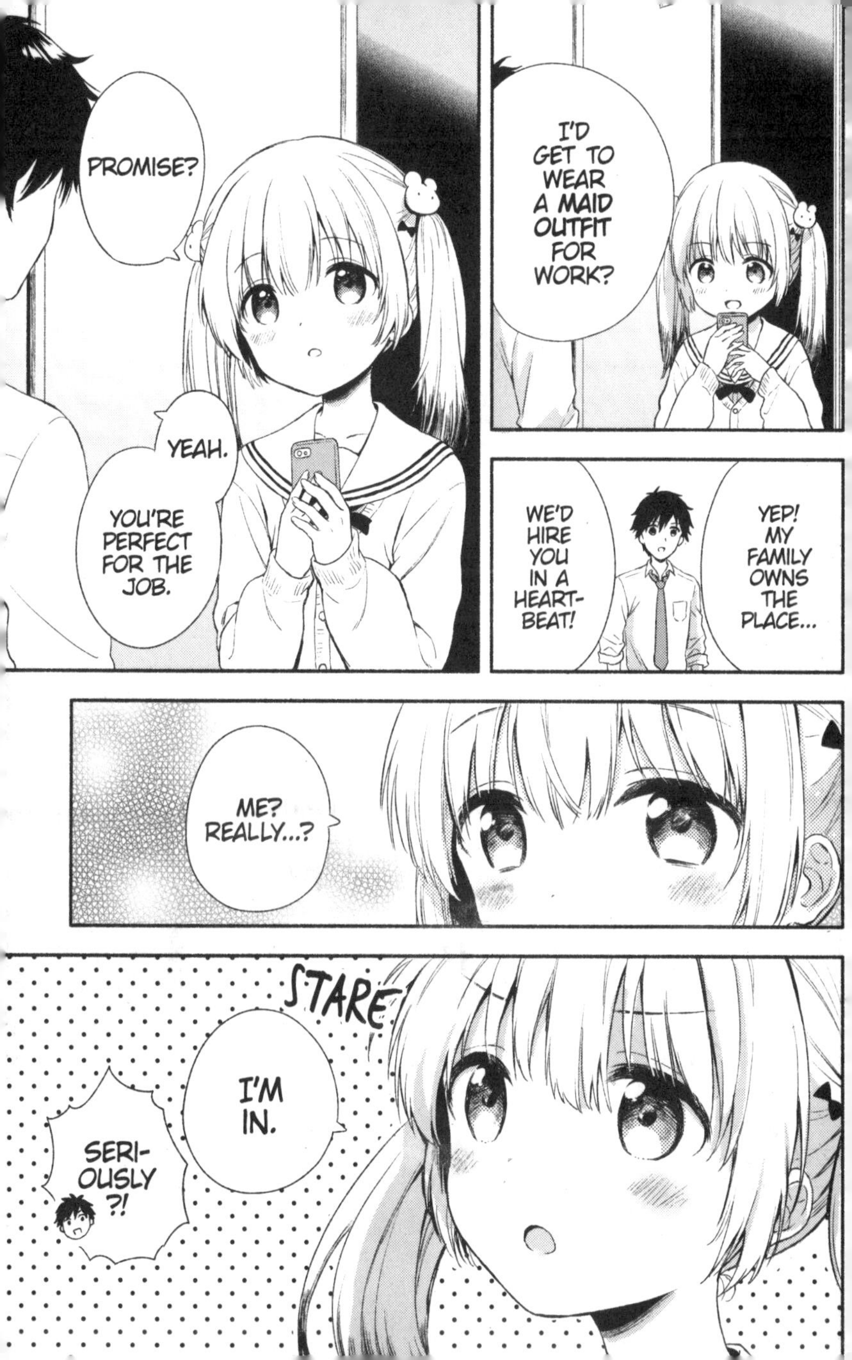
I'D GET TO WEAR A MAID OUTFIT FOR WORK?
YEP! MY FAMILY OWNS THE PLACE...
WE'D HIRE YOU IN A HEART-BEAT!
PROMISE?
YEAH.
YOU'RE PERFECT FOR THE JOB.
ME? REALLY...?
STARE
I'M IN.
SERI-OUSLY?!

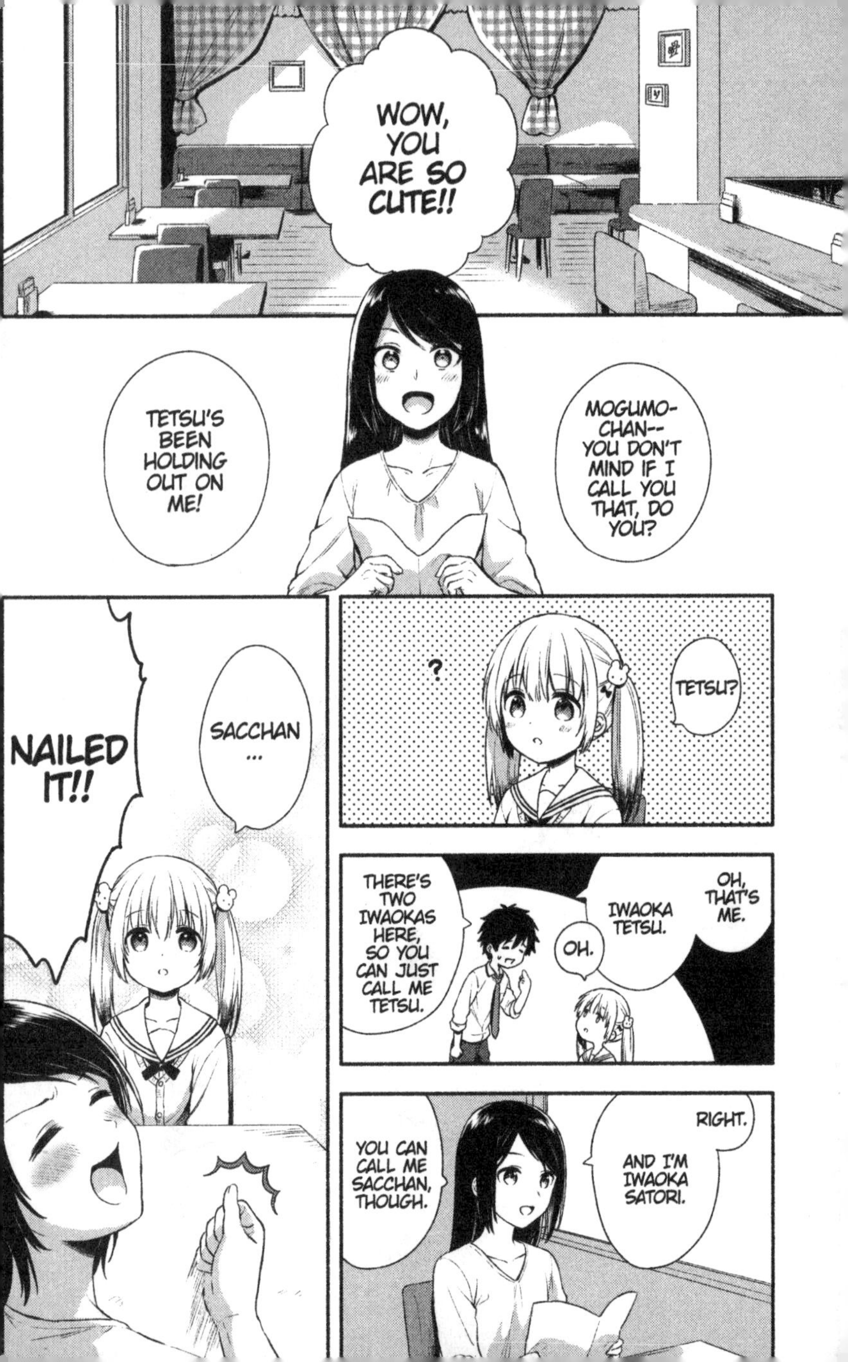
WOW, YOU ARE SO CUTE!!
MOGUMO-CHAN-- YOU DON'T MIND IF I CALL YOU THAT, DO YOU?
TETSU'S BEEN HOLDING OUT ON ME!
TETSU?
?
OH, THAT'S ME.
IWAOKA TETSU.
OH.
THERE'S TWO IWAOKAS HERE, SO YOU CAN JUST CALL ME TETSU.
RIGHT.
AND I'M IWAOKA SATORI.
YOU CAN CALL ME SACCHAN, THOUGH.
SACCHAN ...
NAILED IT!!

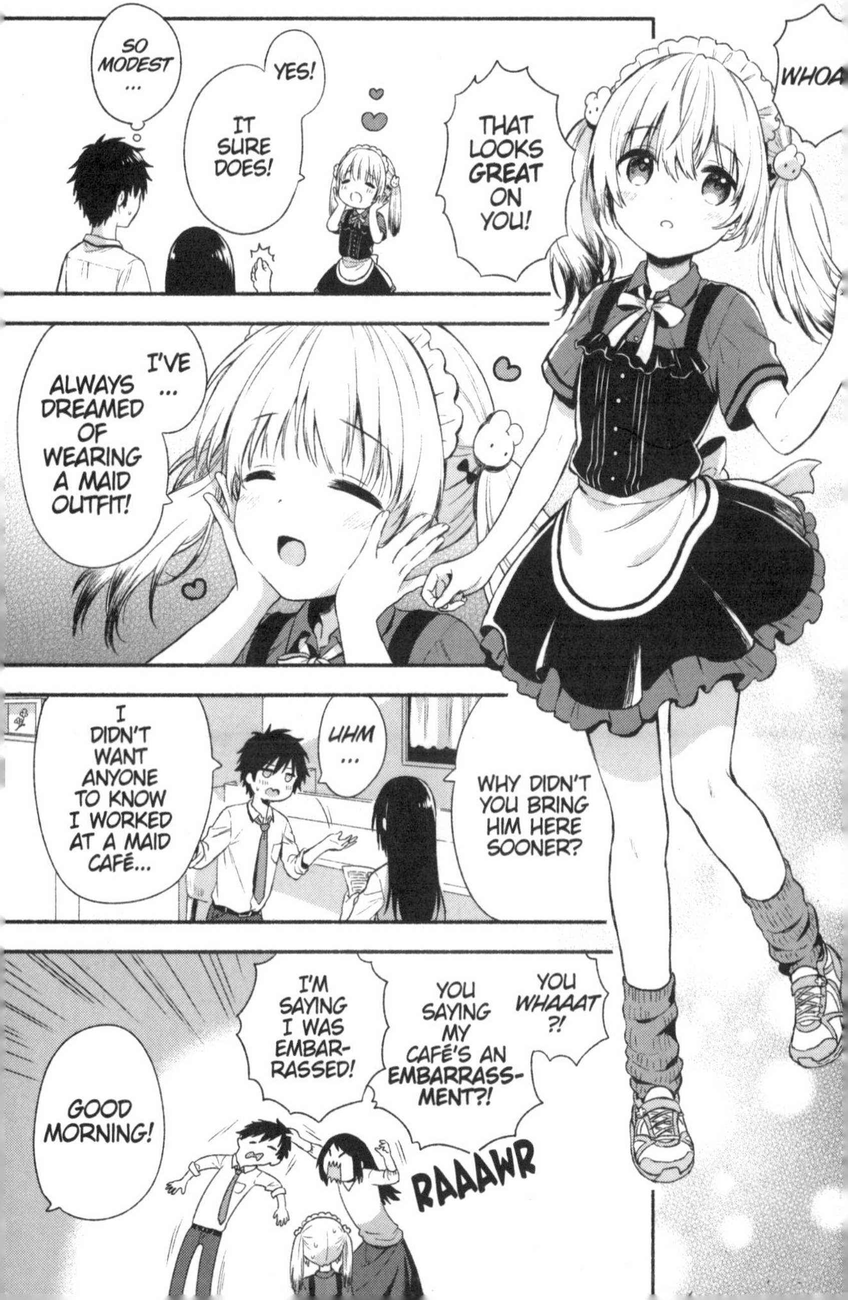
WHOA
THAT LOOKS GREAT ON YOU!
YES!
IT SURE DOES!
SO MODEST ...
I'VE ... ALWAYS DREAMED OF WEARING A MAID OUTFIT!
WHY DIDN'T YOU BRING HIM HERE SOONER?
UHM ...
I DIDN'T WANT ANYONE TO KNOW I WORKED AT A MAID CAFÉ...
YOU WHAAAT ?!
YOU SAYING MY CAFÉ'S AN EMBARRASS-MENT?!
I'M SAYING I WAS EMBAR-RASSED!
GOOD MORNING!
RAAAWR

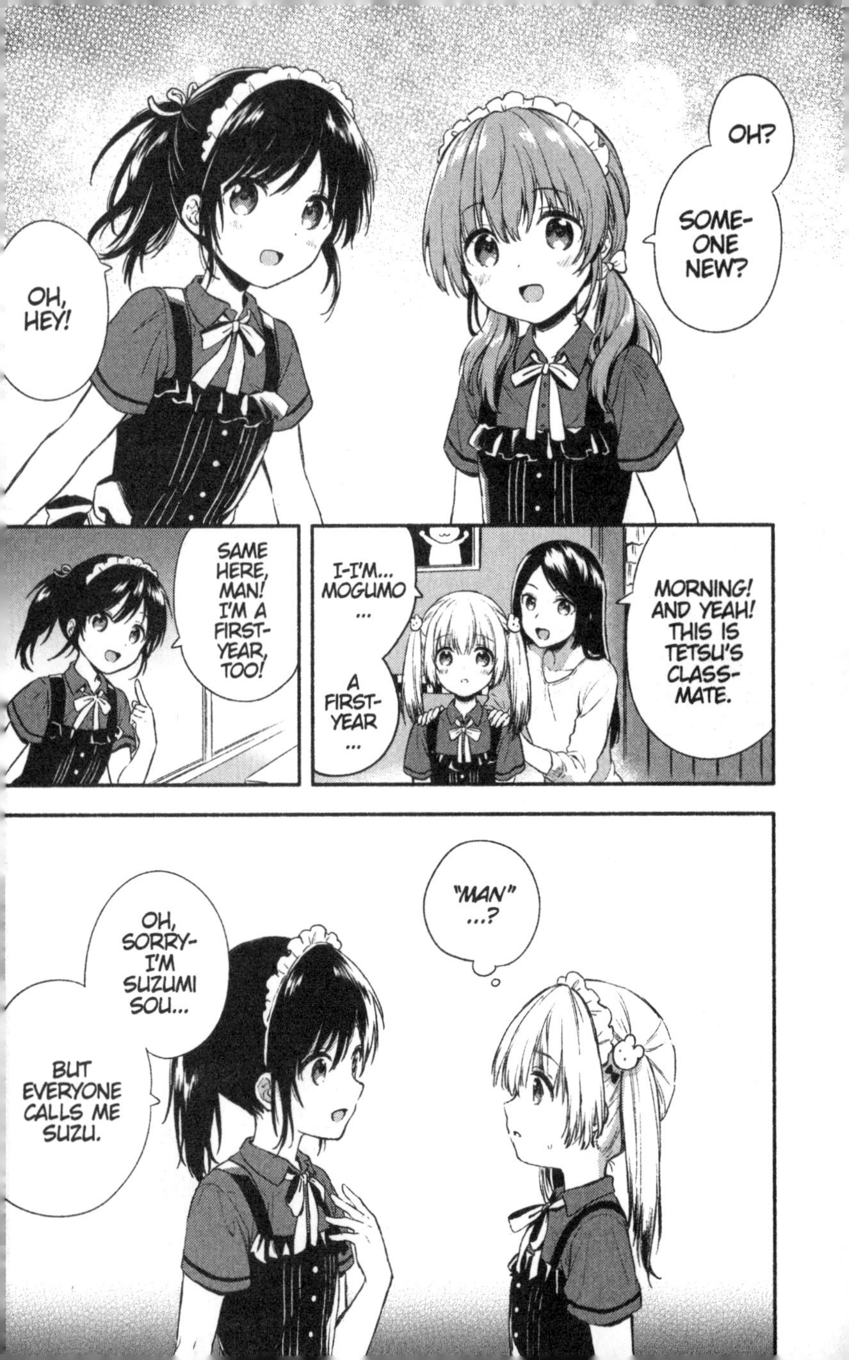
OH?
SOME-ONE NEW?
OH, HEY!
MORNING! AND YEAH! THIS IS TETSU'S CLASS-MATE.
I-I'M... MOGUMO ...
A FIRST-YEAR ...
SAME HERE, MAN! I'M A FIRST-YEAR, TOO!
"MAN" ...?
OH, SORRY- I'M SUZUMI SOU...
BUT EVERYONE CALLS ME SUZU.

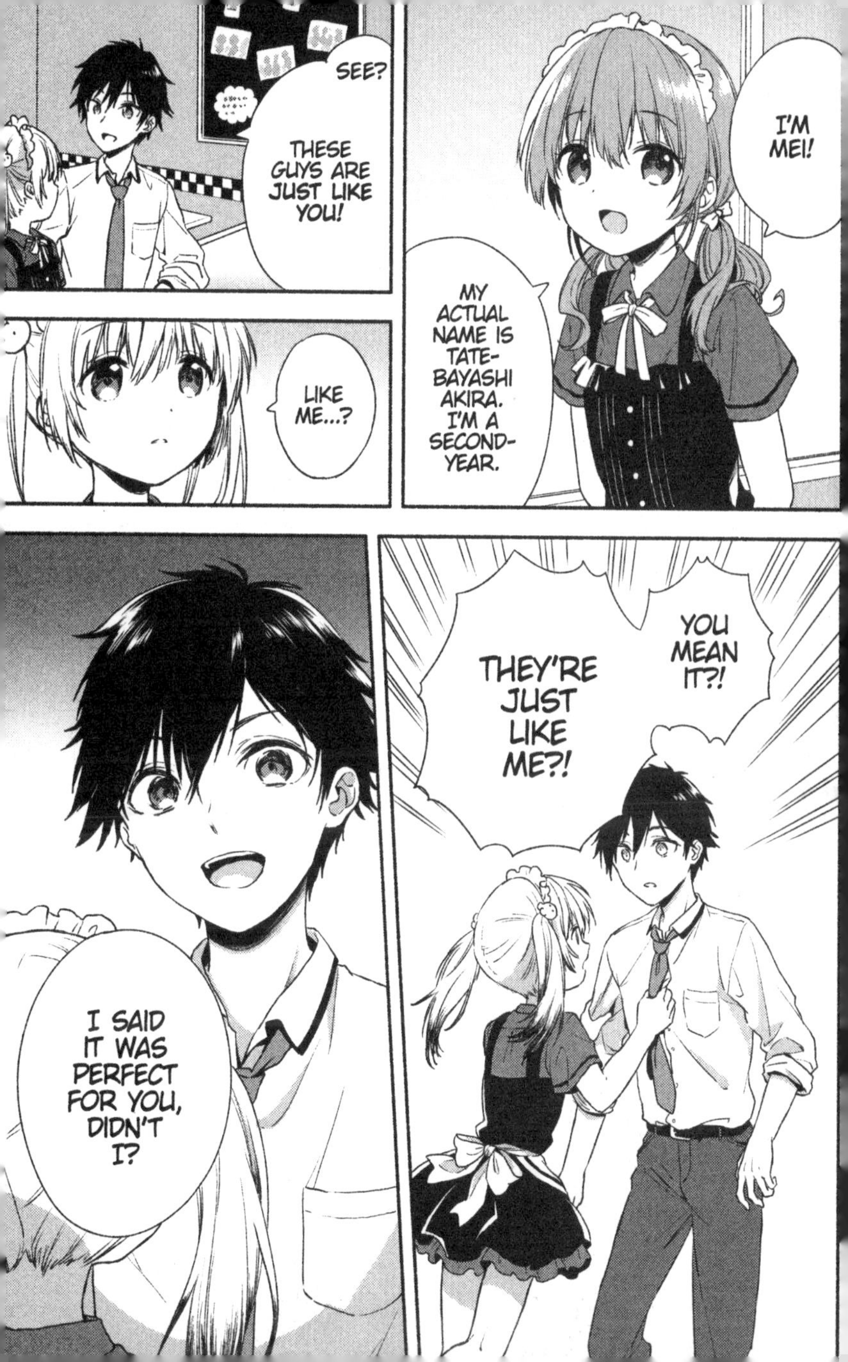
I'M MEI!
MY ACTUAL NAME IS TATE-BAYASHI AKIRA. I'M A SECOND-YEAR.
SEE?
THESE GUYS ARE JUST LIKE YOU!
LIKE ME...?
YOU MEAN IT?!
THEY'RE JUST LIKE ME?!
I SAID IT WAS PERFECT FOR YOU, DIDN'T I?

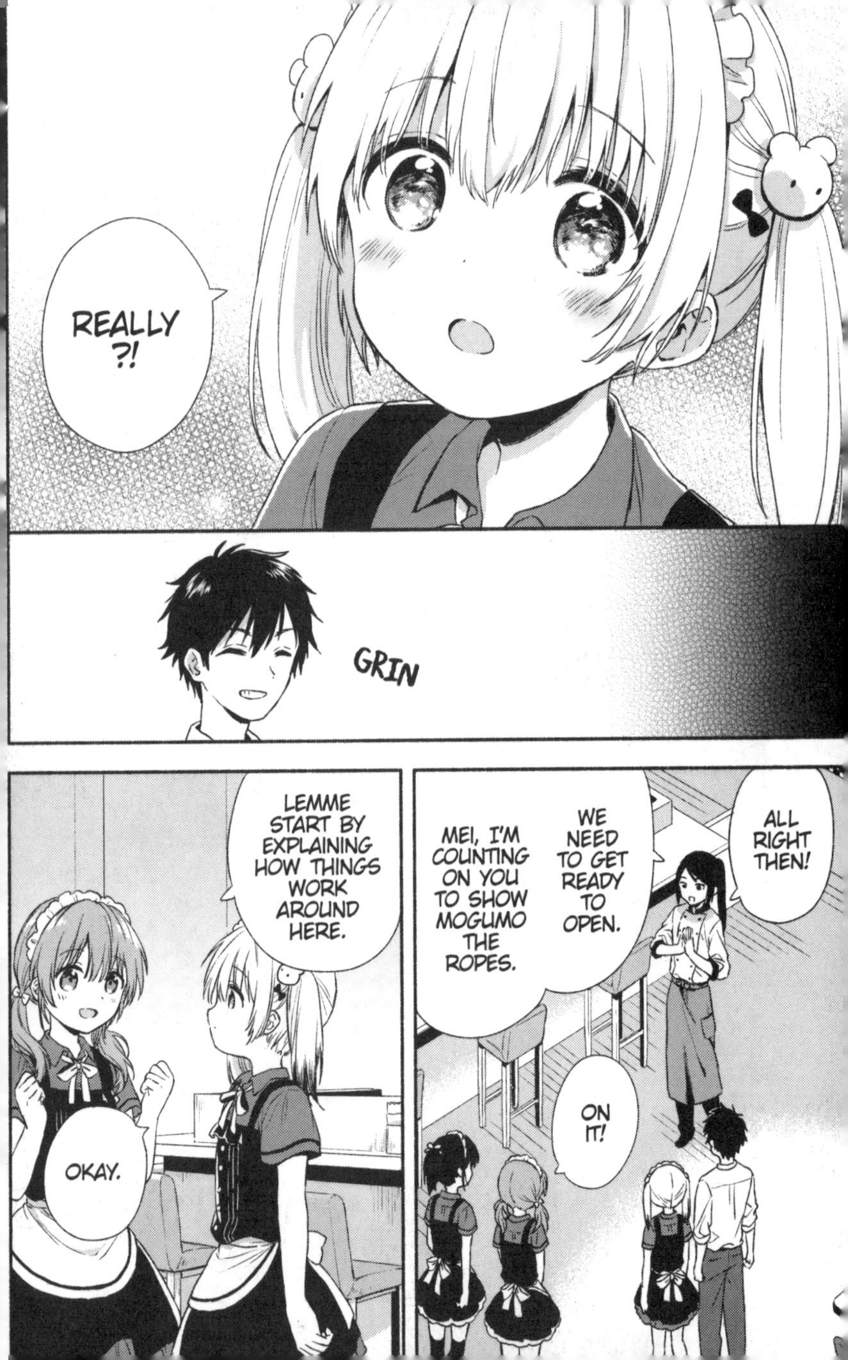
REALLY ?!
GRIN
ALL RIGHT THEN!
WE NEED TO GET READY TO OPEN.
MEI, I'M COUNTING ON YOU TO SHOW MOGUMO THE ROPES.
ON IT!
LEMME START BY EXPLAINING HOW THINGS WORK AROUND HERE.
OKAY.

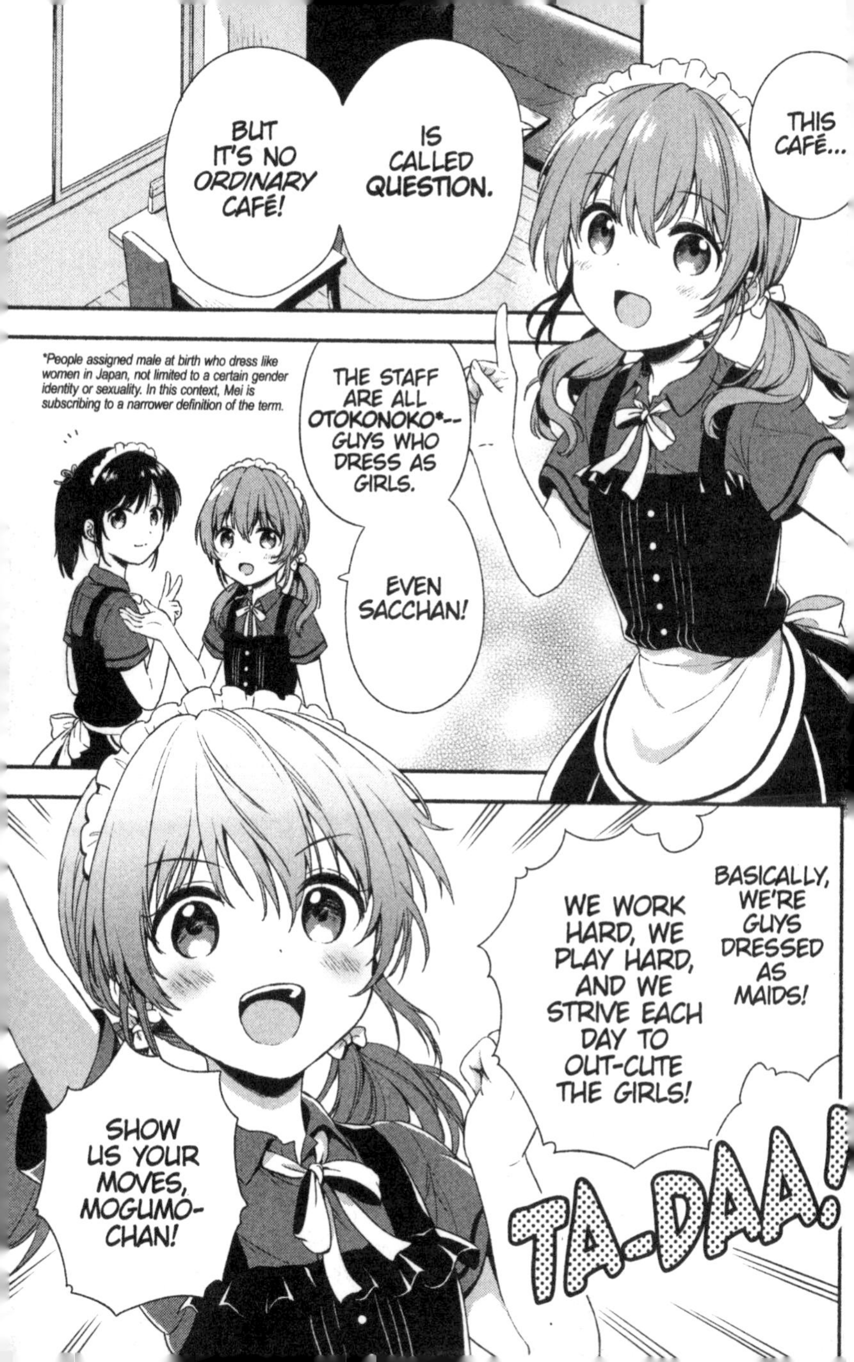
THIS CAFÉ...
IS CALLED QUESTION.
BUT IT'S NO ORDINARY CAFÉ!
THE STAFF ARE ALL OTOKONOKO*--GUYS WHO DRESS AS GIRLS.
EVEN SACCHAN!
*People assigned male at birth who dress like women in Japan, not limited to a certain gender identity or sexuality. In this context, Mei is subscribing to a narrower definition of the term.
BASICALLY, WE'RE GUYS DRESSED AS MAIDS!
WE WORK HARD, WE PLAY HARD, AND WE STRIVE EACH DAY TO OUT-CUTE THE GIRLS!
SHOW US YOUR MOVES, MOGUMO-CHAN!
TA-DAA!

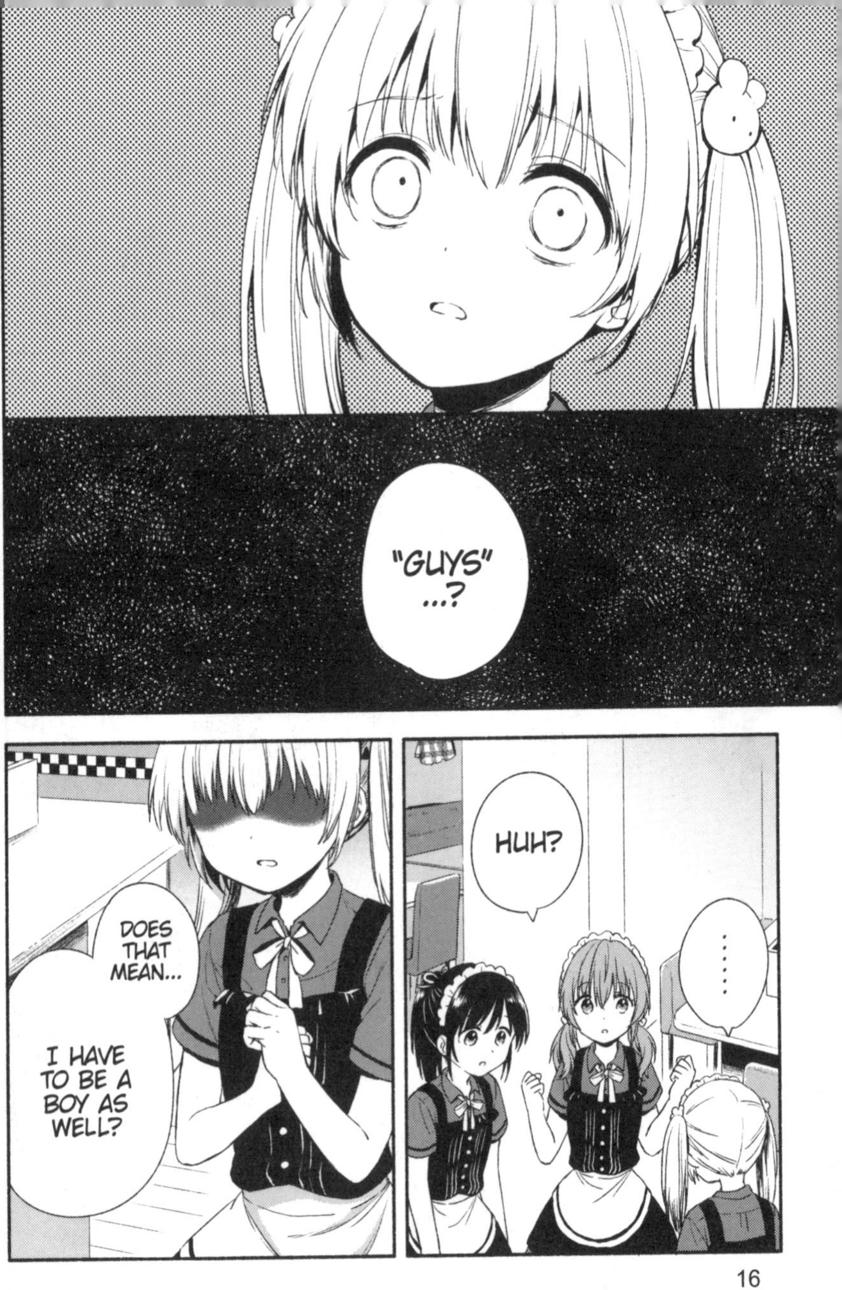
"GUYS" ...?
HUH?
......
DOES THAT MEAN...
I HAVE TO BE A BOY AS WELL?

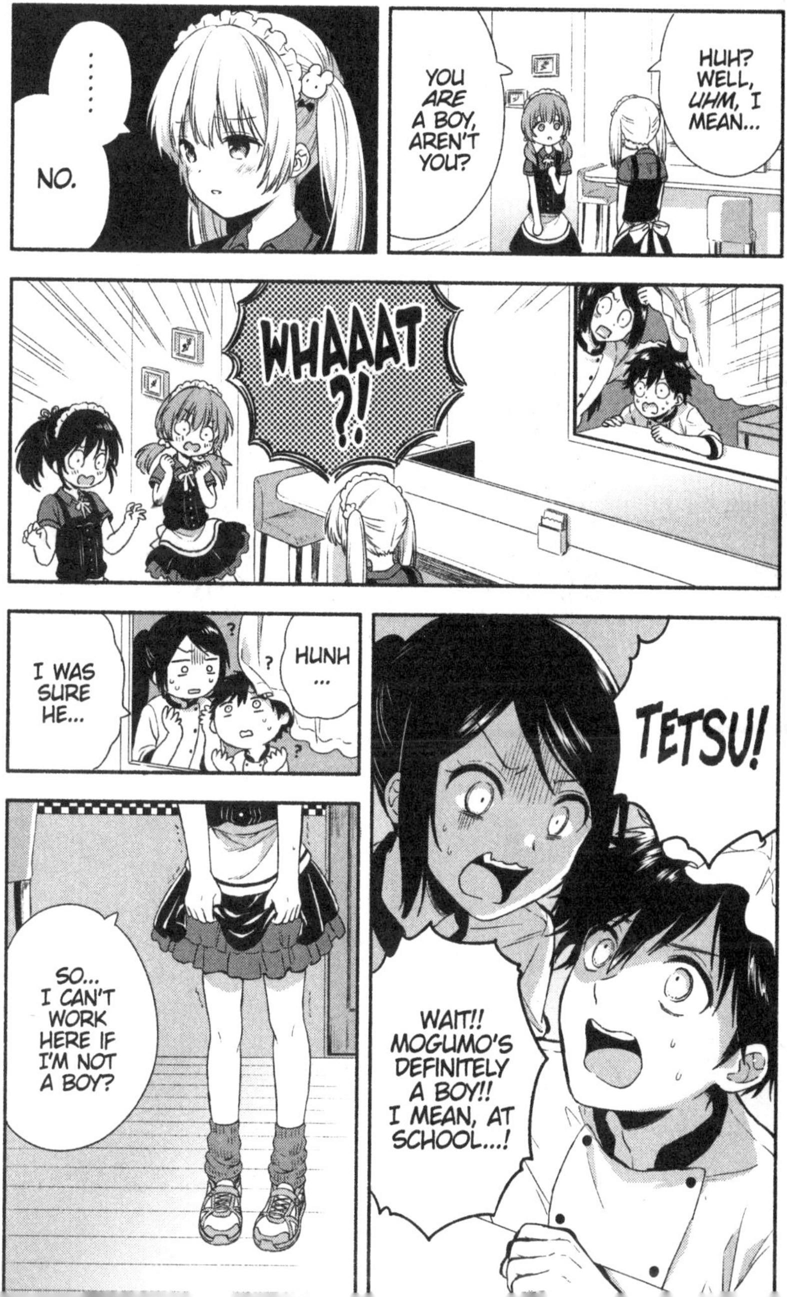
HUH? WELL, UHM, I MEAN...
YOU ARE A BOY, AREN'T YOU?
......
NO.
WHAAAT ?!
TETSU!
WAIT!! MOGUMO'S DEFINITELY A BOY!! I MEAN, AT SCHOOL...!
HUNH ...
I WAS SURE HE...
SO... I CAN'T WORK HERE IF I'M NOT A BOY?

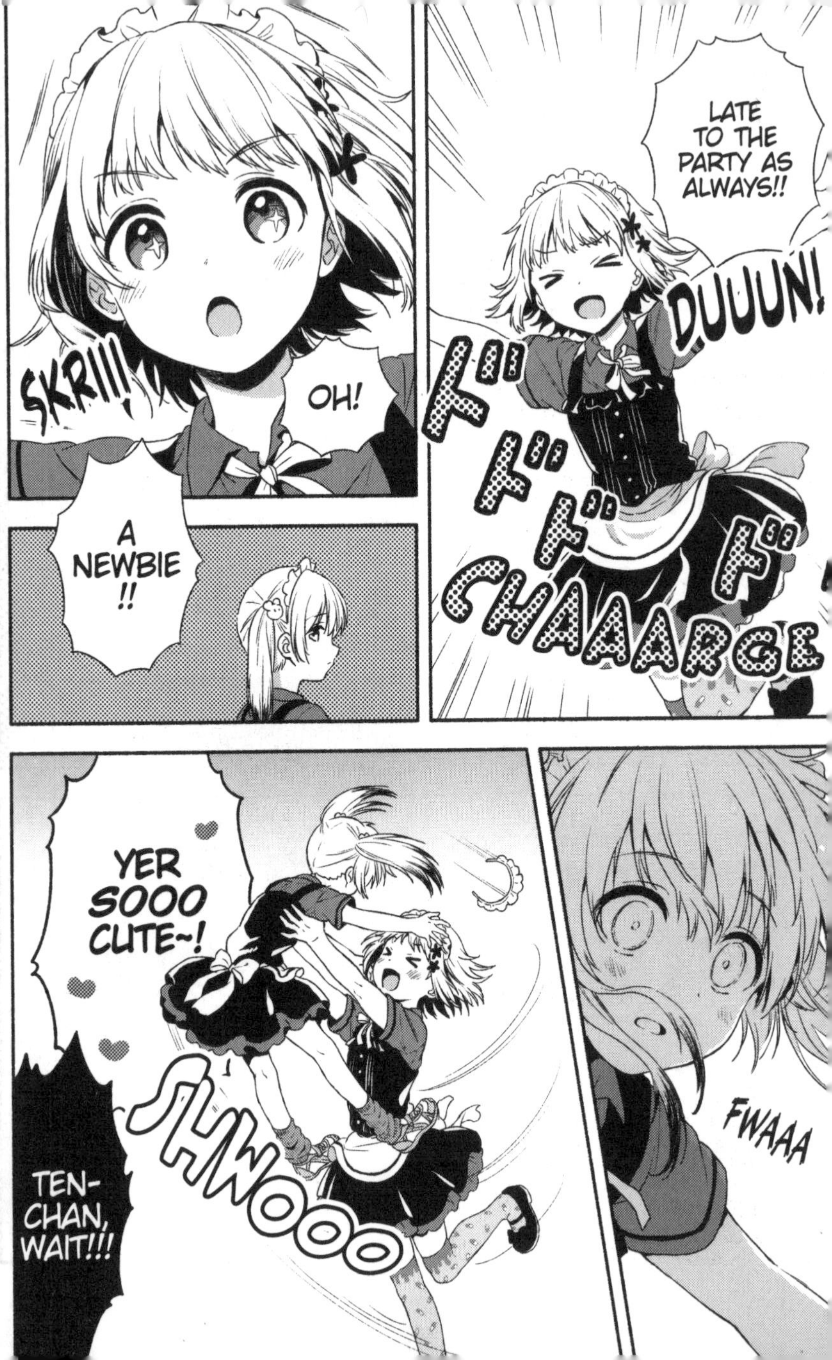
LATE TO THE PARTY AS ALWAYS!!
DUUUN!
ドドドド
CHAAARGE
SKRIII
OH!
A NEWBIE!!
FWAAA
YER SOOO CUTE~!
SHWOOO
TEN-CHAN, WAIT!!!

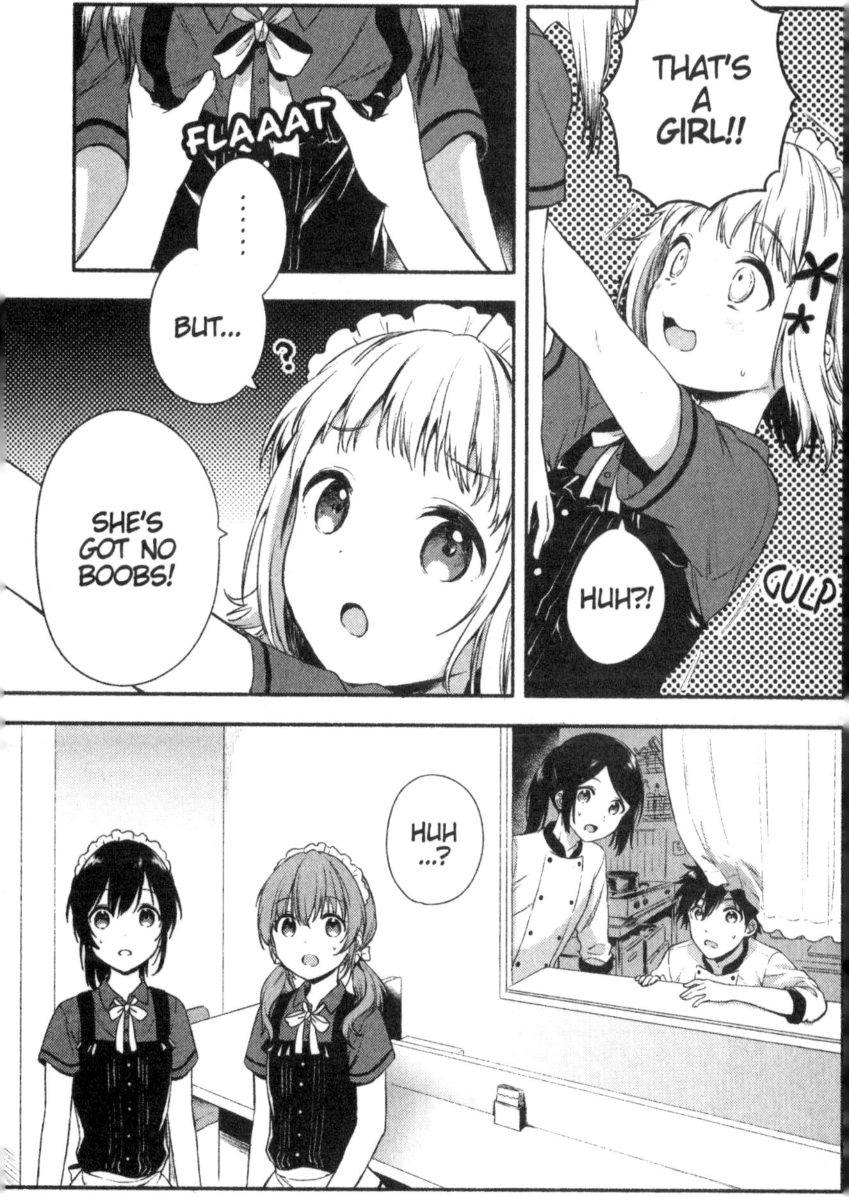

THAT'S A GIRL!!
HUH?!
GULP
FLAAAT
......
BUT...
?
SHE'S GOT NO BOOBS!
HUH ...?

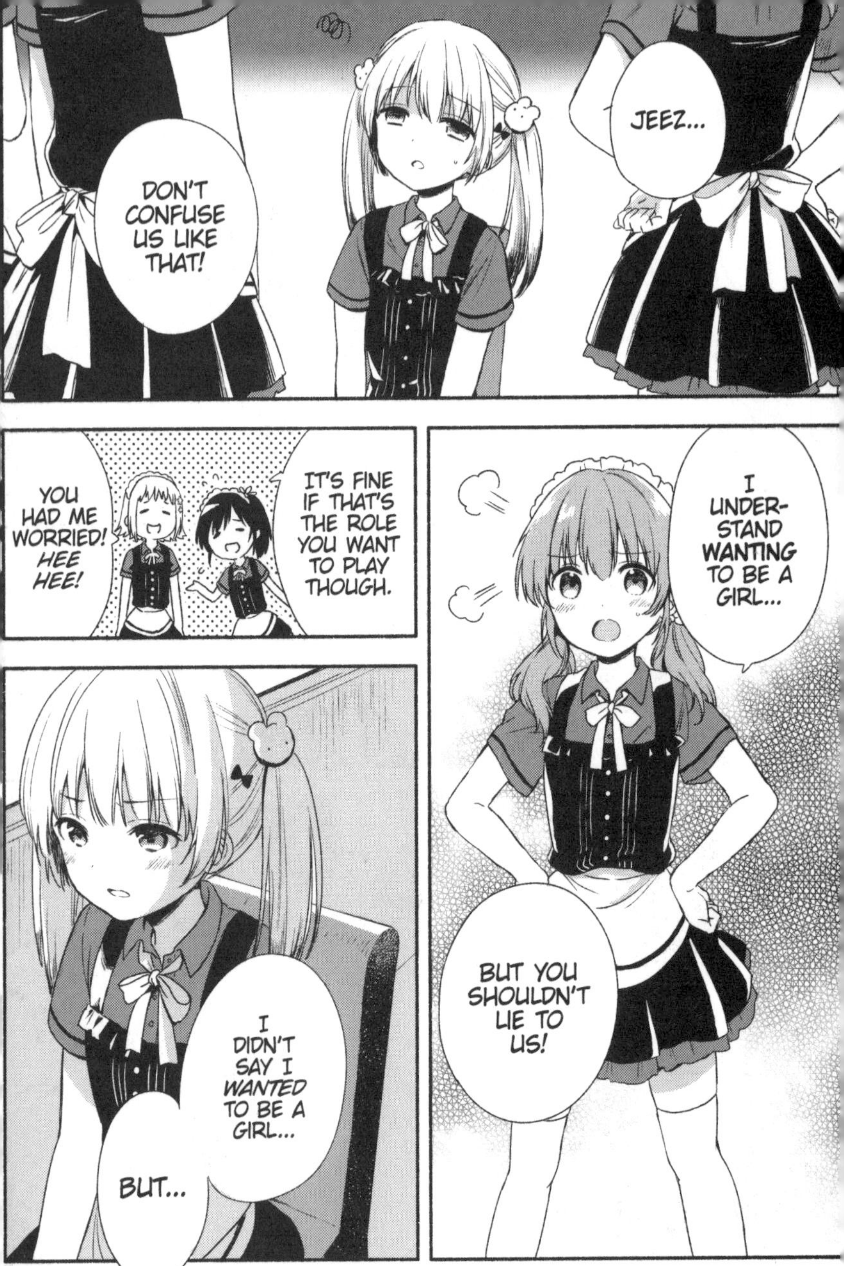
JEEZ...
DON'T CONFUSE US LIKE THAT!
I UNDER-STAND WANTING TO BE A GIRL...
BUT YOU SHOULDN'T LIE TO US!
IT'S FINE IF THAT'S THE ROLE YOU WANT TO PLAY THOUGH.
YOU HAD ME WORRIED! *HEE HEE!*
I DIDN'T SAY I *WANTED* TO BE A GIRL...
BUT...

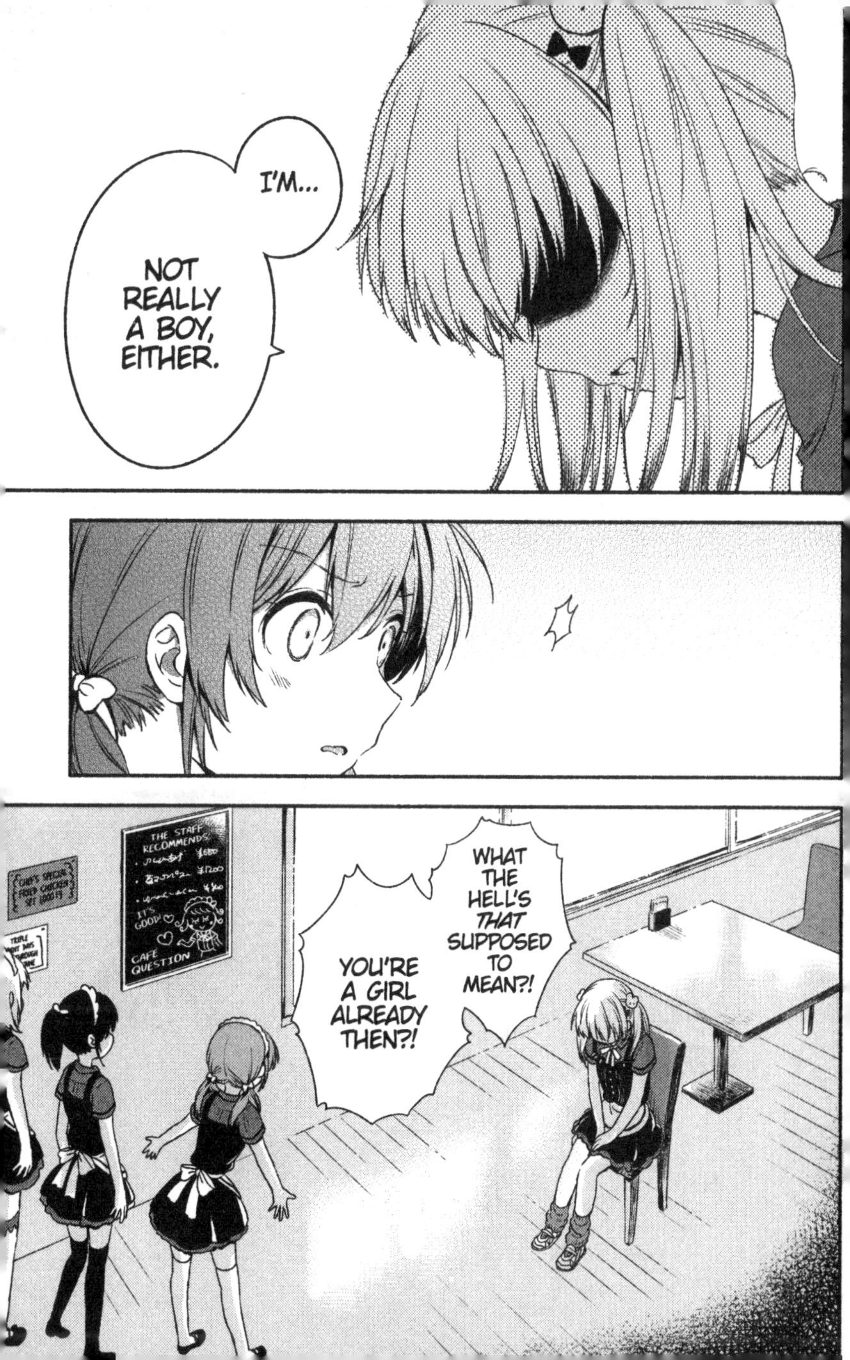
I'M...
NOT REALLY A BOY, EITHER.
WHAT THE HELL'S *THAT* SUPPOSED TO MEAN?!
YOU'RE A GIRL ALREADY THEN?!
THE STAFF RECOMMENDS
IT'S GOOD!
CAFE QUESTION

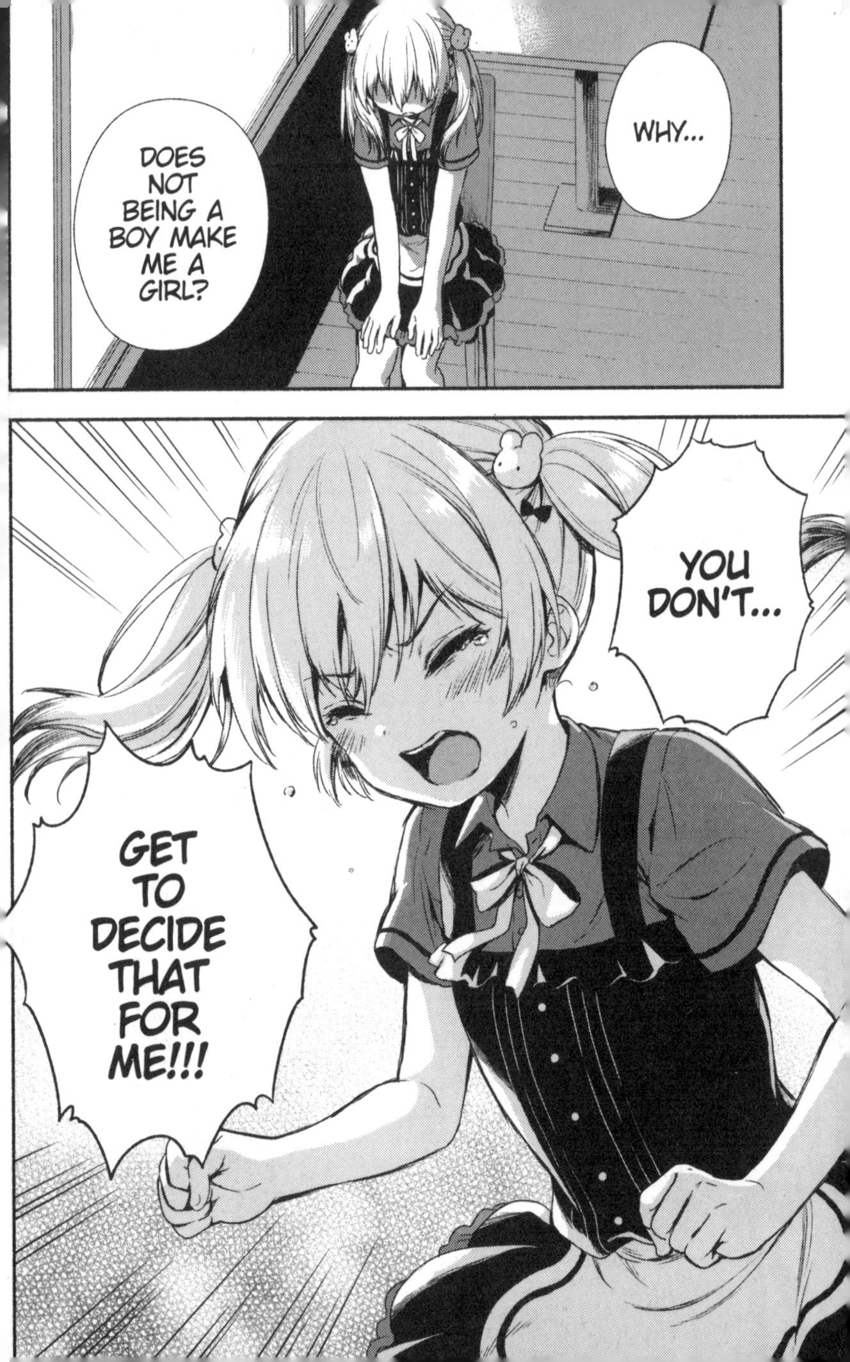
WHY...
DOES NOT BEING A BOY MAKE ME A GIRL?
YOU DON'T...
GET TO DECIDE THAT FOR ME!!!

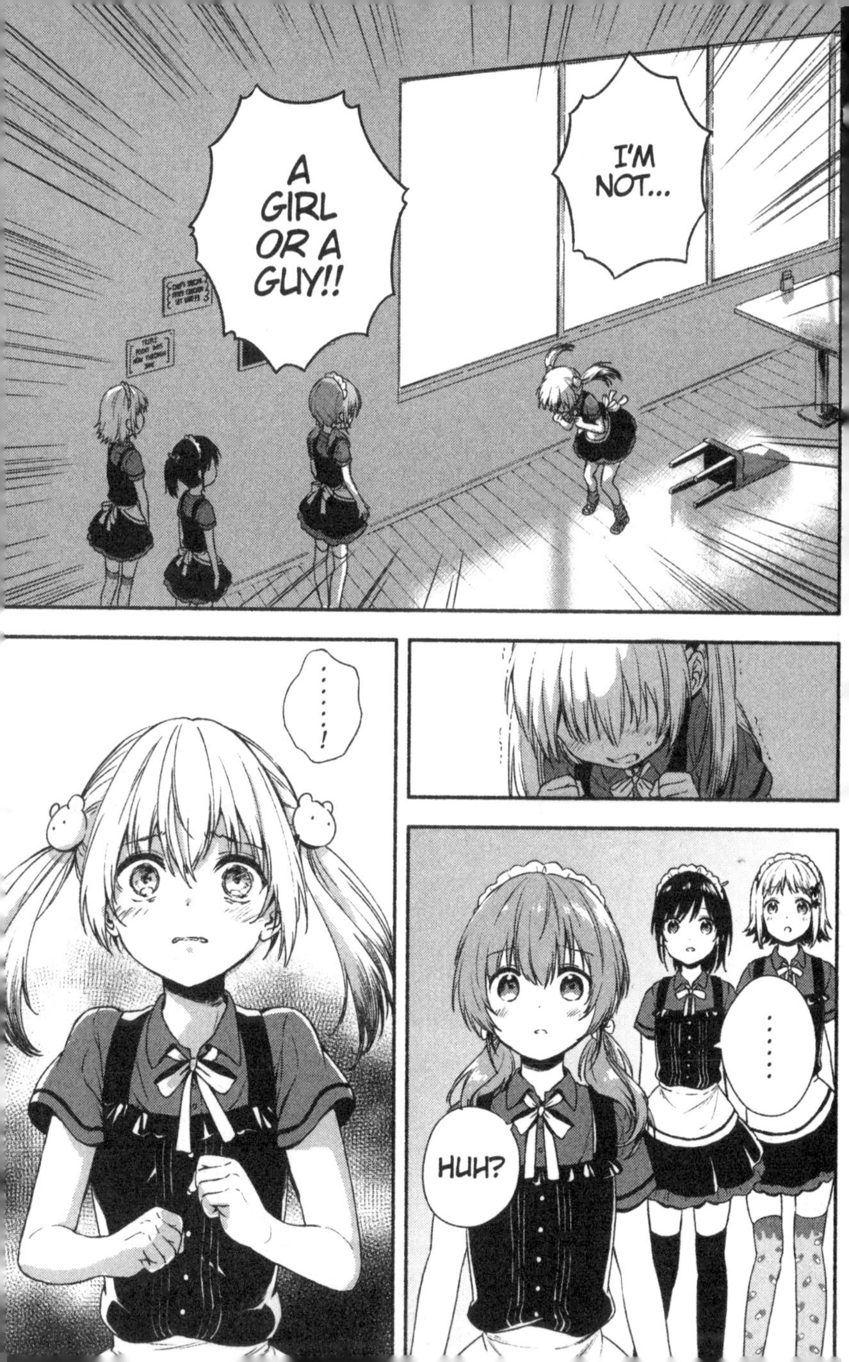
I'M NOT...
A GIRL OR A GUY!!
......
HUH?
......!

MOGU-MO!

I'M SORRY...

TETSU-KUN, I'M SORRY!

I THINK I REALLY SCREWED UP HERE!

NO...

IT'S MY FAULT...

I DIDN'T EVEN KNOW MOGUMO, BUT I TRIED TO MAKE HIM WORK HERE...

I... JUST...

......

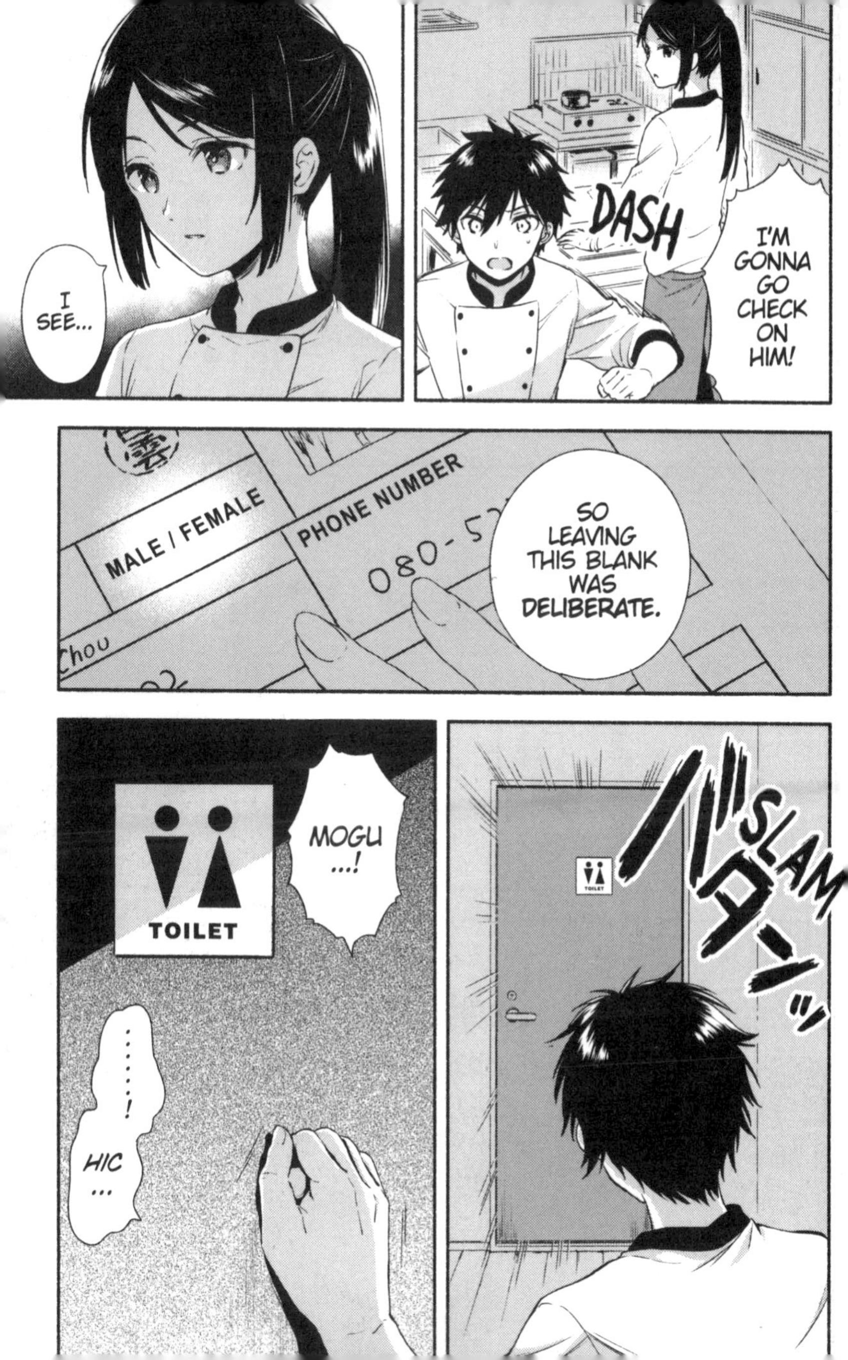
DASH
I'M GONNA GO CHECK ON HIM!
I SEE...
SO LEAVING THIS BLANK WAS DELIBERATE.
PHONE NUMBER
MALE / FEMALE
080-52
Chou
SLAM
MOGU ...!
TOILET
TOILET
.......!
HIC ...

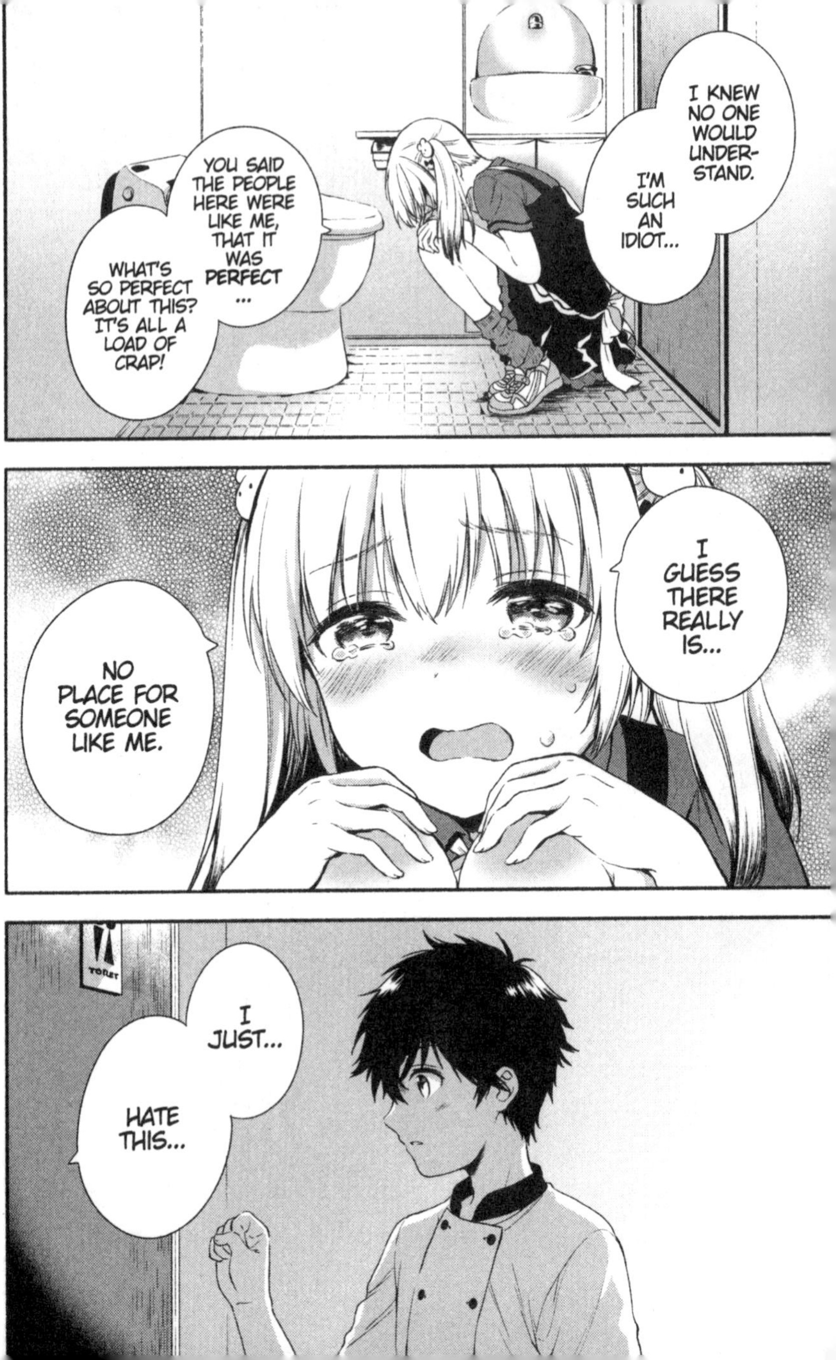
I KNEW NO ONE WOULD UNDER-STAND.
I'M SUCH AN IDIOT...
YOU SAID THE PEOPLE HERE WERE LIKE ME, THAT IT WAS PERFECT ...
WHAT'S SO PERFECT ABOUT THIS? IT'S ALL A LOAD OF CRAP!
I GUESS THERE REALLY IS...
NO PLACE FOR SOMEONE LIKE ME.
TOILET
I JUST...
HATE THIS...

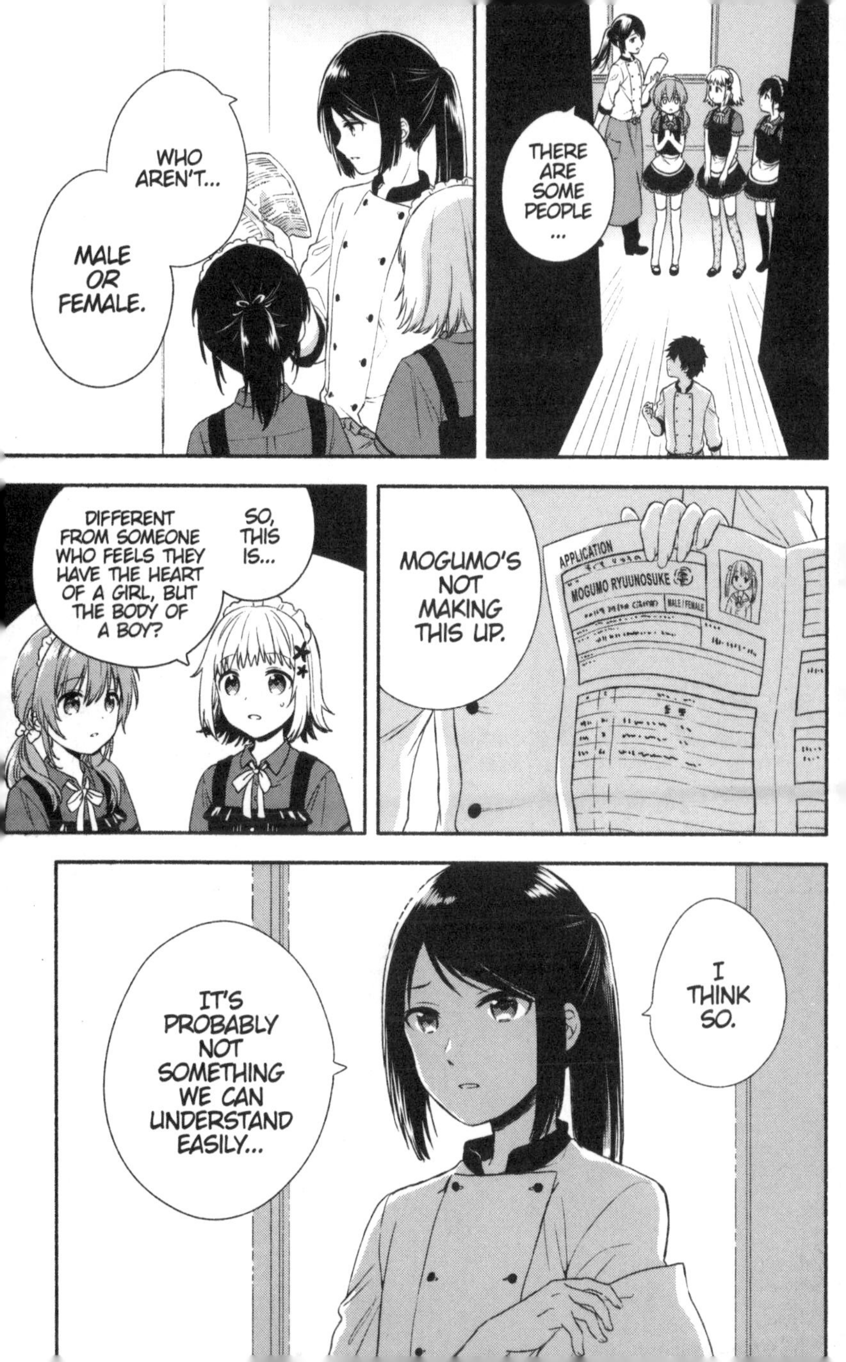
THERE ARE SOME PEOPLE ...
WHO AREN'T...
MALE OR FEMALE.
MOGUMO'S NOT MAKING THIS UP.
APPLICATION
MOGUMO RYUUNOSUKE
MALE / FEMALE
SO, THIS IS...
DIFFERENT FROM SOMEONE WHO FEELS THEY HAVE THE HEART OF A GIRL, BUT THE BODY OF A BOY?
I THINK SO.
IT'S PROBABLY NOT SOMETHING WE CAN UNDERSTAND EASILY...

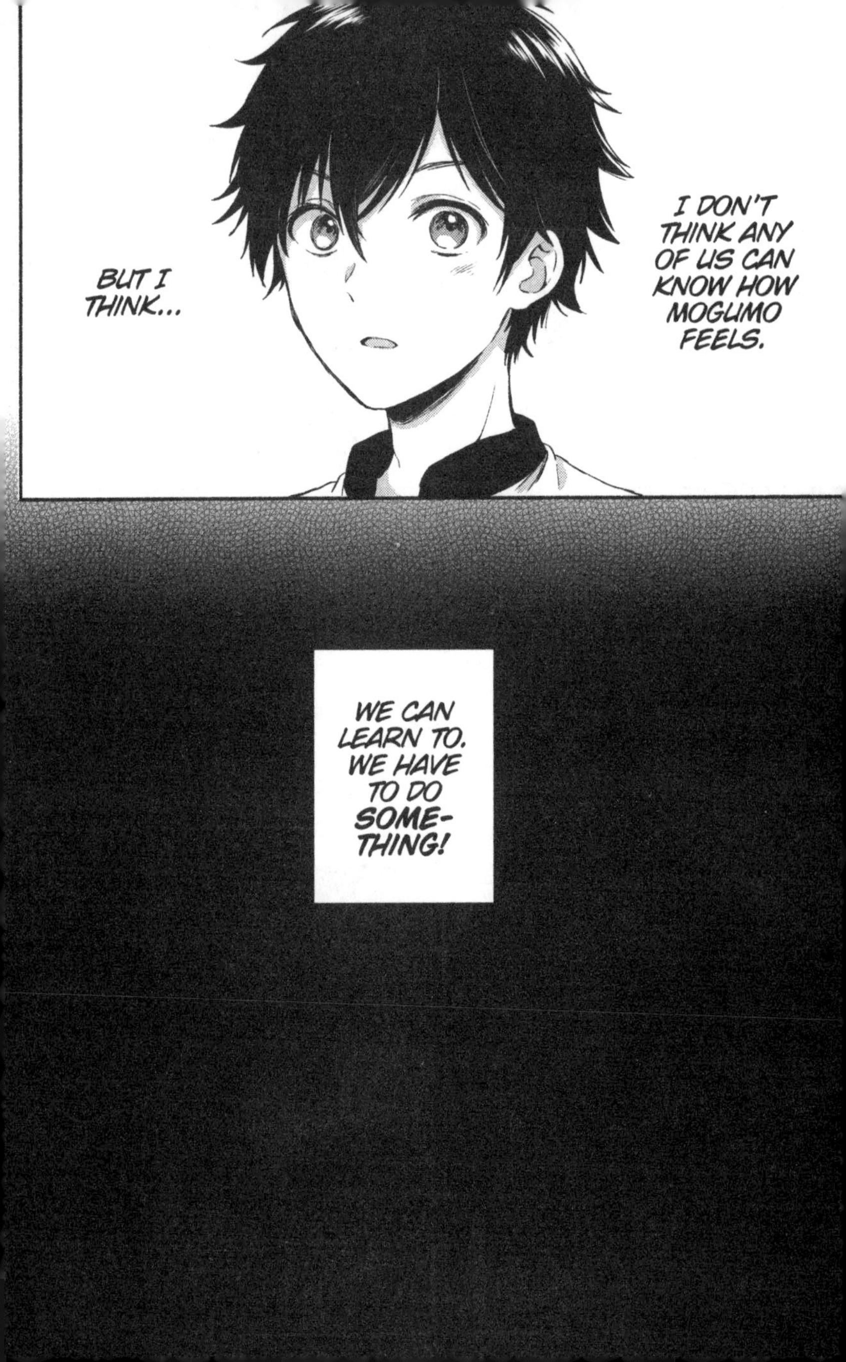
I DON'T THINK ANY OF US CAN KNOW HOW MOGUMO FEELS.
BUT I THINK...
WE CAN LEARN TO. WE HAVE TO DO SOME-THING!

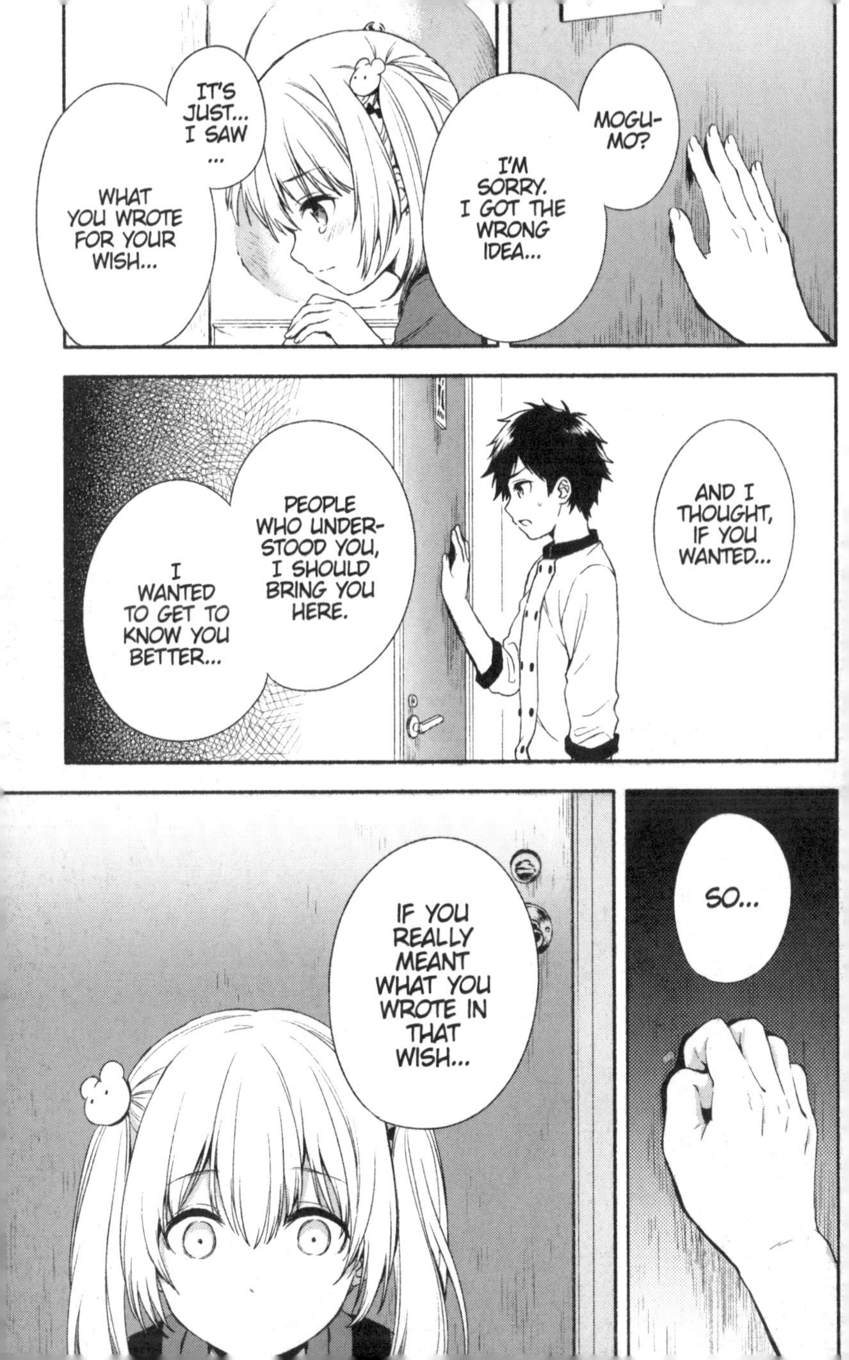
MOGU-MO?
I'M SORRY. I GOT THE WRONG IDEA...
IT'S JUST... I SAW ...
WHAT YOU WROTE FOR YOUR WISH...
AND I THOUGHT, IF YOU WANTED...
PEOPLE WHO UNDER-STOOD YOU, I SHOULD BRING YOU HERE.
I WANTED TO GET TO KNOW YOU BETTER...
SO...
IF YOU REALLY MEANT WHAT YOU WROTE IN THAT WISH...

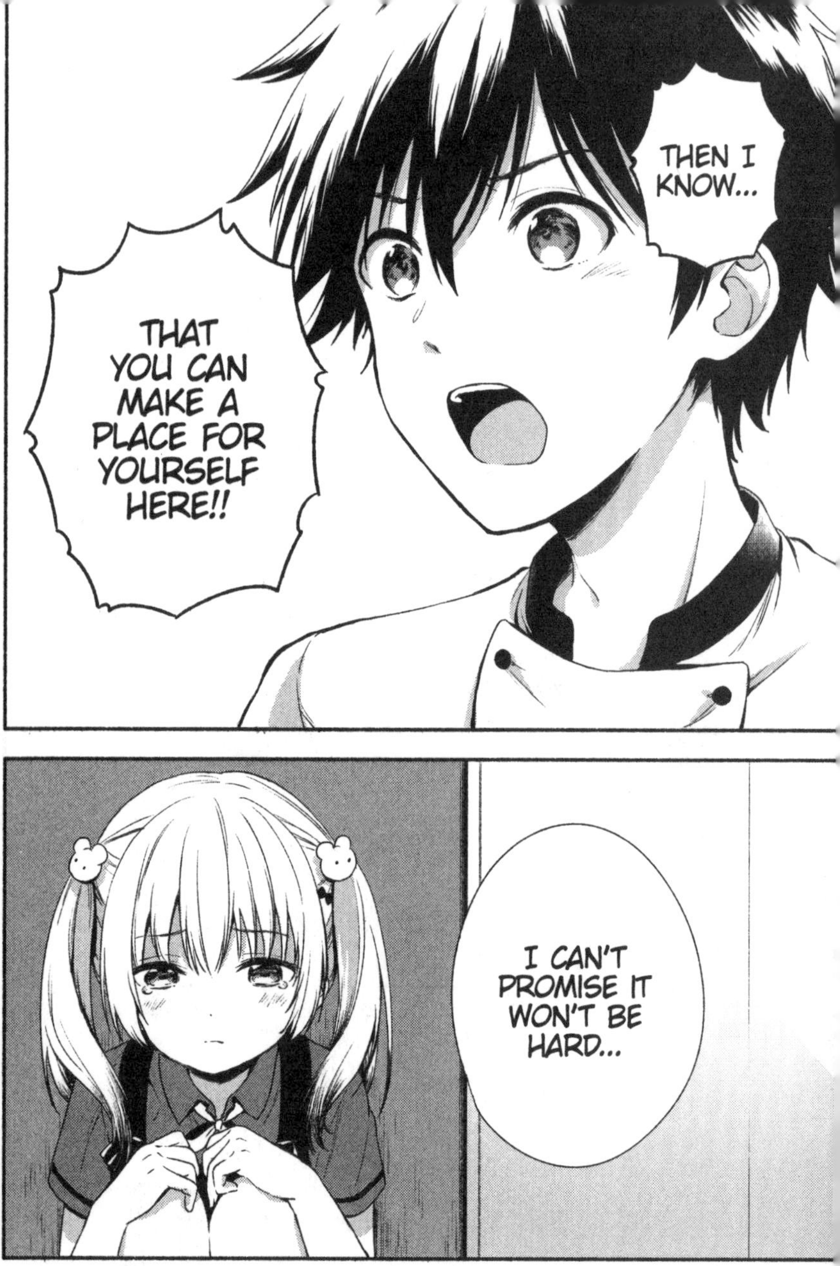
THEN I KNOW...
THAT YOU CAN MAKE A PLACE FOR YOURSELF HERE!!
I CAN'T PROMISE IT WON'T BE HARD...

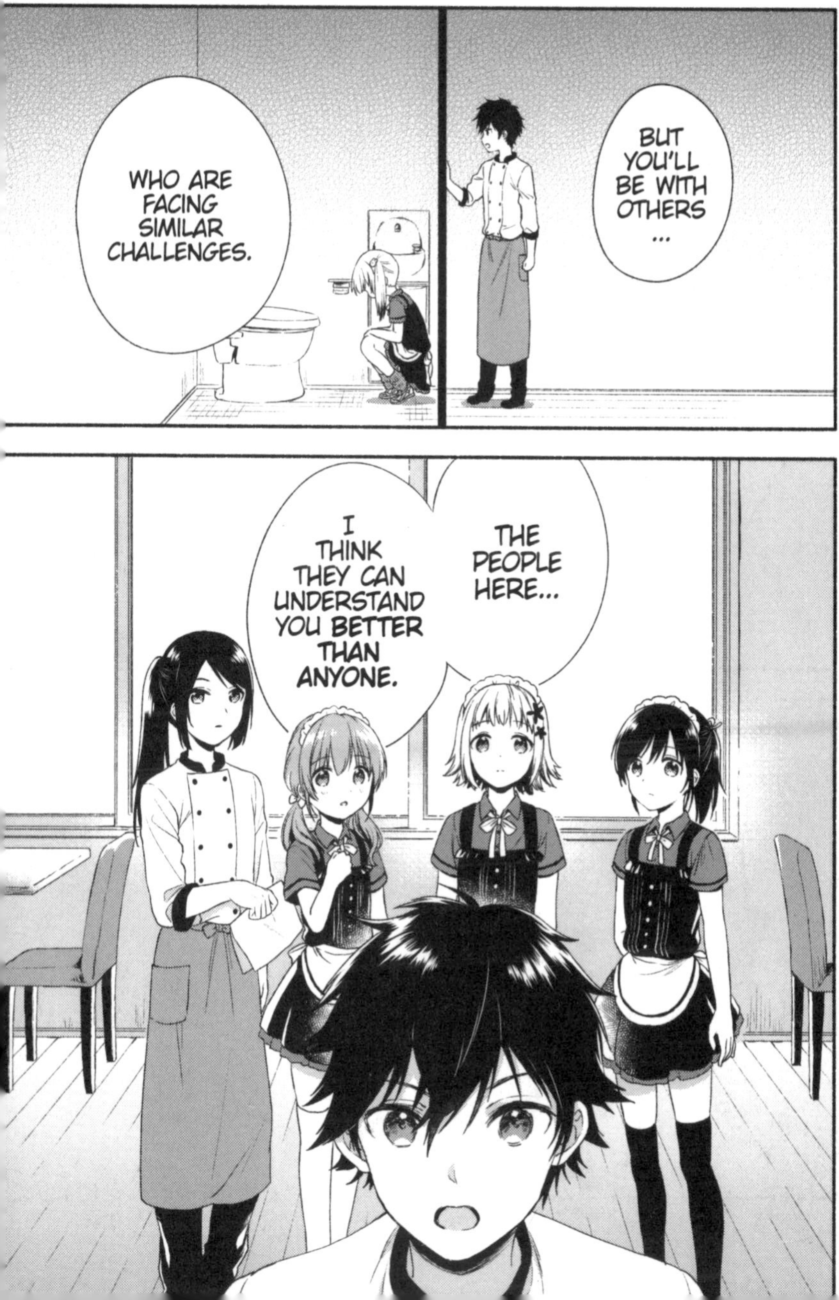
BUT YOU'LL BE WITH OTHERS ...
WHO ARE FACING SIMILAR CHALLENGES.
THE PEOPLE HERE...
I THINK THEY CAN UNDERSTAND YOU BETTER THAN ANYONE.

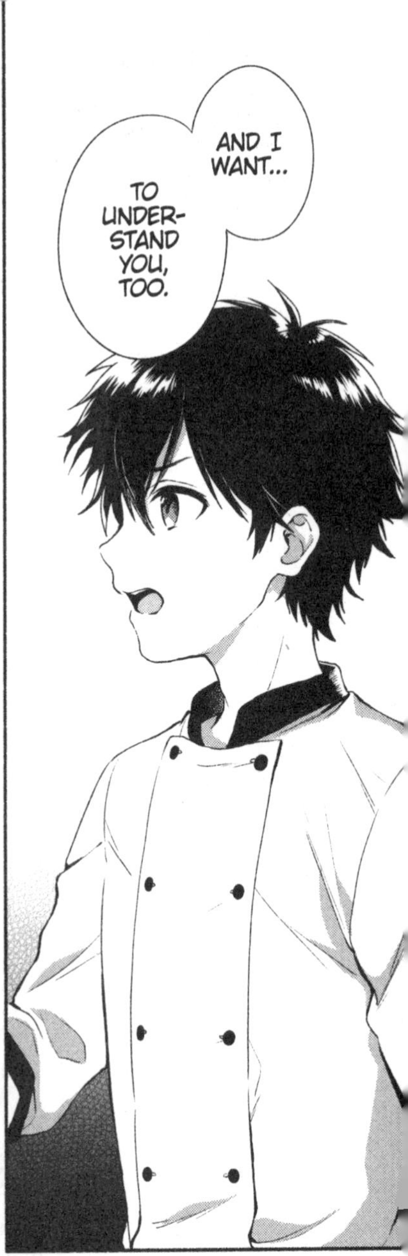
AND I WANT...
TO UNDERSTAND YOU, TOO.

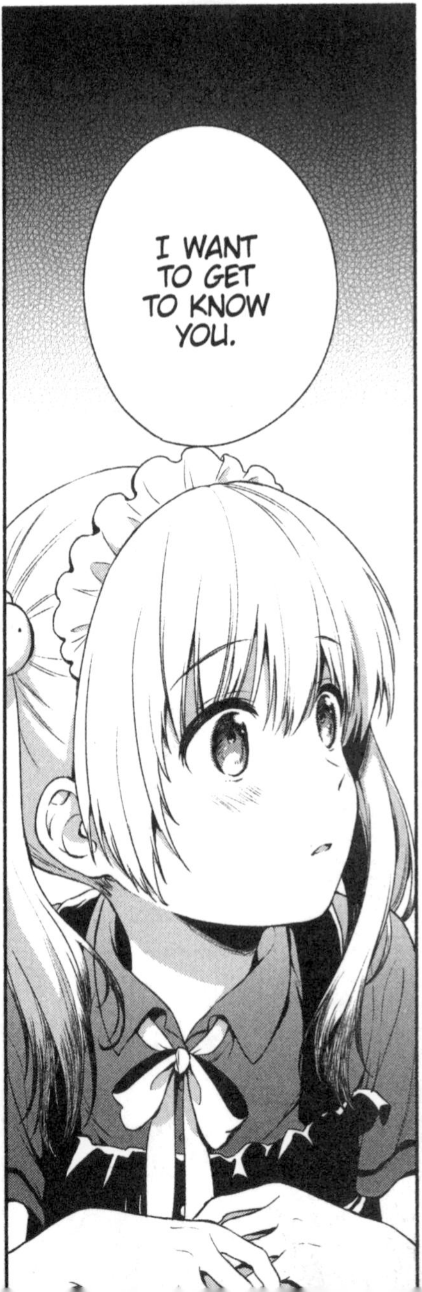
I WANT TO GET TO KNOW YOU.

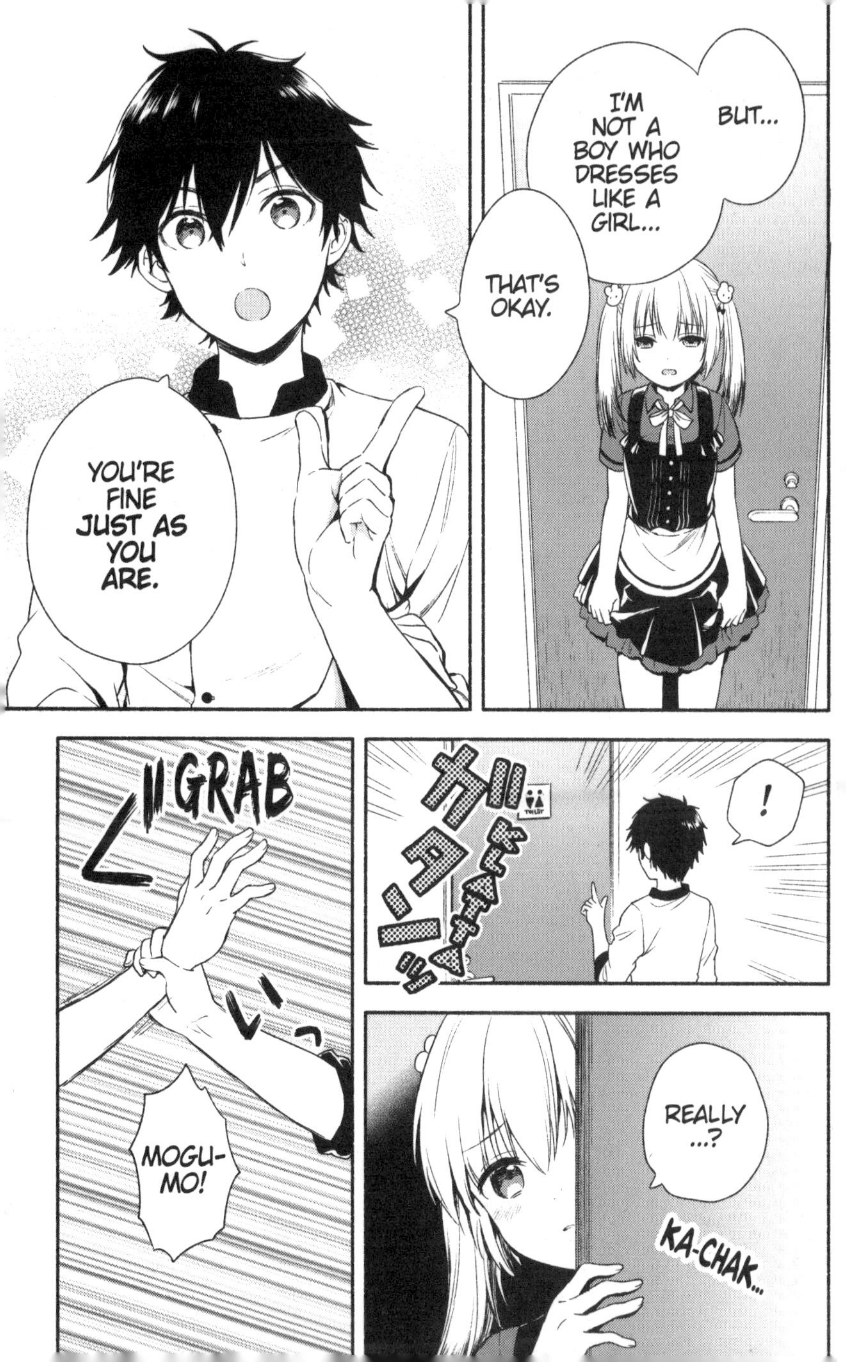
BUT...
I'M NOT A BOY WHO DRESSES LIKE A GIRL...
THAT'S OKAY.
YOU'RE FINE JUST AS YOU ARE.
!
REALLY ...?
KA-CHAK...
GRAB
MOGU-MO!

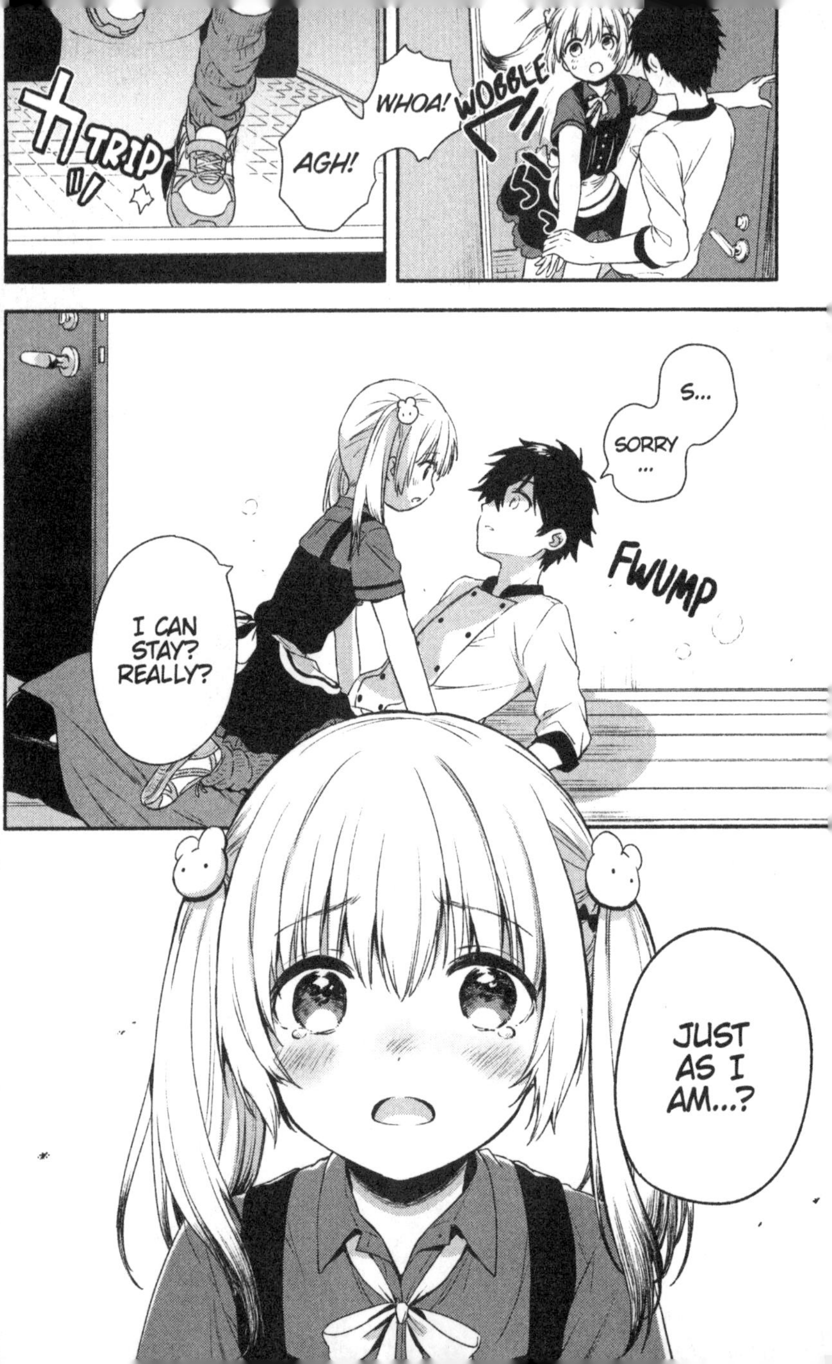
WOBBLE
WHOA! AGH!
TRIP
S... SORRY...
FWUMP
I CAN STAY? REALLY?
JUST AS I AM...?

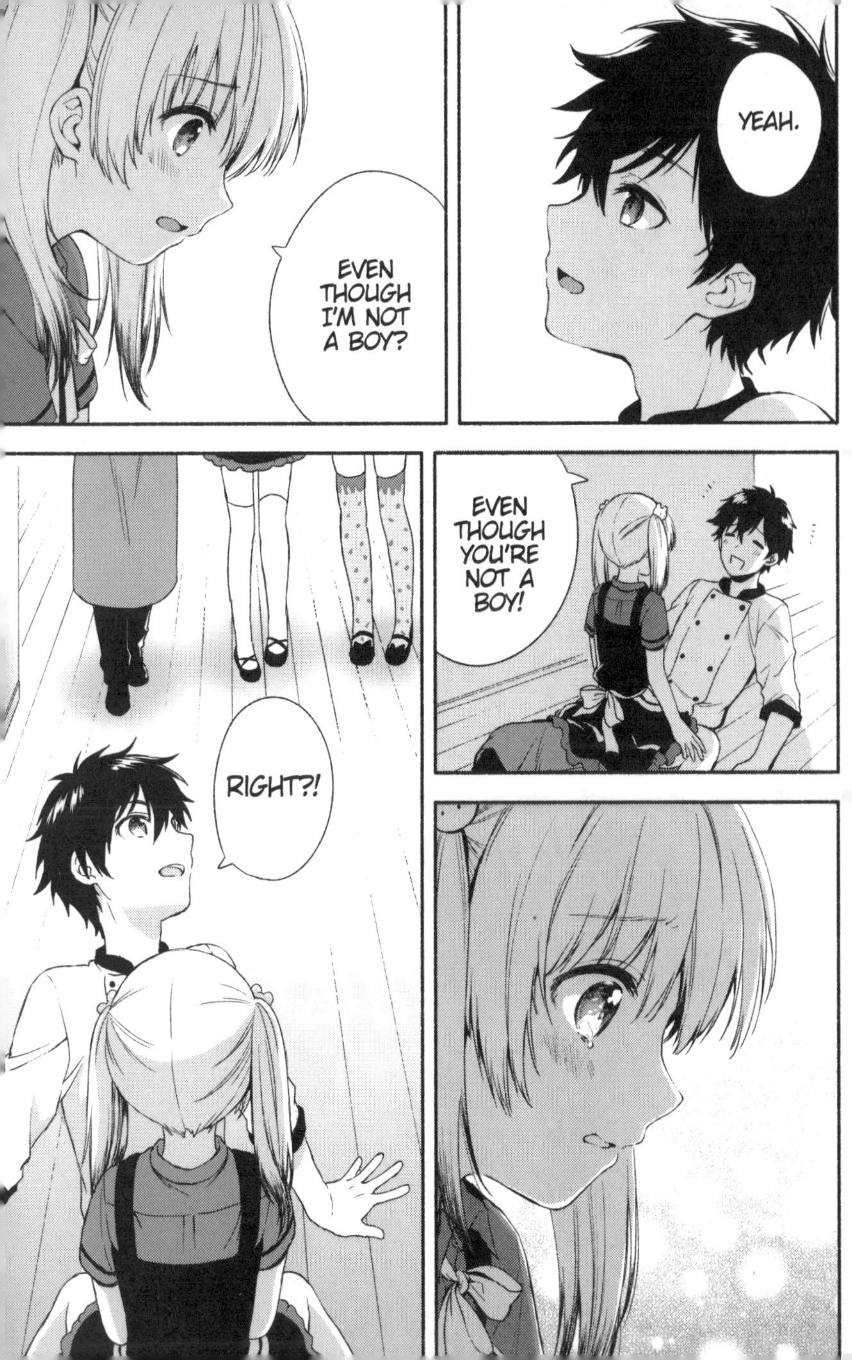
YEAH.
EVEN THOUGH I'M NOT A BOY?
EVEN THOUGH YOU'RE NOT A BOY!
RIGHT?!

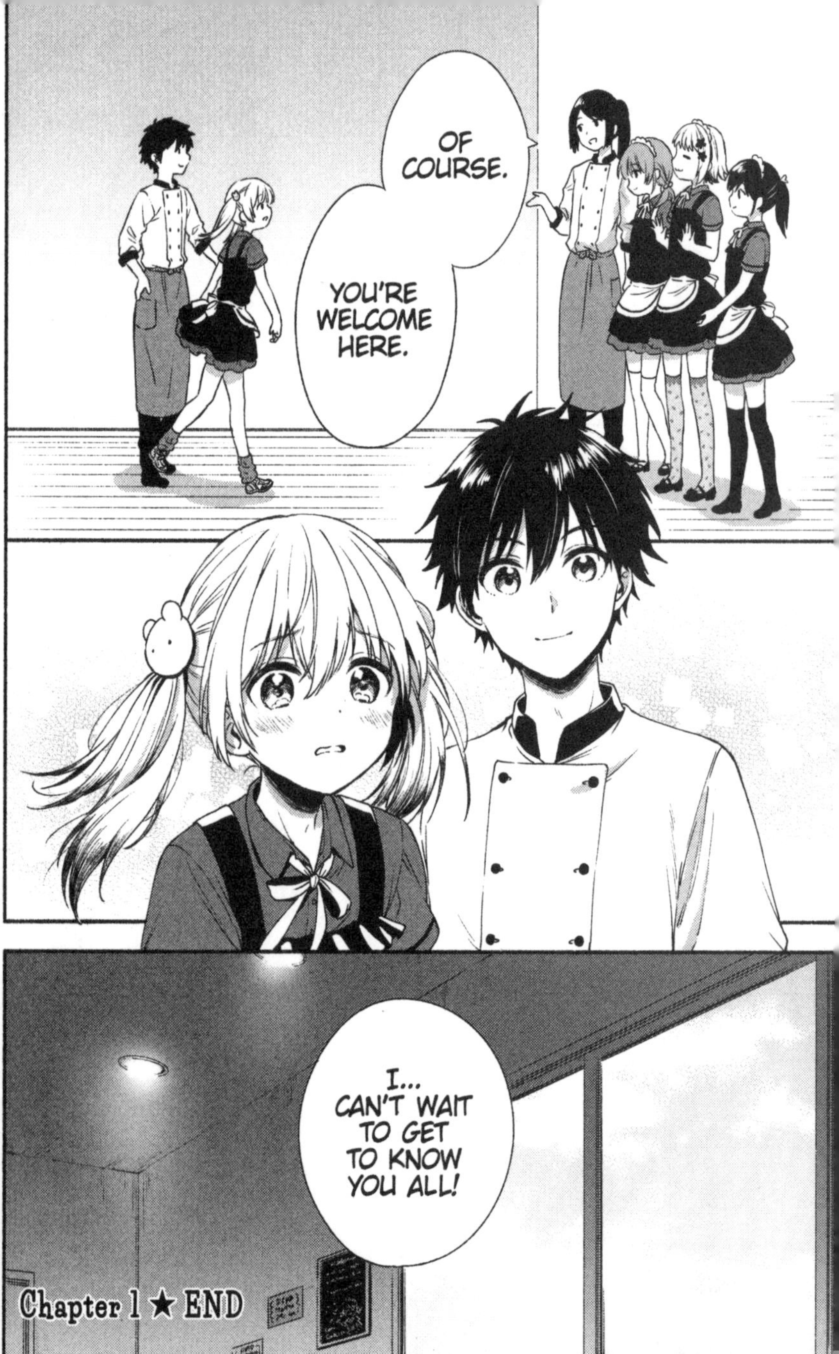
OF COURSE.
YOU'RE WELCOME HERE.
I... CAN'T WAIT TO GET TO KNOW YOU ALL!
Chapter 1 ★ END

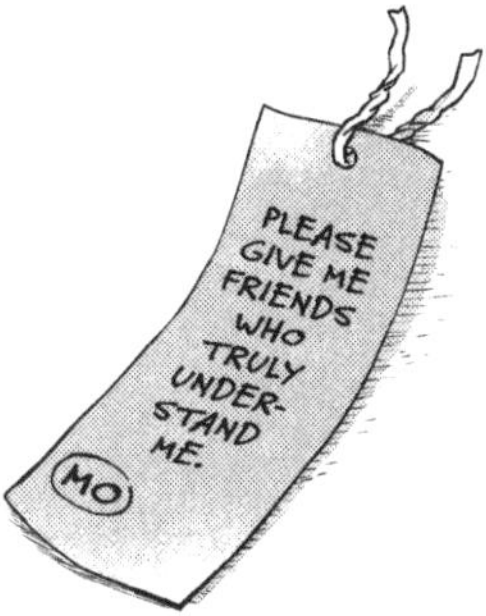
PLEASE GIVE ME FRIENDS WHO TRULY UNDER-STAND ME.
MO

Love me for
who I am

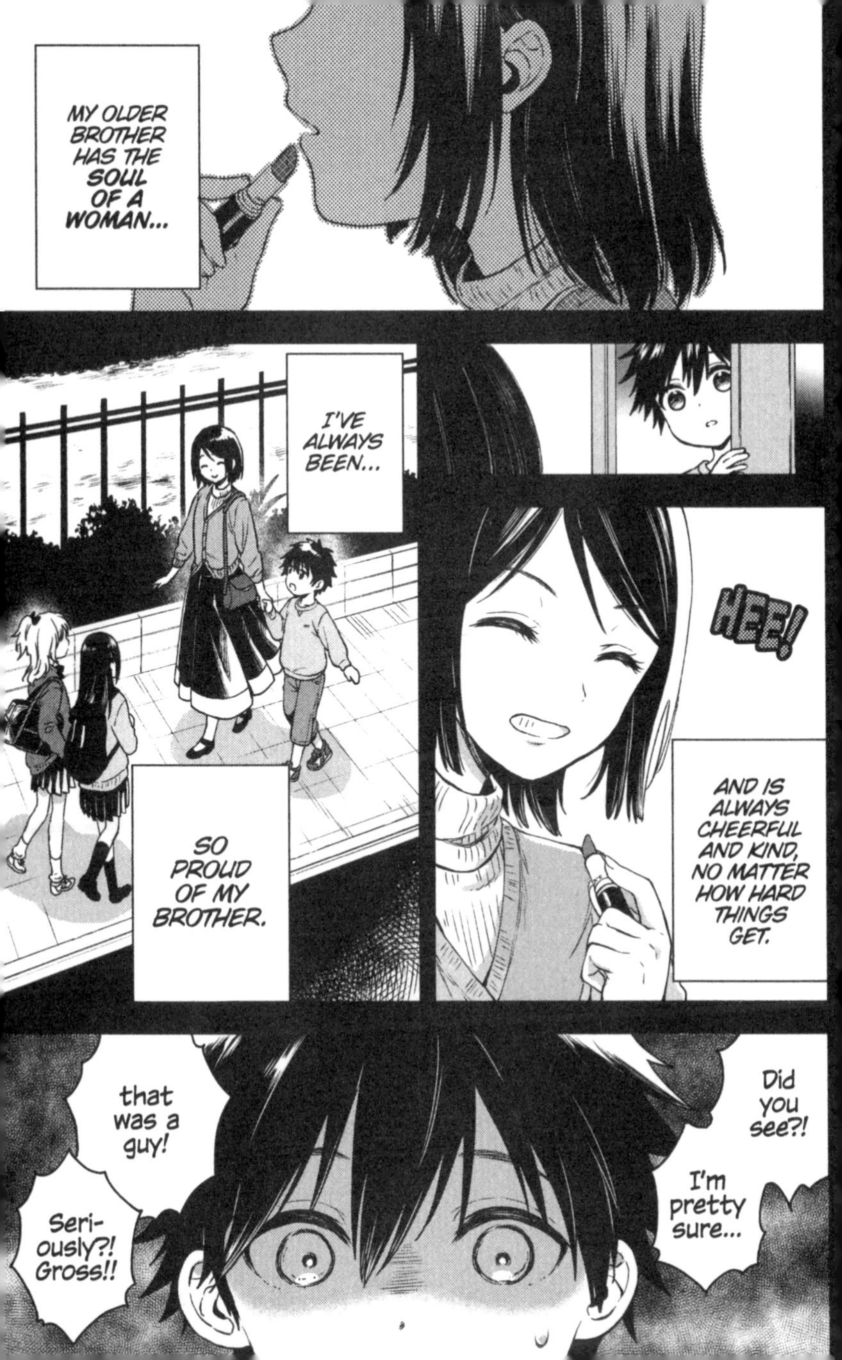
MY OLDER BROTHER HAS THE SOUL OF A WOMAN...
HEE!
AND IS ALWAYS CHEERFUL AND KIND, NO MATTER HOW HARD THINGS GET.
I'VE ALWAYS BEEN...
SO PROUD OF MY BROTHER.
Did you see?!
I'm pretty sure...
that was a guy!
Seri-ously?! Gross!!

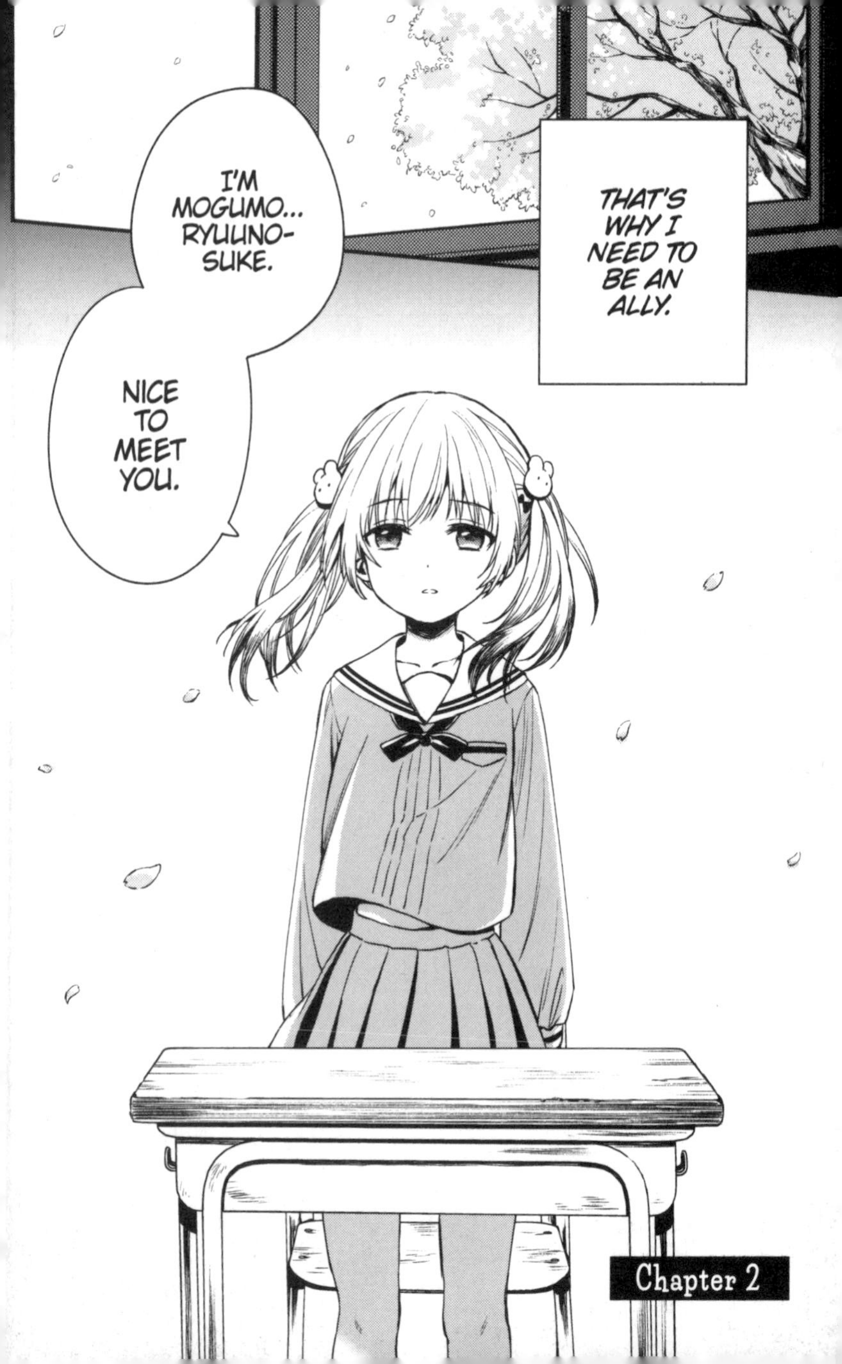
THAT'S WHY I NEED TO BE AN ALLY.
I'M MOGUMO... RYUUNOSUKE.
NICE TO MEET YOU.
Chapter 2

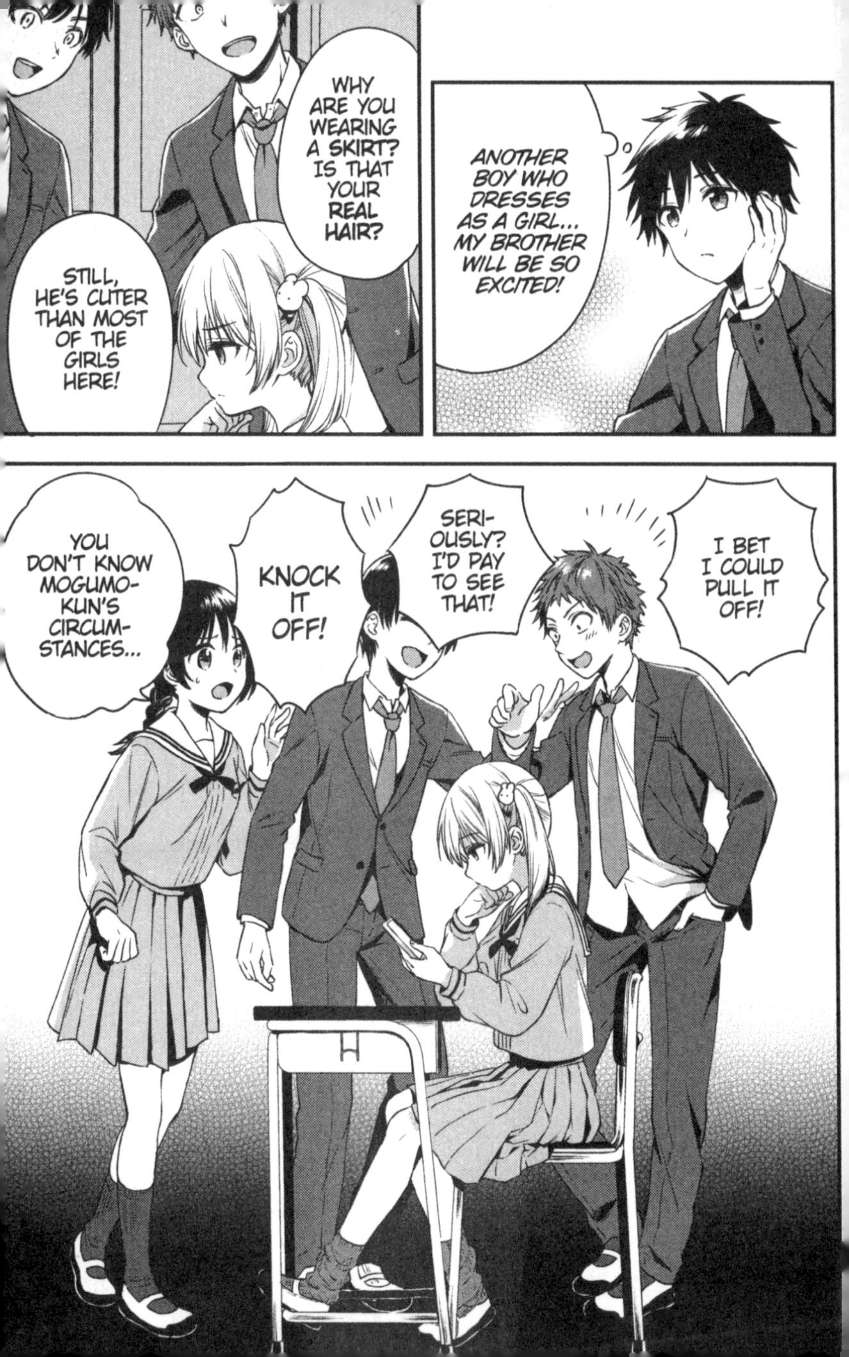
ANOTHER BOY WHO DRESSES AS A GIRL... MY BROTHER WILL BE SO EXCITED!
WHY ARE YOU WEARING A SKIRT? IS THAT YOUR REAL HAIR?
STILL, HE'S CUTER THAN MOST OF THE GIRLS HERE!
I BET I COULD PULL IT OFF!
SERI-OUSLY? I'D PAY TO SEE THAT!
KNOCK IT OFF!
YOU DON'T KNOW MOGUMO-KUN'S CIRCUM-STANCES...

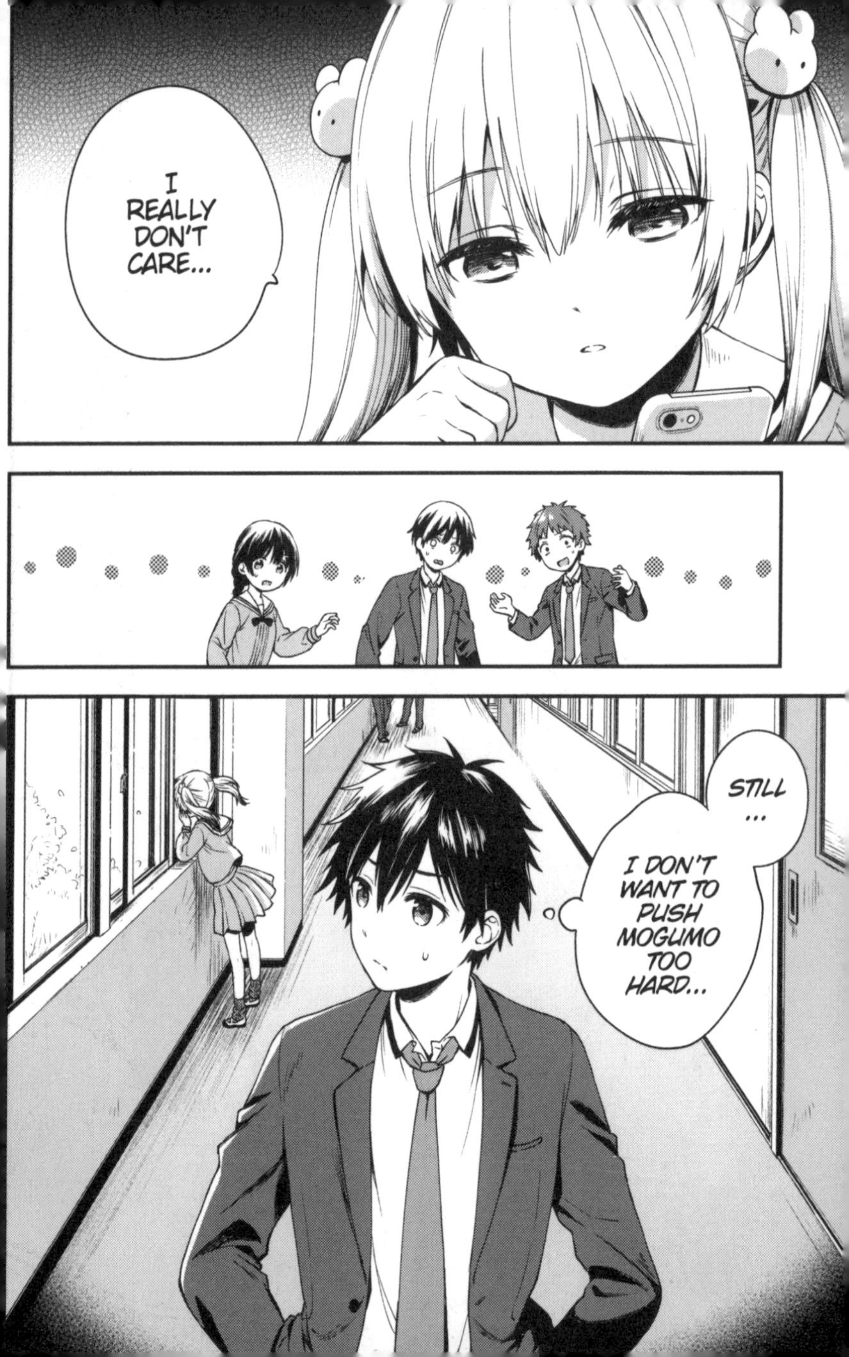
I REALLY DON'T CARE...
STILL ...
I DON'T WANT TO PUSH MOGUMO TOO HARD...

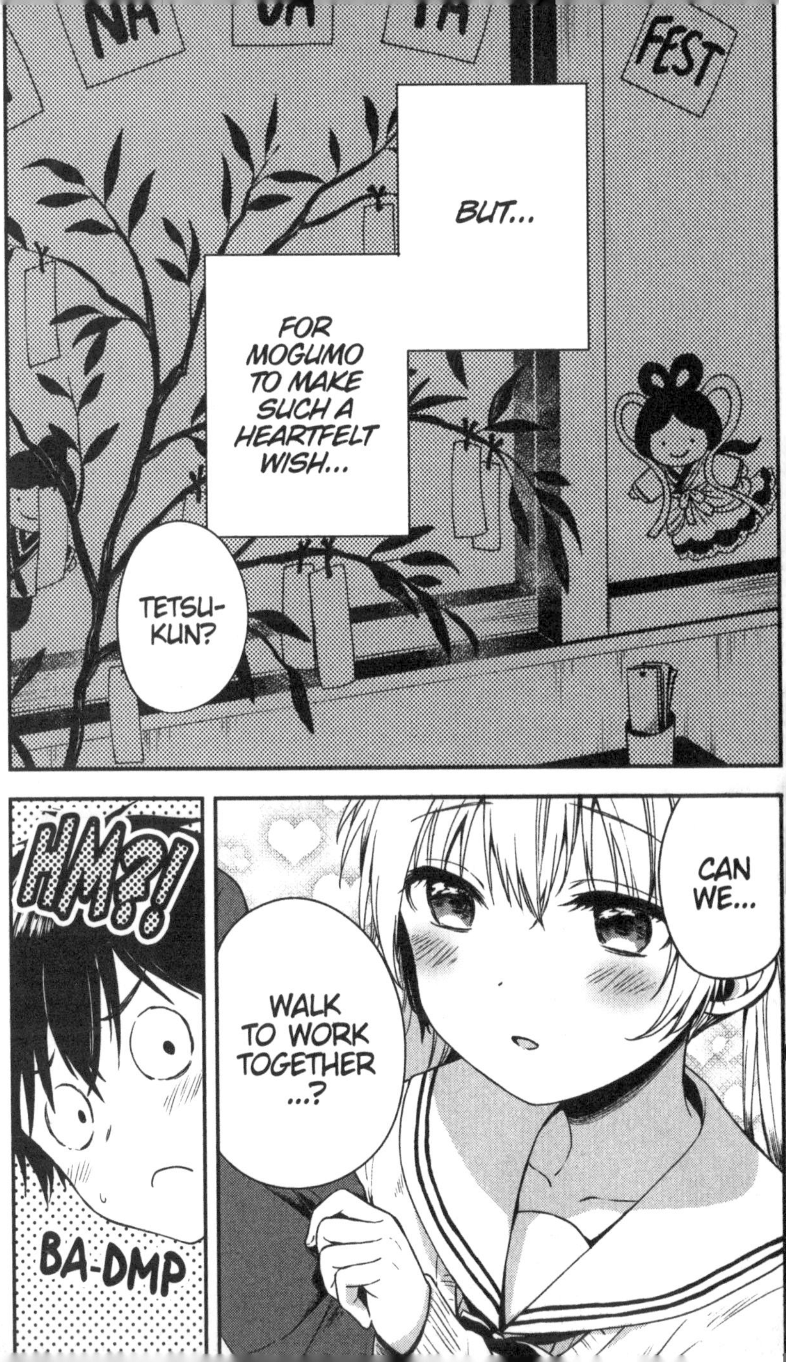
FEST
BUT...
FOR MOGUMO TO MAKE SUCH A HEARTFELT WISH...
TETSU-KUN?
CAN WE...
WALK TO WORK TOGETHER ...?
HM?!
BA-DMP

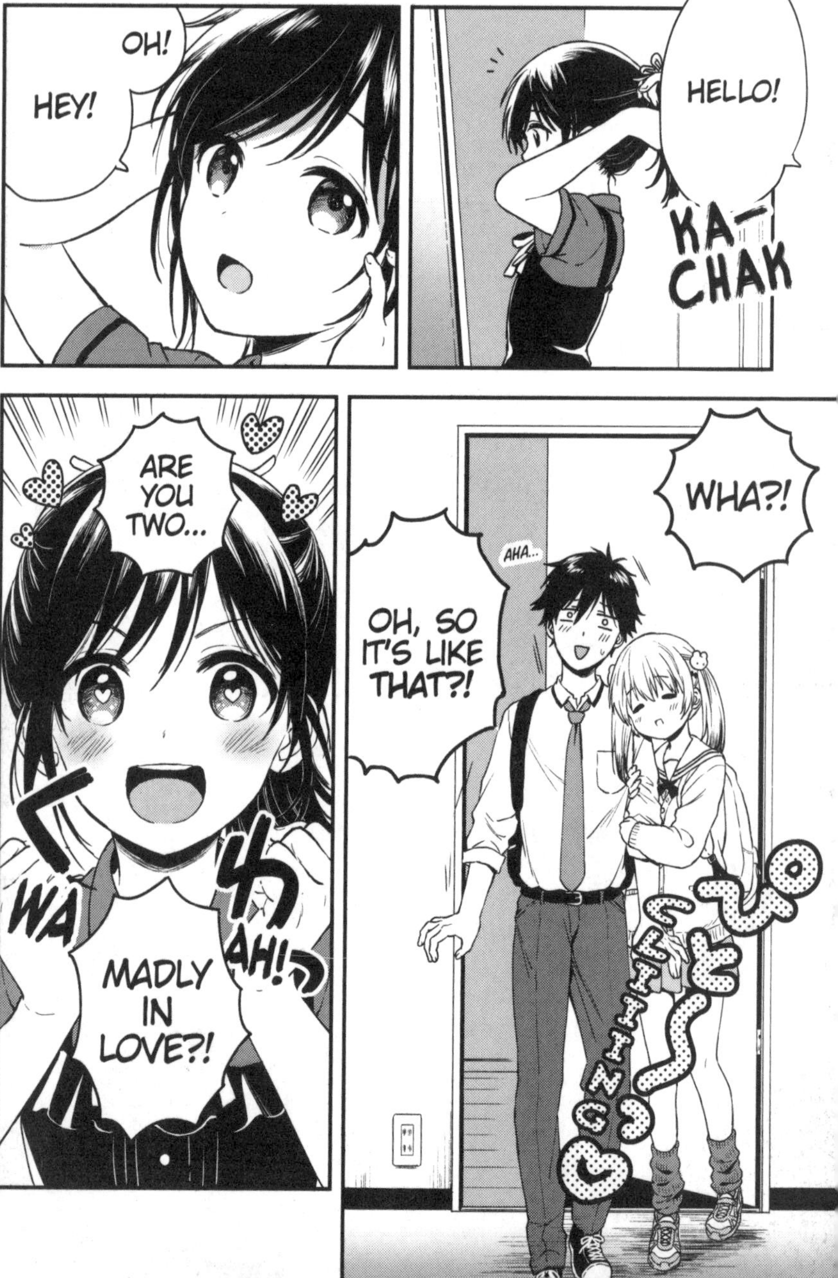
HELLO!
KA-CHAK
OH!
HEY!
WHA?!
AHA...
OH, SO IT'S LIKE THAT?!
ARE YOU TWO...
WA
AH!
MADLY IN LOVE?!

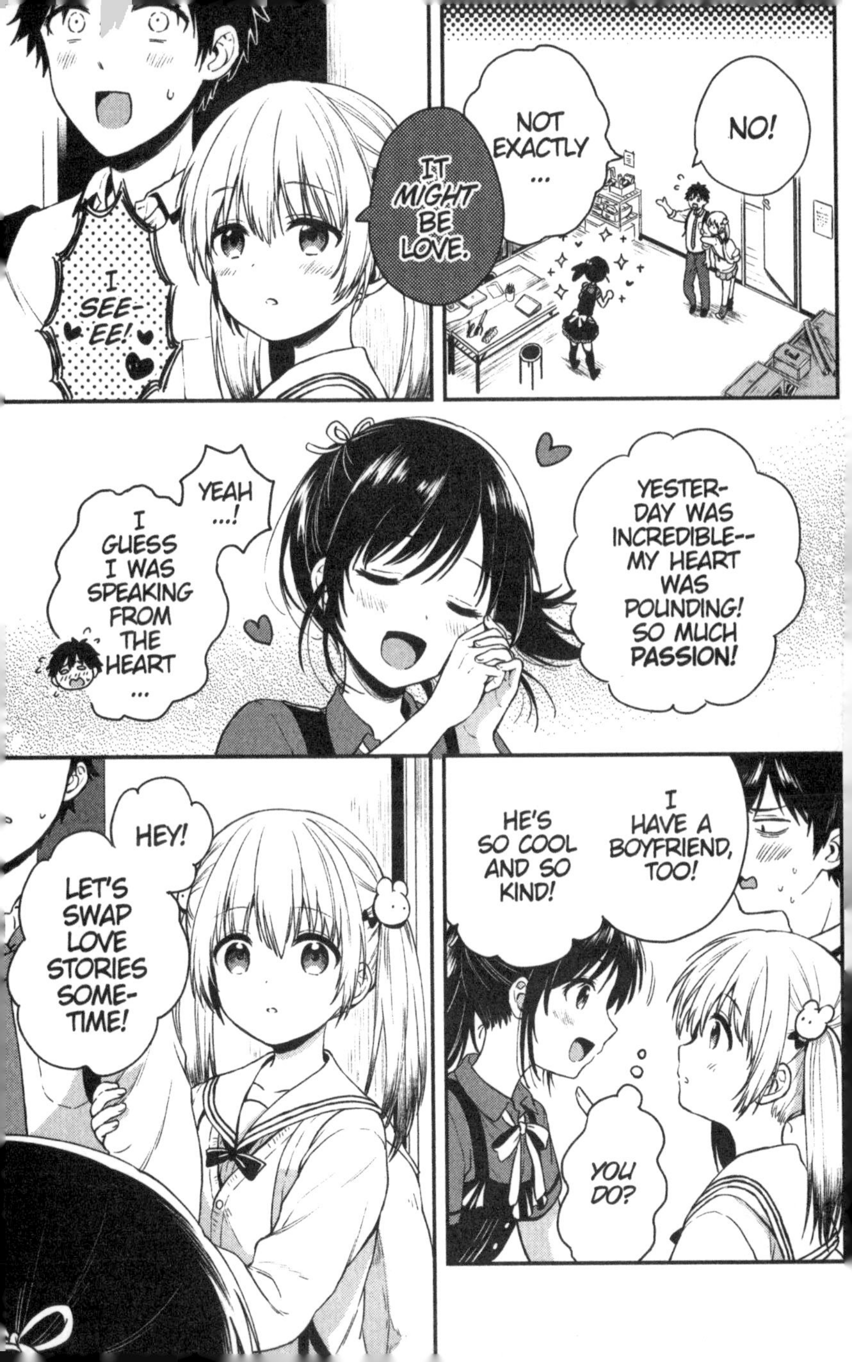
NO!
NOT EXACTLY ...
IT MIGHT BE LOVE.
I SEEE-EE!
YESTER-DAY WAS INCREDIBLE-- MY HEART WAS POUNDING! SO MUCH PASSION!
YEAH ...!
I GUESS I WAS SPEAKING FROM THE HEART ...
I HAVE A BOYFRIEND, TOO!
HE'S SO COOL AND SO KIND!
YOU DO?
HEY!
LET'S SWAP LOVE STORIES SOME-TIME!

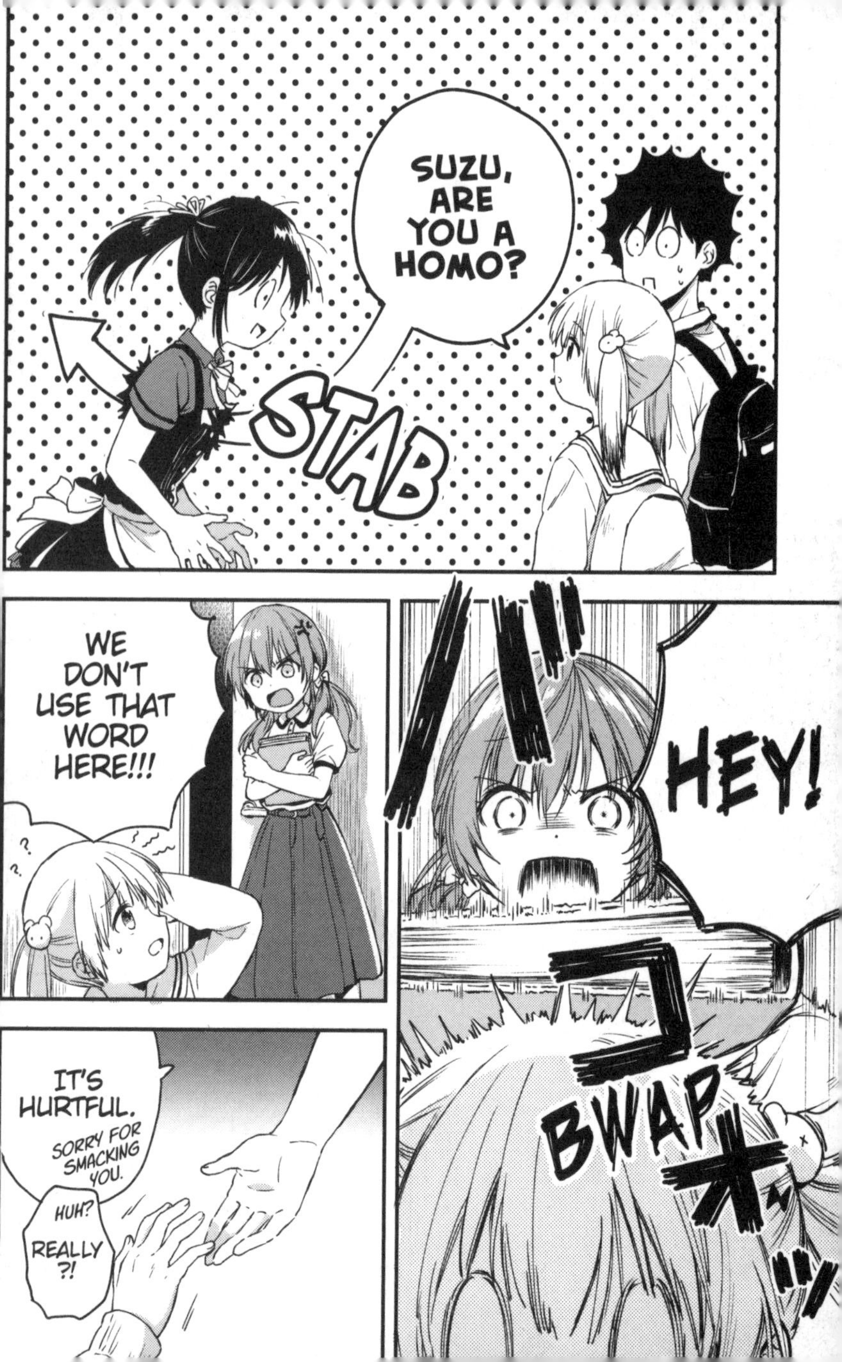
SUZU, ARE YOU A HOMO?
STAB
HEY!
BWAP
WE DON'T USE THAT WORD HERE!!!
IT'S HURTFUL.
SORRY FOR SMACKING YOU.
HUH?
REALLY?!

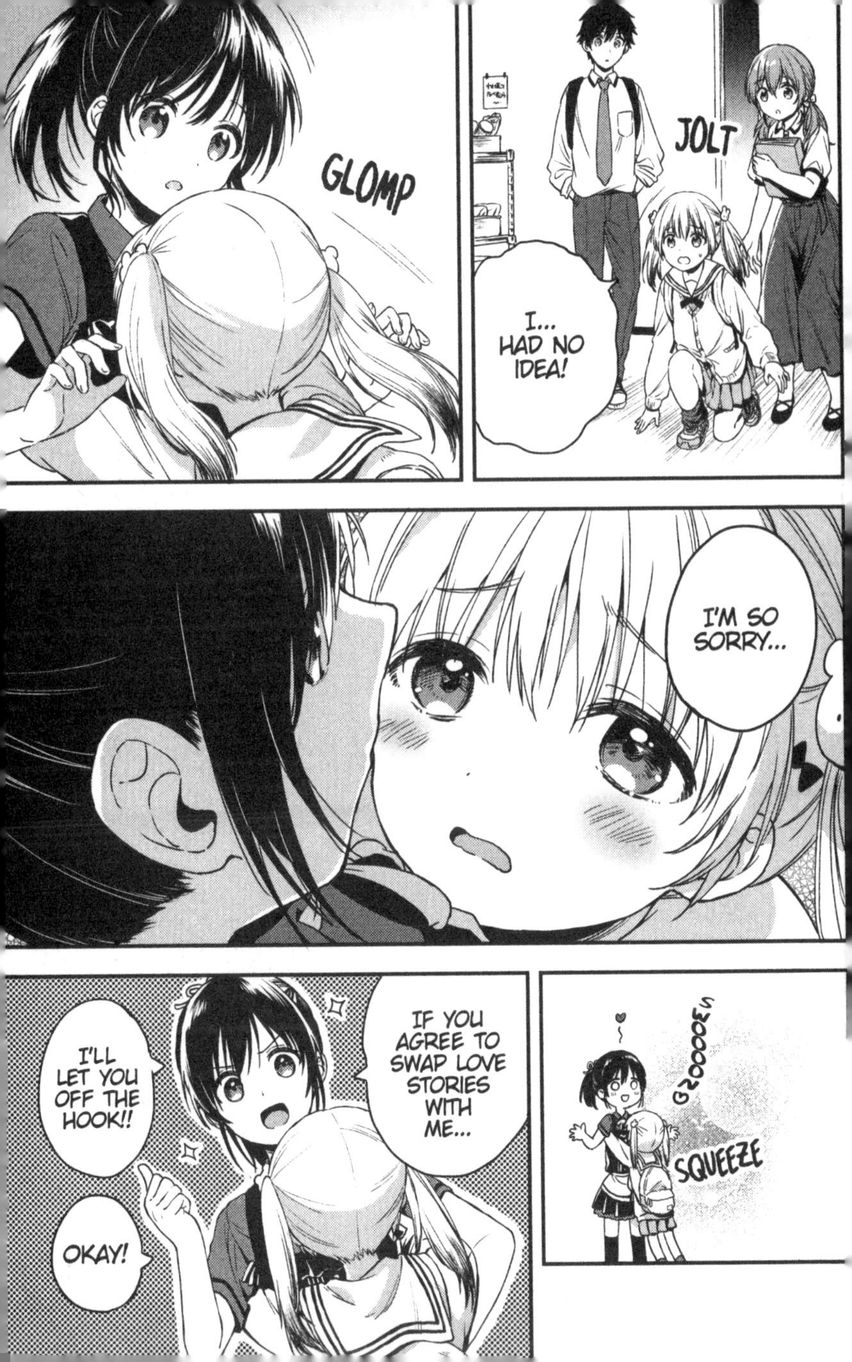
JOLT
I... HAD NO IDEA!
GLOMP
I'M SO SORRY...
SQUEEZE
IF YOU AGREE TO SWAP LOVE STORIES WITH ME...
I'LL LET YOU OFF THE HOOK!!
OKAY!

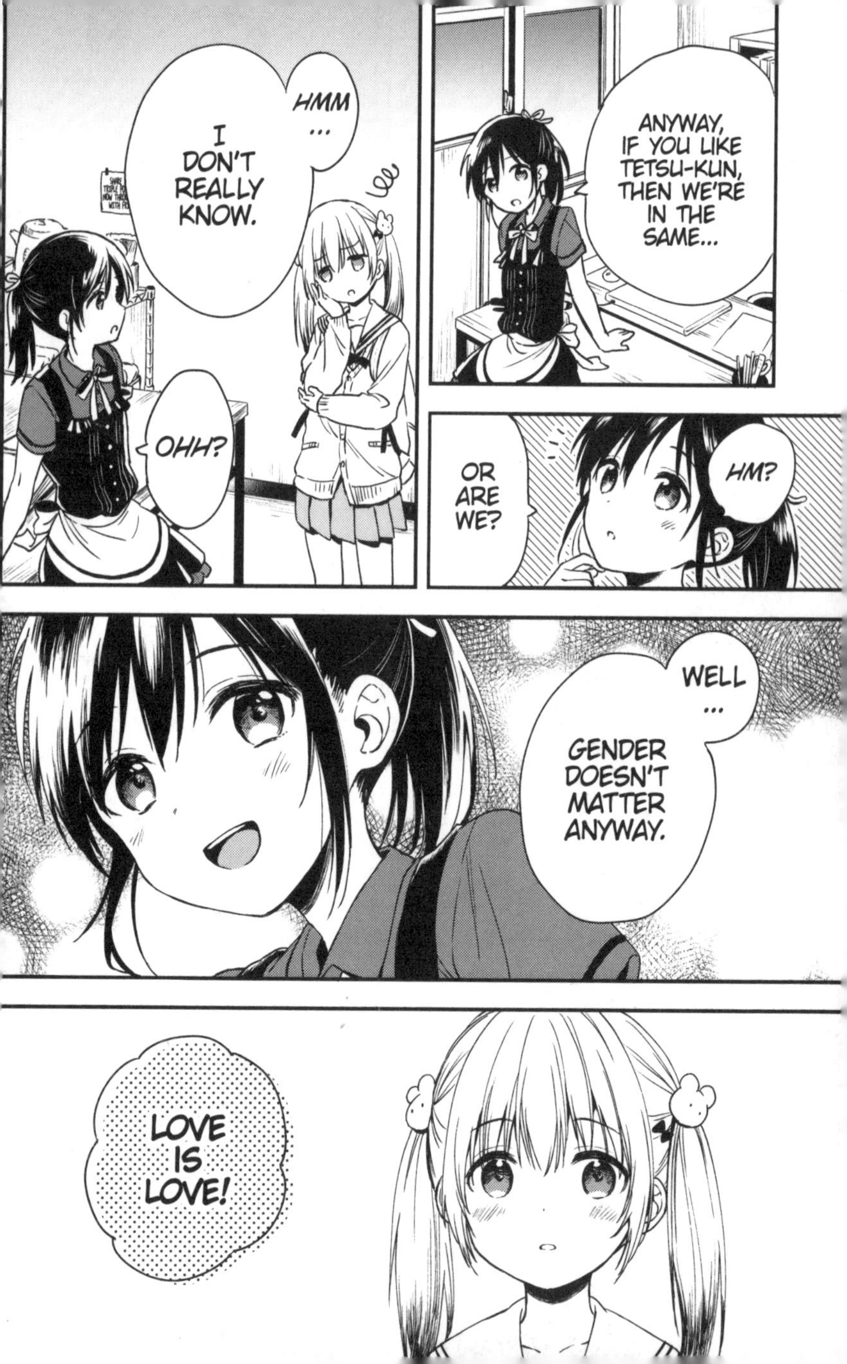
ANYWAY, IF YOU LIKE TETSU-KUN, THEN WE'RE IN THE SAME...
HM?
OR ARE WE?
HMM ...
I DON'T REALLY KNOW.
OHH?
WELL ...
GENDER DOESN'T MATTER ANYWAY.
LOVE IS LOVE!

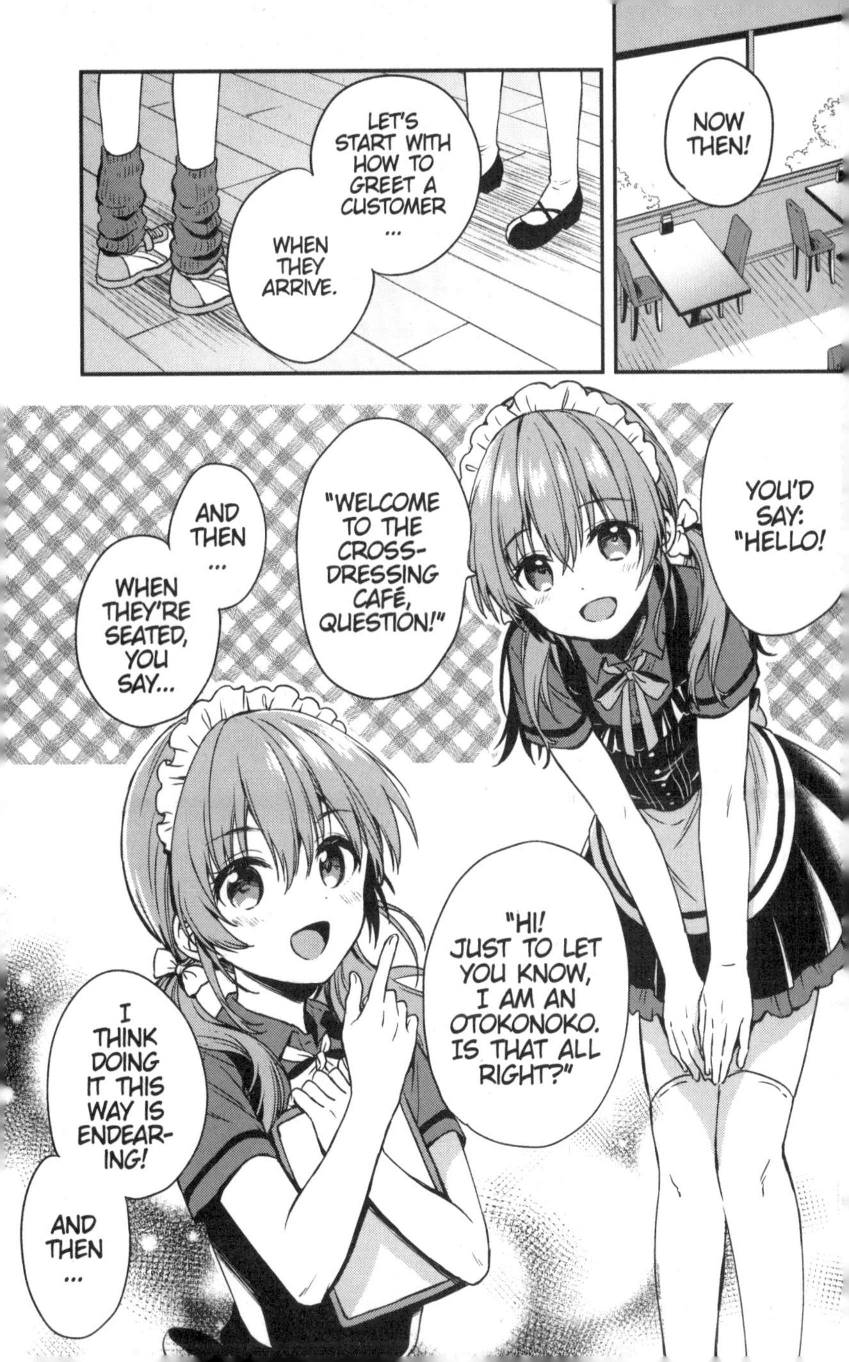
NOW THEN!
LET'S START WITH HOW TO GREET A CUSTOMER...
WHEN THEY ARRIVE.
YOU'D SAY: "HELLO!
"WELCOME TO THE CROSS-DRESSING CAFÉ, QUESTION!"
AND THEN...
WHEN THEY'RE SEATED, YOU SAY...
"HI! JUST TO LET YOU KNOW, I AM AN OTOKONOKO. IS THAT ALL RIGHT?"
I THINK DOING IT THIS WAY IS ENDEAR-ING!
AND THEN...

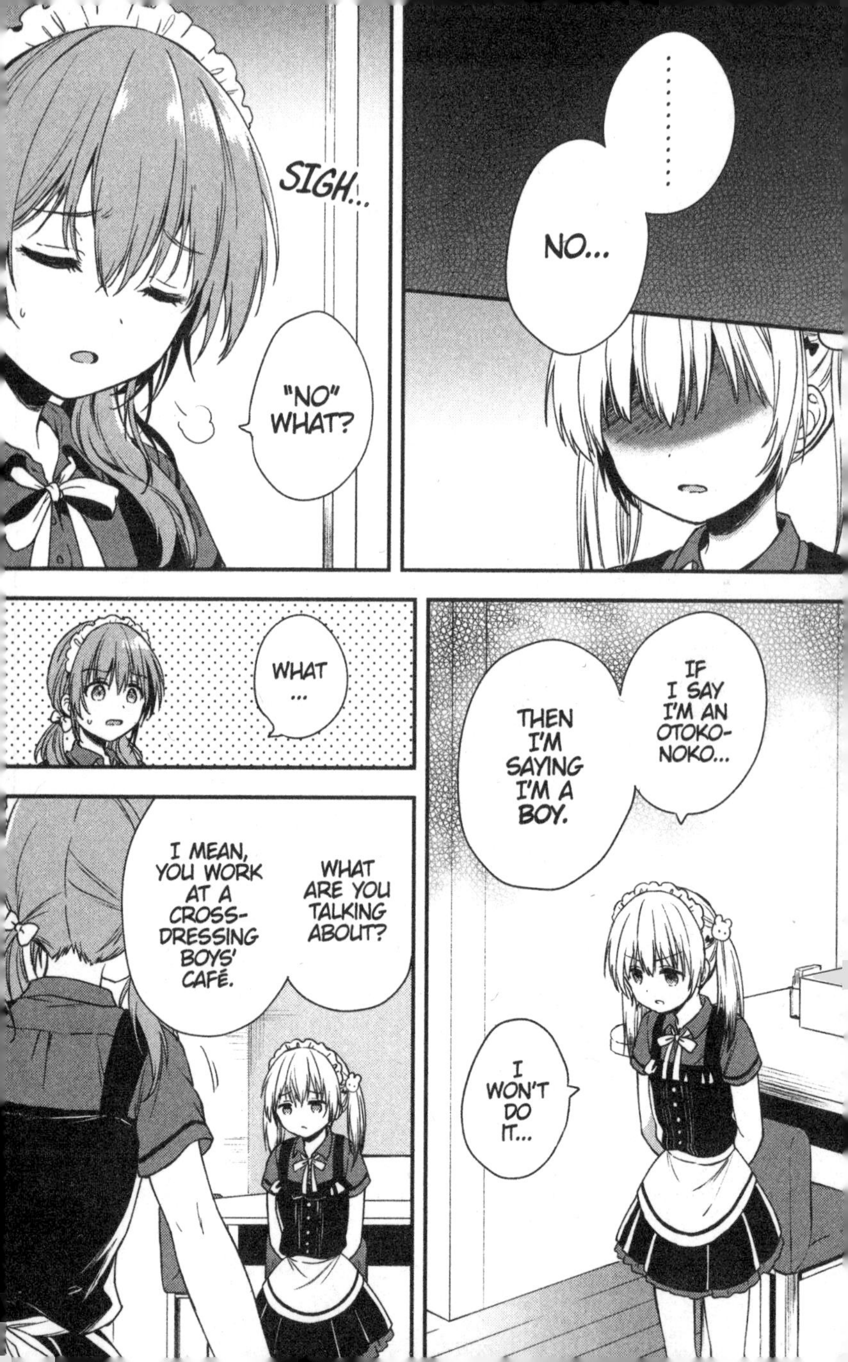
......
NO...
SIGH...
"NO" WHAT?
IF I SAY I'M AN OTOKO-NOKO...
THEN I'M SAYING I'M A BOY.
I WON'T DO IT...
WHAT ...
WHAT ARE YOU TALKING ABOUT?
I MEAN, YOU WORK AT A CROSS-DRESSING BOYS' CAFÉ.

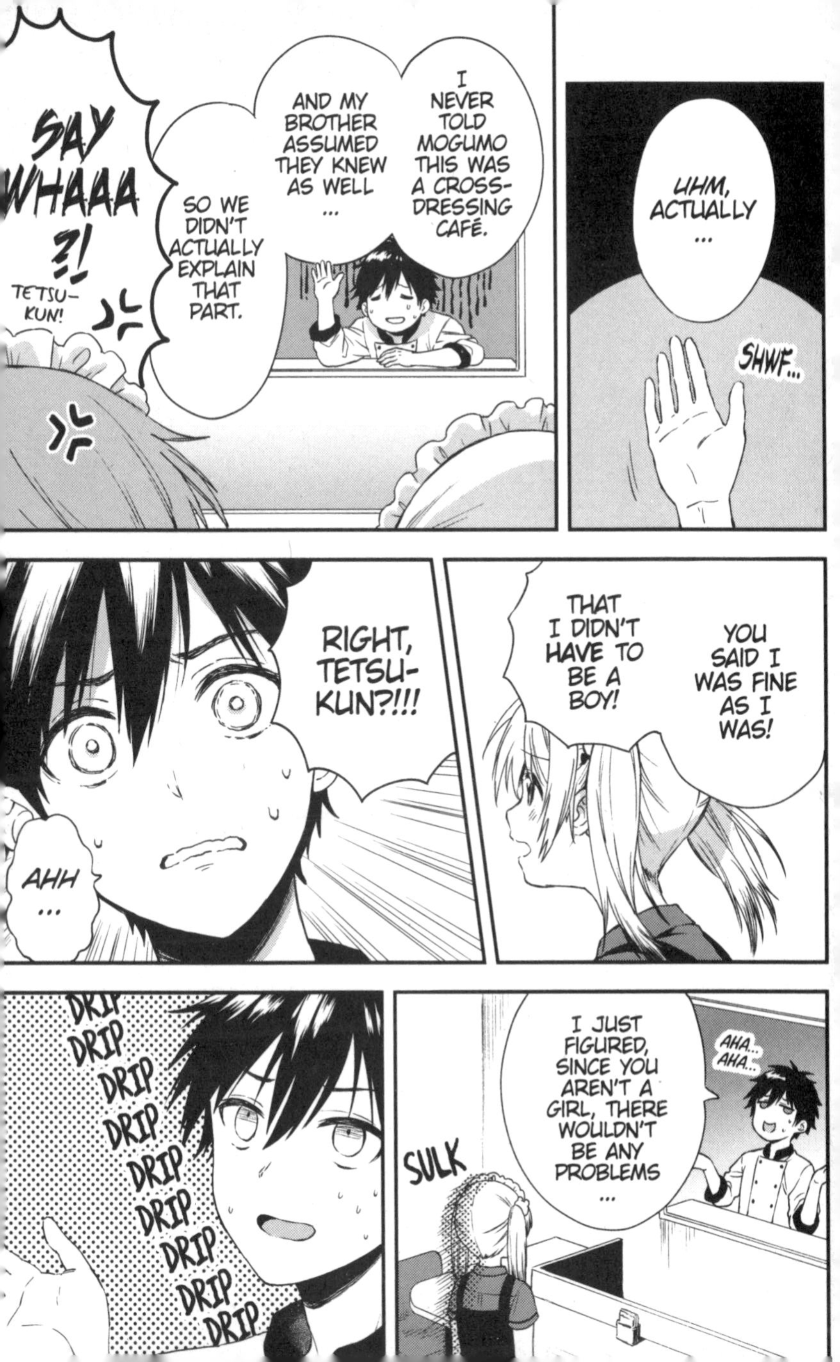
UHM, ACTUALLY ...
SHWF...
I NEVER TOLD MOGUMO THIS WAS A CROSS-DRESSING CAFÉ.
AND MY BROTHER ASSUMED THEY KNEW AS WELL ...
SO WE DIDN'T ACTUALLY EXPLAIN THAT PART.
SAY WHAAA ?!
TETSU-KUN!
YOU SAID I WAS FINE AS I WAS!
THAT I DIDN'T HAVE TO BE A BOY!
RIGHT, TETSU-KUN?!!!
AHH ...
AHA... AHA...
I JUST FIGURED, SINCE YOU AREN'T A GIRL, THERE WOULDN'T BE ANY PROBLEMS ...
SULK
DRIP DRIP DRIP DRIP DRIP DRIP DRIP DRIP DRIP DRIP DRIP

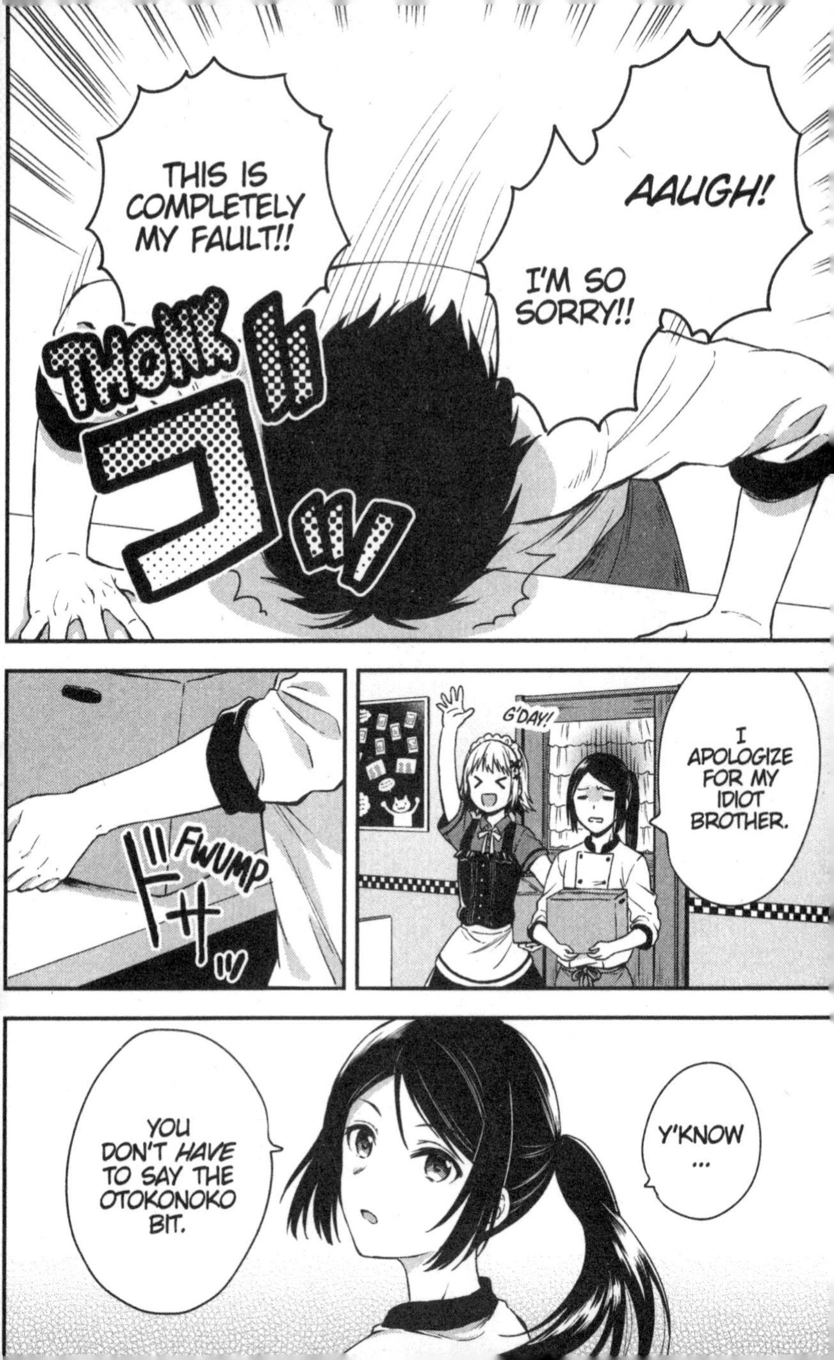
AAUGH!
I'M SO SORRY!!
THIS IS COMPLETELY MY FAULT!!
THONK
I APOLOGIZE FOR MY IDIOT BROTHER.
G'DAY!
FWUMP
Y'KNOW ...
YOU DON'T *HAVE* TO SAY THE OTOKONOKO BIT.

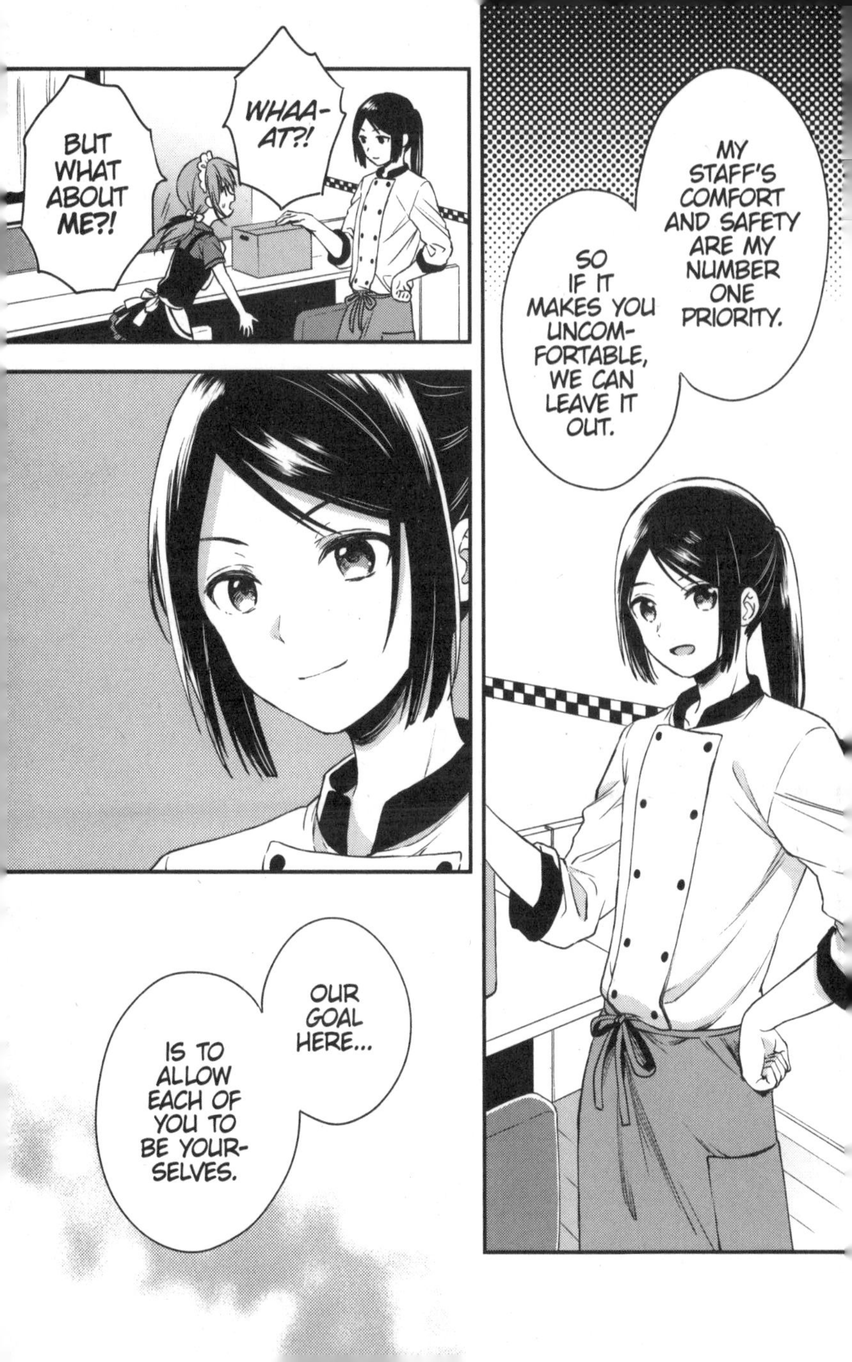
MY STAFF'S COMFORT AND SAFETY ARE MY NUMBER ONE PRIORITY.
SO IF IT MAKES YOU UNCOMFORTABLE, WE CAN LEAVE IT OUT.
WHAA-AT?!
BUT WHAT ABOUT ME?!
OUR GOAL HERE...
IS TO ALLOW EACH OF YOU TO BE YOURSELVES.

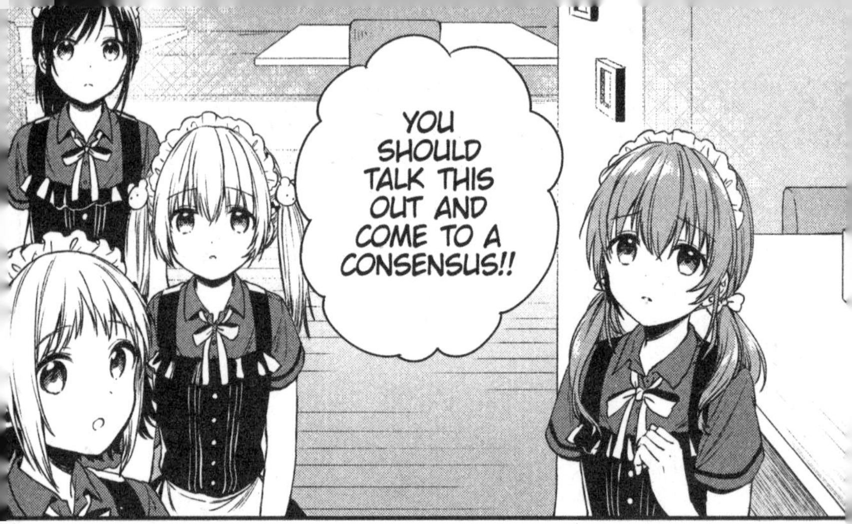
YOU SHOULD TALK THIS OUT AND COME TO A CONSENSUS!!

CASE 1: SUZU'S FEELINGS

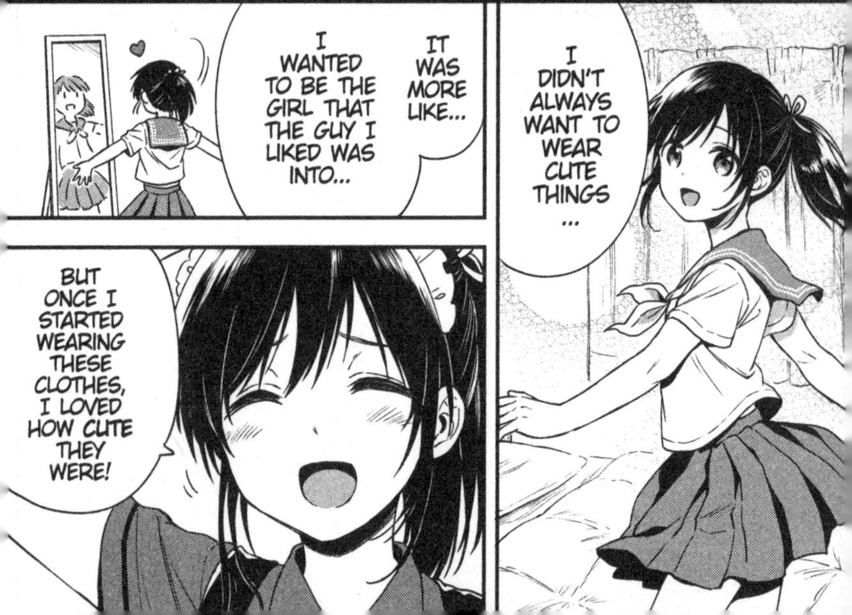
I DIDN'T ALWAYS WANT TO WEAR CUTE THINGS...
IT WAS MORE LIKE...
I WANTED TO BE THE GIRL THAT THE GUY I LIKED WAS INTO...
BUT ONCE I STARTED WEARING THESE CLOTHES, I LOVED HOW CUTE THEY WERE!

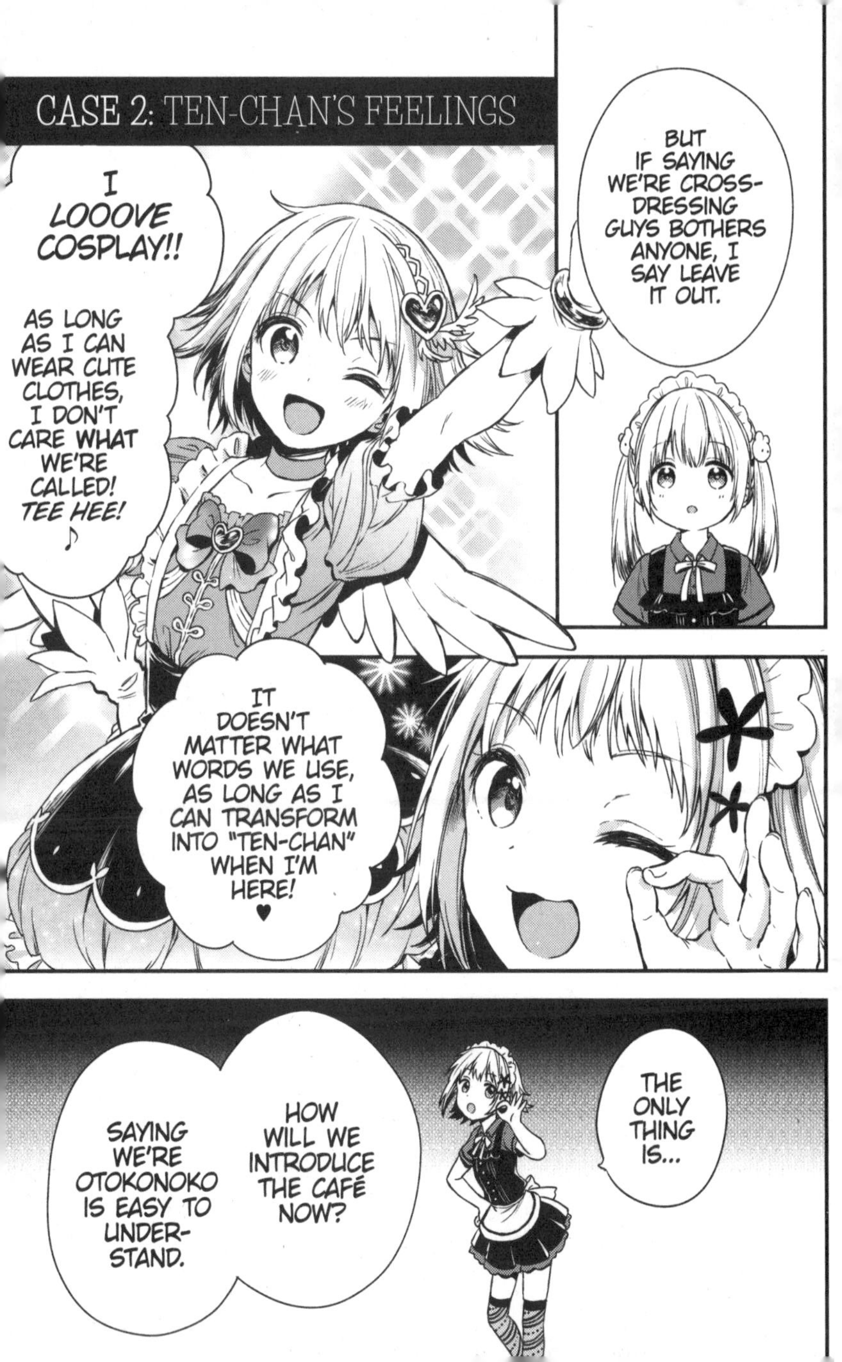
CASE 2: TEN-CHAN'S FEELINGS
BUT IF SAYING WE'RE CROSS-DRESSING GUYS BOTHERS ANYONE, I SAY LEAVE IT OUT.
I LOOOVE COSPLAY!!
AS LONG AS I CAN WEAR CUTE CLOTHES, I DON'T CARE WHAT WE'RE CALLED! TEE HEE! ♪
IT DOESN'T MATTER WHAT WORDS WE USE, AS LONG AS I CAN TRANSFORM INTO "TEN-CHAN" WHEN I'M HERE! ♥
THE ONLY THING IS...
HOW WILL WE INTRODUCE THE CAFÉ NOW?
SAYING WE'RE OTOKONOKO IS EASY TO UNDER-STAND.

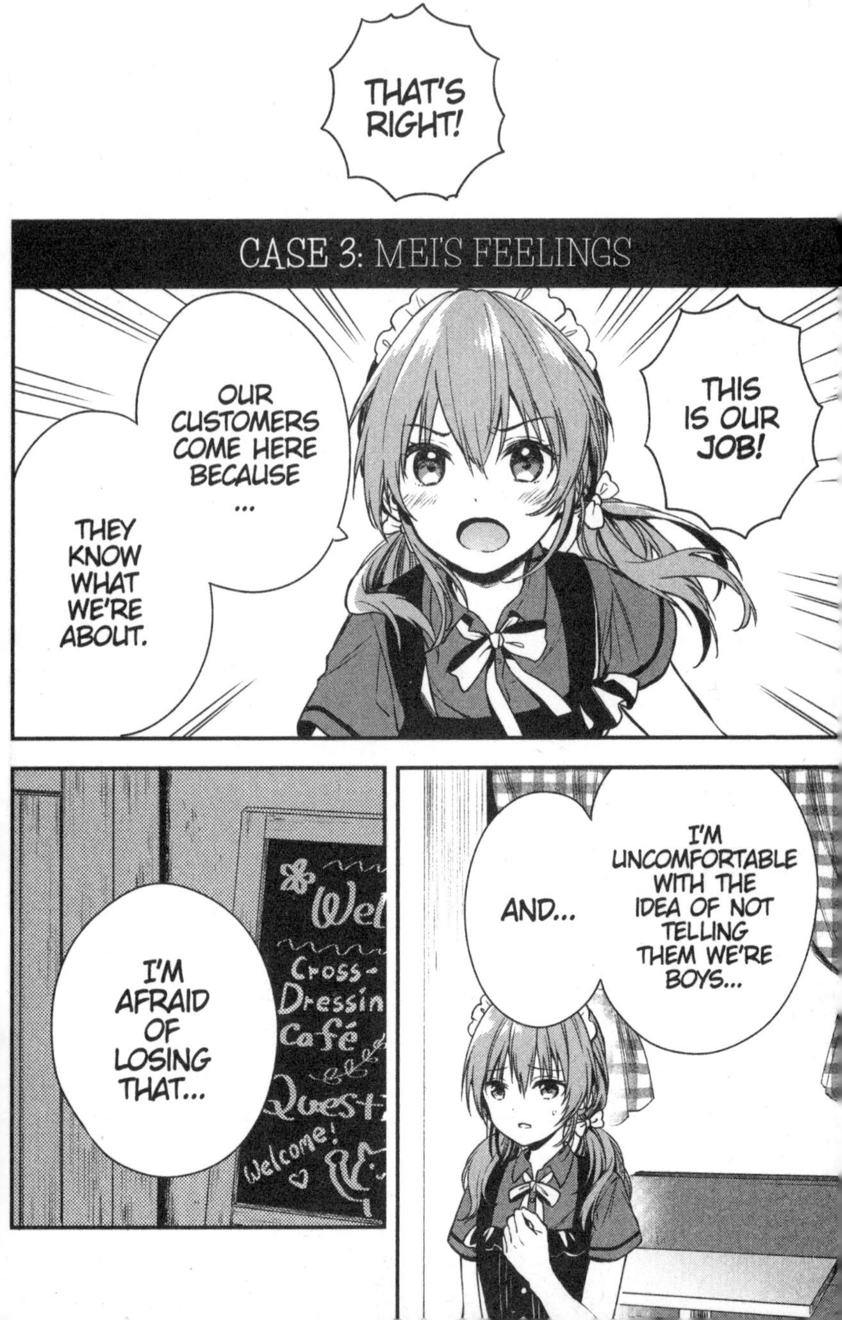
THAT'S RIGHT!
CASE 3: MEI'S FEELINGS
THIS IS OUR JOB!
OUR CUSTOMERS COME HERE BECAUSE ...
THEY KNOW WHAT WE'RE ABOUT.
I'M UNCOMFORTABLE WITH THE IDEA OF NOT TELLING THEM WE'RE BOYS...
AND...
I'M AFRAID OF LOSING THAT...
Wel
Cross-
Dressin
Café
Questi
Welcome!

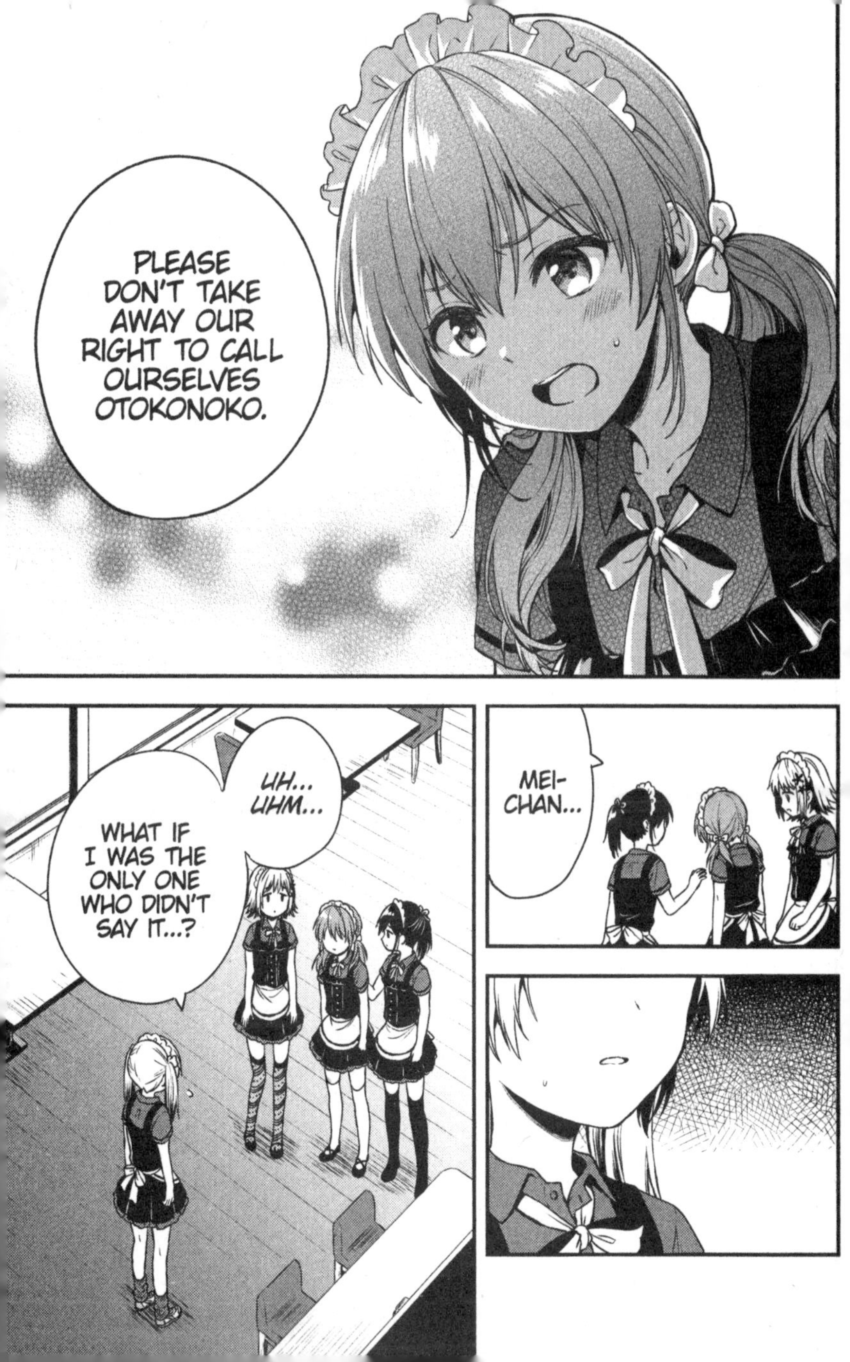
PLEASE DON'T TAKE AWAY OUR RIGHT TO CALL OURSELVES OTOKONOKO.
MEI-CHAN...
UH... UHM...
WHAT IF I WAS THE ONLY ONE WHO DIDN'T SAY IT...?

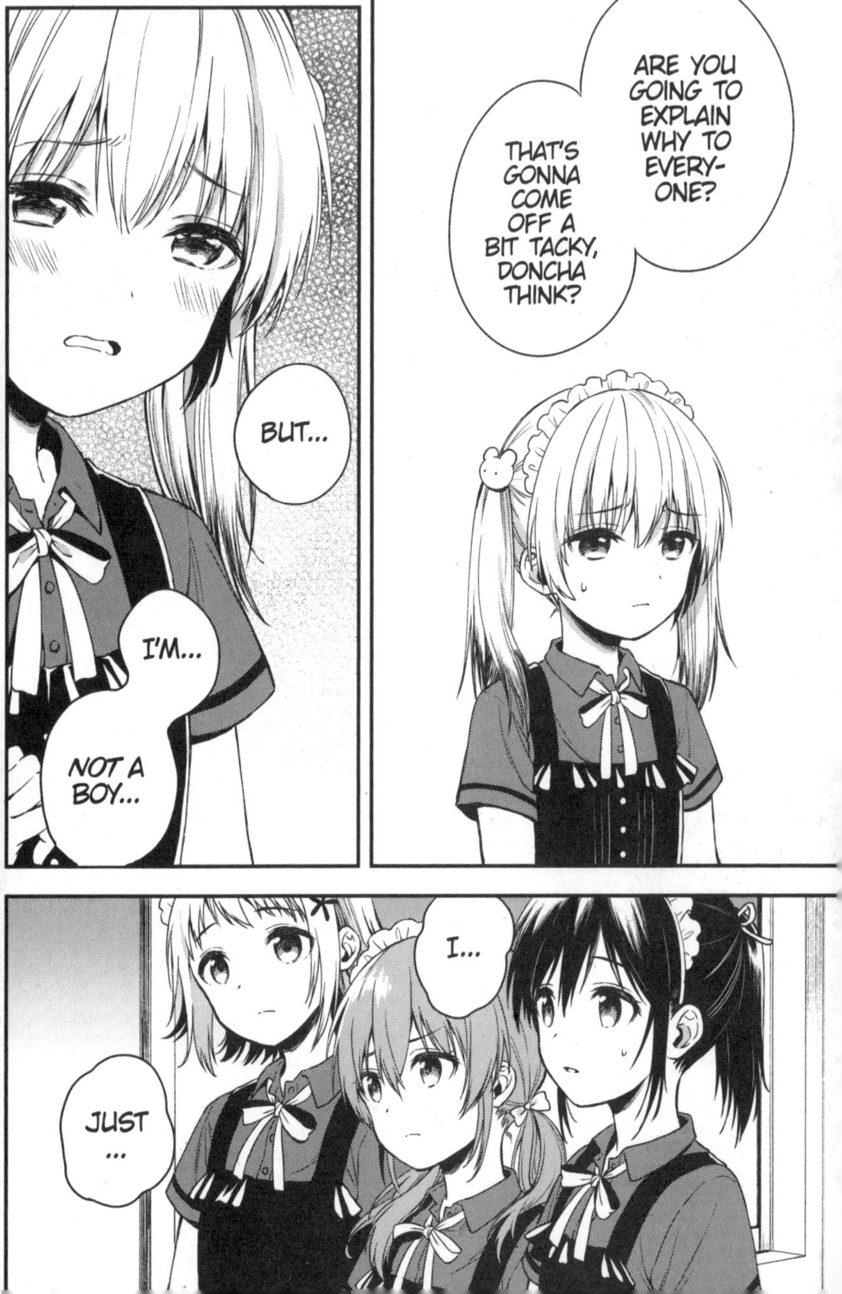
ARE YOU GOING TO EXPLAIN WHY TO EVERY-ONE?
THAT'S GONNA COME OFF A BIT TACKY, DONCHA THINK?
BUT...
I'M...
NOT A BOY...
I...
JUST ...

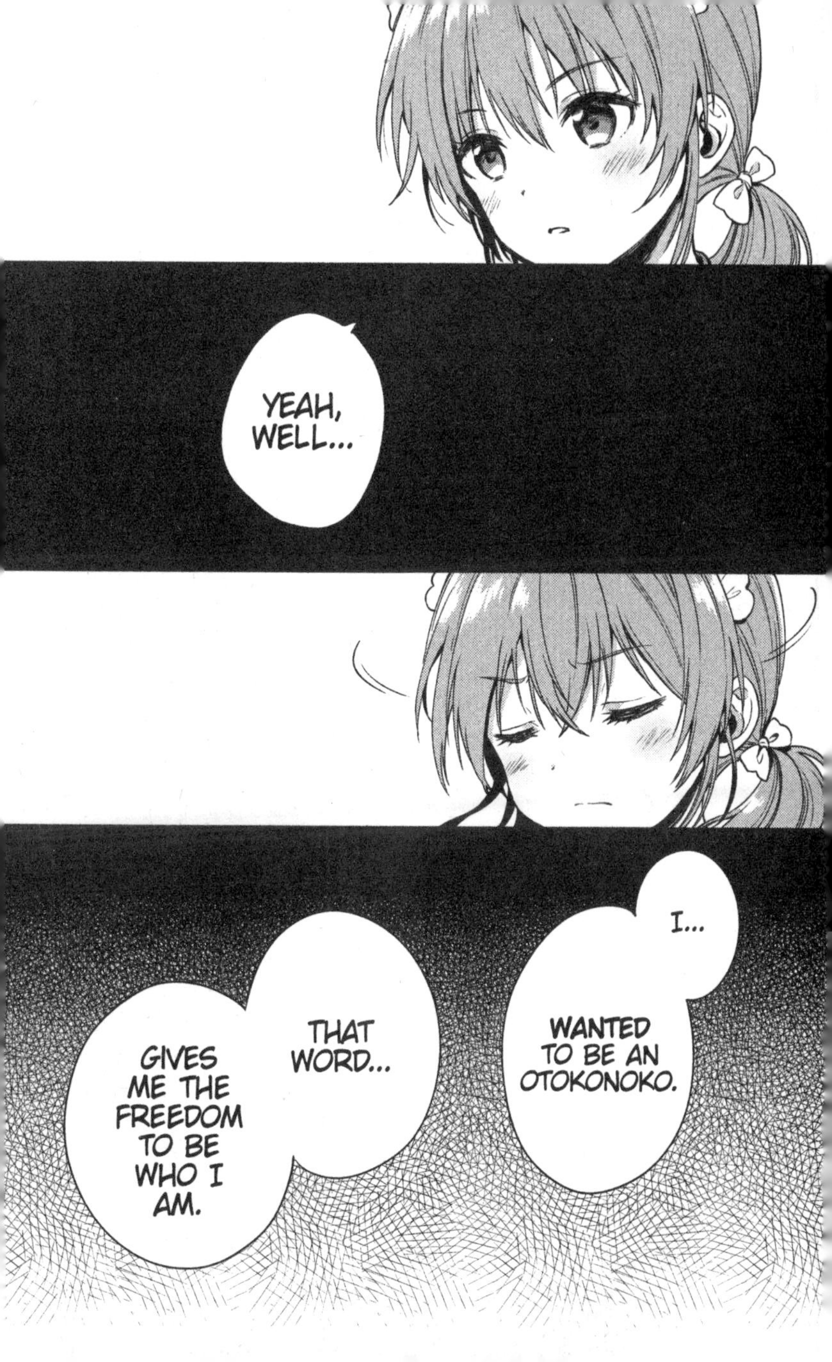
YEAH, WELL...
I...
WANTED TO BE AN OTOKONOKO.
THAT WORD...
GIVES ME THE FREEDOM TO BE WHO I AM.

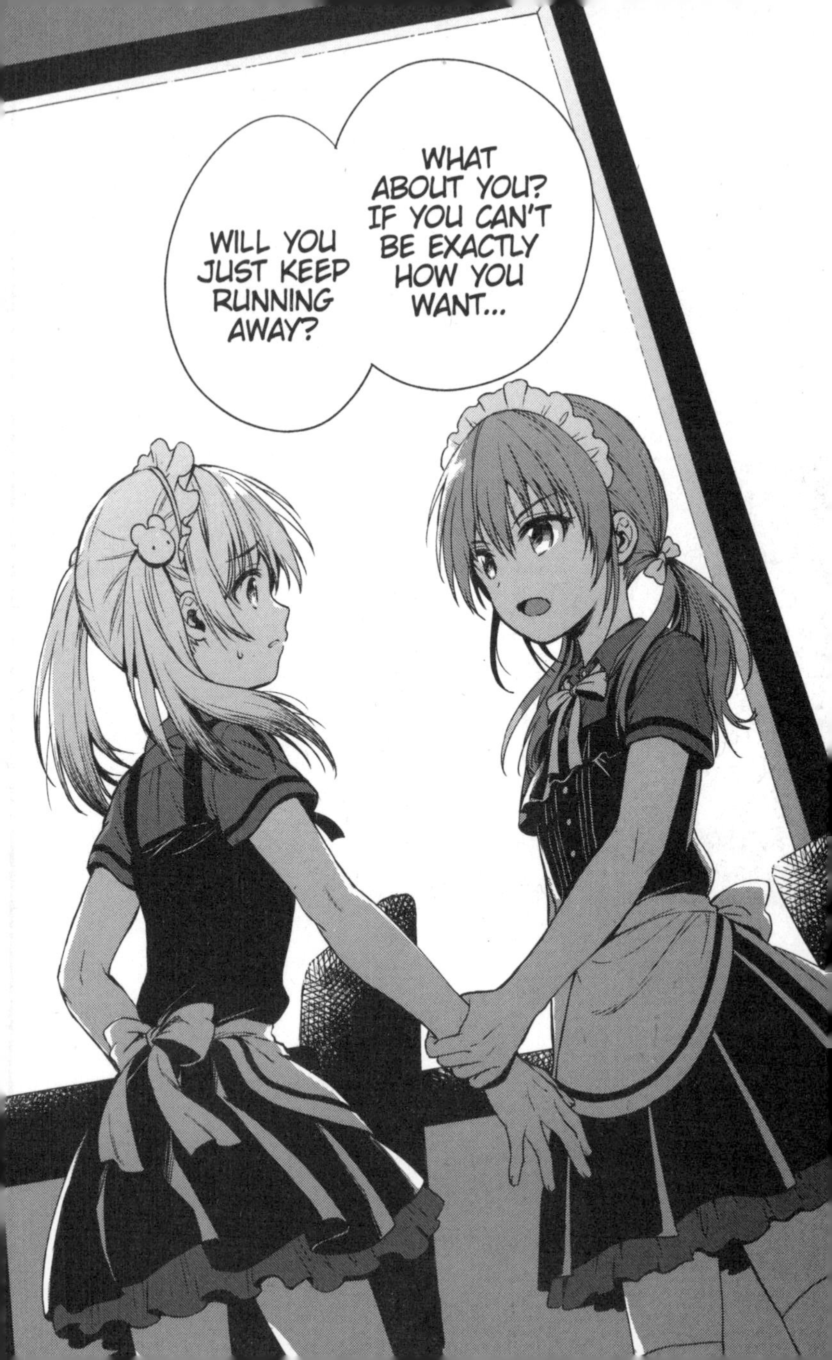
WHAT ABOUT YOU? IF YOU CAN'T BE EXACTLY HOW YOU WANT...
WILL YOU JUST KEEP RUNNING AWAY?

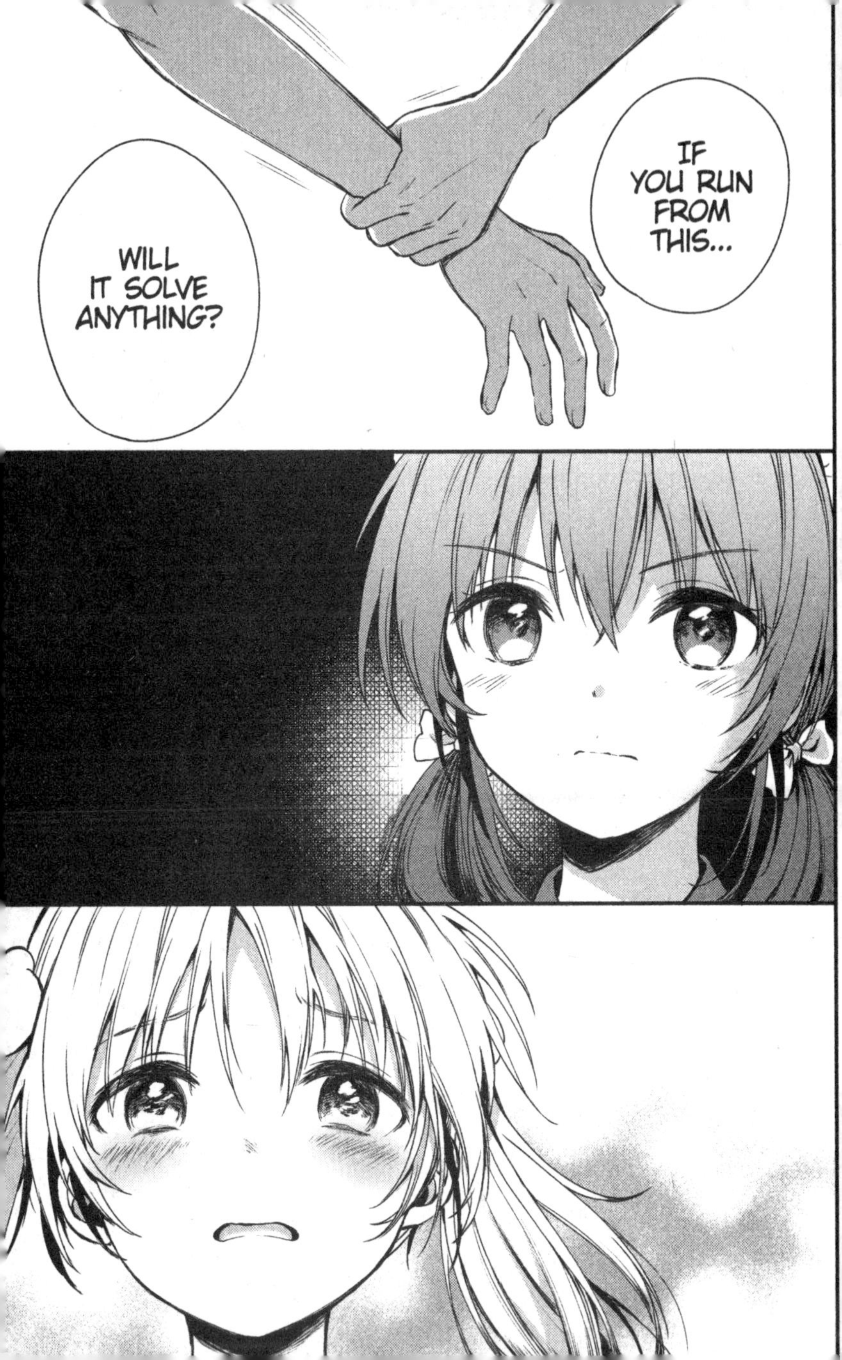
IF YOU RUN FROM THIS...
WILL IT SOLVE ANYTHING?

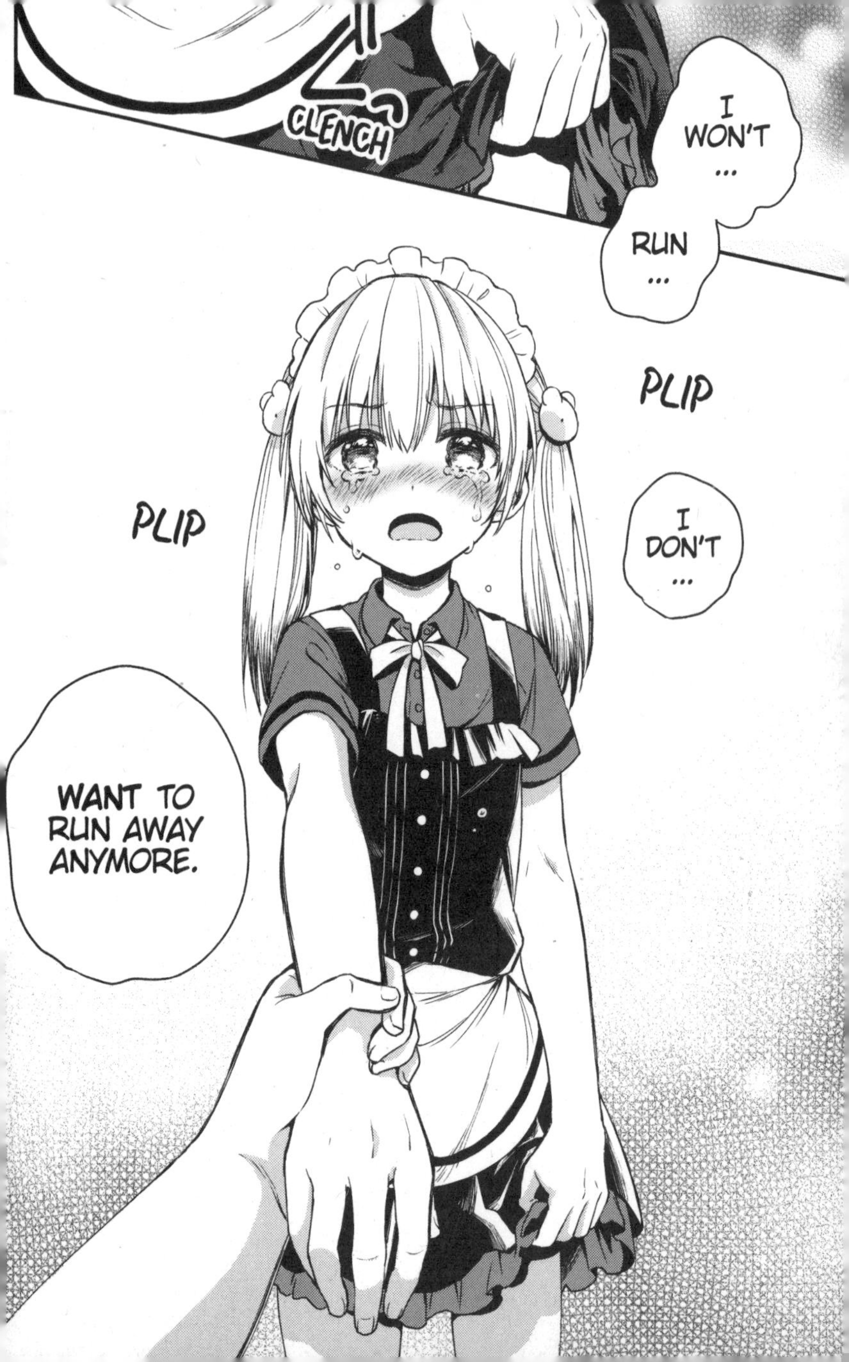
CLENCH
I WON'T ...
RUN ...
PLIP
I DON'T ...
PLIP
WANT TO RUN AWAY ANYMORE.

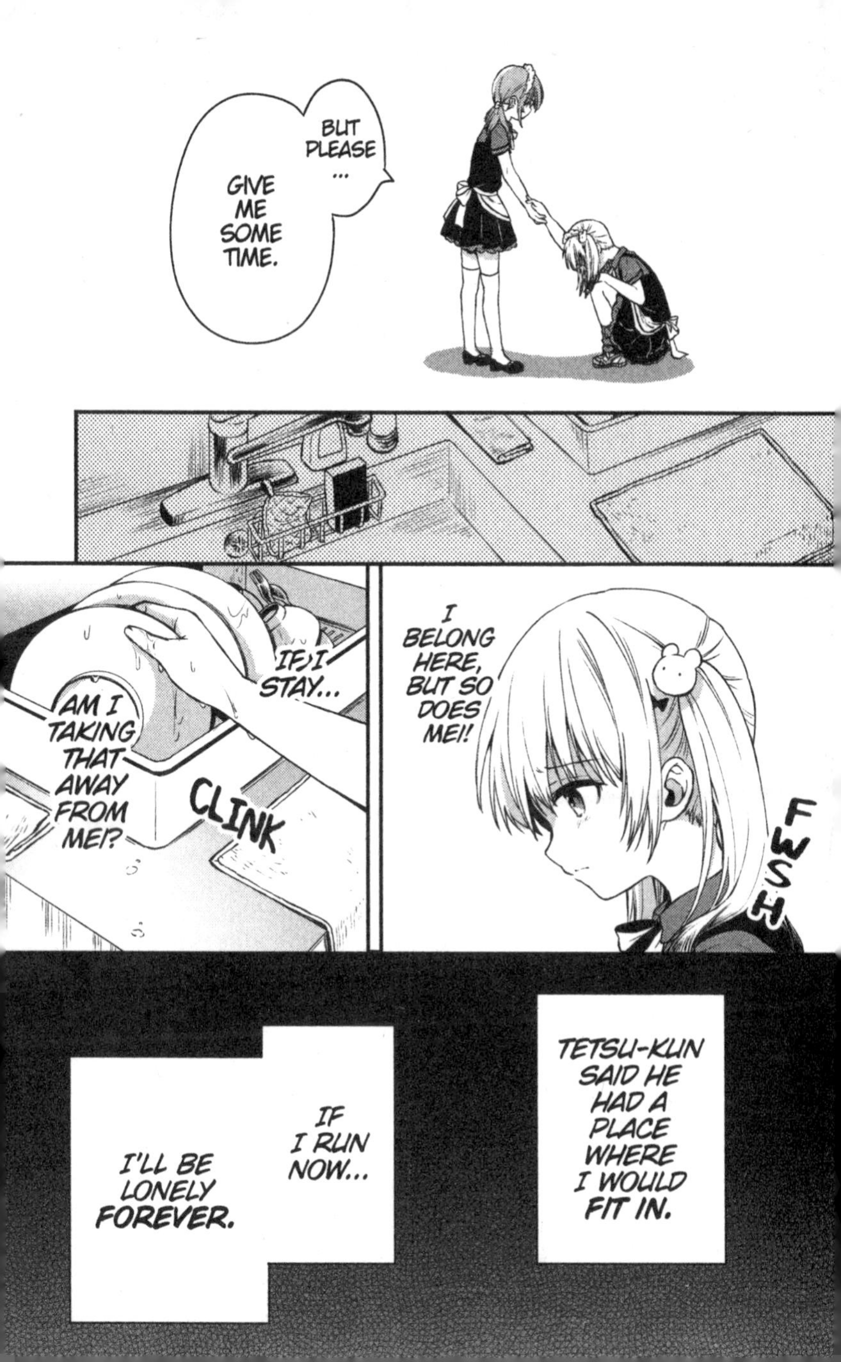
BUT PLEASE... GIVE ME SOME TIME.
I BELONG HERE, BUT SO DOES MEI!
FWSH
IF I STAY...
AM I TAKING THAT AWAY FROM MEI?
CLINK
TETSU-KUN SAID HE HAD A PLACE WHERE I WOULD FIT IN.
IF I RUN NOW...
I'LL BE LONELY FOREVER.

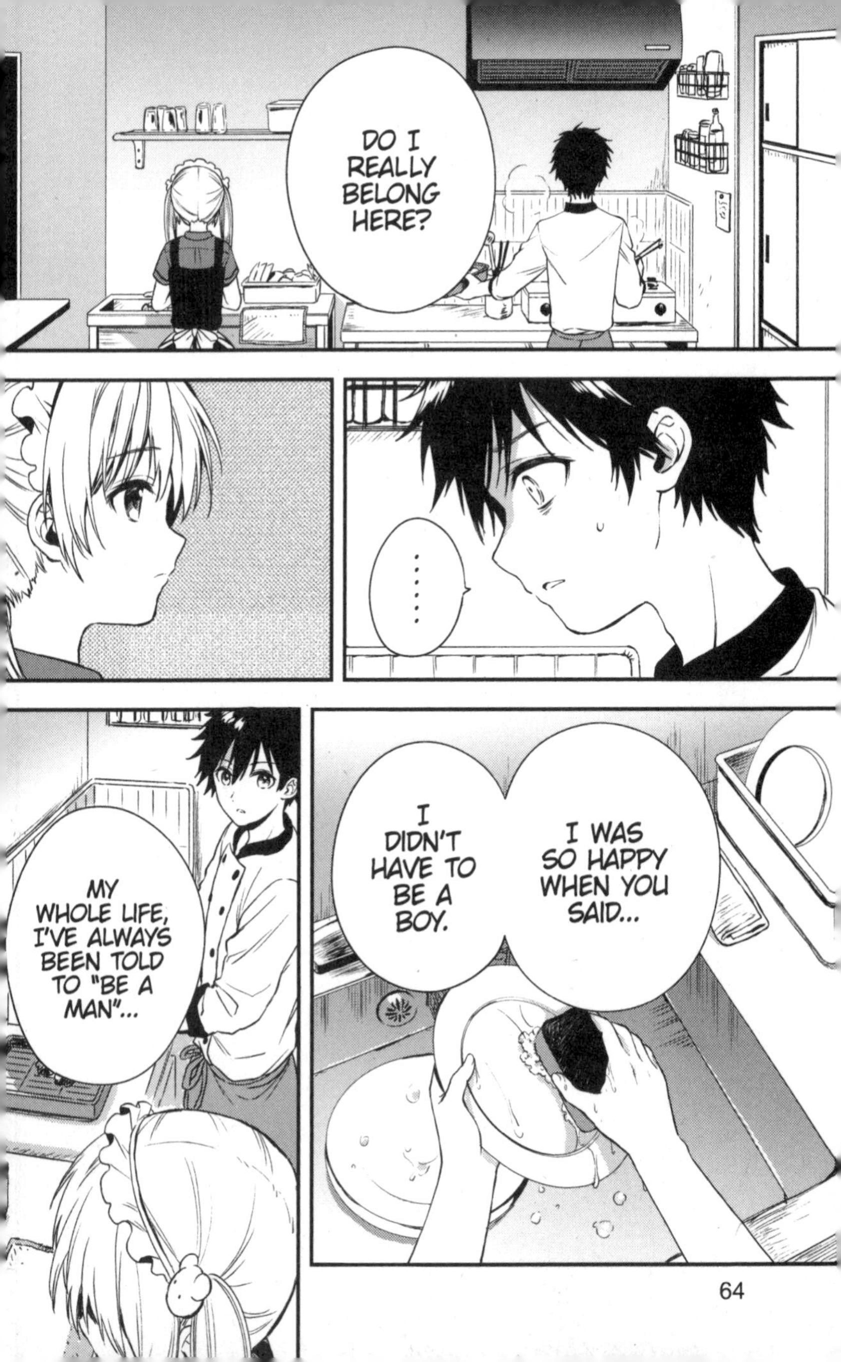
DO I REALLY BELONG HERE?
......
I WAS SO HAPPY WHEN YOU SAID...
I DIDN'T HAVE TO BE A BOY.
MY WHOLE LIFE, I'VE ALWAYS BEEN TOLD TO "BE A MAN"...

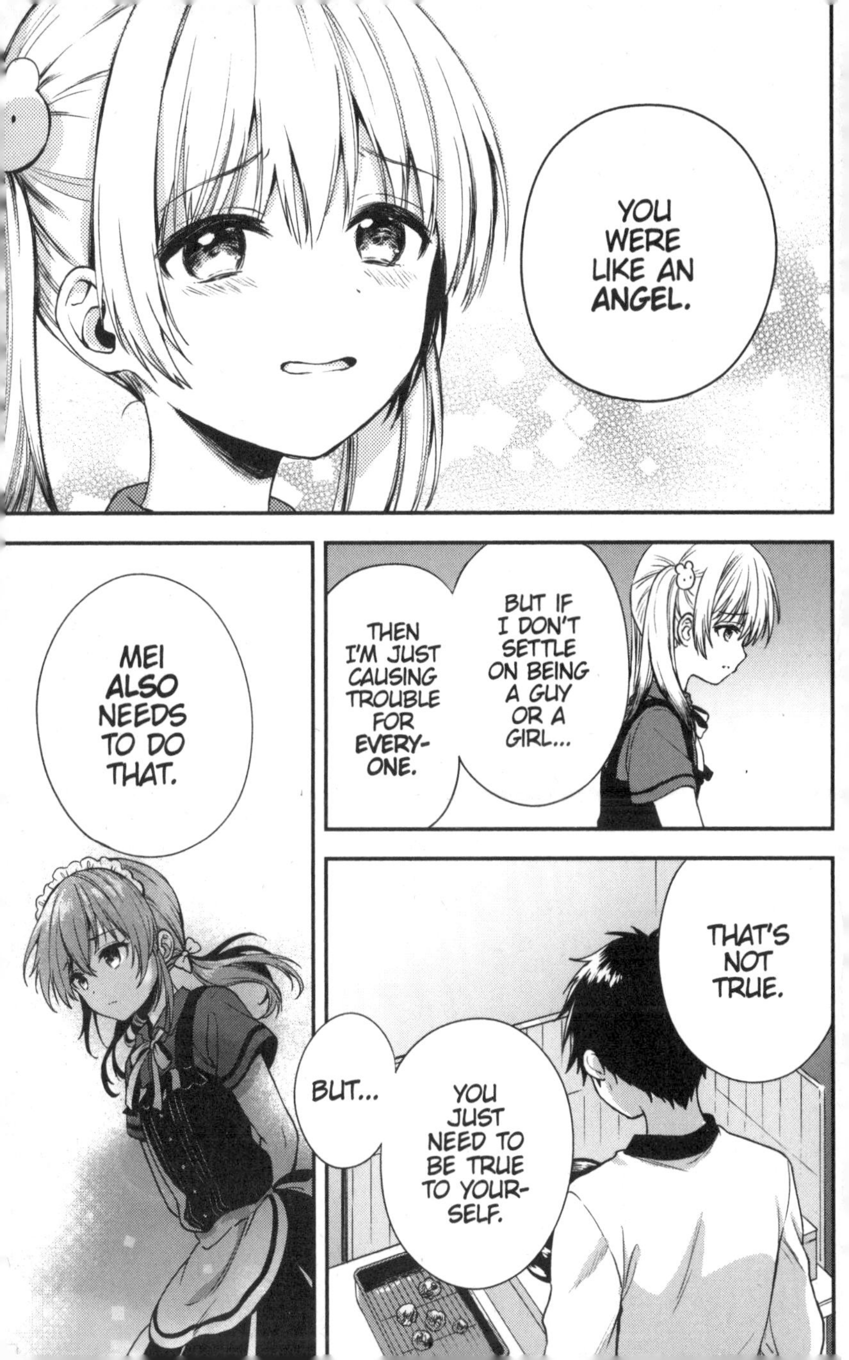
YOU WERE LIKE AN ANGEL.
BUT IF I DON'T SETTLE ON BEING A GUY OR A GIRL...
THEN I'M JUST CAUSING TROUBLE FOR EVERY-ONE.
THAT'S NOT TRUE.
YOU JUST NEED TO BE TRUE TO YOUR-SELF.
BUT...
MEI ALSO NEEDS TO DO THAT.

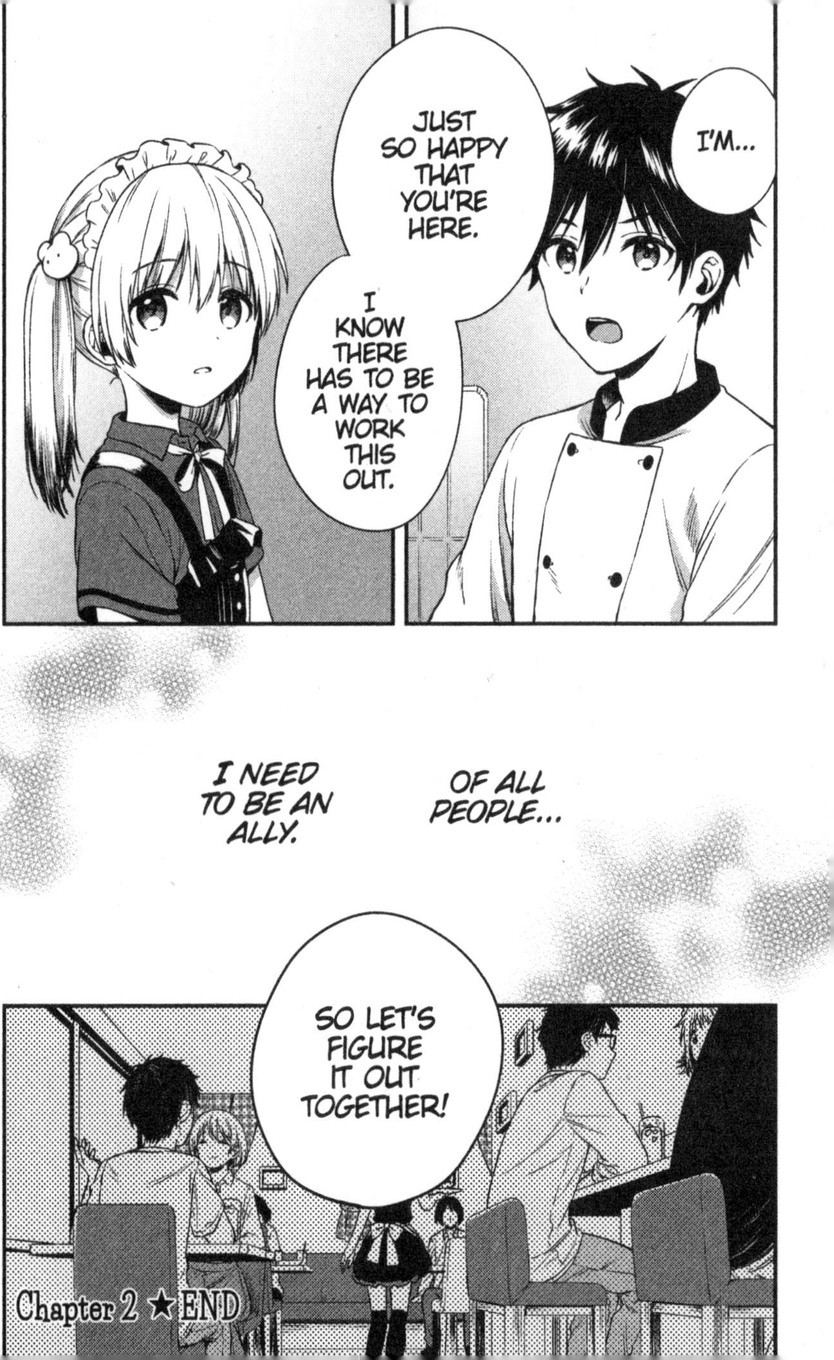
I'M...
JUST SO HAPPY THAT YOU'RE HERE.
I KNOW THERE HAS TO BE A WAY TO WORK THIS OUT.
OF ALL PEOPLE...
I NEED TO BE AN ALLY.
SO LET'S FIGURE IT OUT TOGETHER!
Chapter 2 ★ END

Love me for
who I am

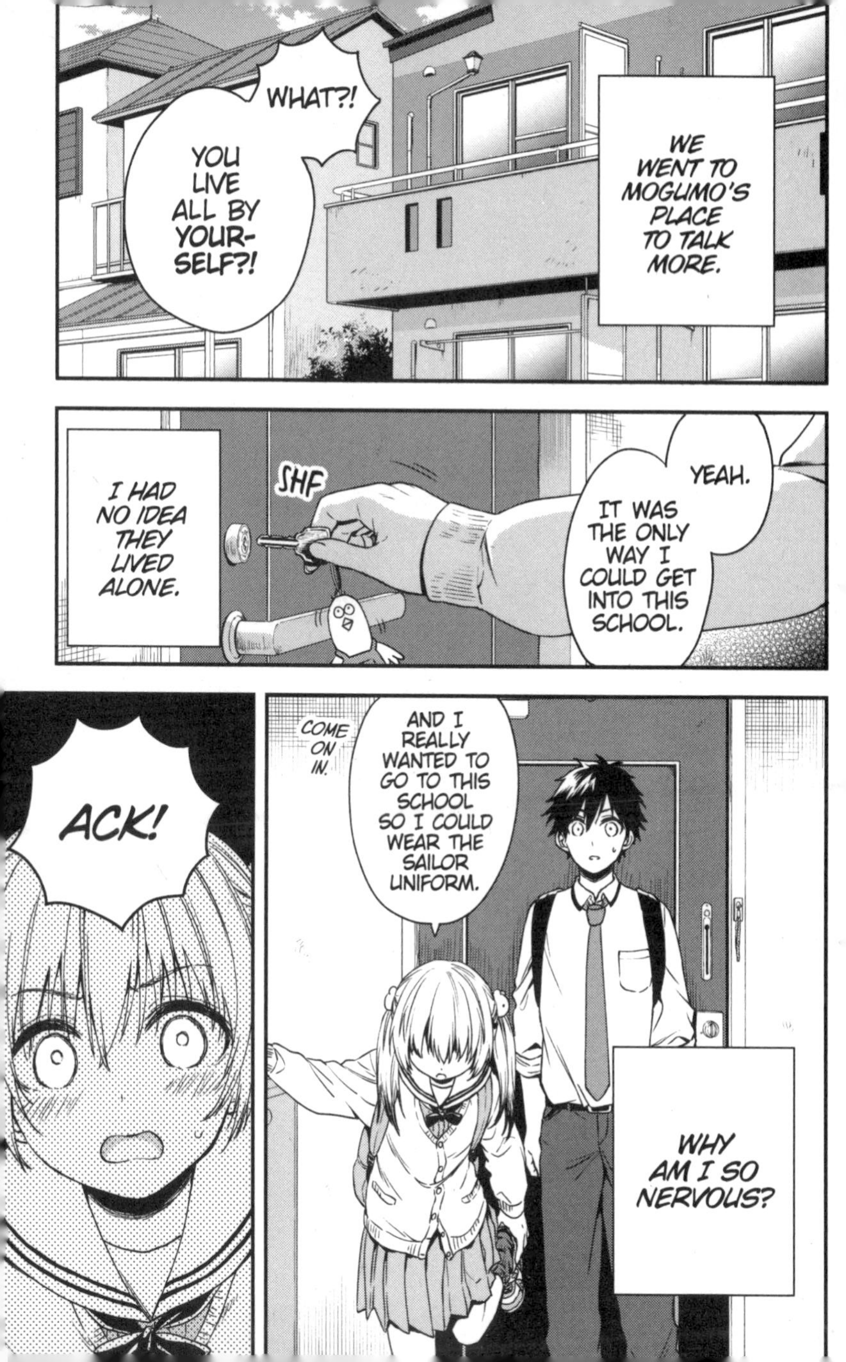
WE WENT TO MOGUMO'S PLACE TO TALK MORE.
WHAT?!
YOU LIVE ALL BY YOURSELF?!
YEAH.
IT WAS THE ONLY WAY I COULD GET INTO THIS SCHOOL.
SHF
I HAD NO IDEA THEY LIVED ALONE.
AND I REALLY WANTED TO GO TO THIS SCHOOL SO I COULD WEAR THE SAILOR UNIFORM.
COME ON IN.
WHY AM I SO NERVOUS?
ACK!

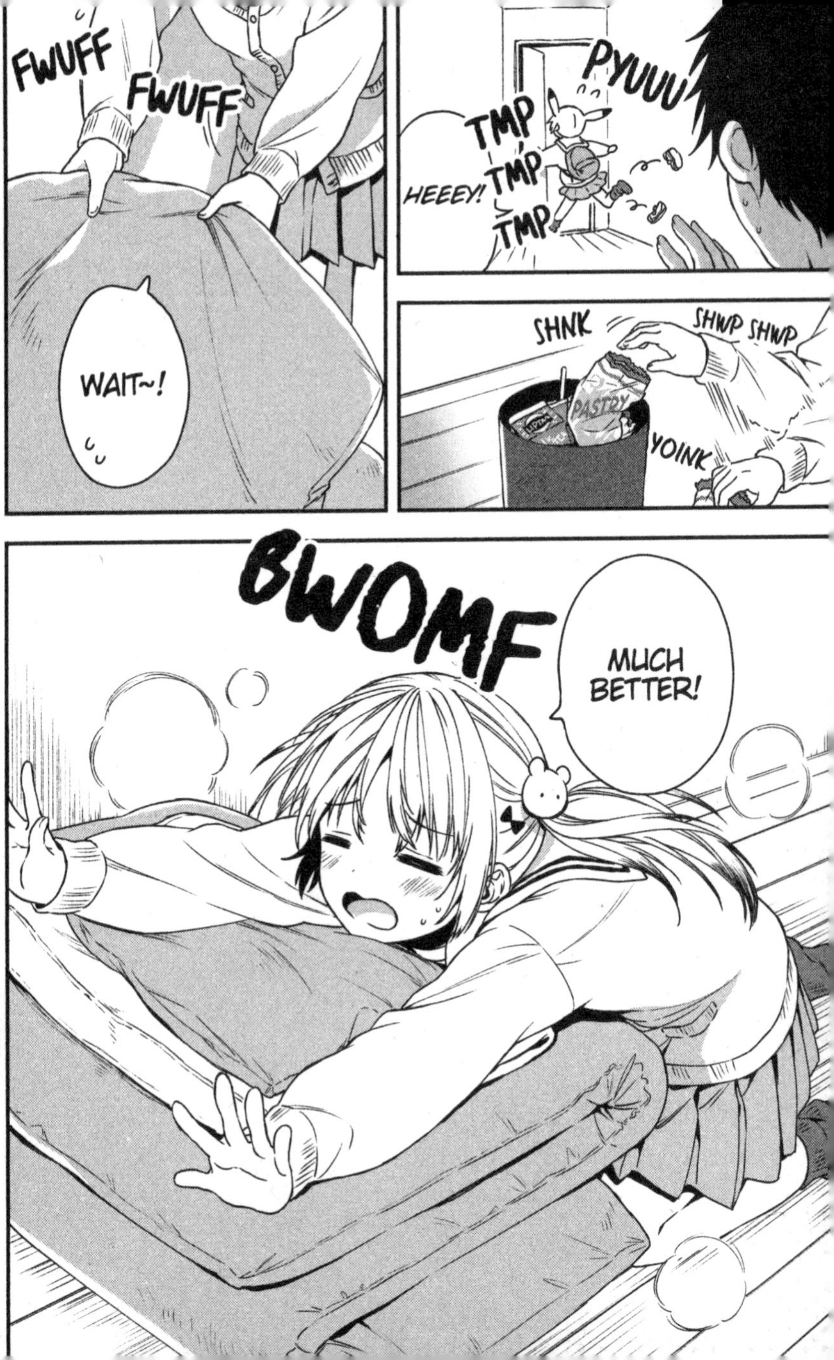
PYUUU
TMP
TMP
HEEEY!
TMP
SHWP SHWP
SHNK
PASTRY
YOINK
FWUFF
FWUFF
WAIT~!
MUCH BETTER!
BWOMF

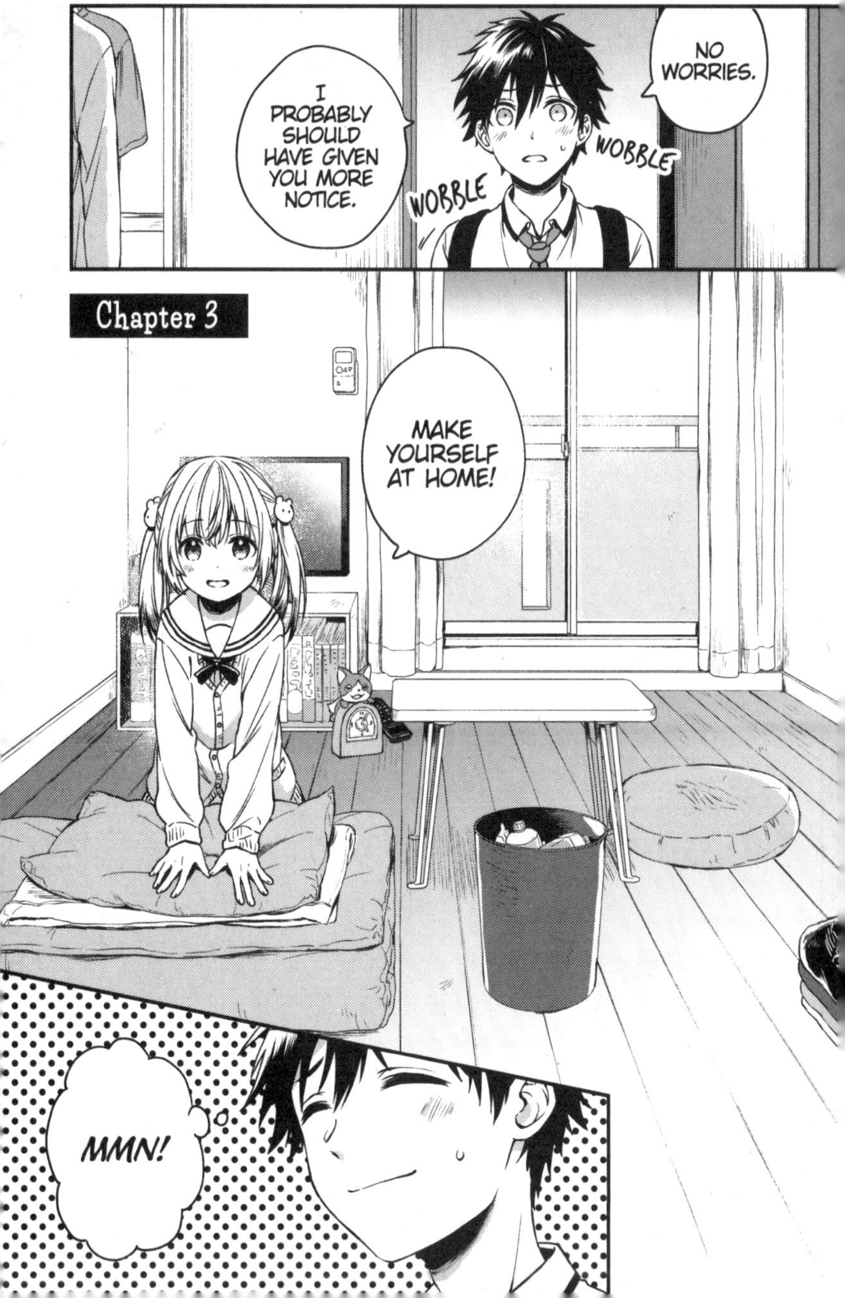
NO WORRIES.
WOBBLE
I PROBABLY SHOULD HAVE GIVEN YOU MORE NOTICE.
WOBBLE
Chapter 3
MAKE YOURSELF AT HOME!
MMN!

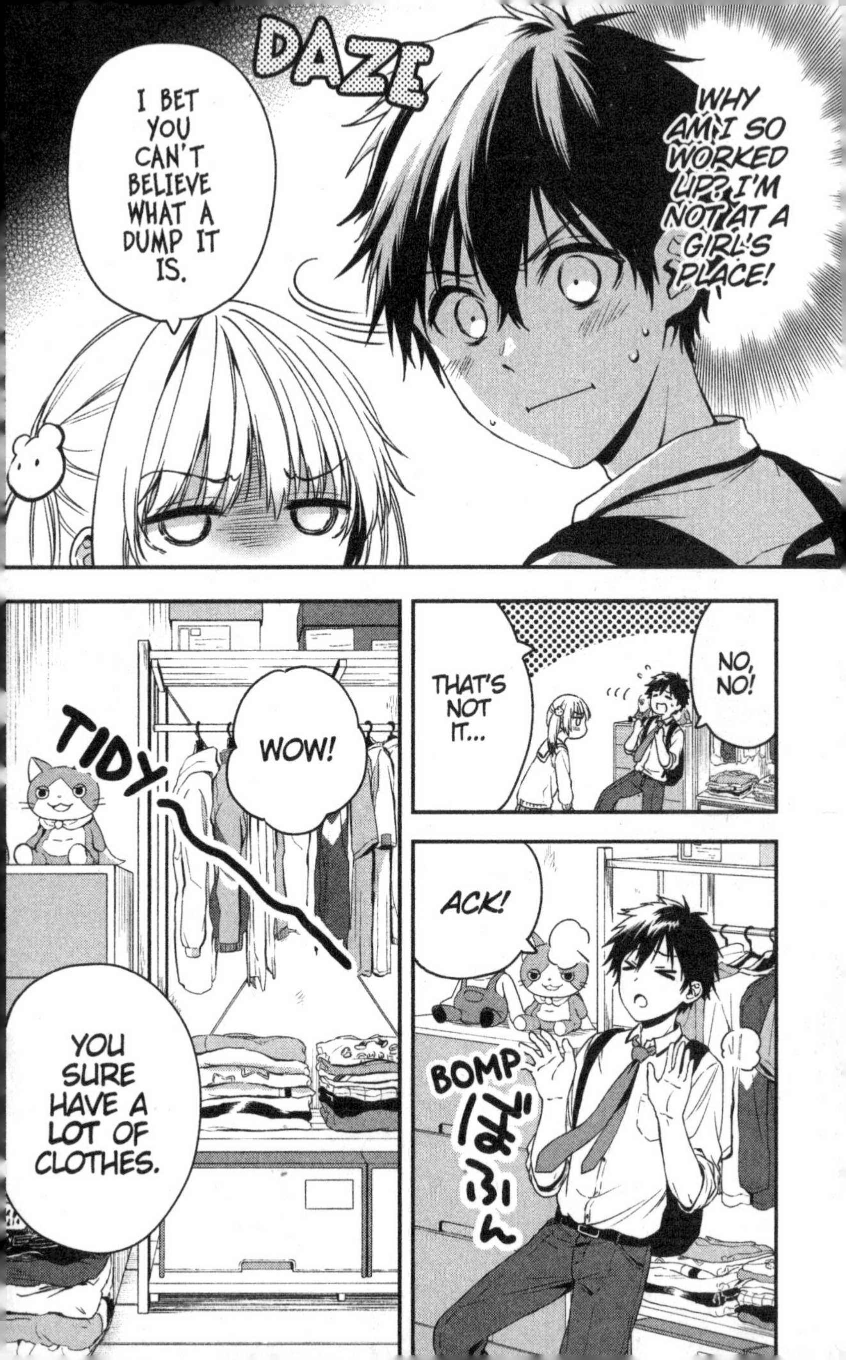
WHY AM I SO WORKED UP? I'M NOT AT A GIRL'S PLACE!
DAZE
I BET YOU CAN'T BELIEVE WHAT A DUMP IT IS.
NO, NO!
THAT'S NOT IT...
ACK!
BOMP
ぽふん
TIDY
WOW!
YOU SURE HAVE A LOT OF CLOTHES.

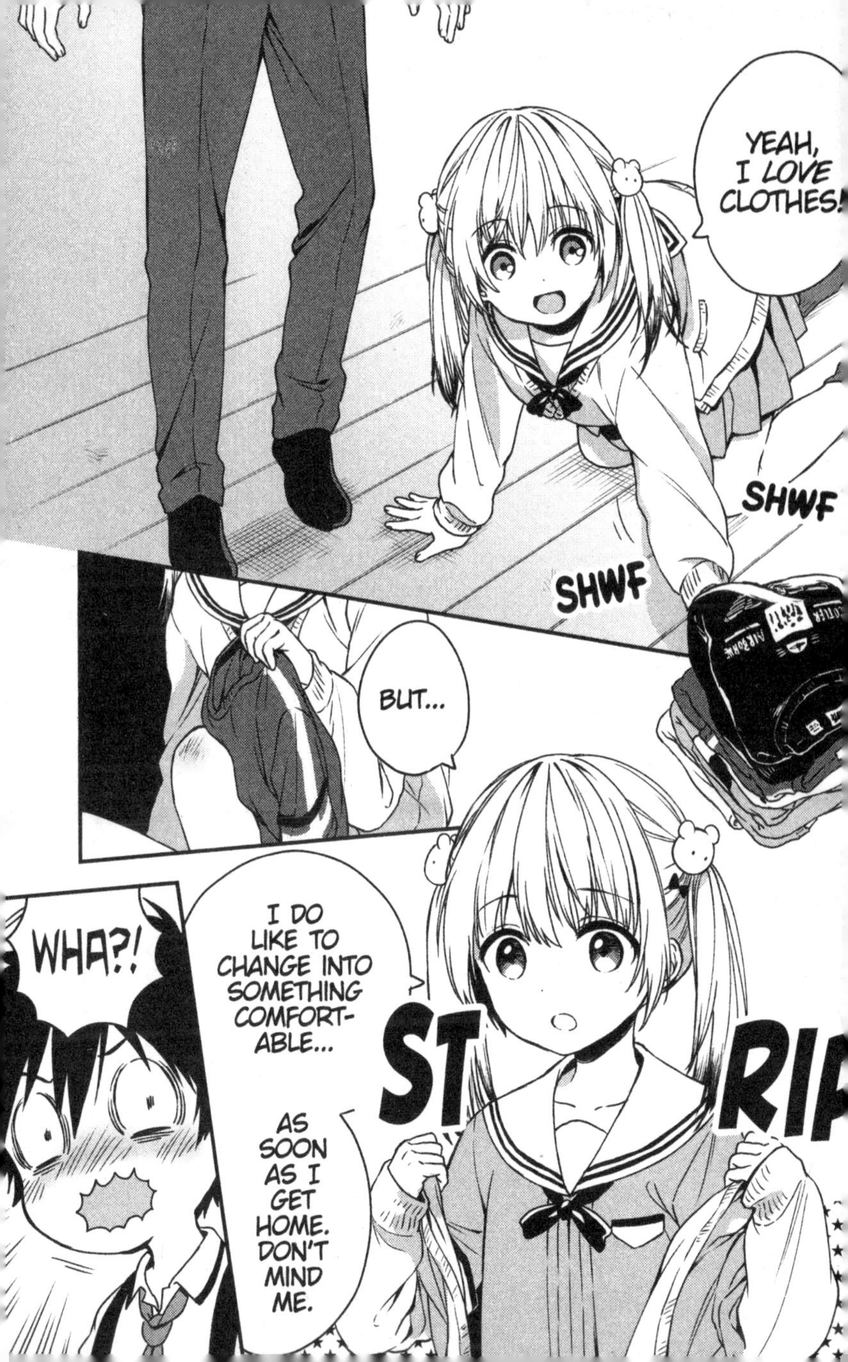
YEAH, I LOVE CLOTHES!
SHWF
SHWF
BUT...
I DO LIKE TO CHANGE INTO SOMETHING COMFORT-ABLE...
AS SOON AS I GET HOME. DON'T MIND ME.
STRIP
WHA?!

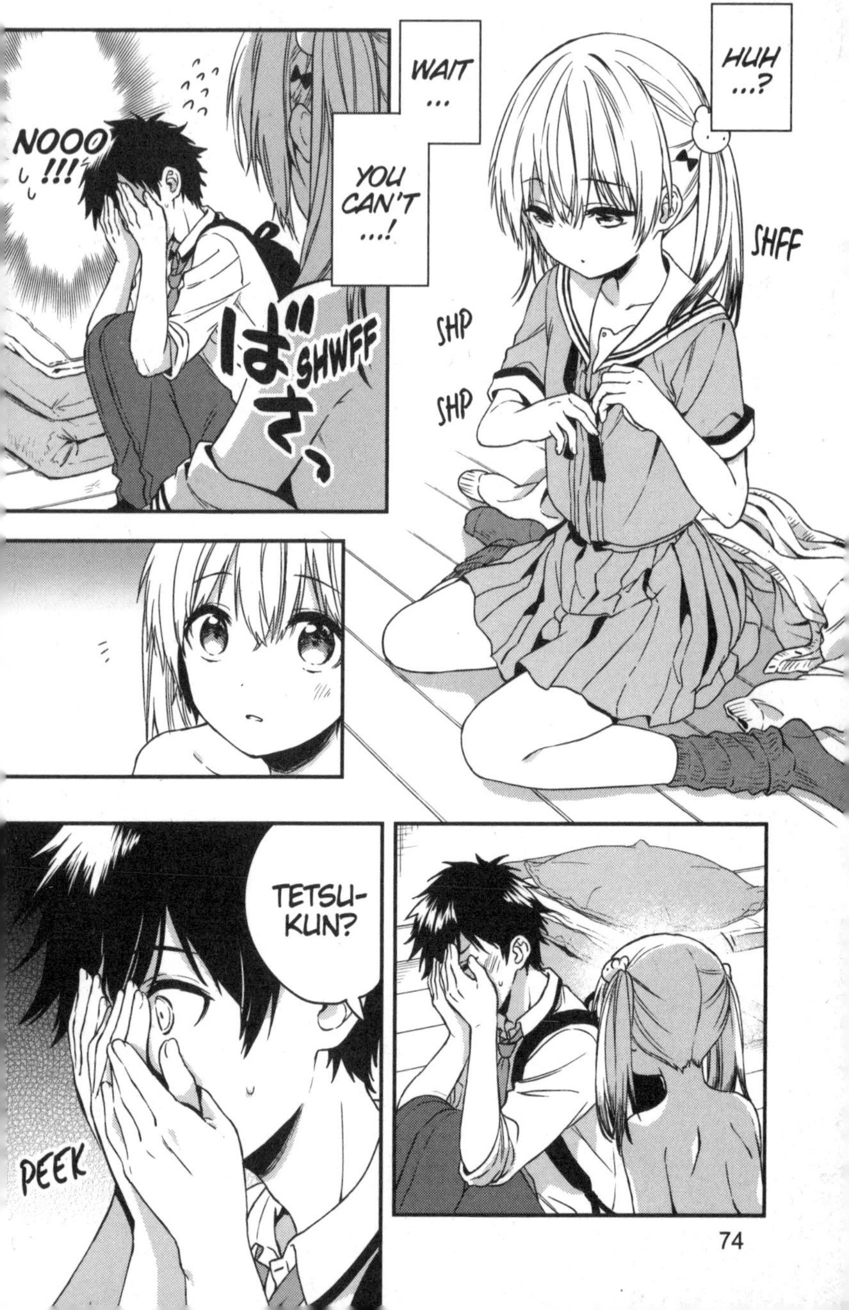
HUH ...?
SHFF
SHP
SHP
WAIT ...
YOU CAN'T ...!
ばさっ
SHWFF
NOOO !!!
TETSU-KUN?
PEEK

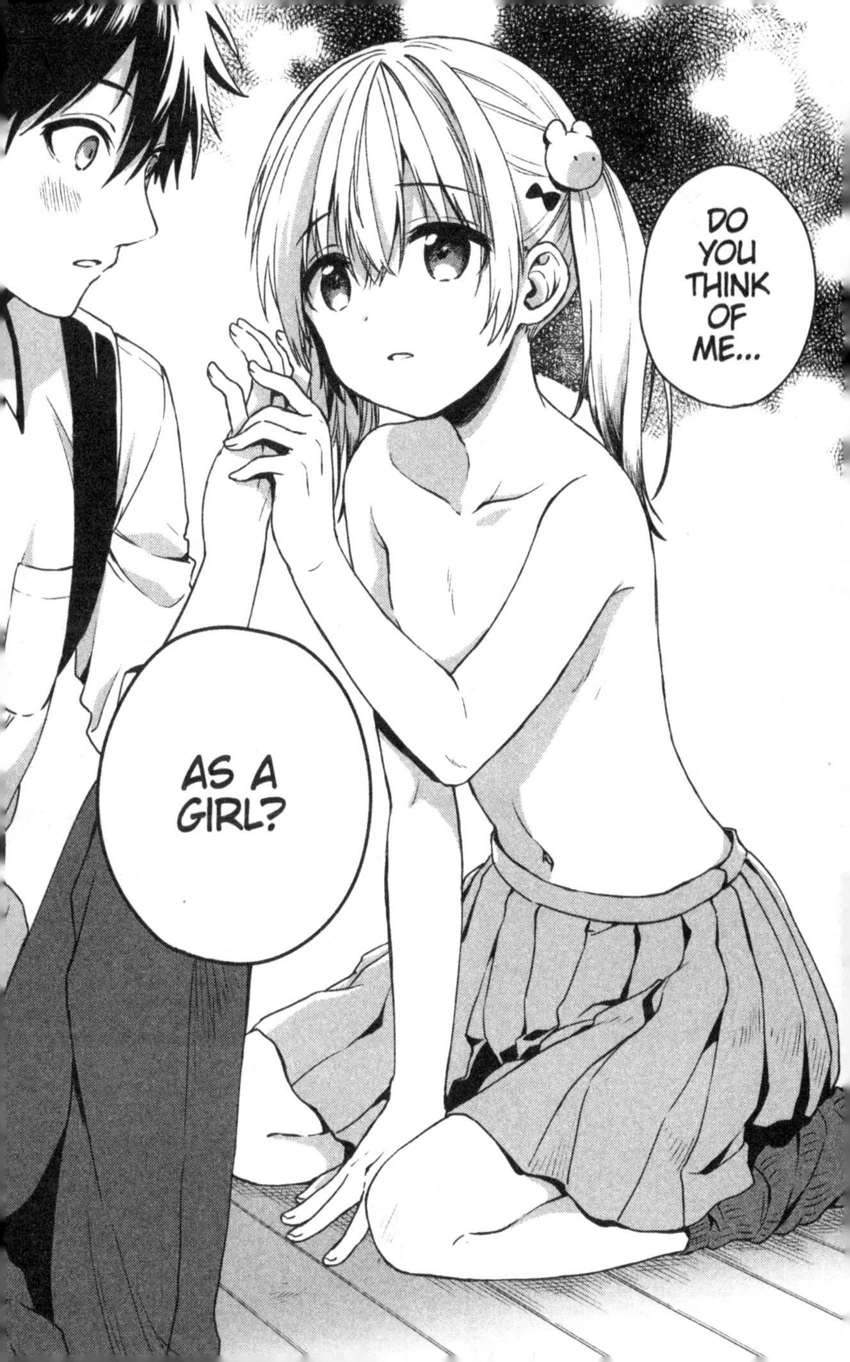
DO YOU THINK OF ME...
AS A GIRL?

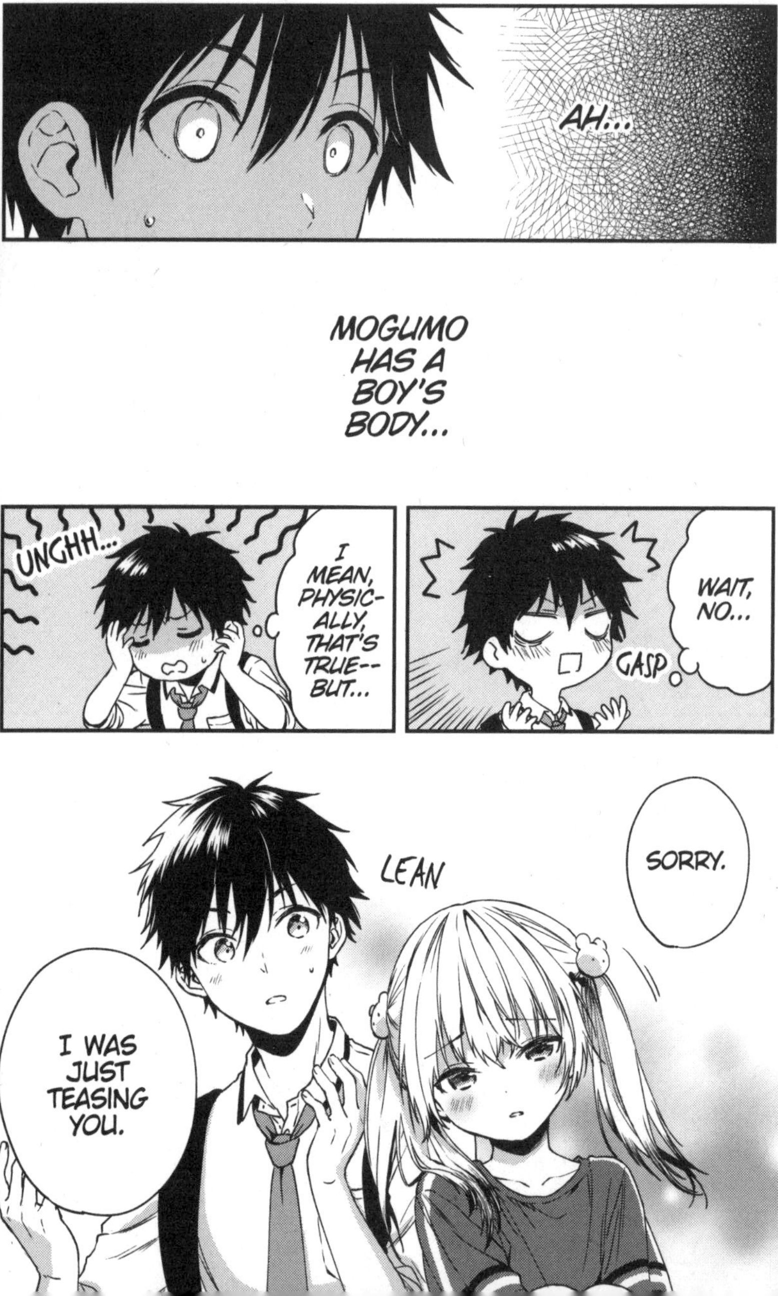
AH...
MOGUMO HAS A BOY'S BODY...
WAIT, NO...
GASP
UNGHH...
I MEAN, PHYSIC-ALLY, THAT'S TRUE-- BUT...
SORRY.
LEAN
I WAS JUST TEASING YOU.

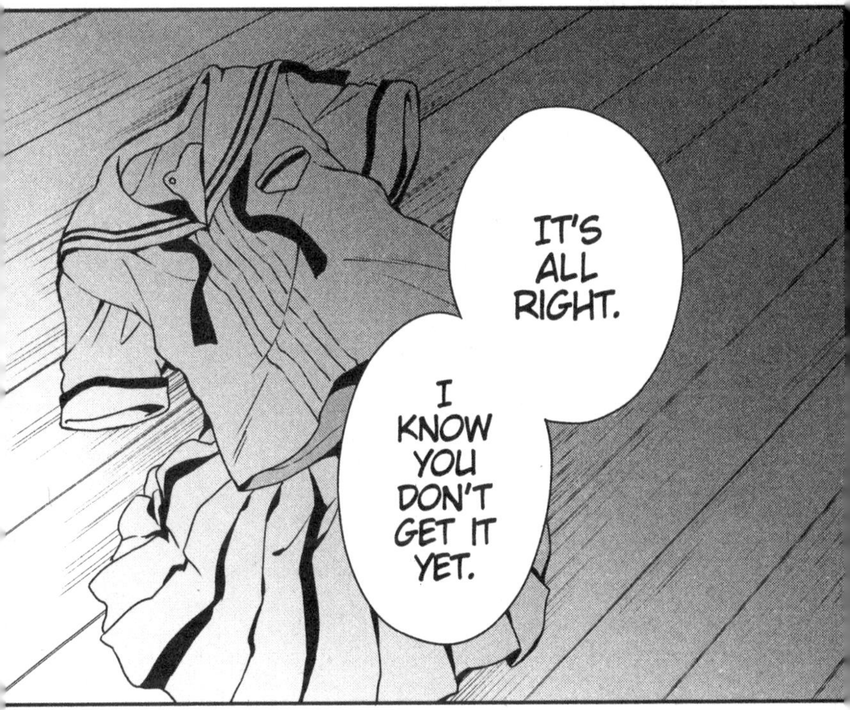
IT'S ALL RIGHT.
I KNOW YOU DON'T GET IT YET.
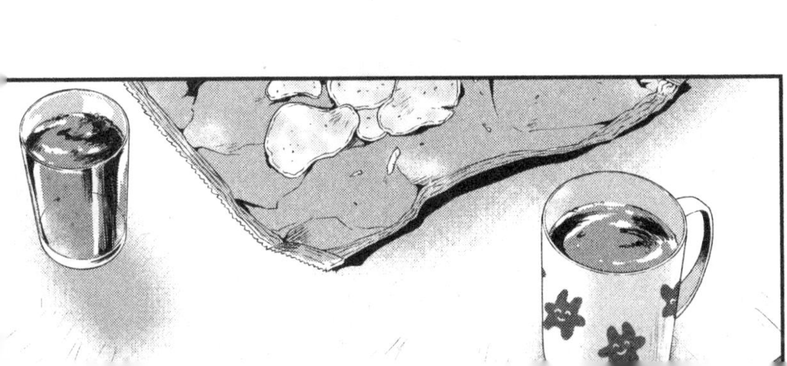

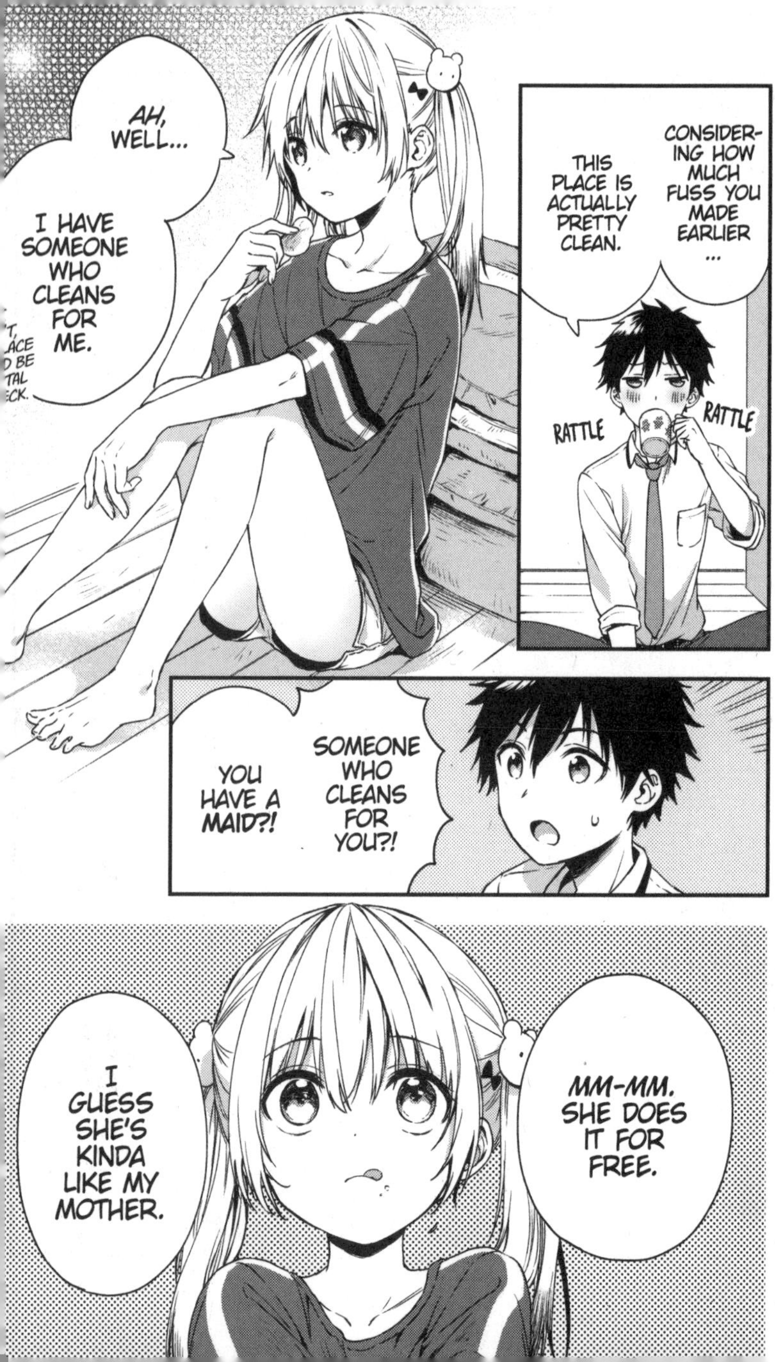
CONSIDERING HOW MUCH FUSS YOU MADE EARLIER ...
THIS PLACE IS ACTUALLY PRETTY CLEAN.
RATTLE
RATTLE
AH, WELL...
I HAVE SOMEONE WHO CLEANS FOR ME.
SOMEONE WHO CLEANS FOR YOU?!
YOU HAVE A MAID?!
MM-MM. SHE DOES IT FOR FREE.
I GUESS SHE'S KINDA LIKE MY MOTHER.

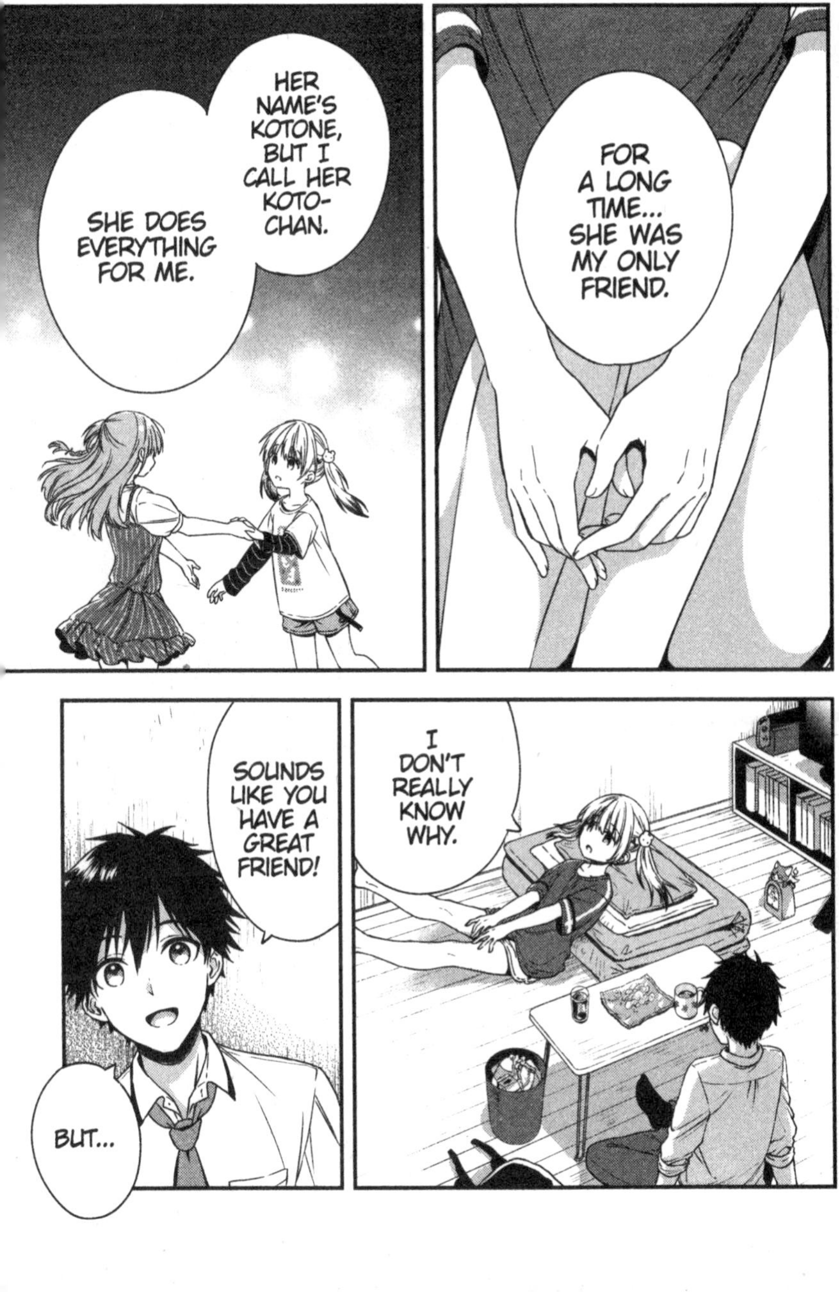
FOR A LONG TIME... SHE WAS MY ONLY FRIEND.
HER NAME'S KOTONE, BUT I CALL HER KOTO-CHAN.
SHE DOES EVERYTHING FOR ME.
I DON'T REALLY KNOW WHY.
SOUNDS LIKE YOU HAVE A GREAT FRIEND!
BUT...

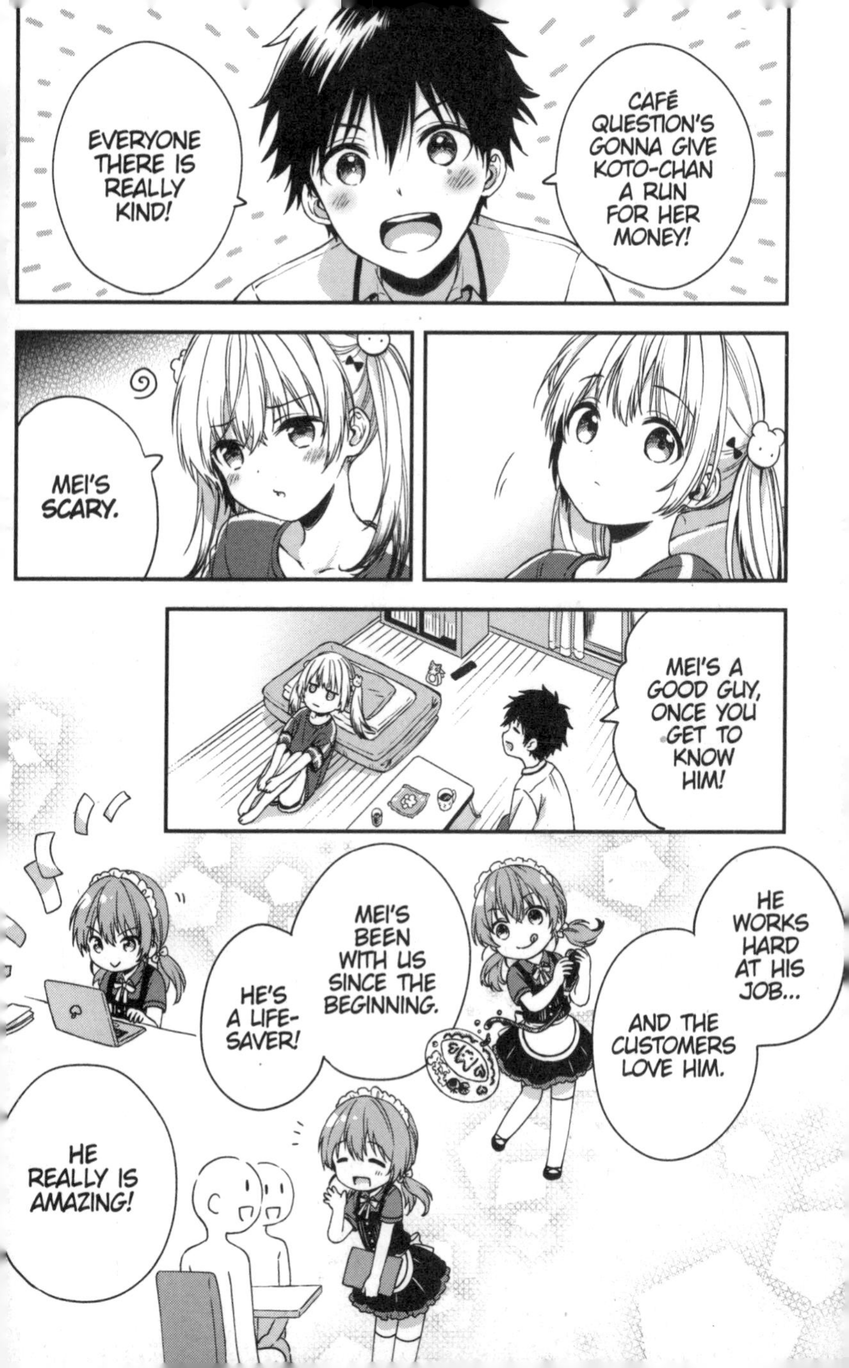
CAFÉ QUESTION'S GONNA GIVE KOTO-CHAN A RUN FOR HER MONEY!
EVERYONE THERE IS REALLY KIND!
MEI'S SCARY.
MEI'S A GOOD GUY, ONCE YOU GET TO KNOW HIM!
HE WORKS HARD AT HIS JOB...
AND THE CUSTOMERS LOVE HIM.
MEI'S BEEN WITH US SINCE THE BEGINNING.
HE'S A LIFE-SAVER!
HE REALLY IS AMAZING!

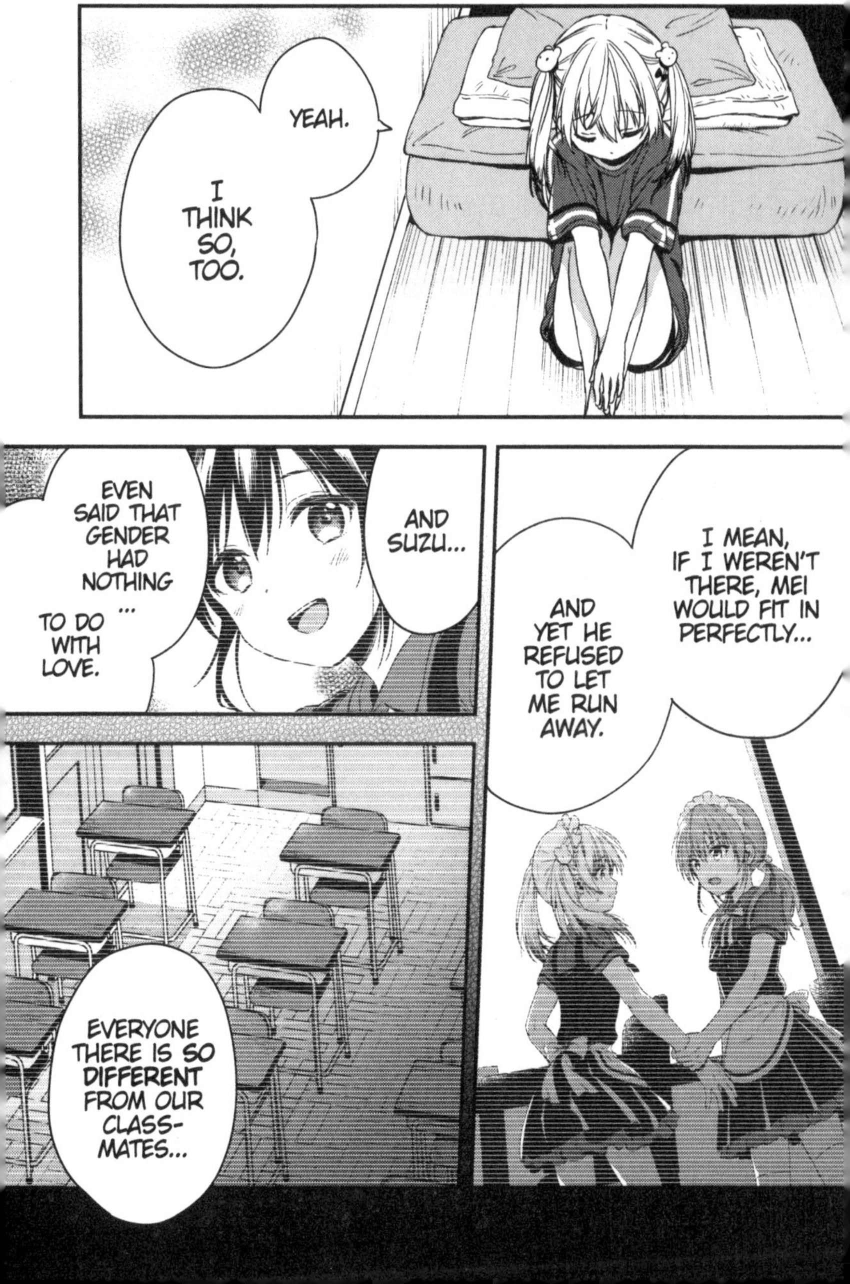
YEAH.
I THINK SO, TOO.
I MEAN, IF I WEREN'T THERE, MEI WOULD FIT IN PERFECTLY...
AND YET HE REFUSED TO LET ME RUN AWAY.
AND SUZU...
EVEN SAID THAT GENDER HAD NOTHING ...
TO DO WITH LOVE.
EVERYONE THERE IS SO DIFFERENT FROM OUR CLASS-MATES...

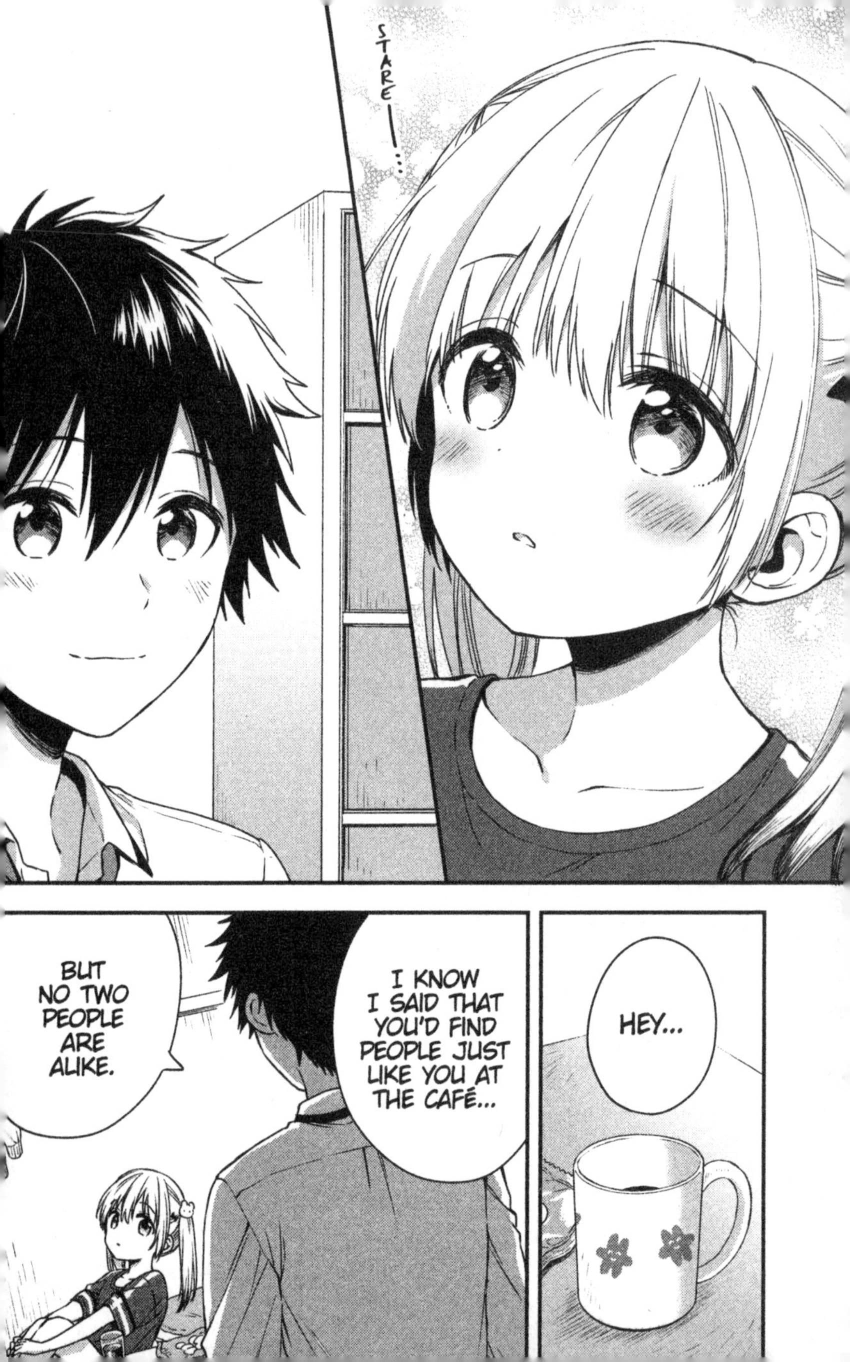
STARE—...
HEY...
I KNOW I SAID THAT YOU'D FIND PEOPLE JUST LIKE YOU AT THE CAFÉ...
BUT NO TWO PEOPLE ARE ALIKE.

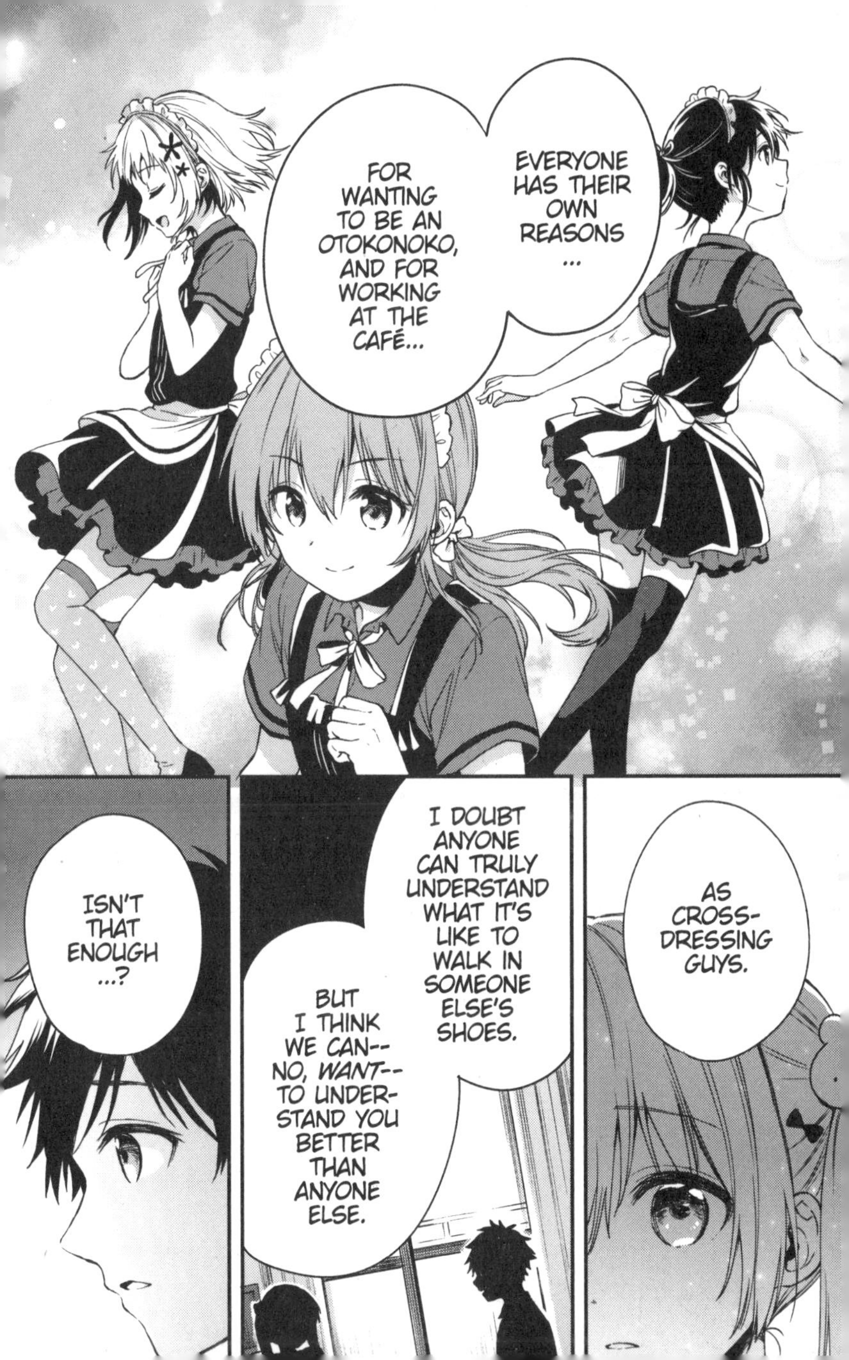
EVERYONE HAS THEIR OWN REASONS ...
FOR WANTING TO BE AN OTOKONOKO, AND FOR WORKING AT THE CAFÉ...
AS CROSS-DRESSING GUYS.
I DOUBT ANYONE CAN TRULY UNDERSTAND WHAT IT'S LIKE TO WALK IN SOMEONE ELSE'S SHOES.
BUT I THINK WE CAN-- NO, *WANT*-- TO UNDERSTAND YOU BETTER THAN ANYONE ELSE.
ISN'T THAT ENOUGH ...?

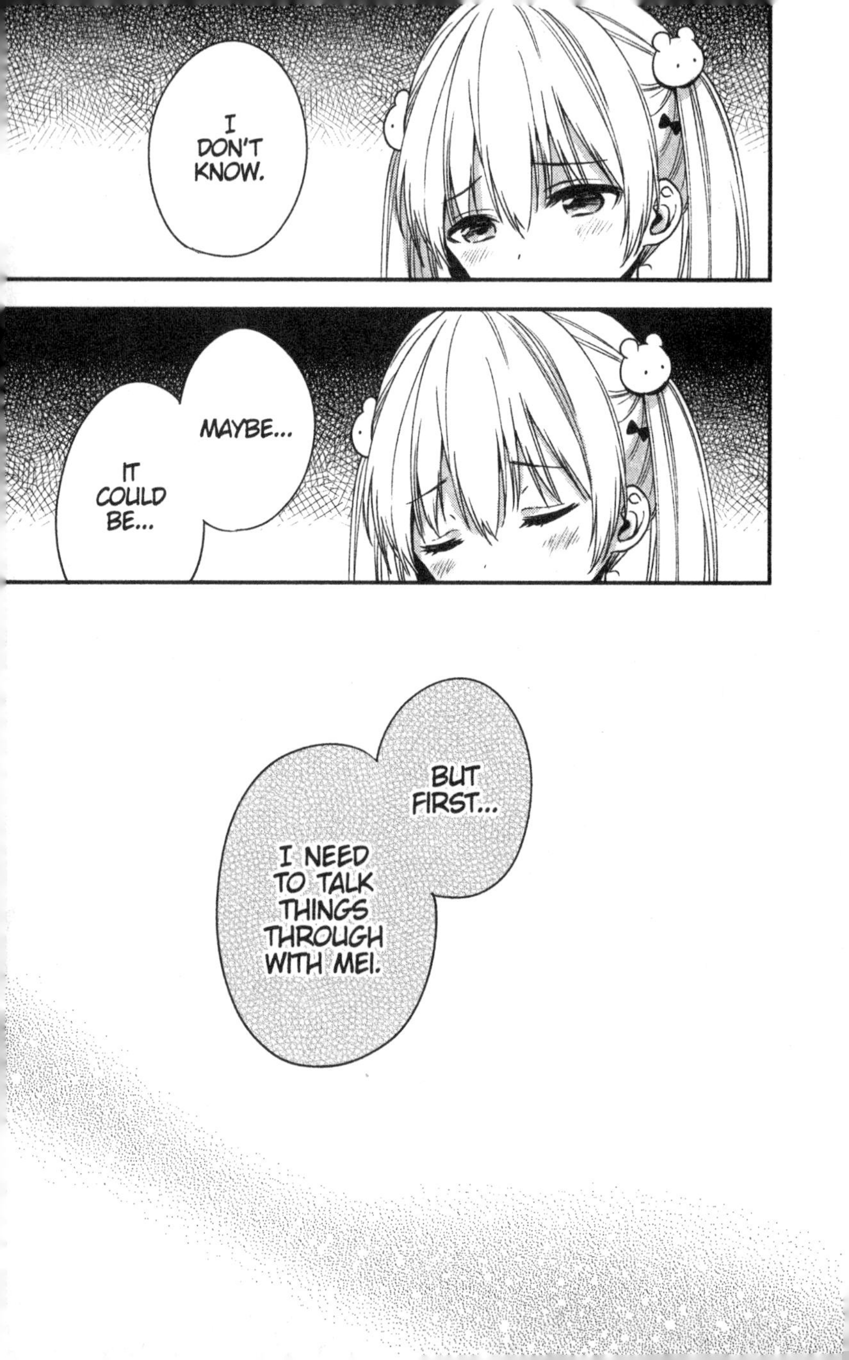
I DON'T KNOW.
MAYBE...
IT COULD BE...
BUT FIRST...
I NEED TO TALK THINGS THROUGH WITH MEI.

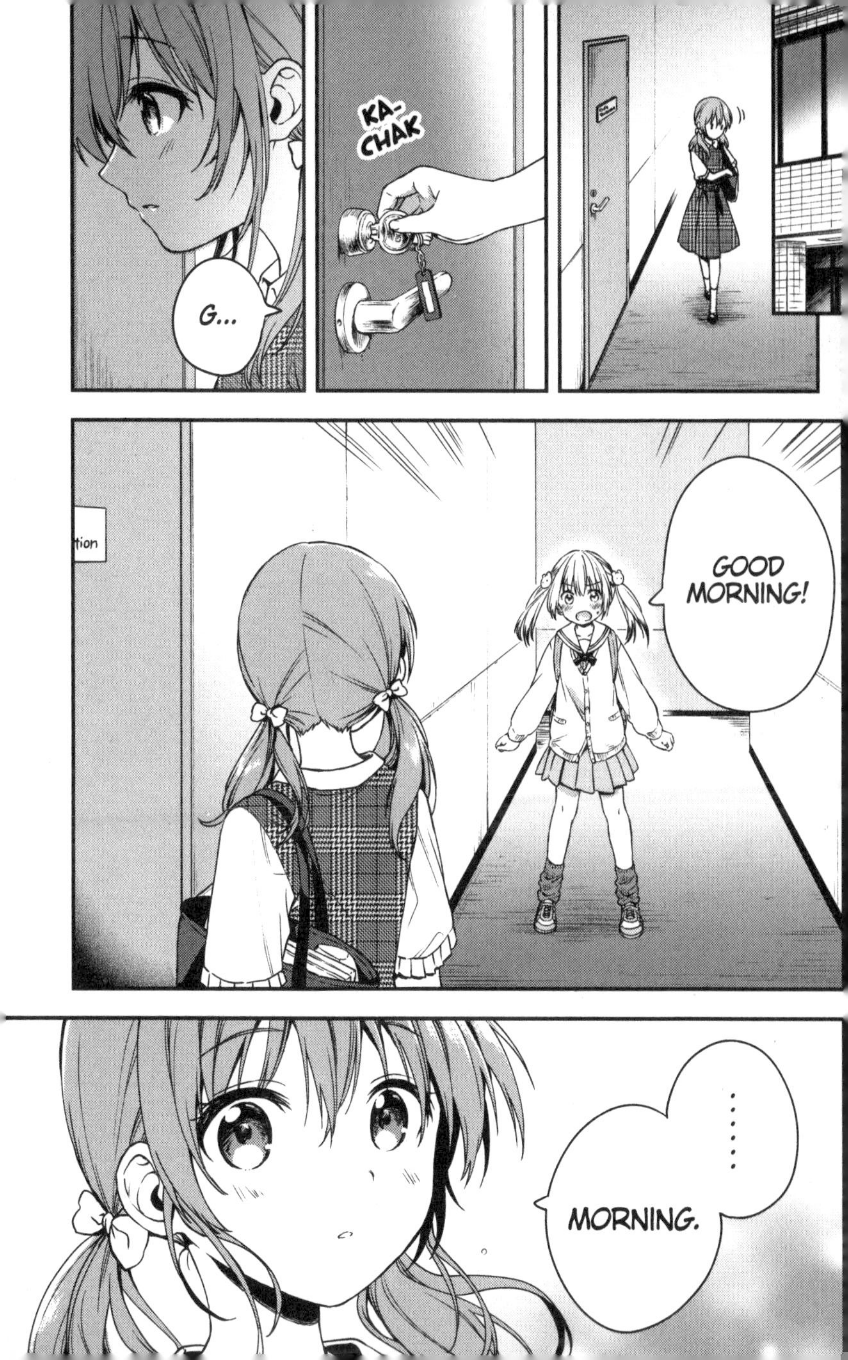
KA-CHAK
G...
GOOD MORNING!
......
MORNING.

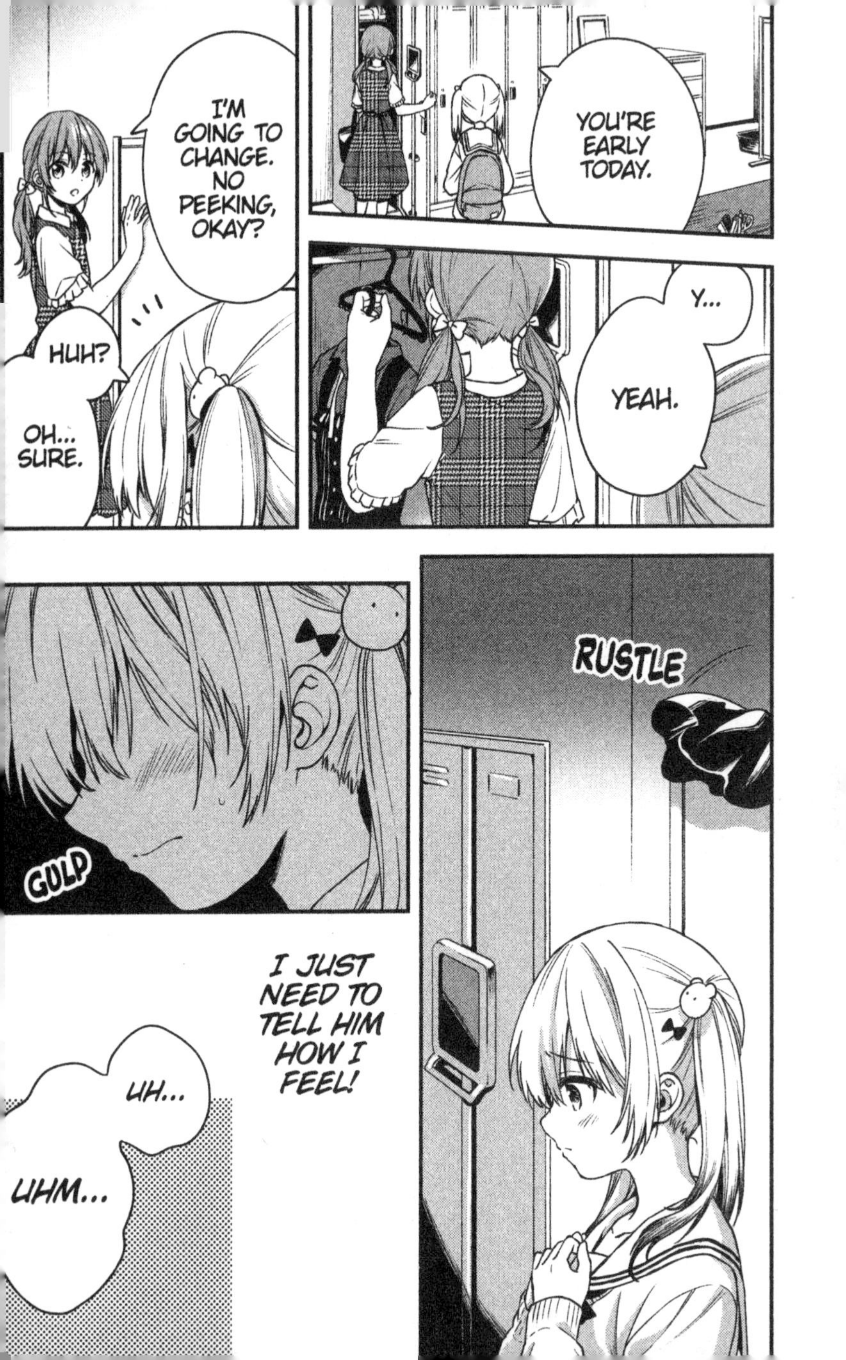

YOU'RE EARLY TODAY.
Y...
YEAH.
I'M GOING TO CHANGE. NO PEEKING, OKAY?
HUH?
OH... SURE.
RUSTLE
GULP
I JUST NEED TO TELL HIM HOW I FEEL!
UH...
UHM...

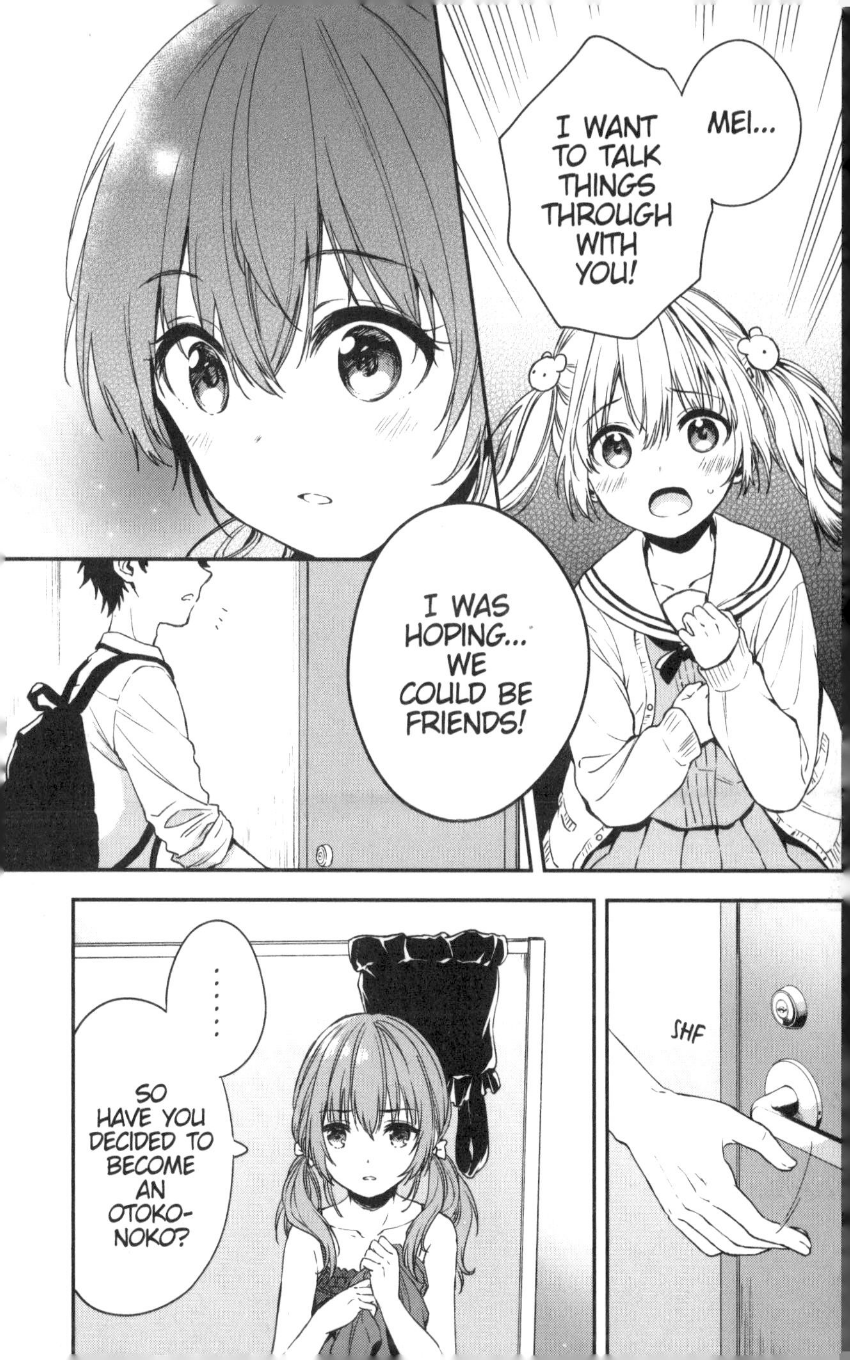
MEI...
I WANT TO TALK THINGS THROUGH WITH YOU!
I WAS HOPING... WE COULD BE FRIENDS!
SHF
......
SO HAVE YOU DECIDED TO BECOME AN OTOKO-NOKO?

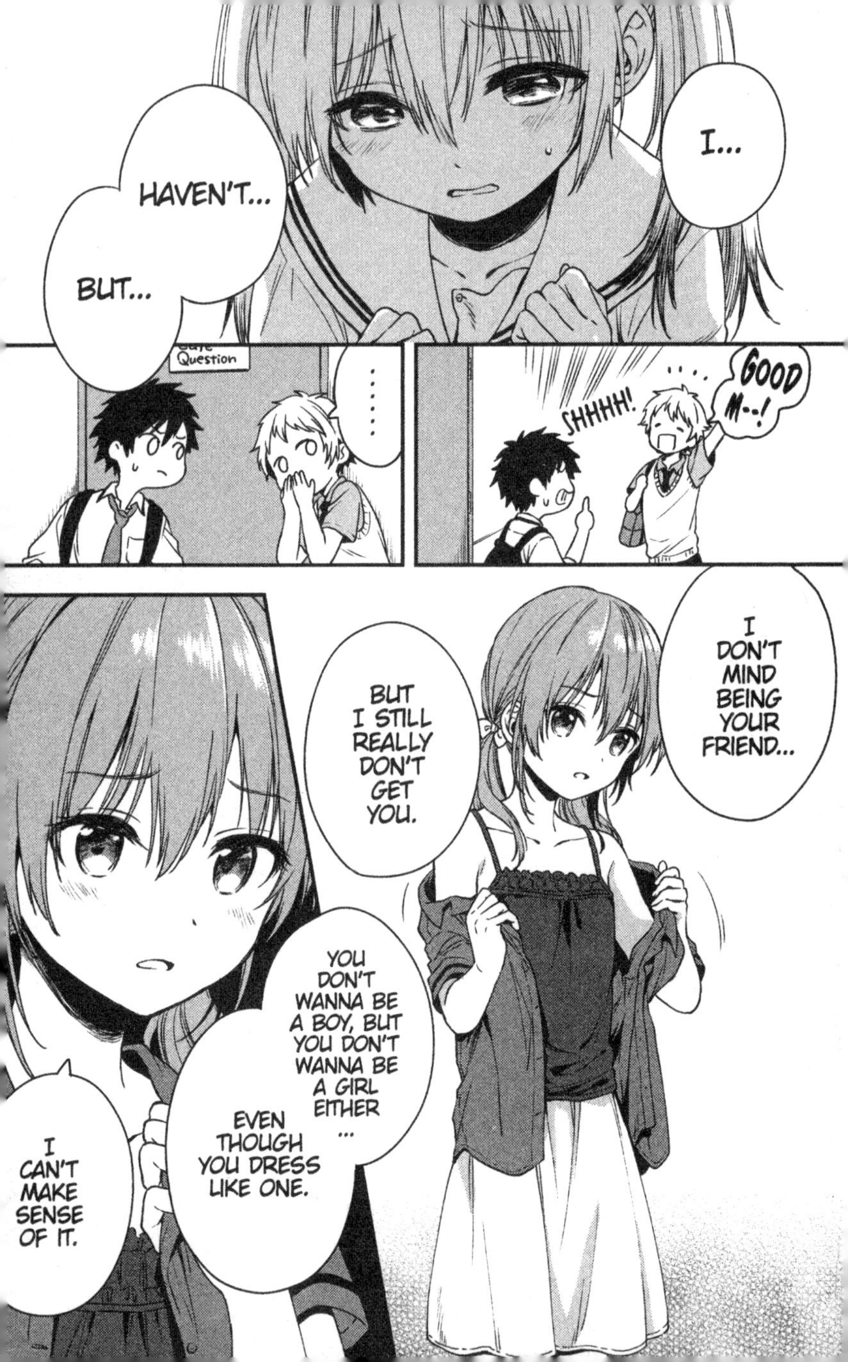
I...
HAVEN'T...
BUT...
GOOD M--!
...
SHHHH!
Question
......
I DON'T MIND BEING YOUR FRIEND...
BUT I STILL REALLY DON'T GET YOU.
YOU DON'T WANNA BE A BOY, BUT YOU DON'T WANNA BE A GIRL EITHER...
EVEN THOUGH YOU DRESS LIKE ONE.
I CAN'T MAKE SENSE OF IT.

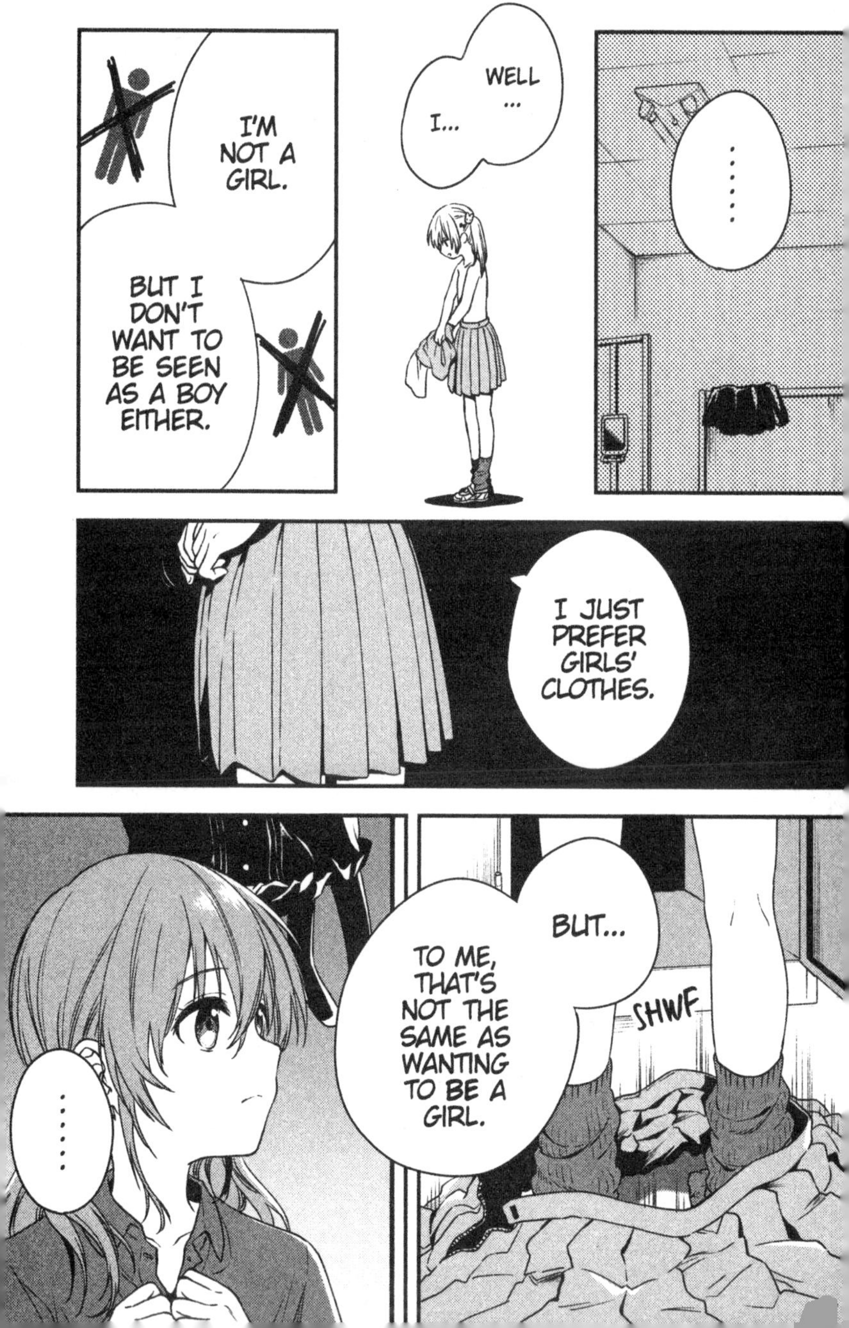
......
WELL... I...
I'M NOT A GIRL.
BUT I DON'T WANT TO BE SEEN AS A BOY EITHER.
I JUST PREFER GIRLS' CLOTHES.
BUT...
TO ME, THAT'S NOT THE SAME AS WANTING TO BE A GIRL.
SHWF
......

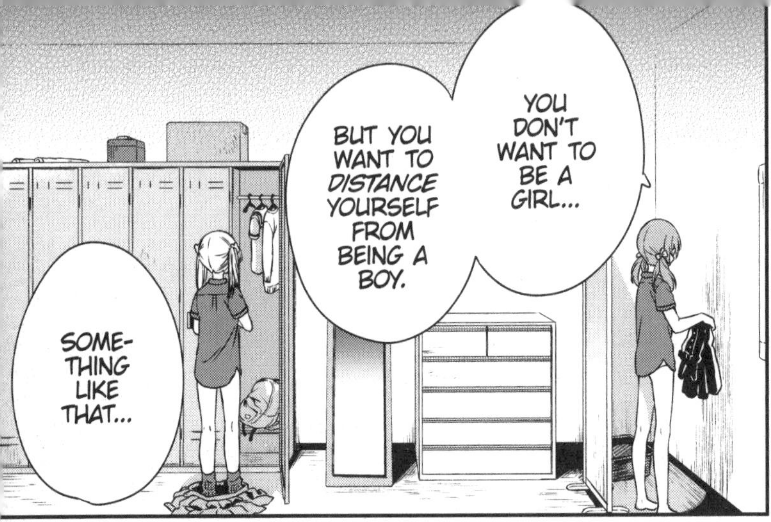
YOU DON'T WANT TO BE A GIRL...
BUT YOU WANT TO *DISTANCE* YOURSELF FROM BEING A BOY.
SOME-THING LIKE THAT...

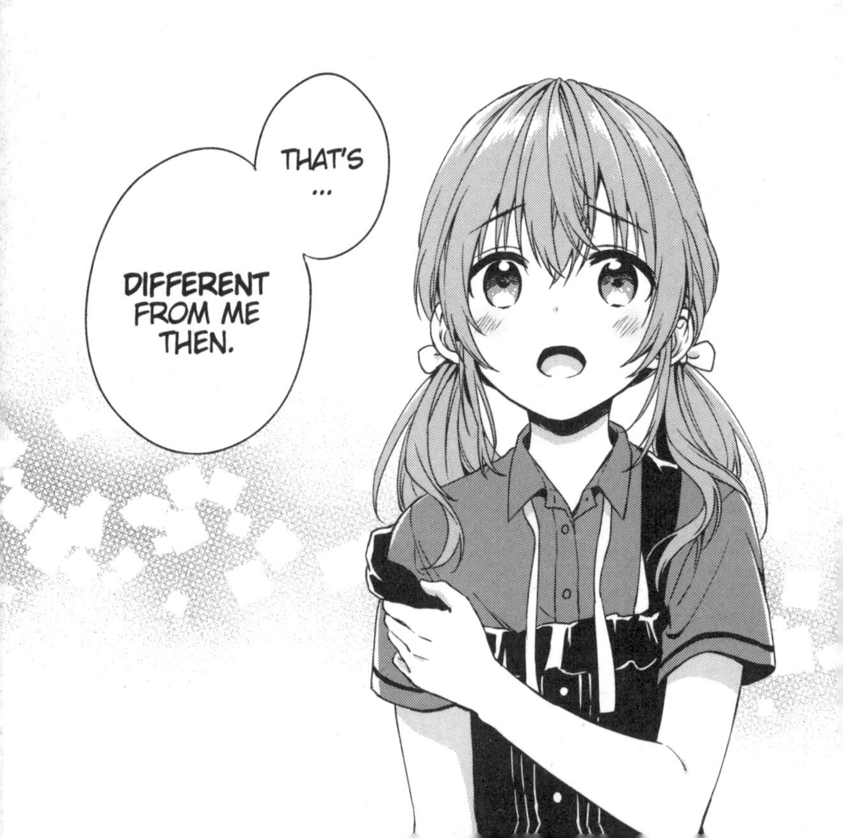
THAT'S ...
DIFFERENT FROM ME THEN.

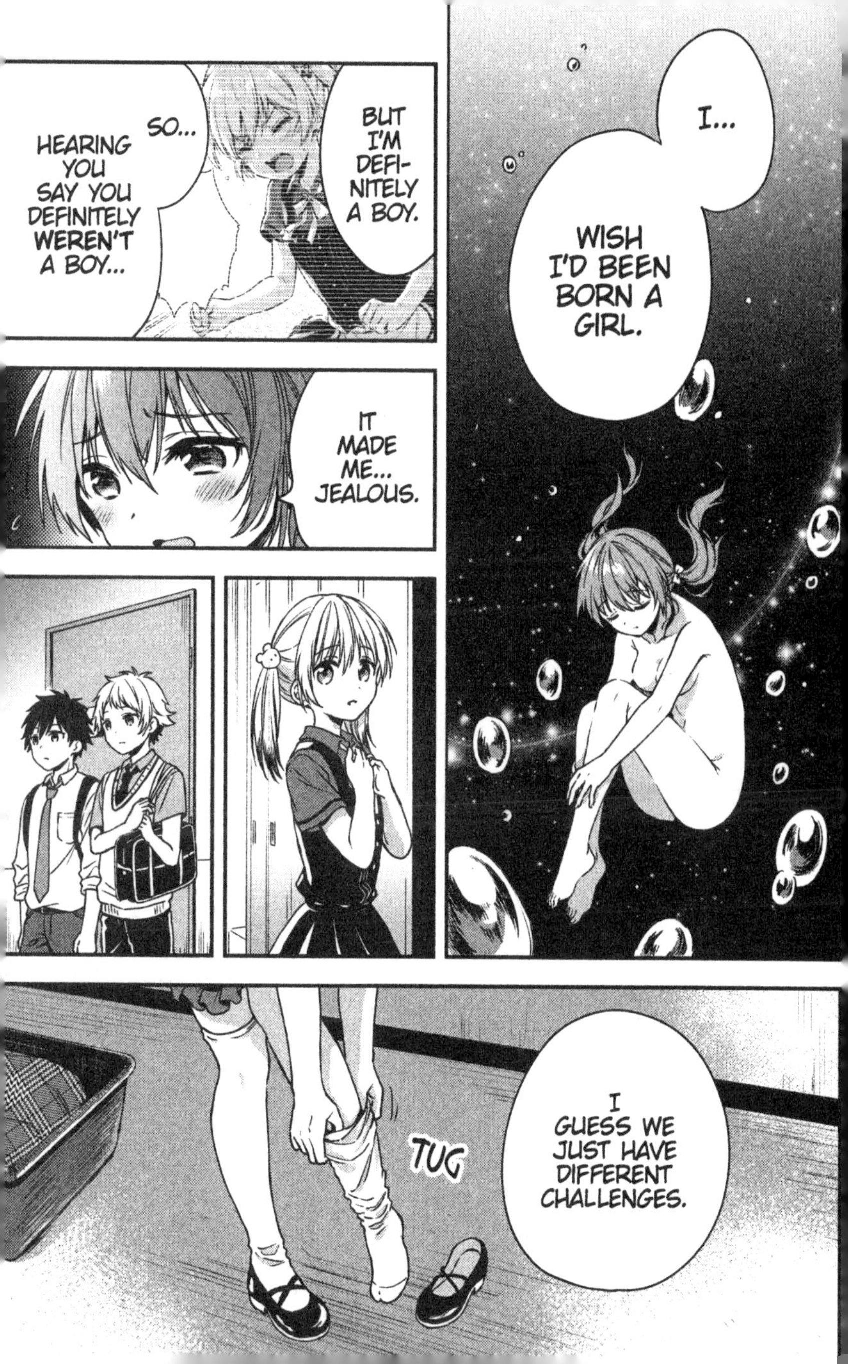
I...
WISH I'D BEEN BORN A GIRL.
BUT I'M DEFINITELY A BOY.
SO...
HEARING YOU SAY YOU DEFINITELY WEREN'T A BOY...
IT MADE ME... JEALOUS.
I GUESS WE JUST HAVE DIFFERENT CHALLENGES.
TUG

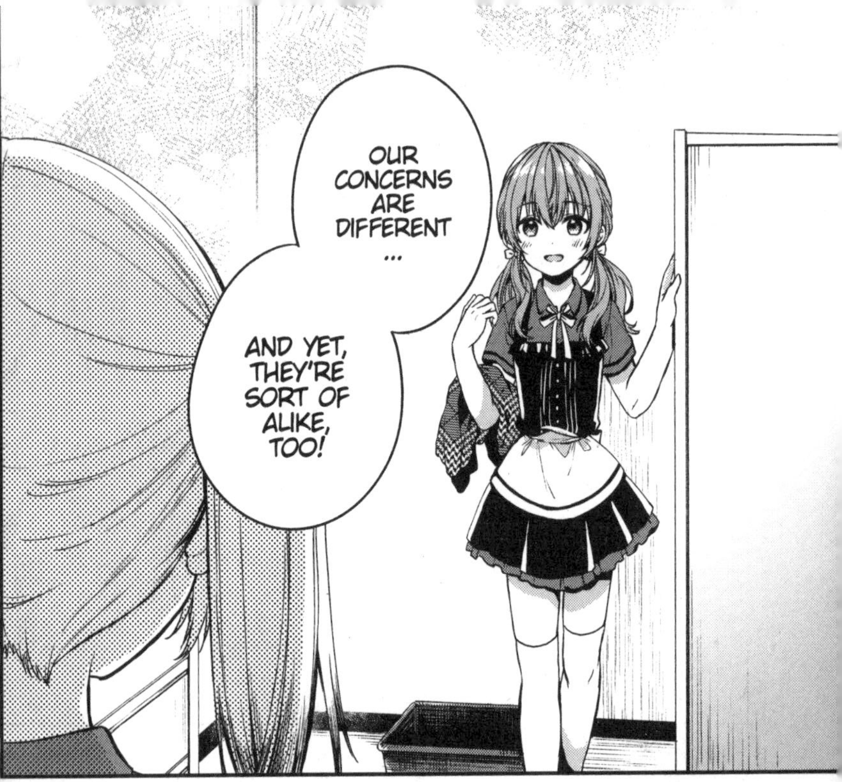
OUR CONCERNS ARE DIFFERENT ...
AND YET, THEY'RE SORT OF ALIKE, TOO!
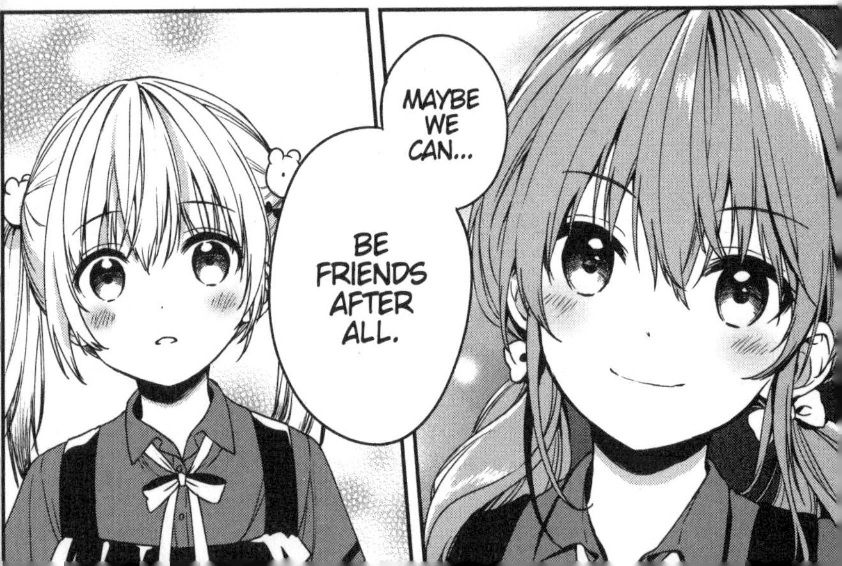
MAYBE WE CAN...
BE FRIENDS AFTER ALL.

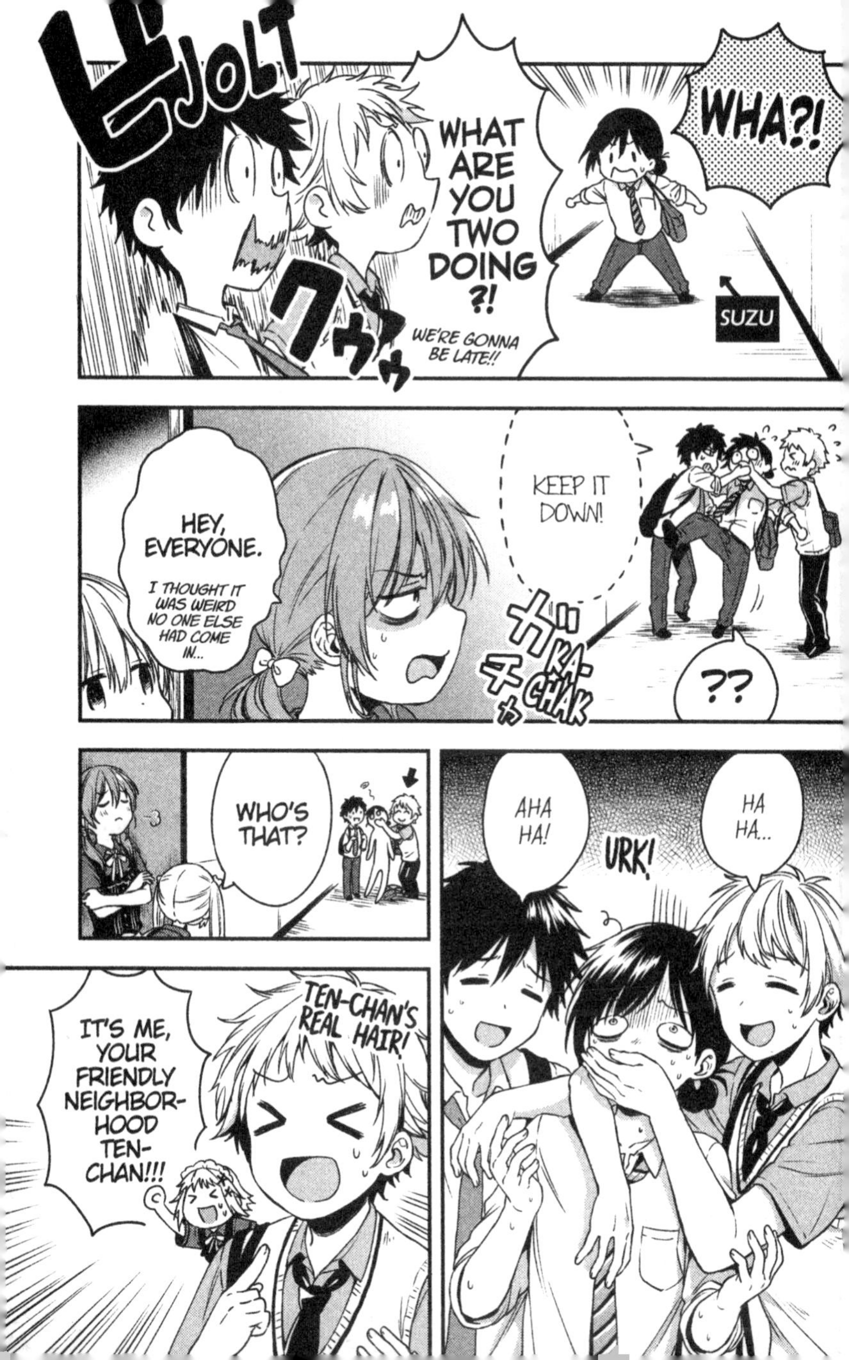
WHA?!
SUZU
WHAT ARE YOU TWO DOING?!
WE'RE GONNA BE LATE!!
JOLT
KEEP IT DOWN!
??
KA-CHAK
HEY, EVERYONE.
I THOUGHT IT WAS WEIRD NO ONE ELSE HAD COME IN...
HA HA...
AHA HA!
URK!
WHO'S THAT?
TEN-CHAN'S REAL HAIR!
IT'S ME, YOUR FRIENDLY NEIGHBORHOOD TEN-CHAN!!!

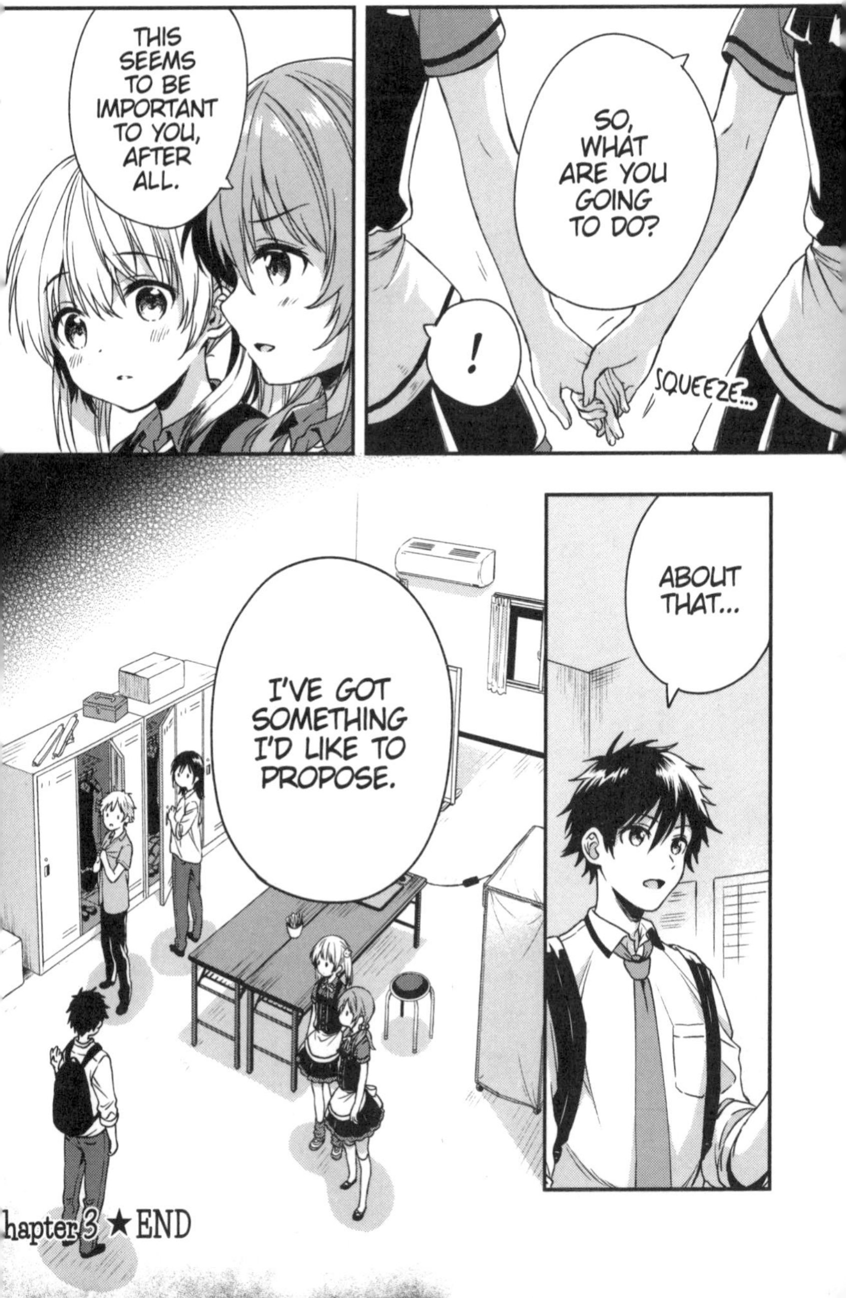
SO, WHAT ARE YOU GOING TO DO?
!
SQUEEZE...
THIS SEEMS TO BE IMPORTANT TO YOU, AFTER ALL.
ABOUT THAT...
I'VE GOT SOMETHING I'D LIKE TO PROPOSE.
hapter 3 ★ END

Love me for
who I am

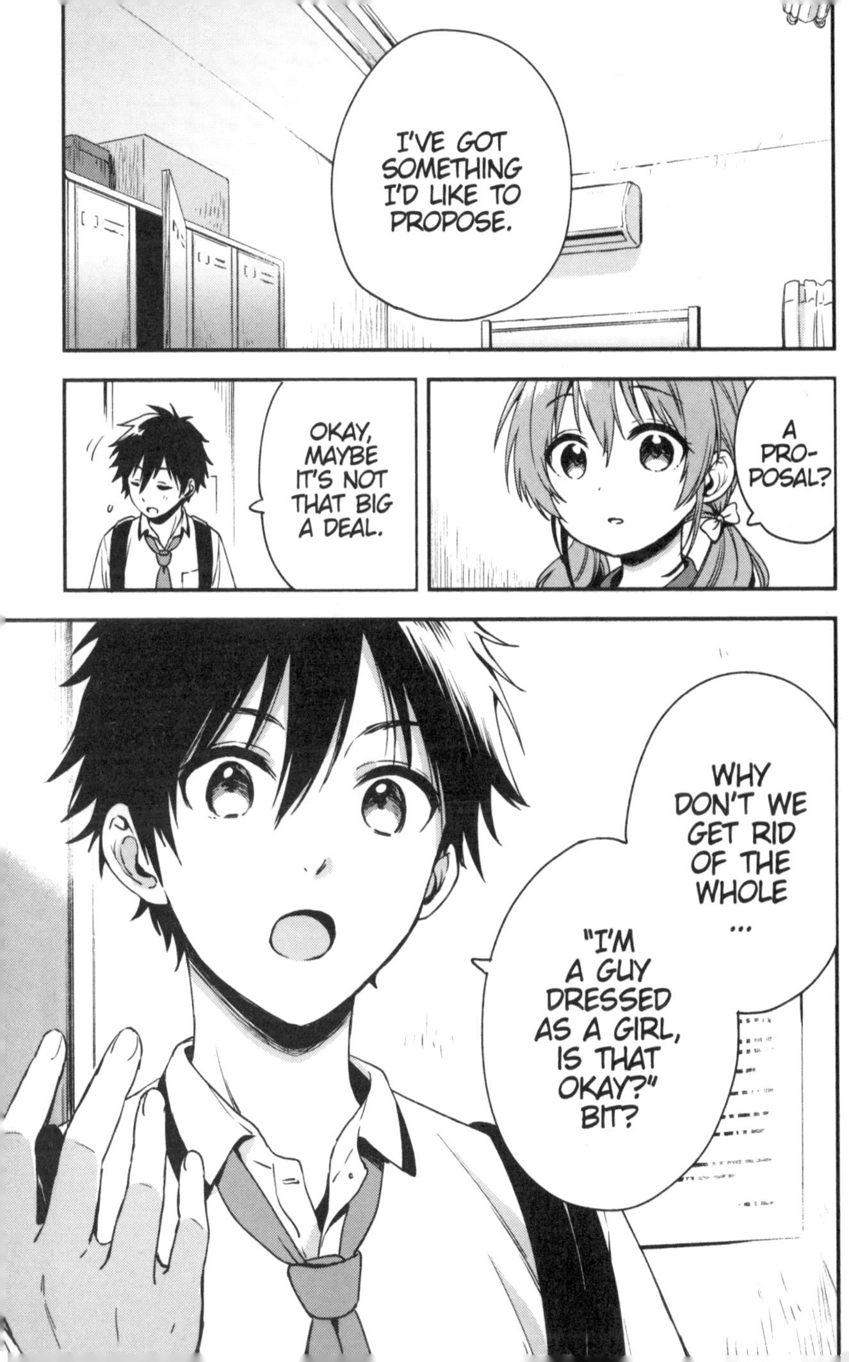
I'VE GOT SOMETHING I'D LIKE TO PROPOSE.
A PRO-POSAL?
OKAY, MAYBE IT'S NOT THAT BIG A DEAL.
WHY DON'T WE GET RID OF THE WHOLE ...
"I'M A GUY DRESSED AS A GIRL, IS THAT OKAY?" BIT?

Chapter 4

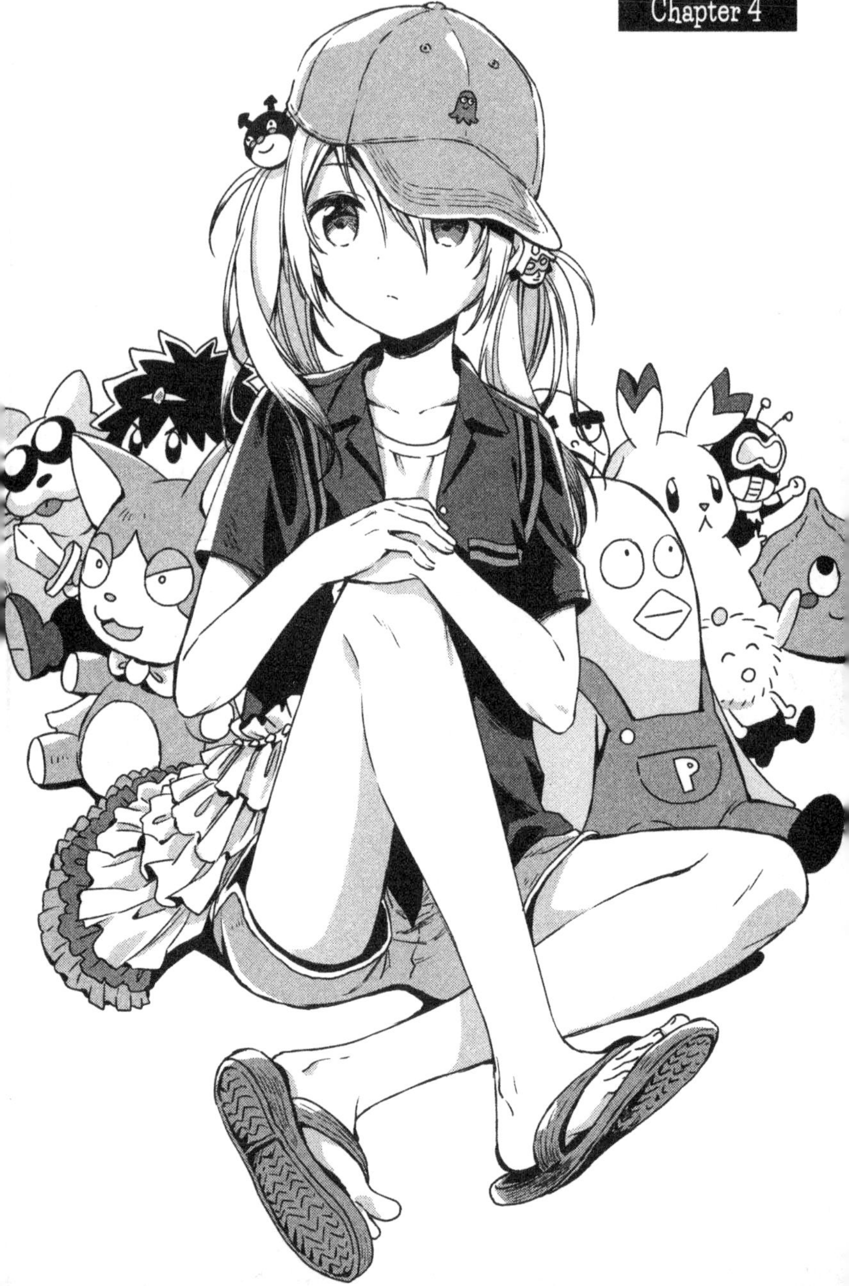

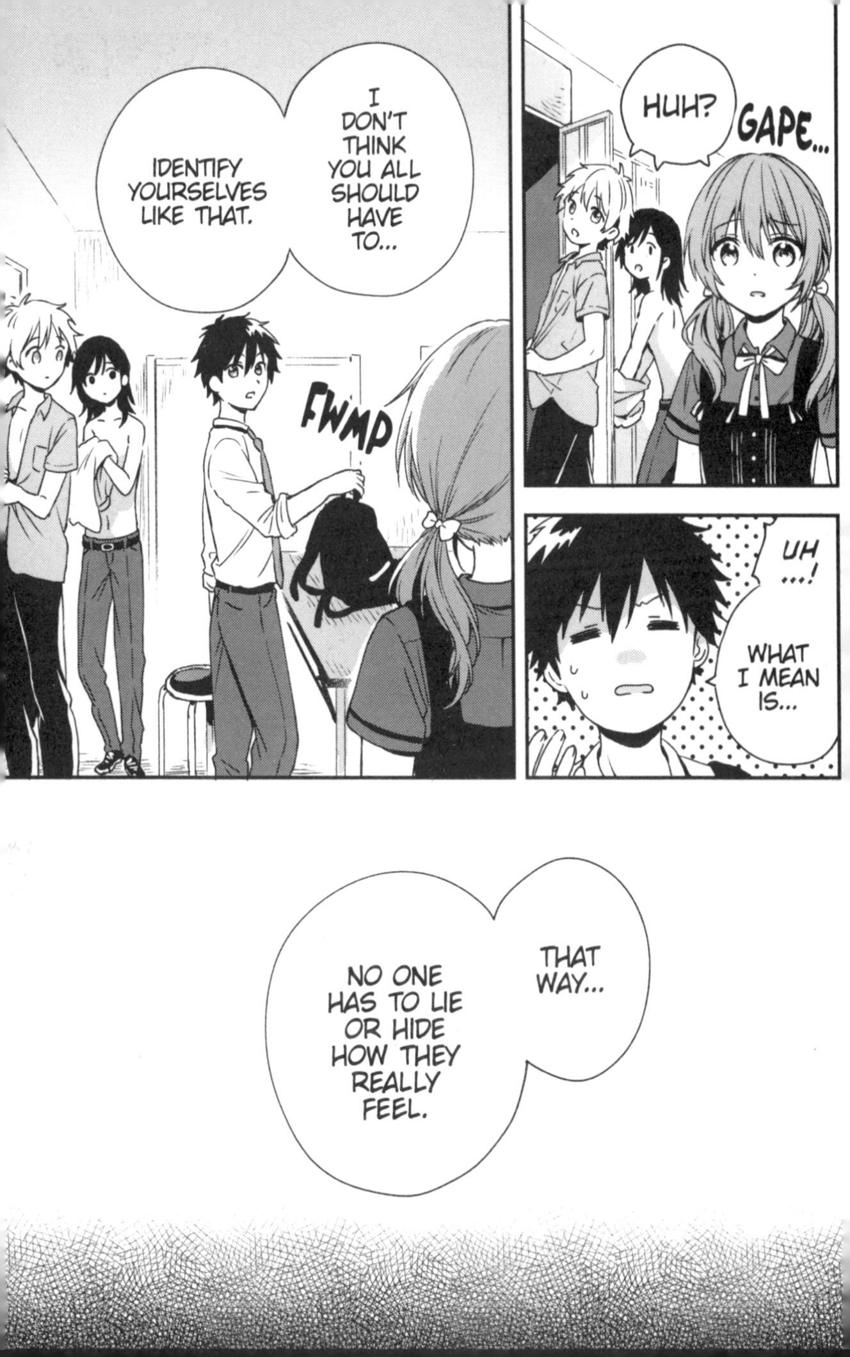
HUH?
GAPE...
UH ...!
WHAT I MEAN IS...
I DON'T THINK YOU ALL SHOULD HAVE TO...
IDENTIFY YOURSELVES LIKE THAT.
FWMP
THAT WAY...
NO ONE HAS TO LIE OR HIDE HOW THEY REALLY FEEL.

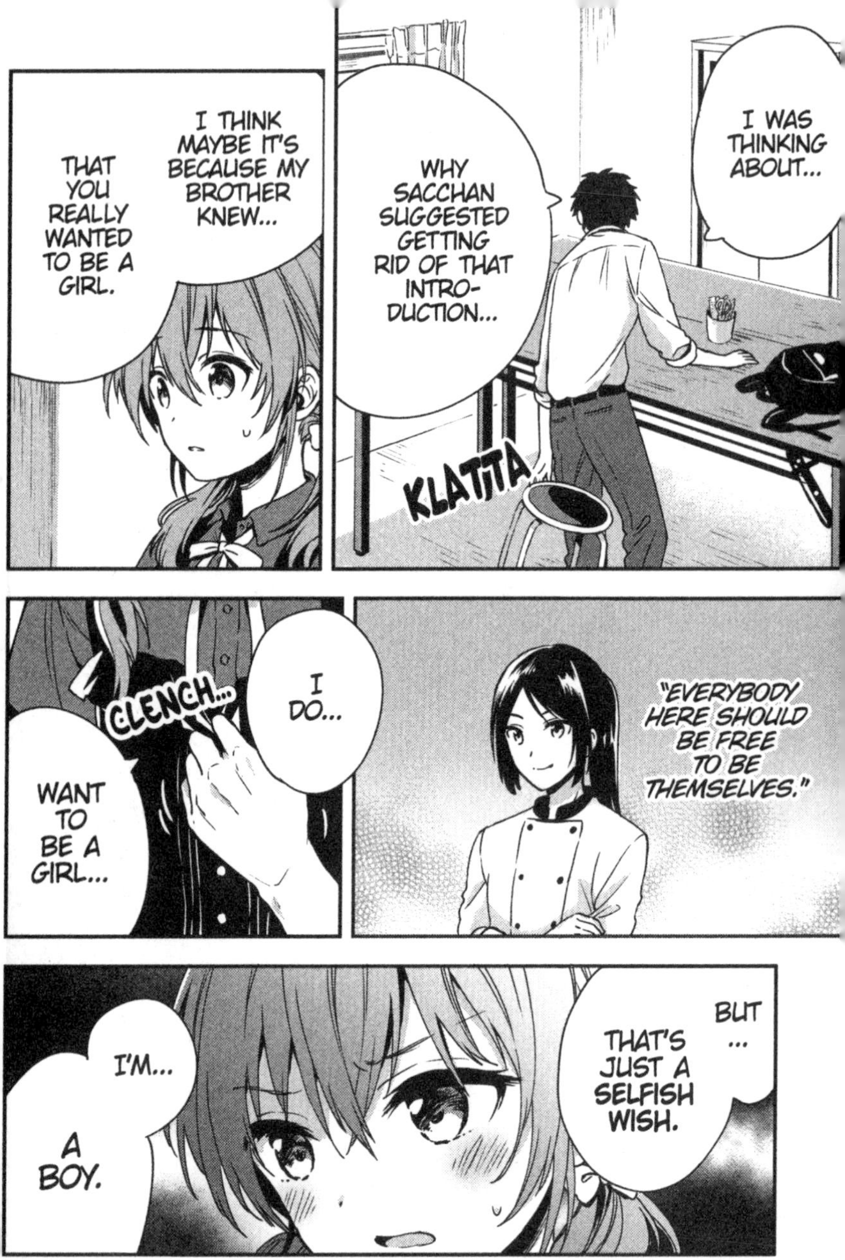
I WAS THINKING ABOUT...
WHY SACCHAN SUGGESTED GETTING RID OF THAT INTRO-DUCTION...
KLATTA
I THINK MAYBE IT'S BECAUSE MY BROTHER KNEW...
THAT YOU REALLY WANTED TO BE A GIRL.
"EVERYBODY HERE SHOULD BE FREE TO BE THEMSELVES."
I DO...
CLENCH...
WANT TO BE A GIRL...
BUT...
THAT'S JUST A SELFISH WISH.
I'M...
A BOY.

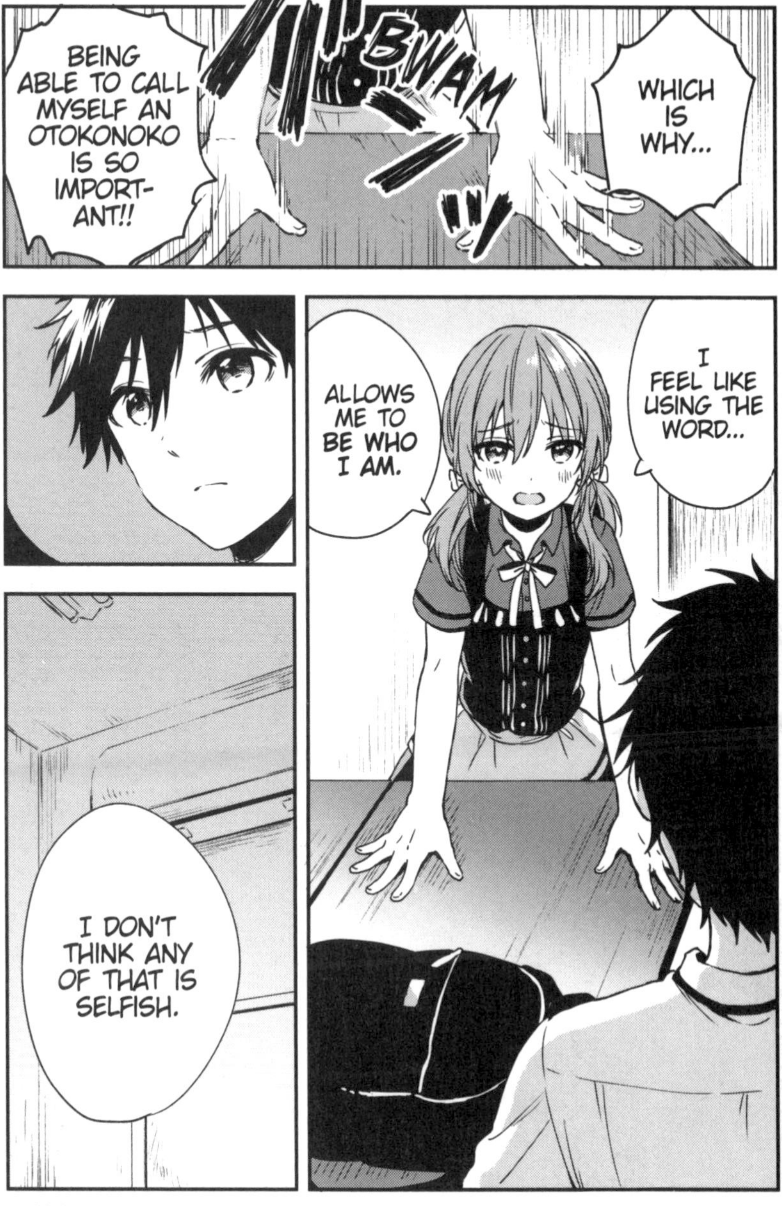
BEING ABLE TO CALL MYSELF AN OTOKONOKO IS SO IMPORTANT!!
BWAM
WHICH IS WHY...
I FEEL LIKE USING THE WORD...
ALLOWS ME TO BE WHO I AM.
I DON'T THINK ANY OF THAT IS SELFISH.

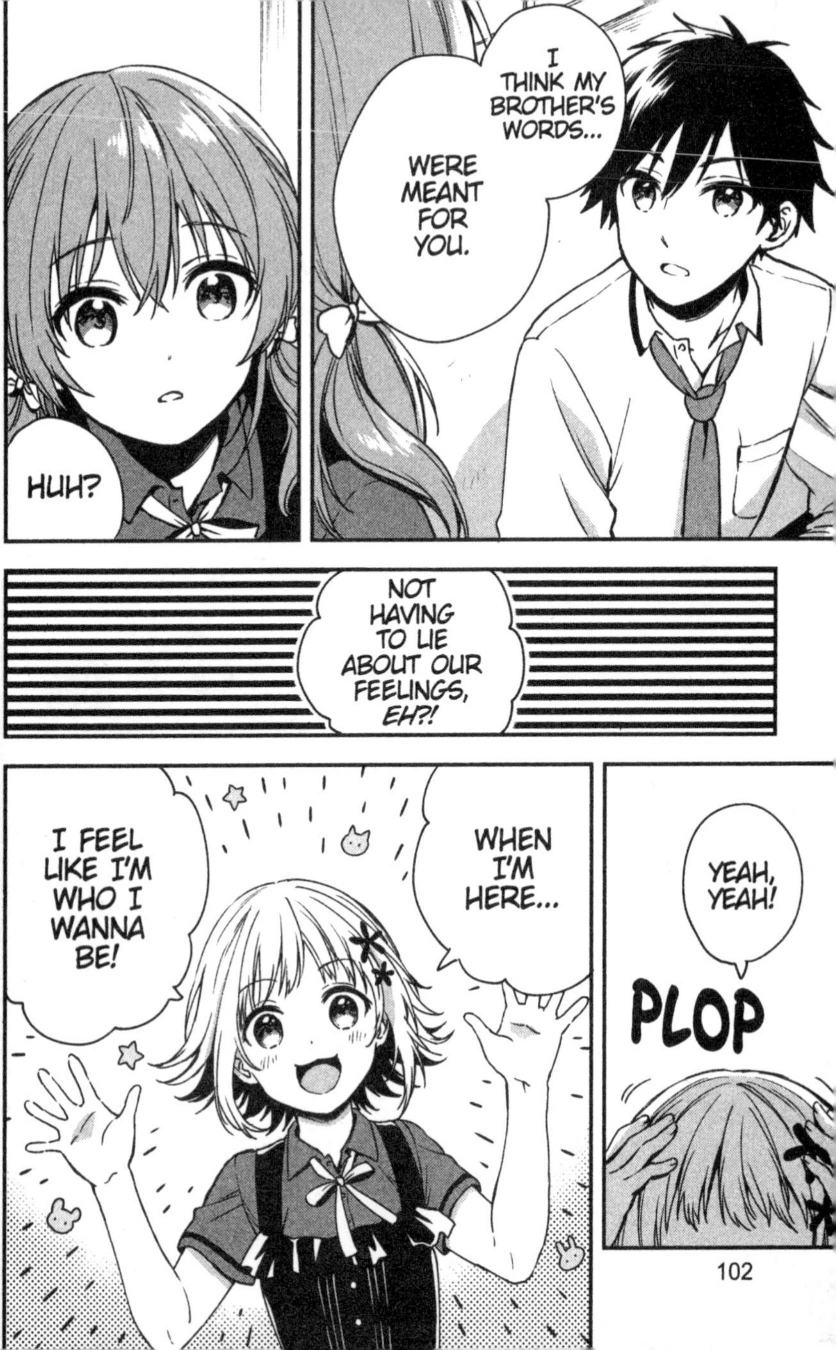
I THINK MY BROTHER'S WORDS...
WERE MEANT FOR YOU.
HUH?
NOT HAVING TO LIE ABOUT OUR FEELINGS, *EH?!*
YEAH, YEAH!
PLOP
WHEN I'M HERE...
I FEEL LIKE I'M WHO I WANNA BE!

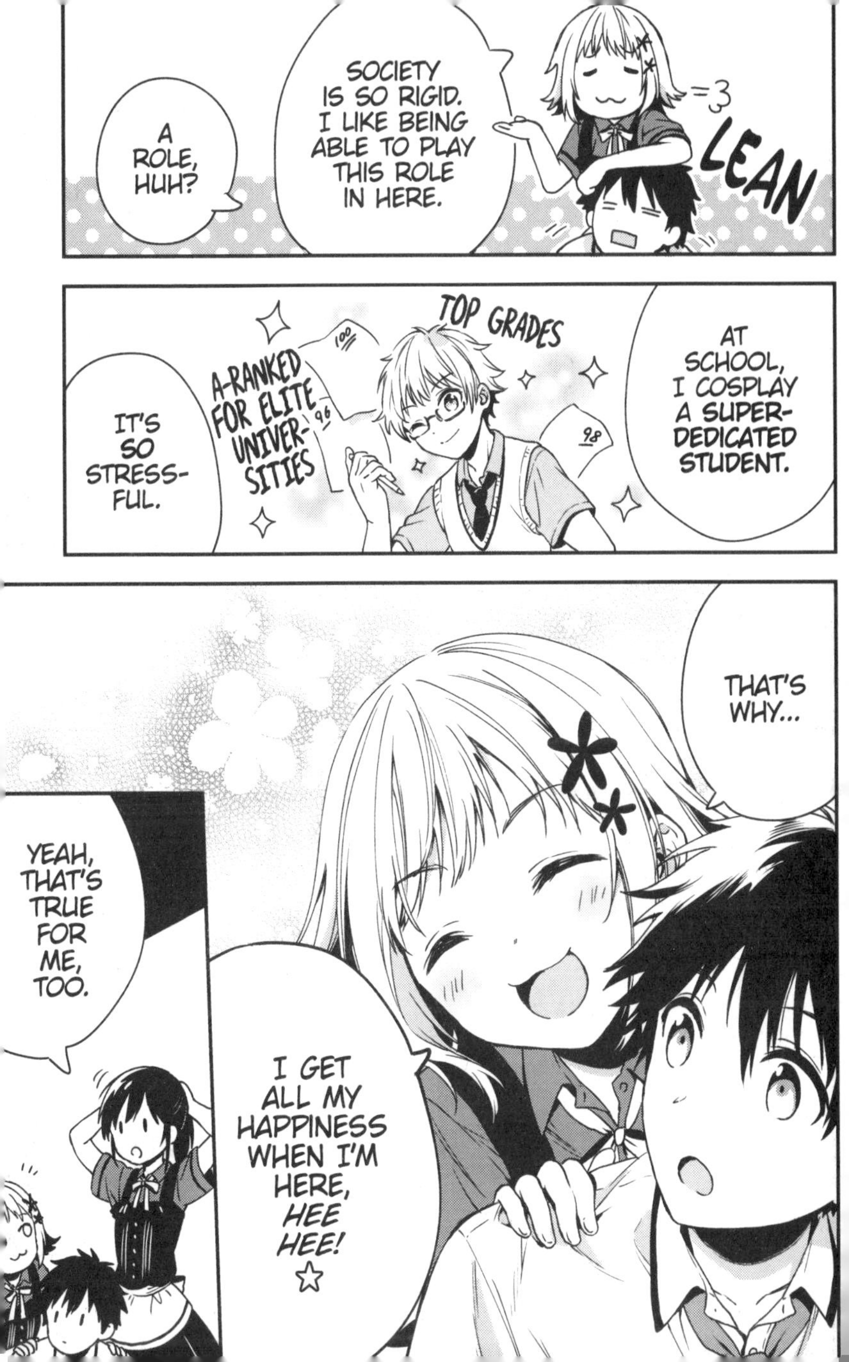
LEAN
SOCIETY IS SO RIGID. I LIKE BEING ABLE TO PLAY THIS ROLE IN HERE.
A ROLE, HUH?
AT SCHOOL, I COSPLAY A SUPER-DEDICATED STUDENT.
TOP GRADES
98
100
A-RANKED FOR ELITE UNIVERSITIES
96
IT'S SO STRESSFUL.
THAT'S WHY...
I GET ALL MY HAPPINESS WHEN I'M HERE, HEE HEE! ☆
YEAH, THAT'S TRUE FOR ME, TOO.

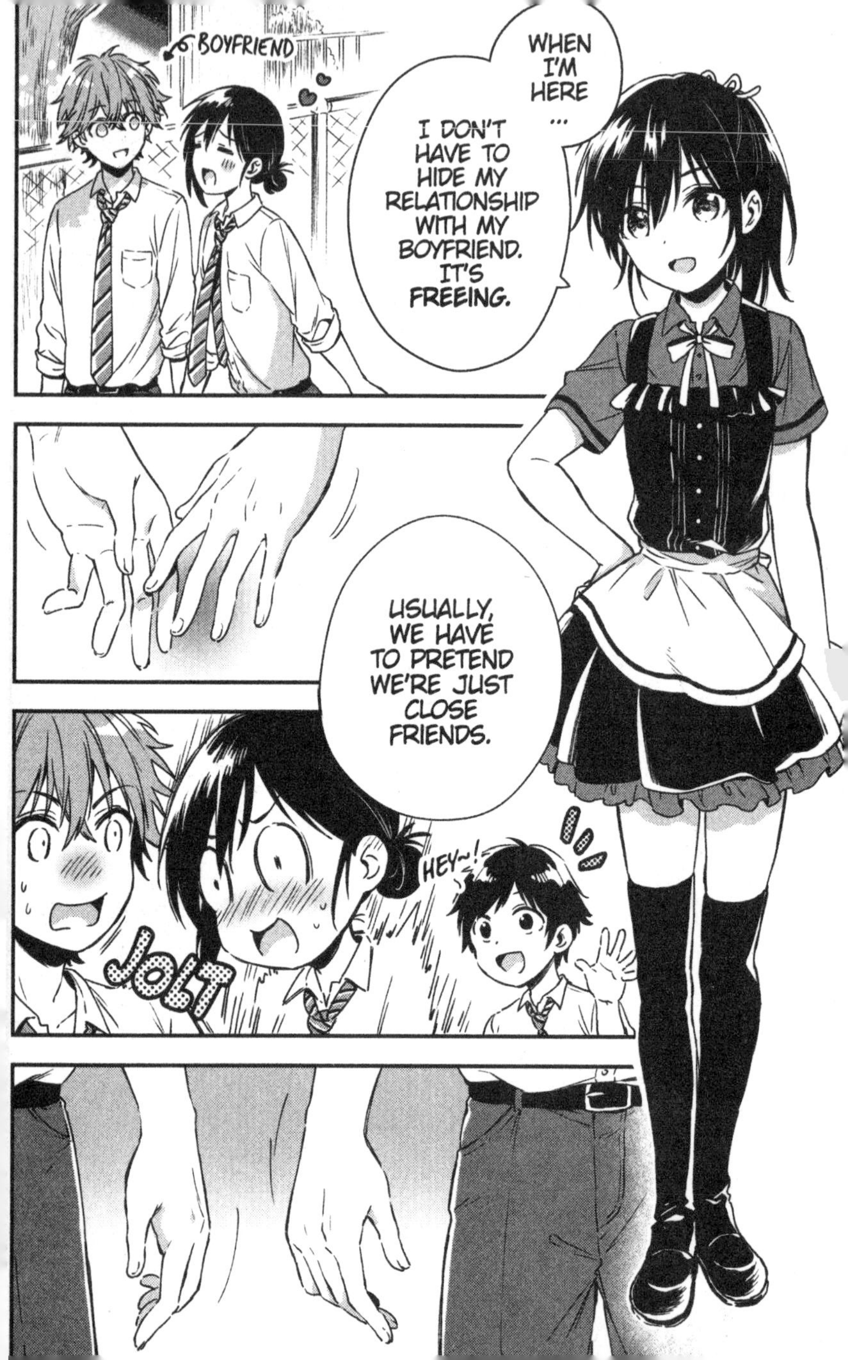
WHEN I'M HERE ...
I DON'T HAVE TO HIDE MY RELATIONSHIP WITH MY BOYFRIEND. IT'S FREEING.
USUALLY, WE HAVE TO PRETEND WE'RE JUST CLOSE FRIENDS.
BOYFRIEND
HEY~!
JOLT

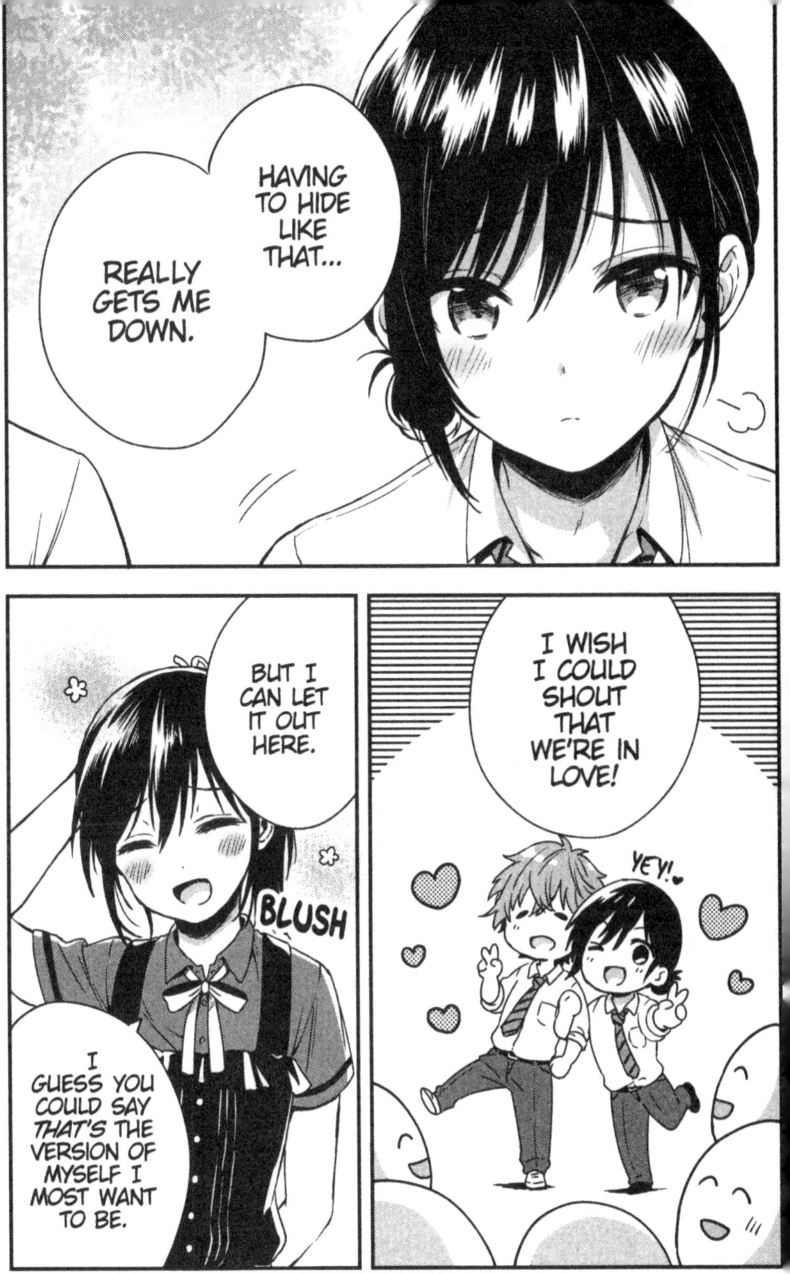
HAVING TO HIDE LIKE THAT...
REALLY GETS ME DOWN.
I WISH I COULD SHOUT THAT WE'RE IN LOVE!
YEY!♥
BUT I CAN LET IT OUT HERE.
BLUSH
I GUESS YOU COULD SAY *THAT'S* THE VERSION OF MYSELF I MOST WANT TO BE.

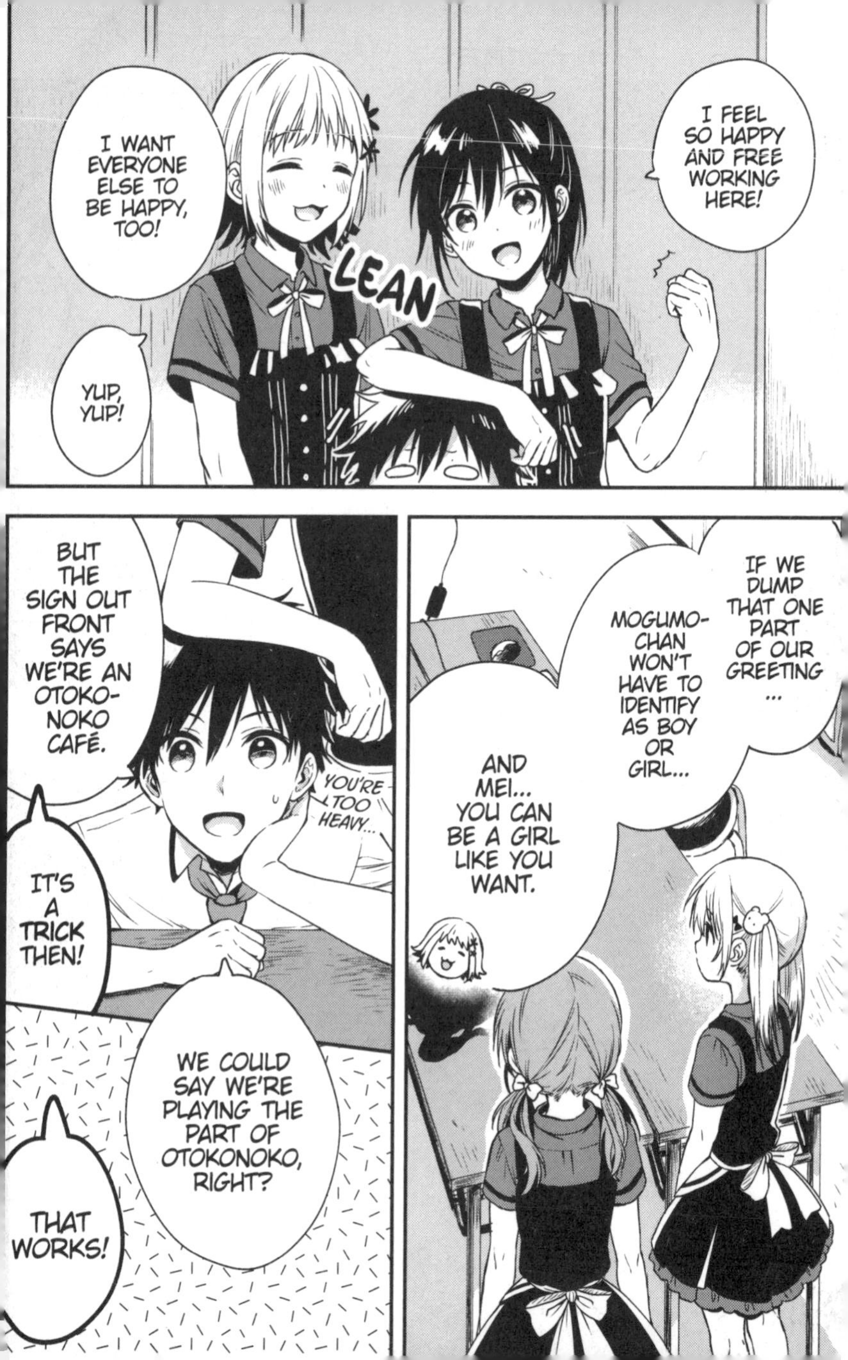
I FEEL SO HAPPY AND FREE WORKING HERE!
I WANT EVERYONE ELSE TO BE HAPPY, TOO!
LEAN
YUP, YUP!
IF WE DUMP THAT ONE PART OF OUR GREETING...
MOGUMO-CHAN WON'T HAVE TO IDENTIFY AS BOY OR GIRL...
AND MEI... YOU CAN BE A GIRL LIKE YOU WANT.
BUT THE SIGN OUT FRONT SAYS WE'RE AN OTOKO-NOKO CAFÉ.
YOU'RE TOO HEAVY...
IT'S A TRICK THEN!
WE COULD SAY WE'RE PLAYING THE PART OF OTOKONOKO, RIGHT?
THAT WORKS!

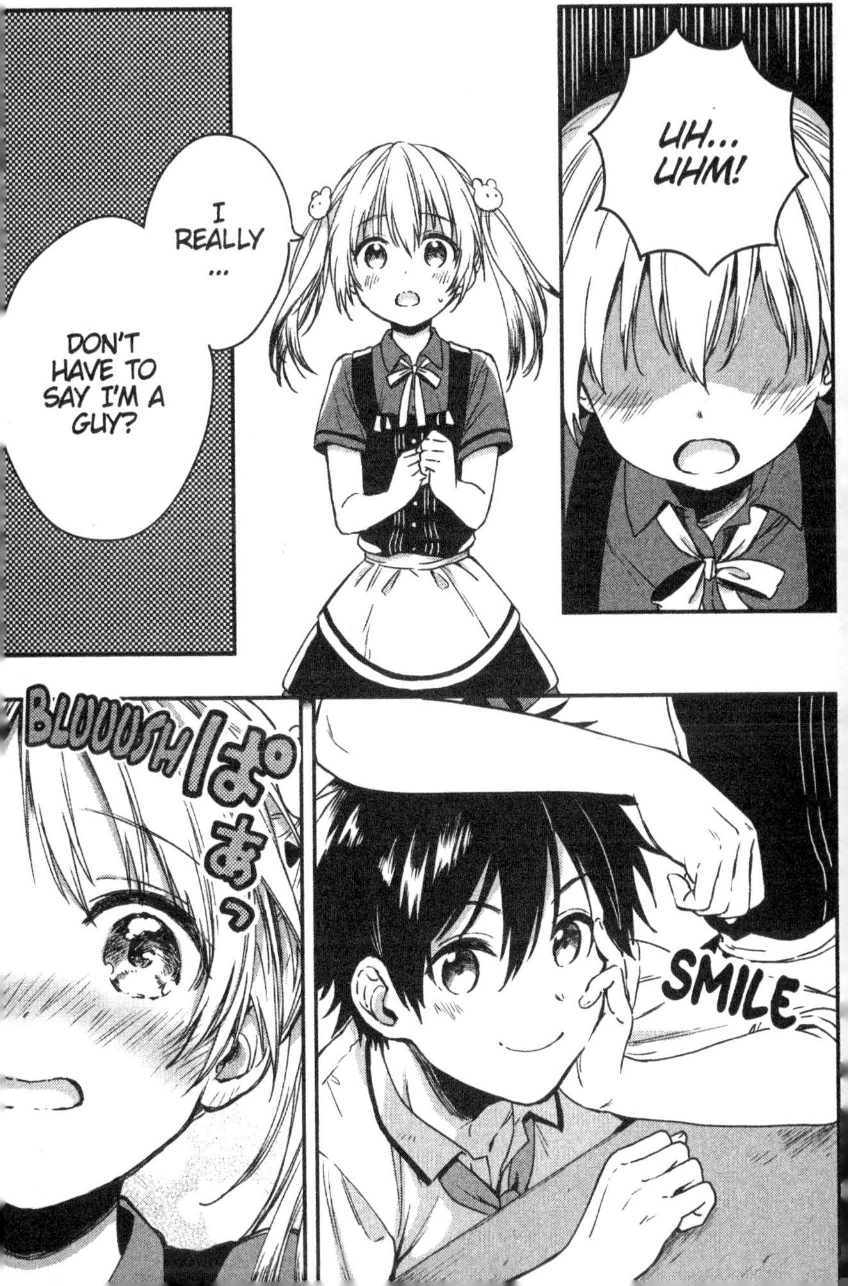
UH... UHM!
I REALLY ...
DON'T HAVE TO SAY I'M A GUY?
SMILE
BLUUUSH
ぽあっ

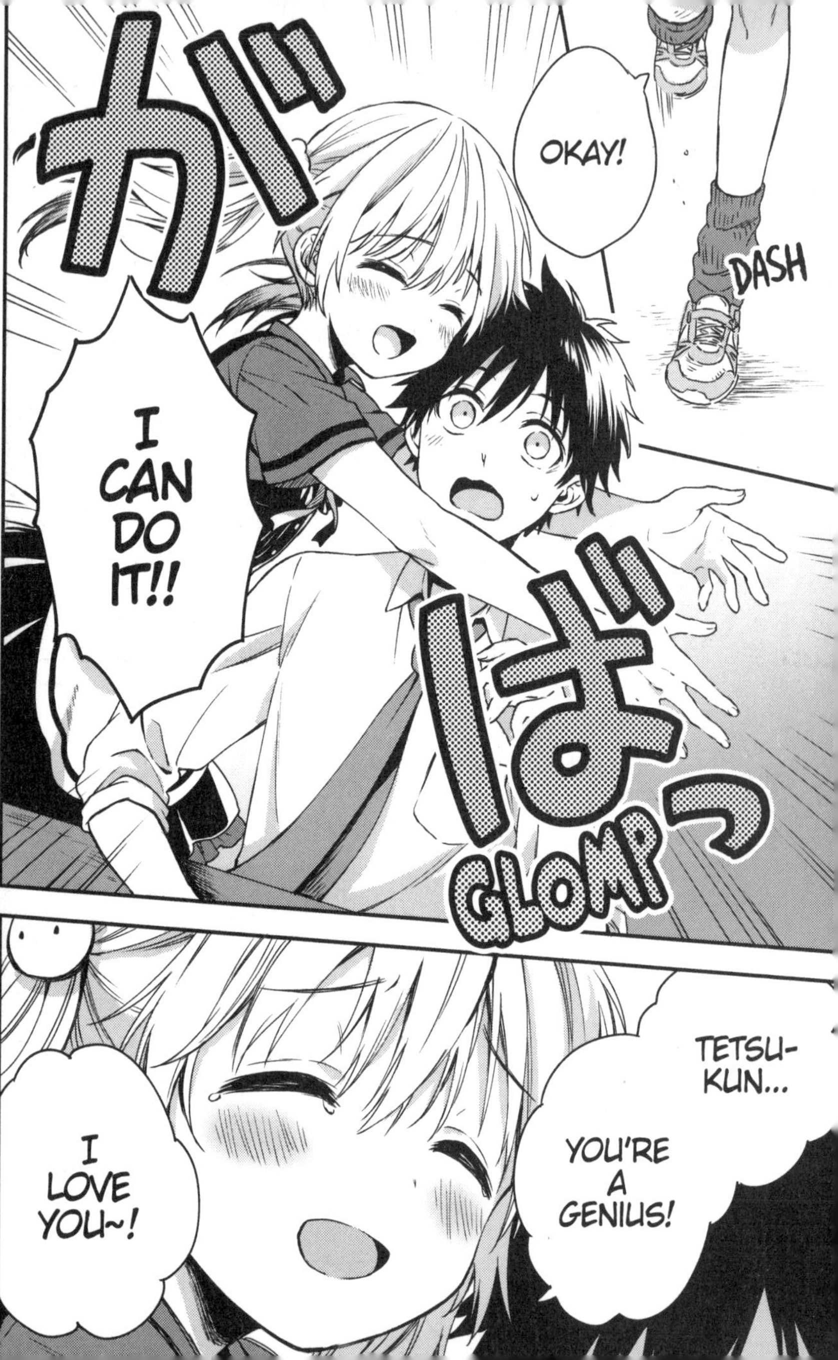

OKAY!
DASH
ガ
I CAN DO IT!!
ばっ
GLOMP
TETSU-KUN...
YOU'RE A GENIUS!
I LOVE YOU~!

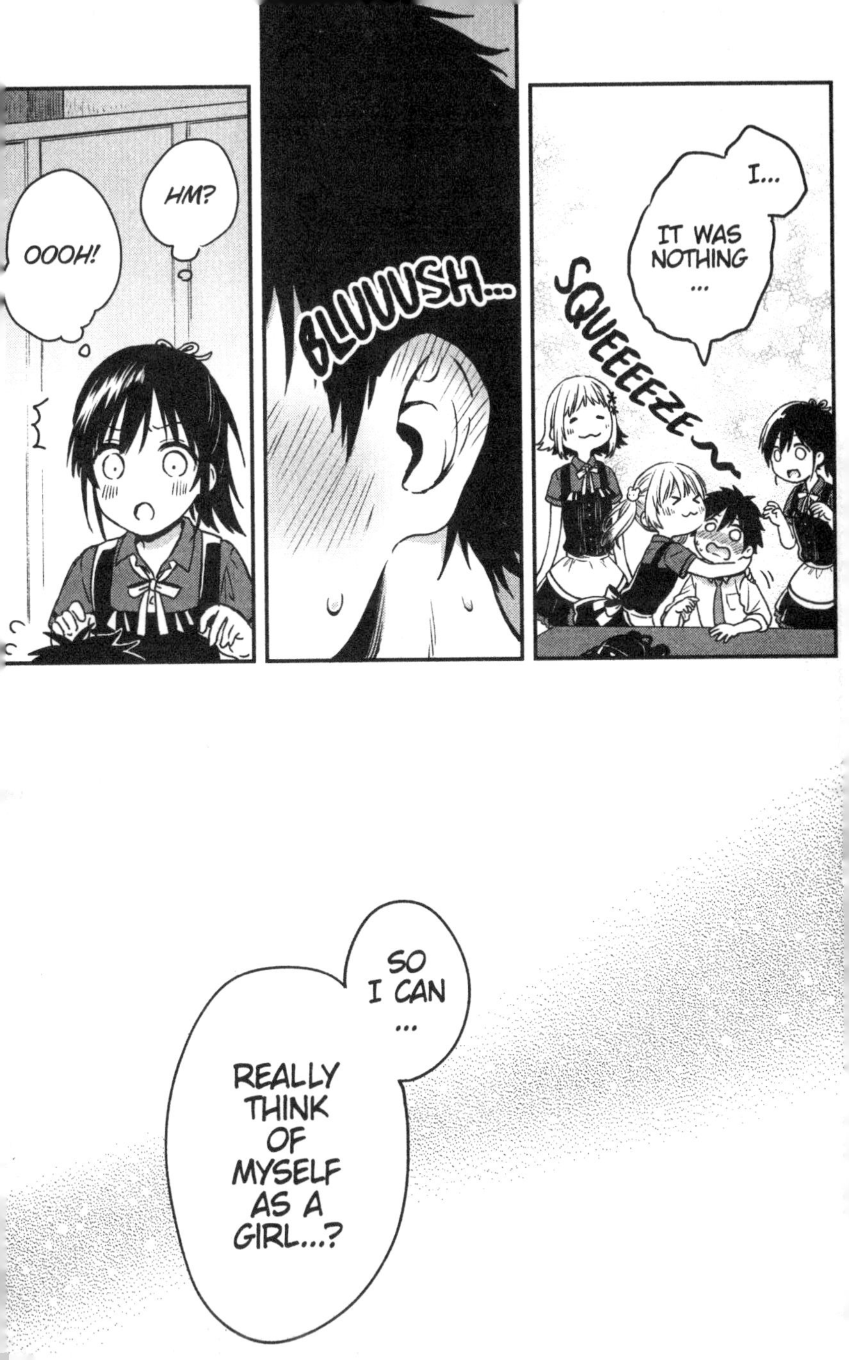
I...
IT WAS NOTHING ...
SQUEEEEEZE~
BLUUUSH...
HM?
OOOH!
SO I CAN ...
REALLY THINK OF MYSELF AS A GIRL...?

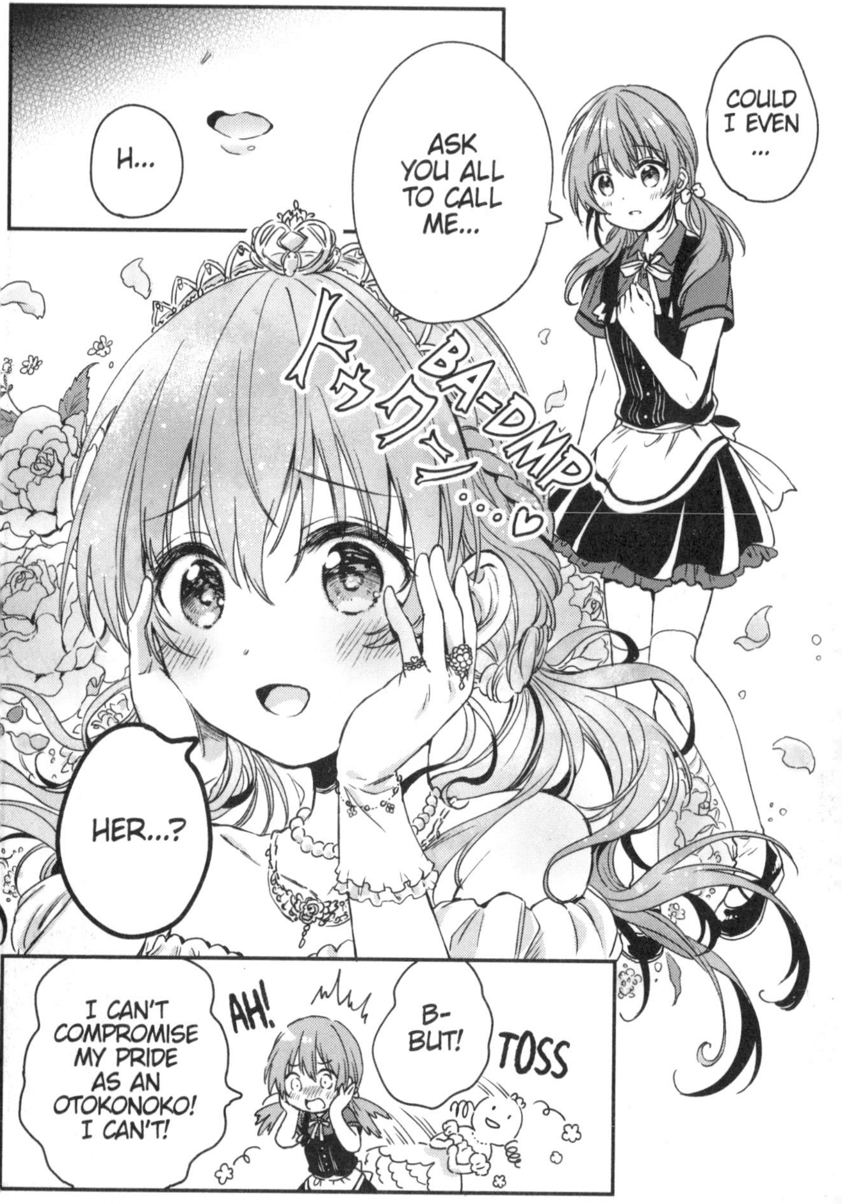
COULD I EVEN ...
ASK YOU ALL TO CALL ME...
H...
トゥクン
BA-DMP...♥
HER...?
B- BUT!
TOSS
AH!
I CAN'T COMPROMISE MY PRIDE AS AN OTOKONOKO! I CAN'T!

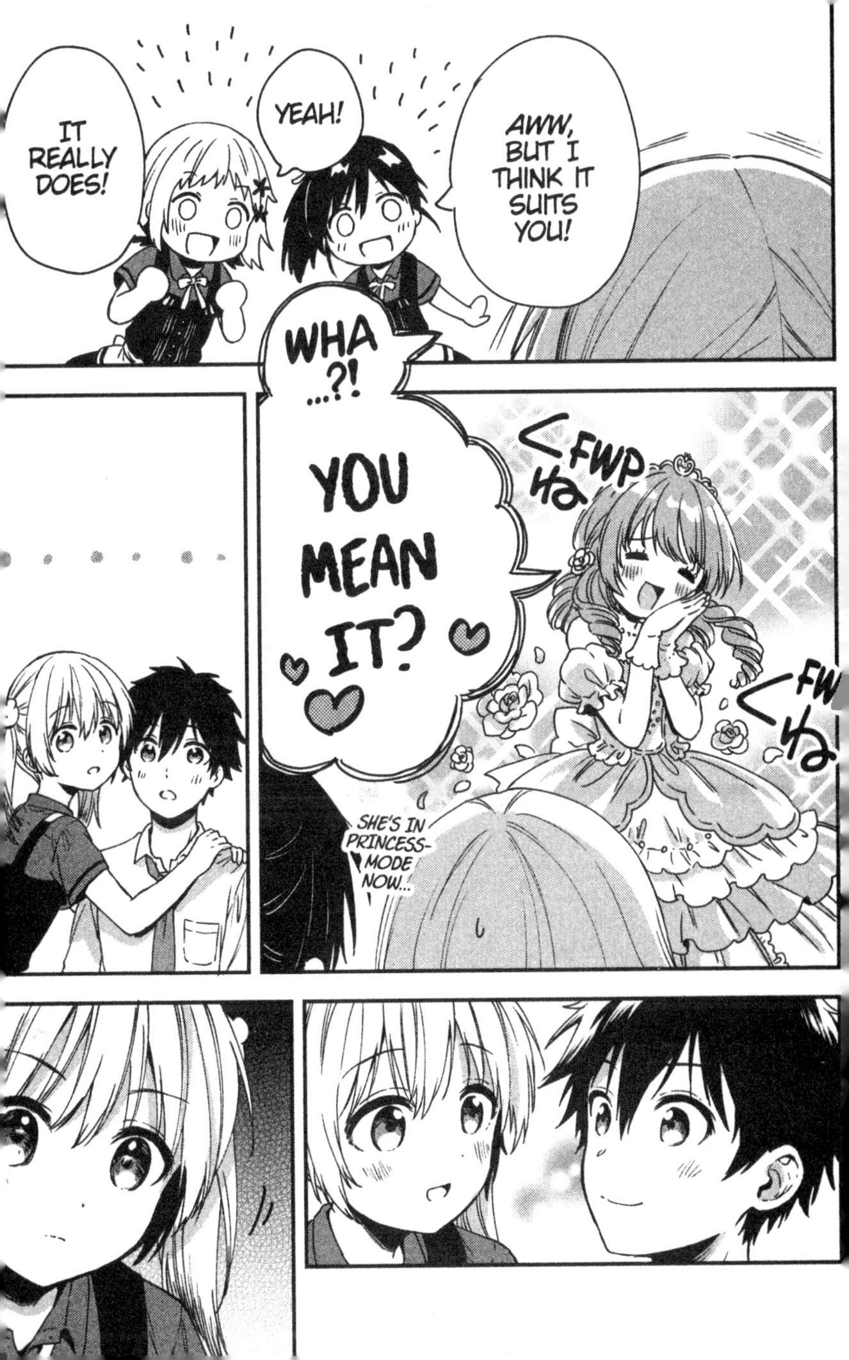
AWW, BUT I THINK IT SUITS YOU!
YEAH!
IT REALLY DOES!
WHA ...?!
YOU MEAN IT?
くね FWP
くね FW
SHE'S IN PRINCESS-MODE NOW...

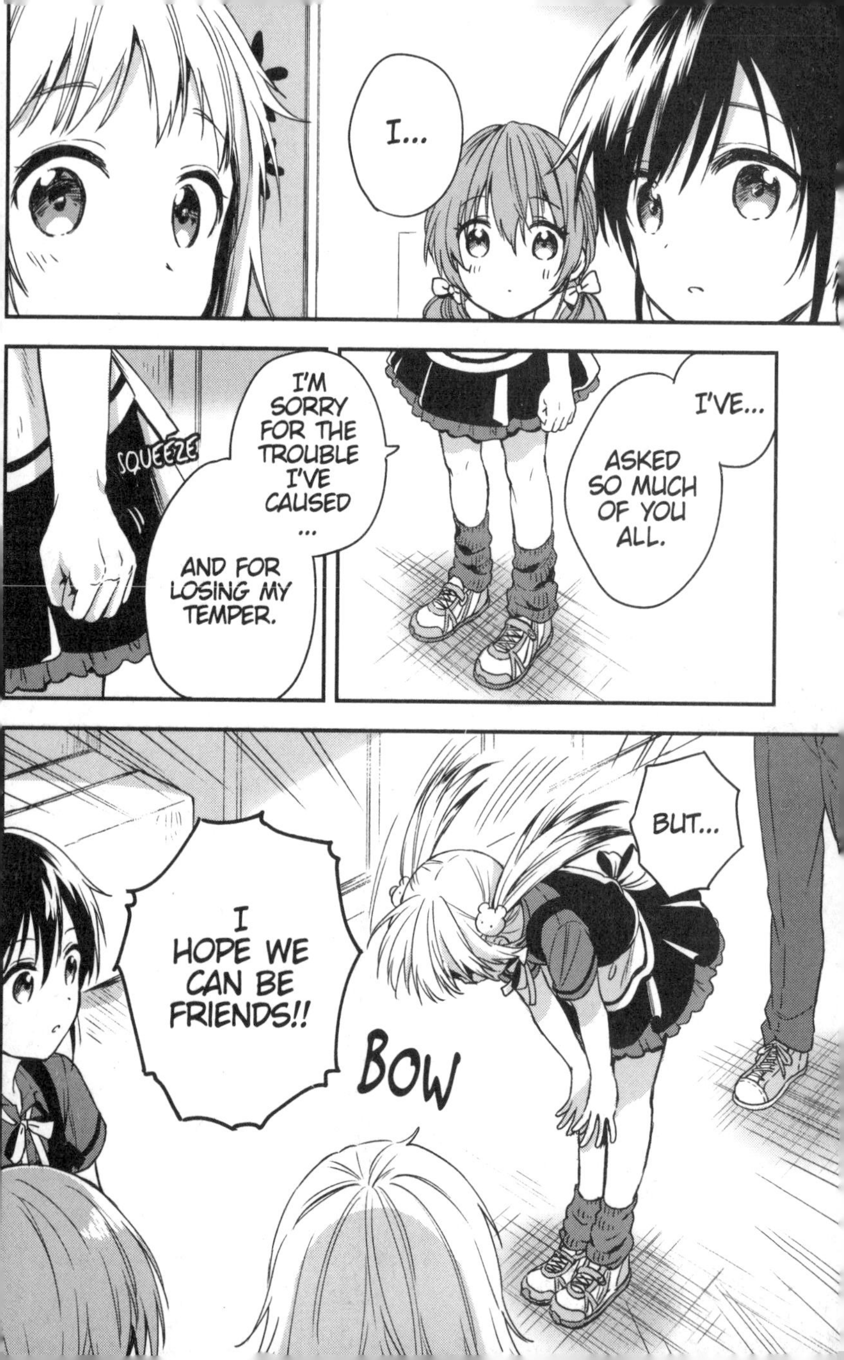
I...
I'VE...
ASKED SO MUCH OF YOU ALL.
I'M SORRY FOR THE TROUBLE I'VE CAUSED ...
SQUEEZE
AND FOR LOSING MY TEMPER.
BUT...
I HOPE WE CAN BE FRIENDS!!
BOW

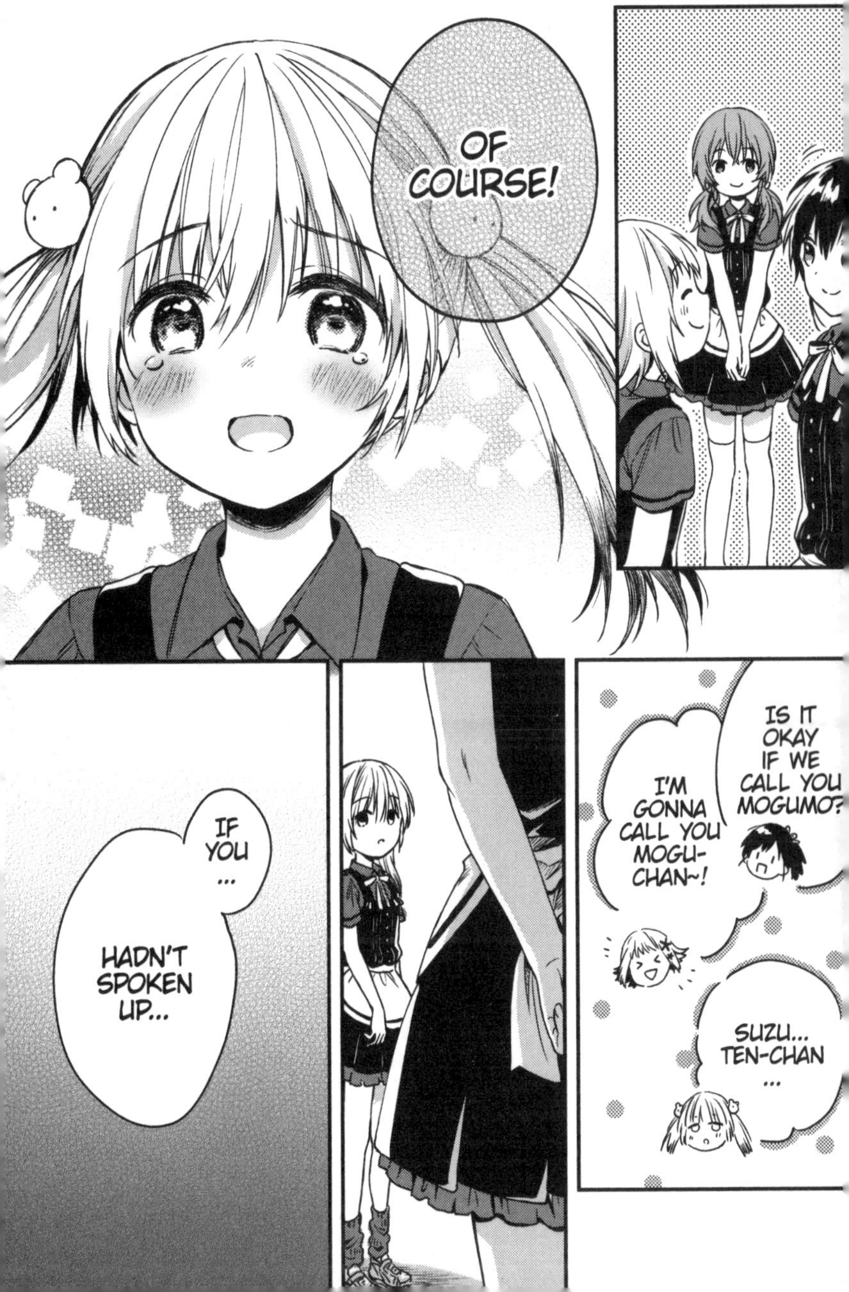
OF COURSE!
IS IT OKAY IF WE CALL YOU MOGUMO?
I'M GONNA CALL YOU MOGU-CHAN~!
SUZU... TEN-CHAN...
IF YOU...
HADN'T SPOKEN UP...

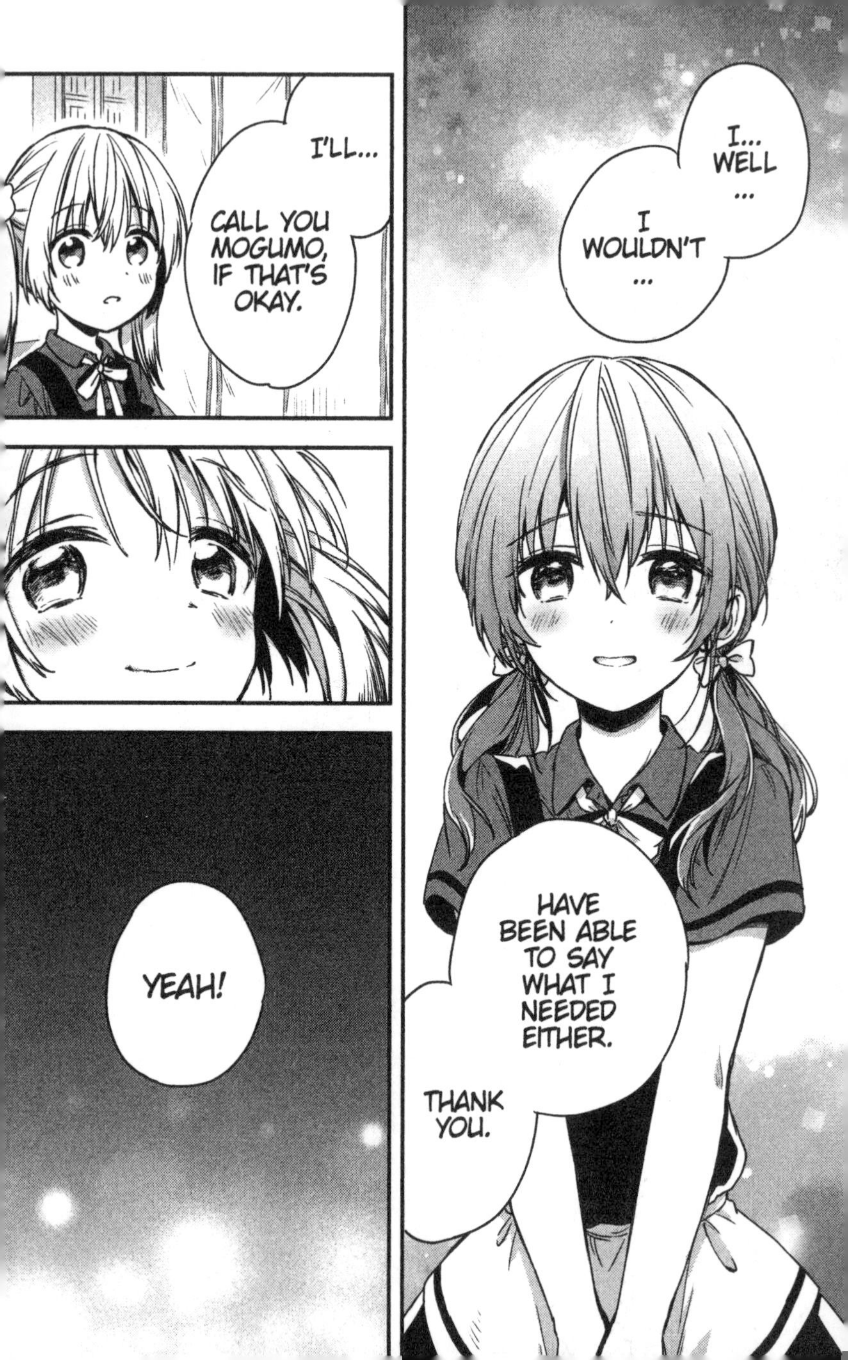
I... WELL ...
I WOULDN'T ...
HAVE BEEN ABLE TO SAY WHAT I NEEDED EITHER.
THANK YOU.
I'LL...
CALL YOU MOGUMO, IF THAT'S OKAY.
YEAH!

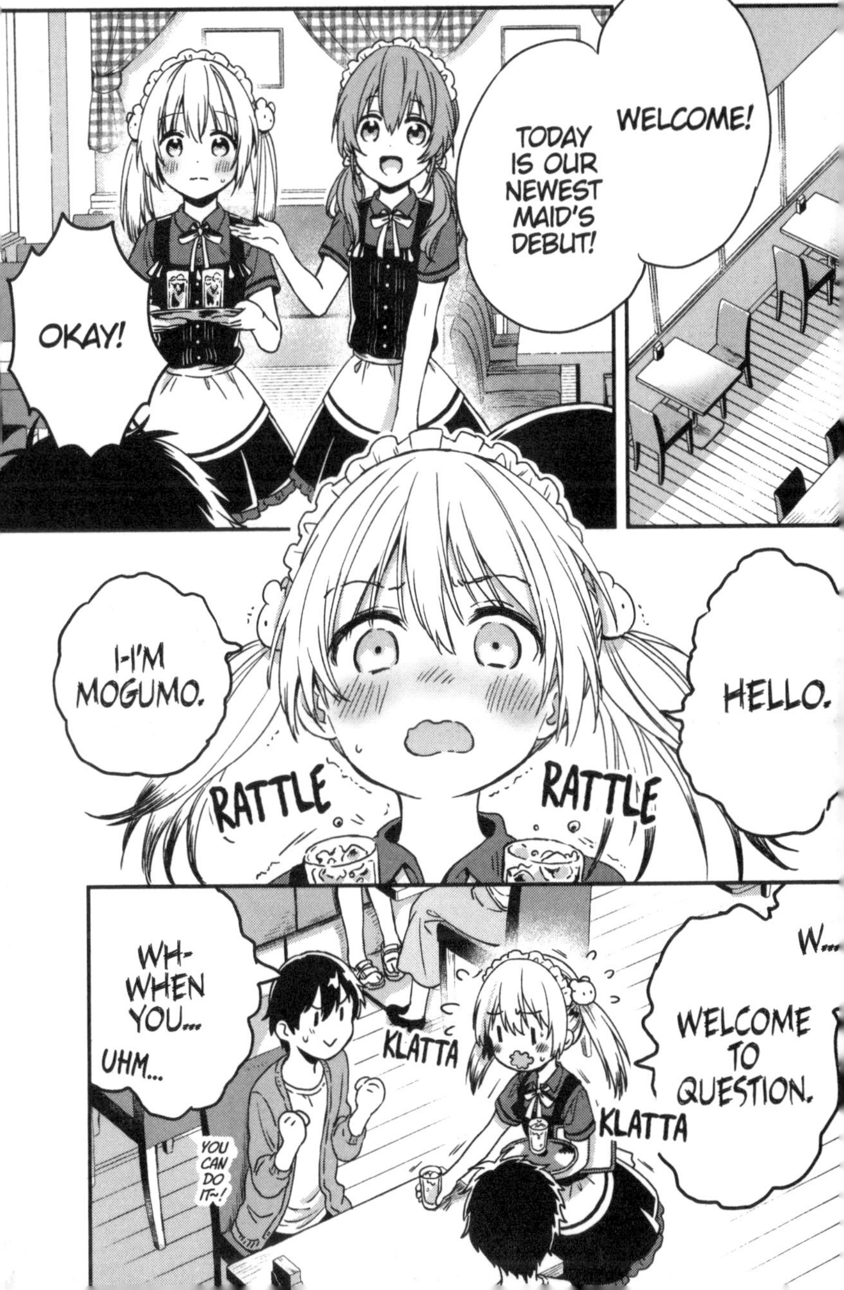
WELCOME!
TODAY IS OUR NEWEST MAID'S DEBUT!
OKAY!
HELLO.
I-I'M MOGUMO.
RATTLE
RATTLE
W... WELCOME TO QUESTION.
KLATTA
KLATTA
WH- WHEN YOU... UHM...
YOU CAN DO IT~!

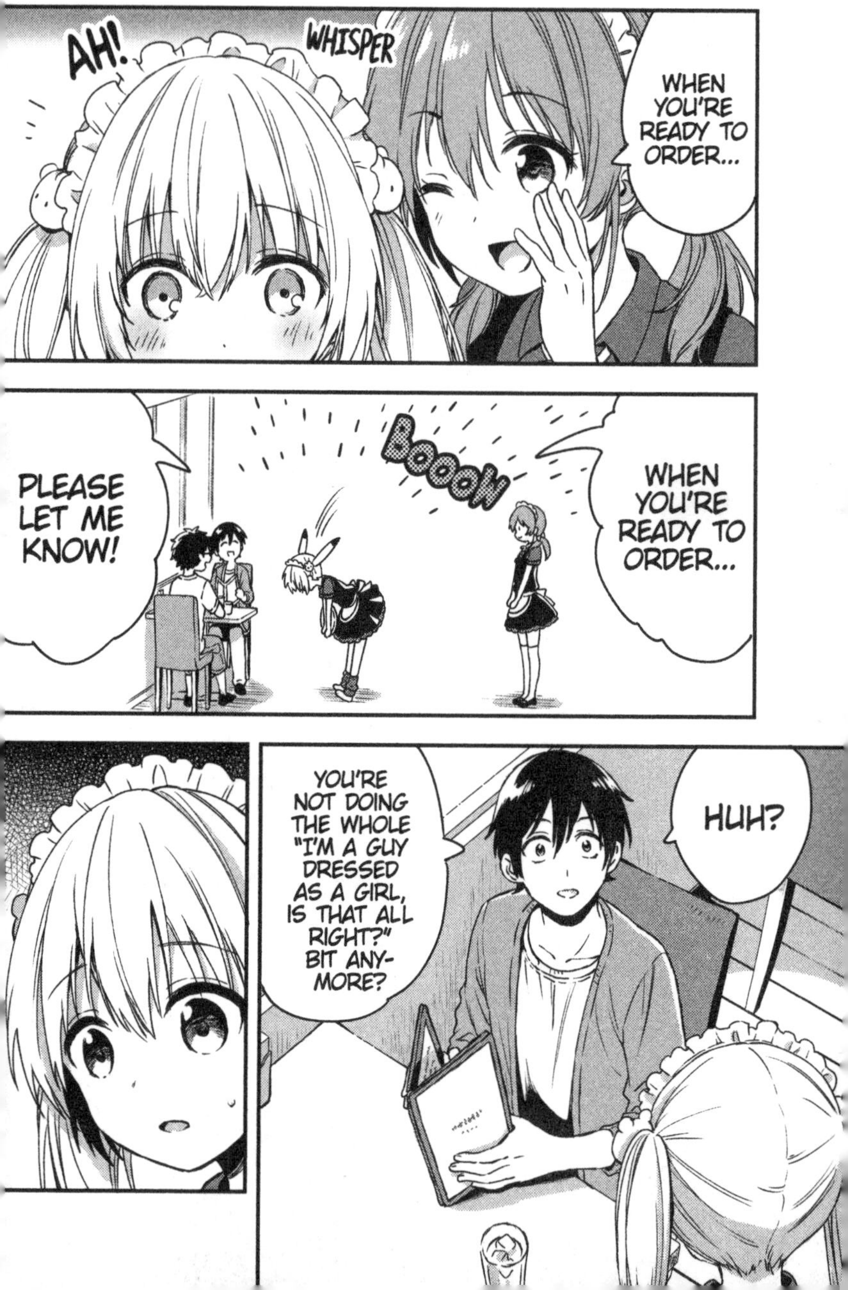
WHEN YOU'RE READY TO ORDER...
WHISPER
AH!
WHEN YOU'RE READY TO ORDER...
BOOOW
PLEASE LET ME KNOW!
HUH?
YOU'RE NOT DOING THE WHOLE "I'M A GUY DRESSED AS A GIRL, IS THAT ALL RIGHT?" BIT ANY-MORE?

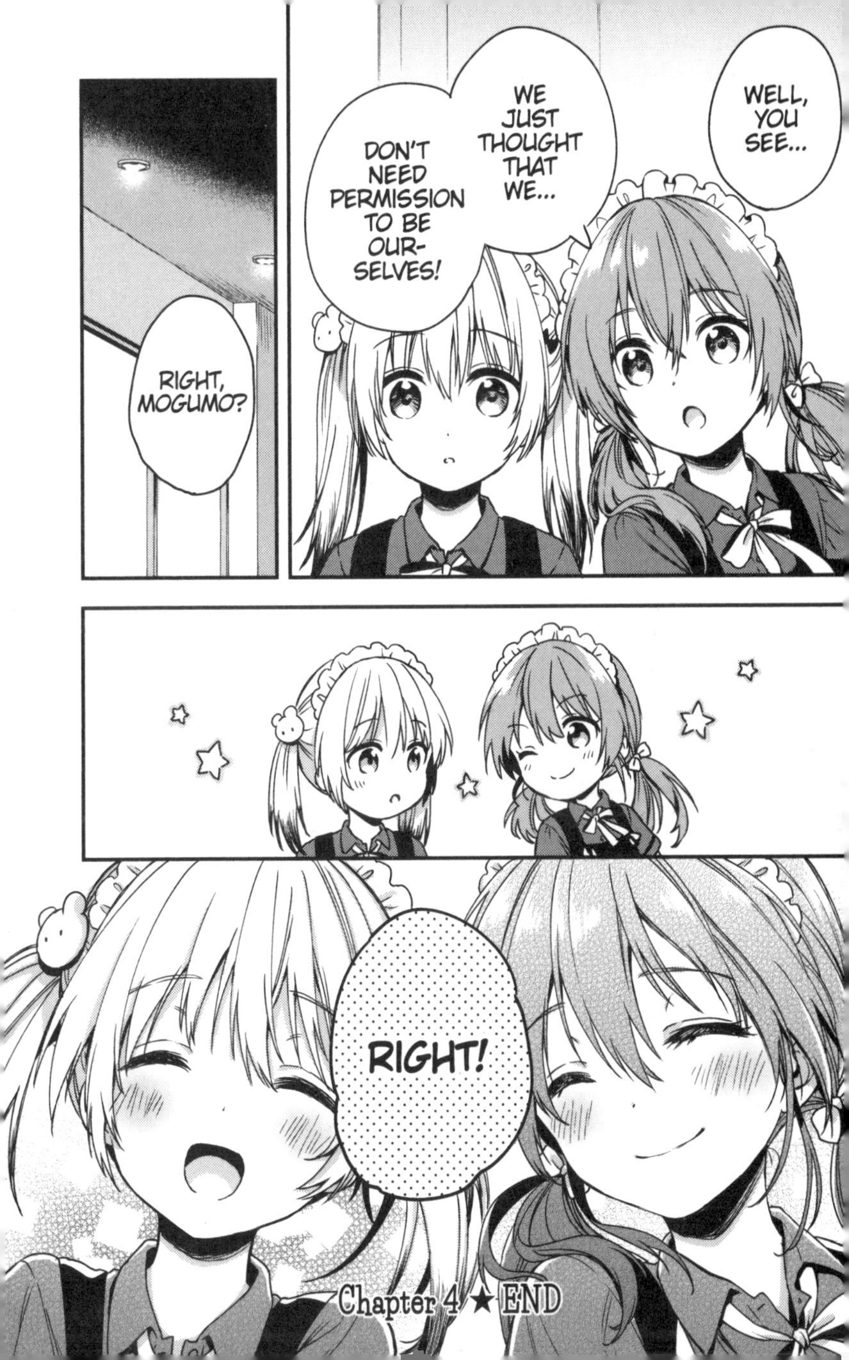
WELL, YOU SEE...
WE JUST THOUGHT THAT WE...
DON'T NEED PERMISSION TO BE OUR-SELVES!
RIGHT, MOGUMO?
RIGHT!
Chapter 4 ★ END

Love me for
who I am

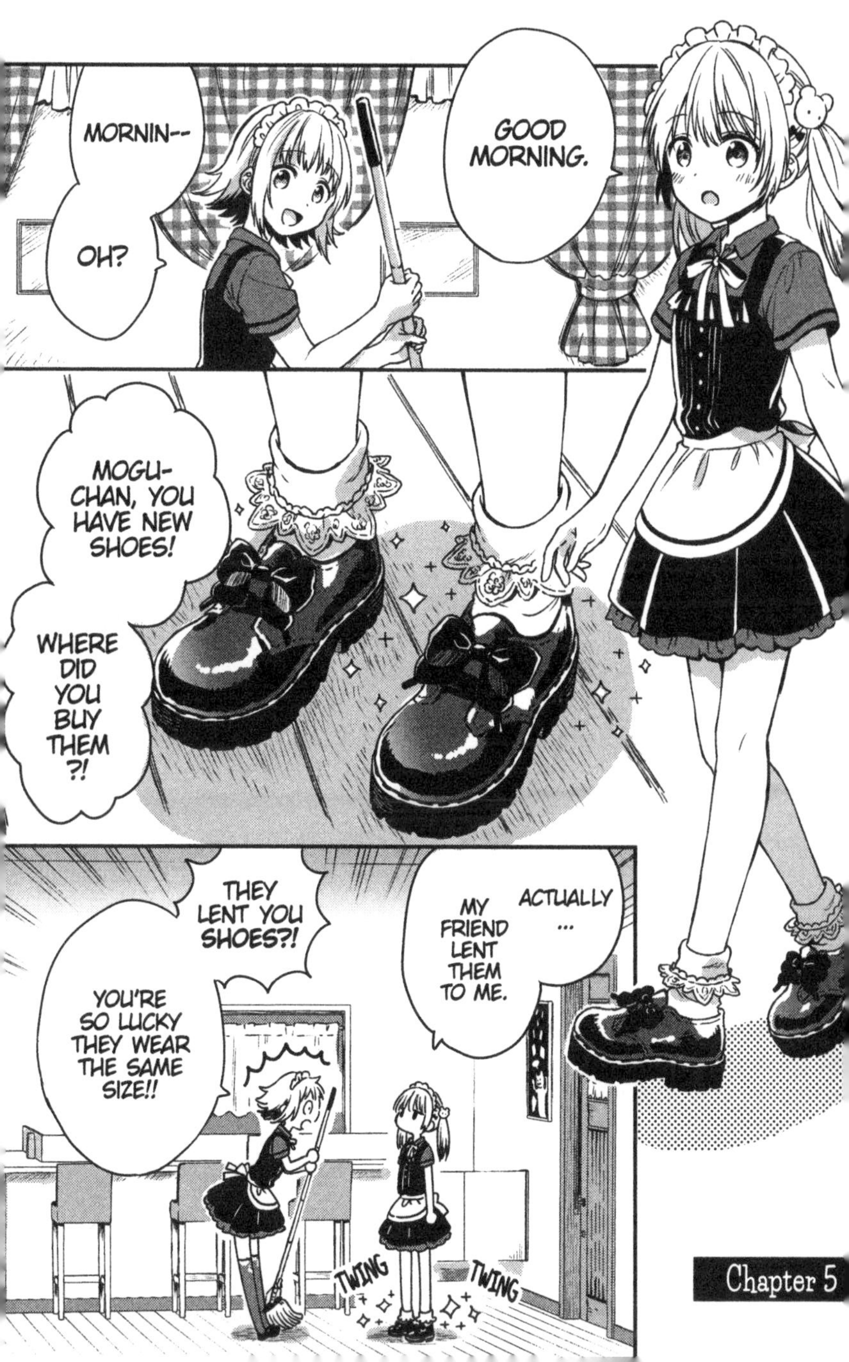
GOOD MORNING.
MORNIN--
OH?
MOGU-CHAN, YOU HAVE NEW SHOES!
WHERE DID YOU BUY THEM?!
ACTUALLY...
MY FRIEND LENT THEM TO ME.
THEY LENT YOU SHOES?!
YOU'RE SO LUCKY THEY WEAR THE SAME SIZE!!
TWING
TWING

Chapter 5

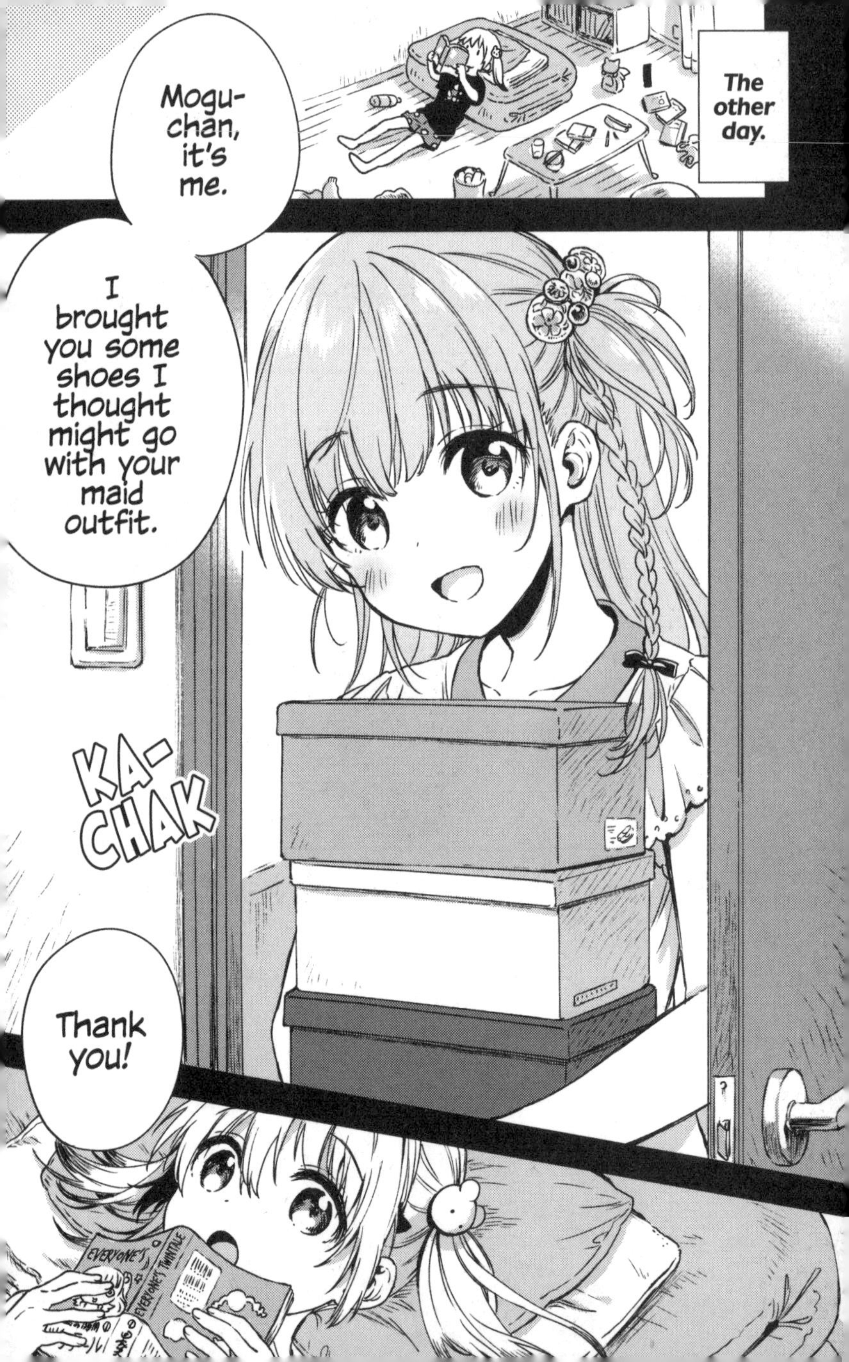
The other day.
Mogu-chan, it's me.
I brought you some shoes I thought might go with your maid outfit.
KA-CHAK
Thank you!

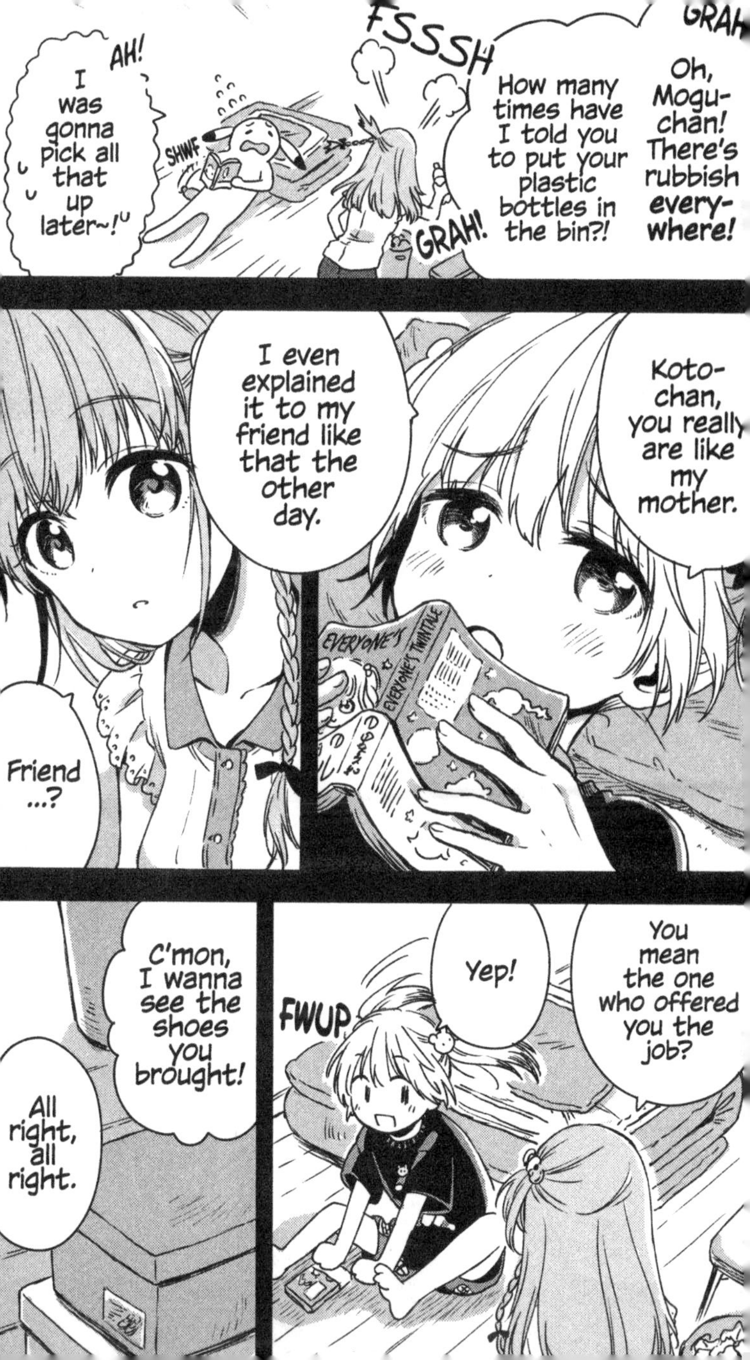
GRAH
Oh, Mogu-chan! There's rubbish every-where!
How many times have I told you to put your plastic bottles in the bin?!
FSSSH
GRAH!
SHWF
AH!
I was gonna pick all that up later~!
Koto-chan, you really are like my mother.
EVERYONE'S TWINTALE
I even explained it to my friend like that the other day.
Friend ...?
You mean the one who offered you the job?
Yep!
FWUP
C'mon, I wanna see the shoes you brought!
All right, all right.

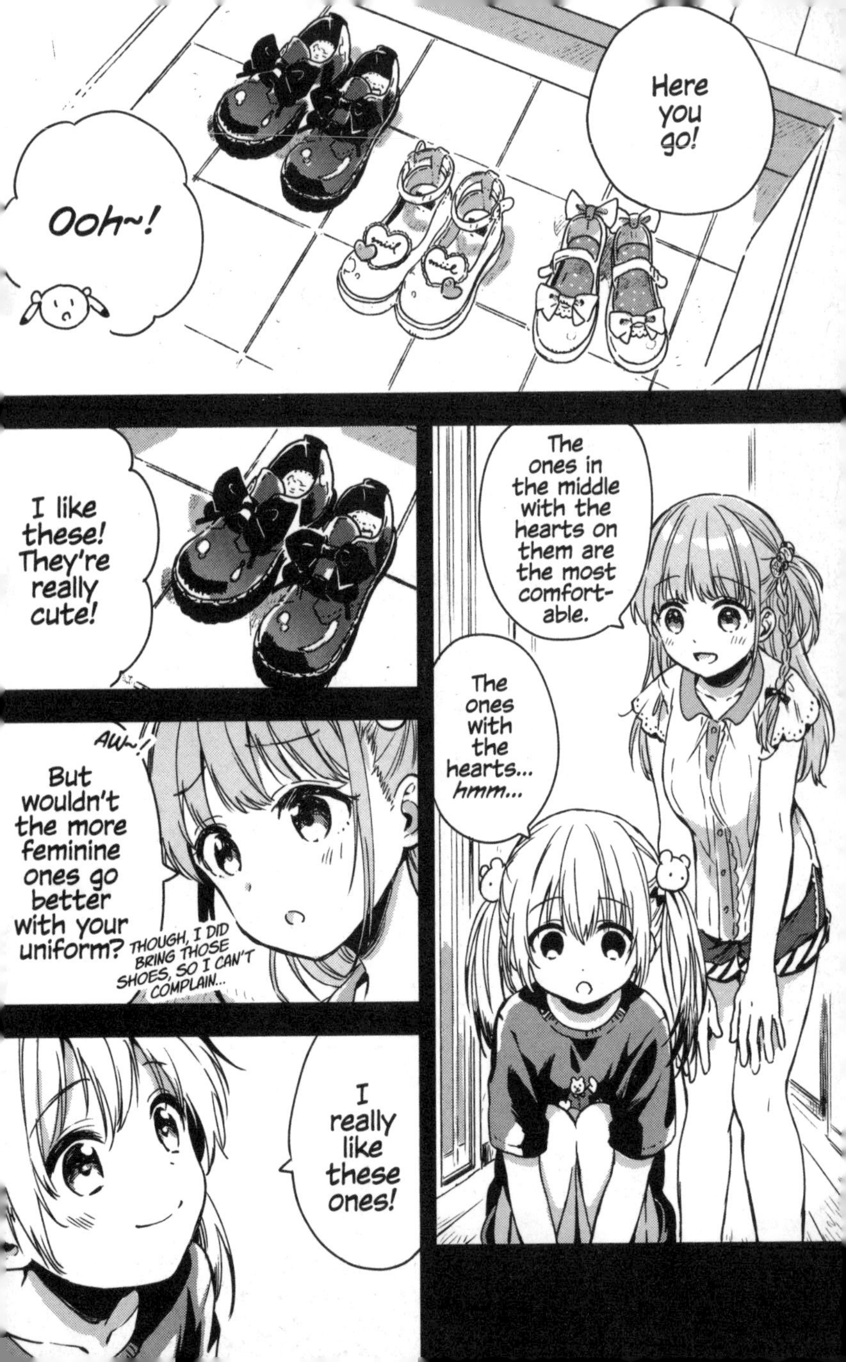
Here you go!
Ooh~!
The ones in the middle with the hearts on them are the most comfortable.
The ones with the hearts... *hmm...*
I like these! They're really cute!
AW~!
But wouldn't the more feminine ones go better with your uniform?
THOUGH, I DID BRING THOSE SHOES, SO I CAN'T COMPLAIN...
I really like these ones!

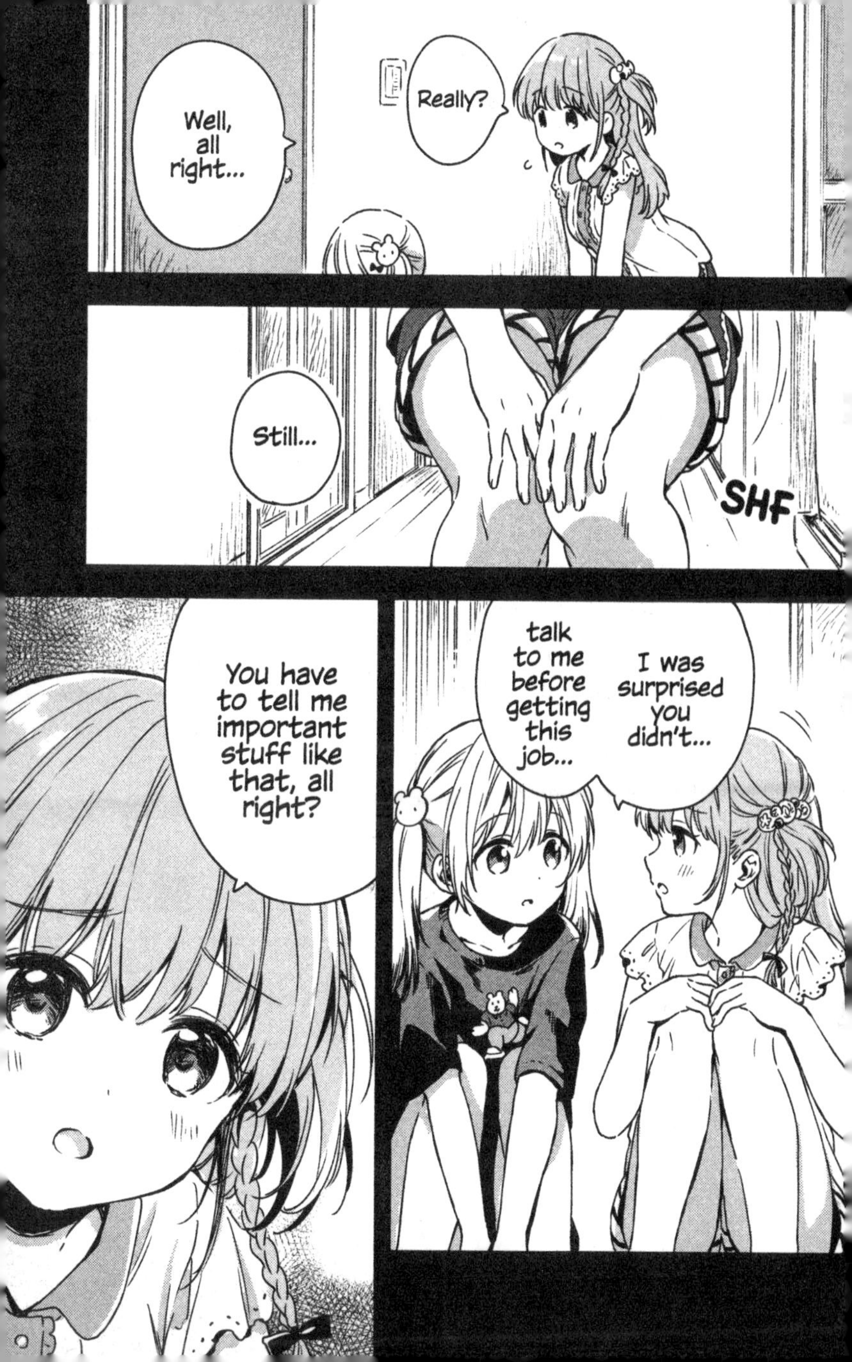
Really?
Well, all right...
Still...
SHF
I was surprised you didn't...
talk to me before getting this job...
You have to tell me important stuff like that, all right?

Okay...

I'm sorry.

NO SPOILERS, ALL RIGHT?!!

I'VE BEEN DYING TO SEE THAT MOVIE, TOO!!

WAH!!

THAT'S GREAT!

HERE YOU GO.

TNK

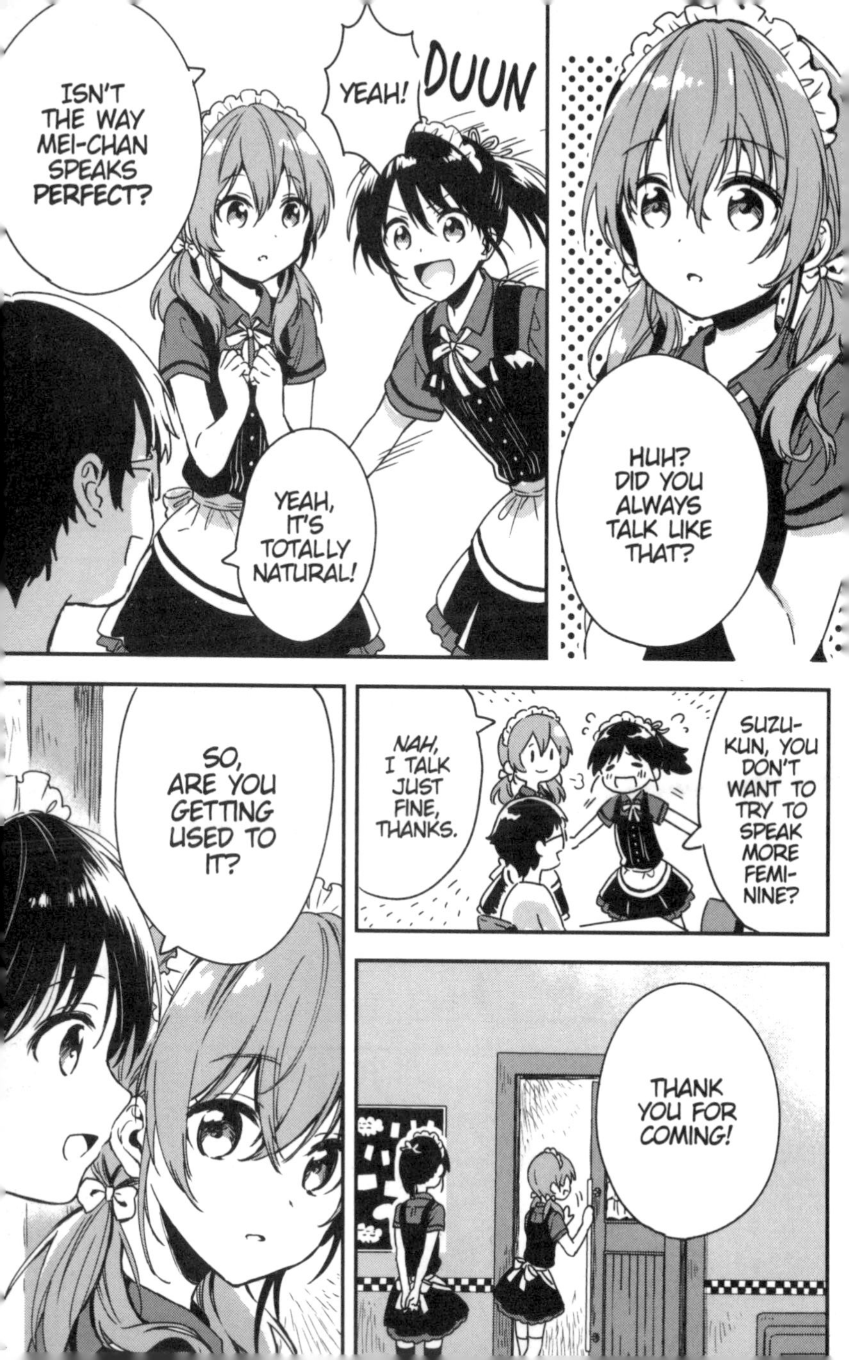
HUH? DID YOU ALWAYS TALK LIKE THAT?
DUUN
YEAH!
ISN'T THE WAY MEI-CHAN SPEAKS PERFECT?
YEAH, IT'S TOTALLY NATURAL!
SUZU-KUN, YOU DON'T WANT TO TRY TO SPEAK MORE FEMI-NINE?
NAH, I TALK JUST FINE, THANKS.
THANK YOU FOR COMING!
SO, ARE YOU GETTING USED TO IT?

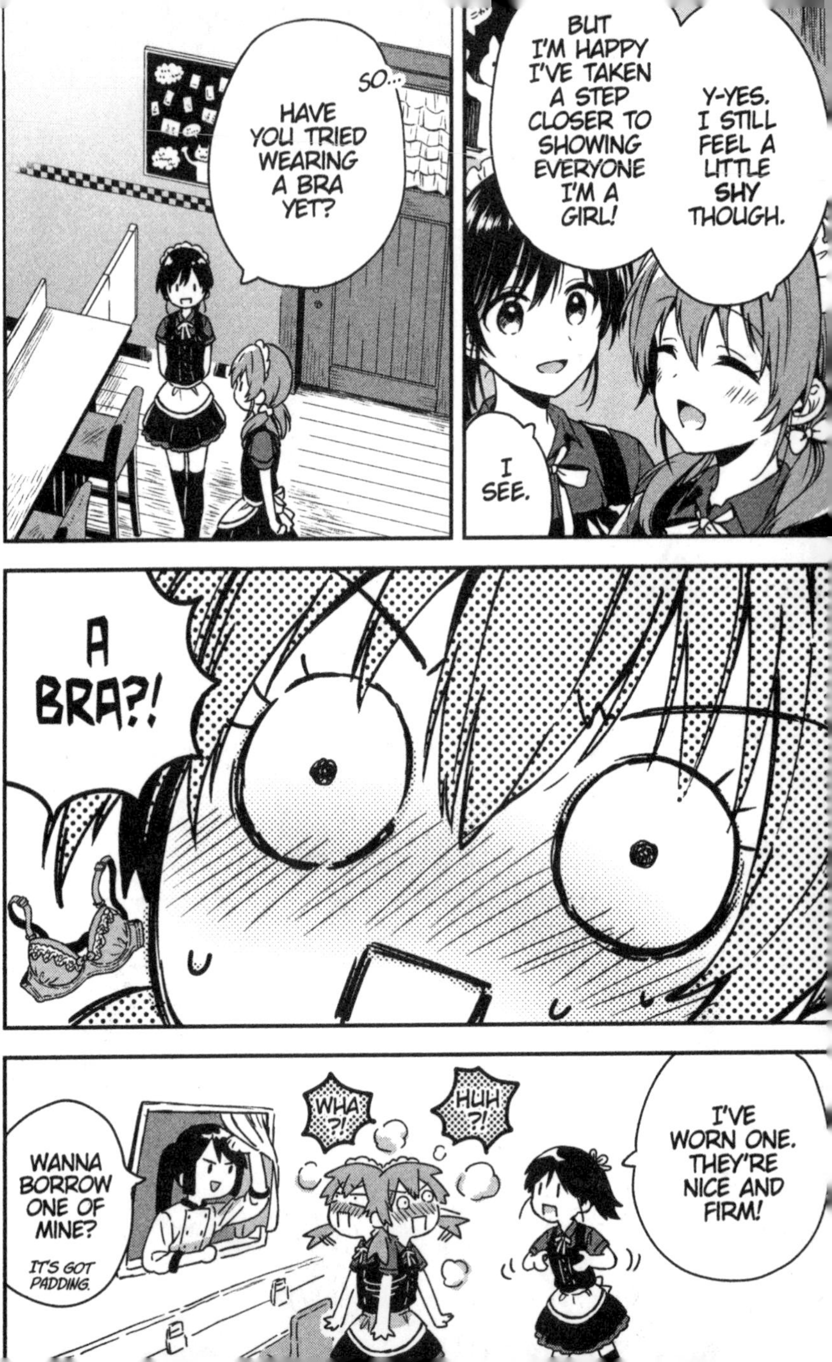
Y-YES. I STILL FEEL A LITTLE SHY THOUGH.
BUT I'M HAPPY I'VE TAKEN A STEP CLOSER TO SHOWING EVERYONE I'M A GIRL!
I SEE.
SO...
HAVE YOU TRIED WEARING A BRA YET?
A BRA?!
I'VE WORN ONE. THEY'RE NICE AND FIRM!
HUH?!
WHA?!
WANNA BORROW ONE OF MINE?
IT'S GOT PADDING.

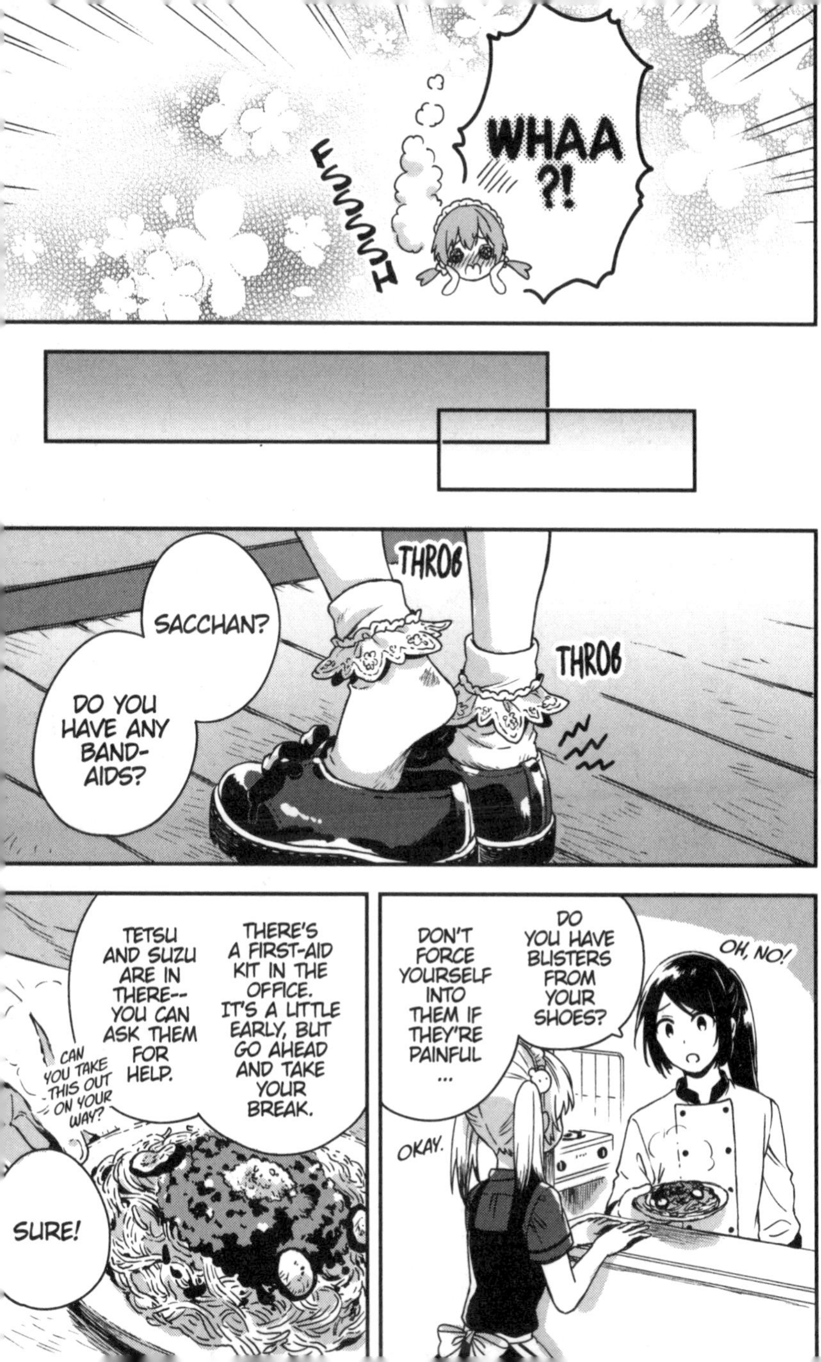
WHAA?!
FSSSSSH
THROB
THROB
SACCHAN?
DO YOU HAVE ANY BAND-AIDS?
OH, NO!
DO YOU HAVE BLISTERS FROM YOUR SHOES?
DON'T FORCE YOURSELF INTO THEM IF THEY'RE PAINFUL...
OKAY.
THERE'S A FIRST-AID KIT IN THE OFFICE. IT'S A LITTLE EARLY, BUT GO AHEAD AND TAKE YOUR BREAK.
TETSU AND SUZU ARE IN THERE--YOU CAN ASK THEM FOR HELP.
CAN YOU TAKE THIS OUT ON YOUR WAY?
SURE!

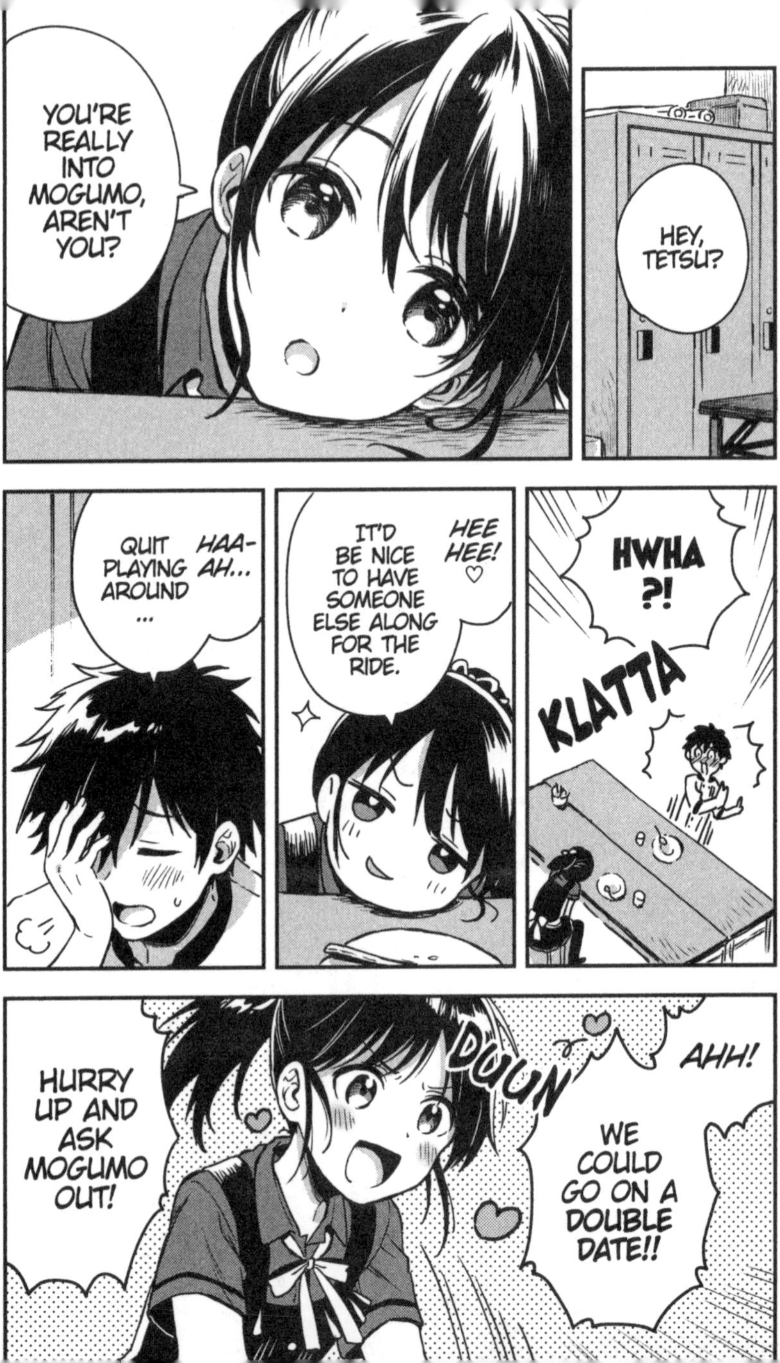
HEY, TETSU?
YOU'RE REALLY INTO MOGUMO, AREN'T YOU?
HWHA ?!
KLATTA
HEE HEE! ♡
IT'D BE NICE TO HAVE SOMEONE ELSE ALONG FOR THE RIDE.
HAA-AH...
QUIT PLAYING AROUND ...
AHH!
DUUN
WE COULD GO ON A DOUBLE DATE!!
HURRY UP AND ASK MOGUMO OUT!

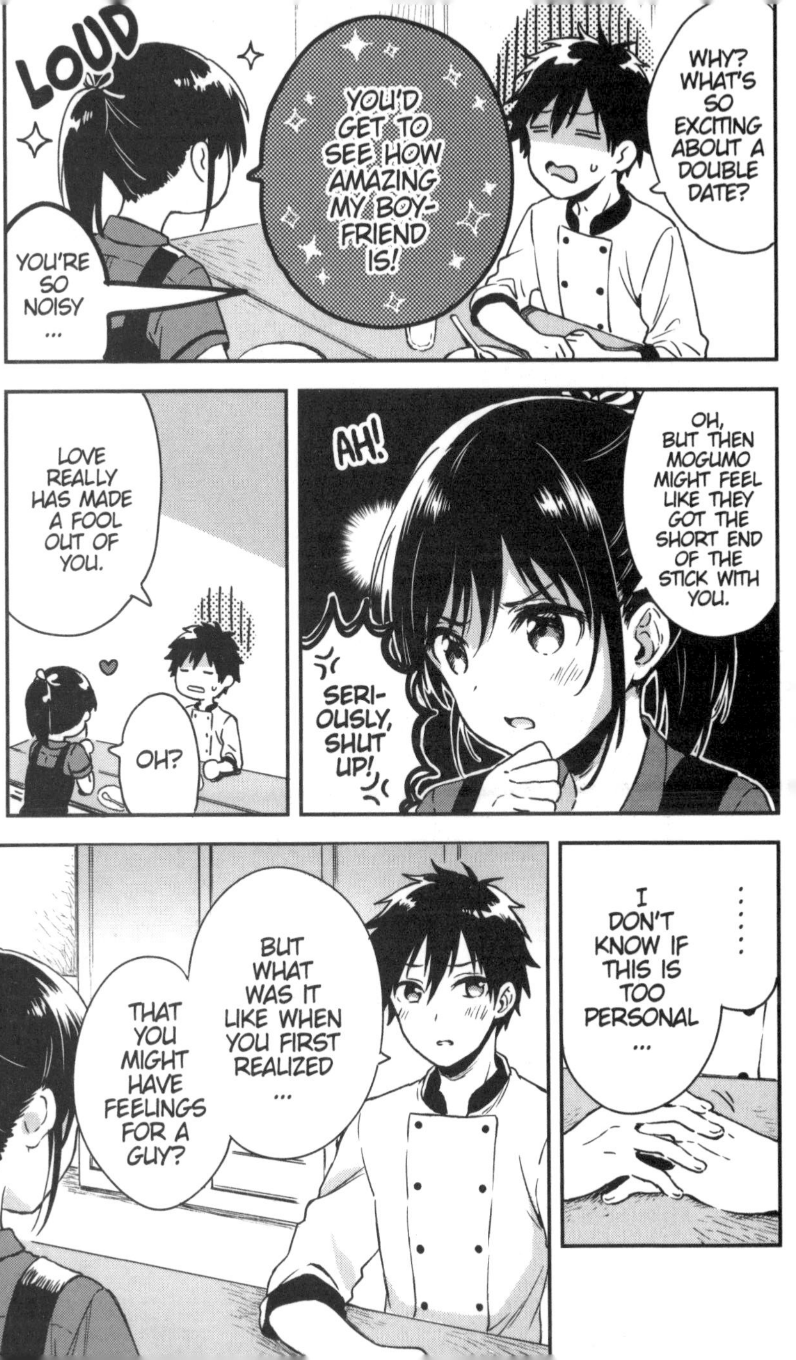
WHY? WHAT'S SO EXCITING ABOUT A DOUBLE DATE?
YOU'D GET TO SEE HOW AMAZING MY BOY-FRIEND IS!
LOUD
YOU'RE SO NOISY ...
OH, BUT THEN MOGUMO MIGHT FEEL LIKE THEY GOT THE SHORT END OF THE STICK WITH YOU.
AH!
SERI-OUSLY, SHUT UP!
LOVE REALLY HAS MADE A FOOL OUT OF YOU.
OH?
......
I DON'T KNOW IF THIS IS TOO PERSONAL ...
BUT WHAT WAS IT LIKE WHEN YOU FIRST REALIZED ...
THAT YOU MIGHT HAVE FEELINGS FOR A GUY?

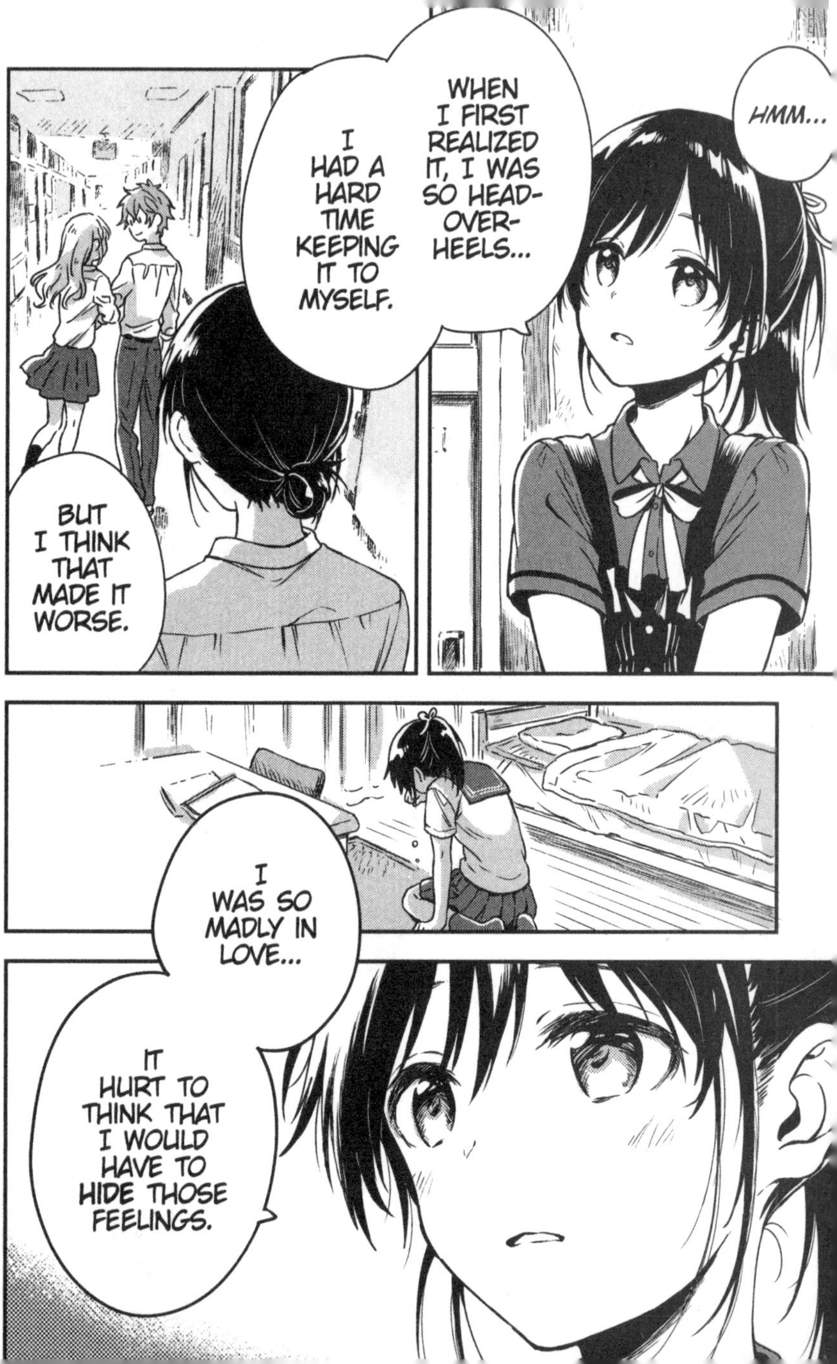
HMM...
WHEN I FIRST REALIZED IT, I WAS SO HEAD-OVER-HEELS... I HAD A HARD TIME KEEPING IT TO MYSELF.
BUT I THINK THAT MADE IT WORSE.
I WAS SO MADLY IN LOVE...
IT HURT TO THINK THAT I WOULD HAVE TO HIDE THOSE FEELINGS.

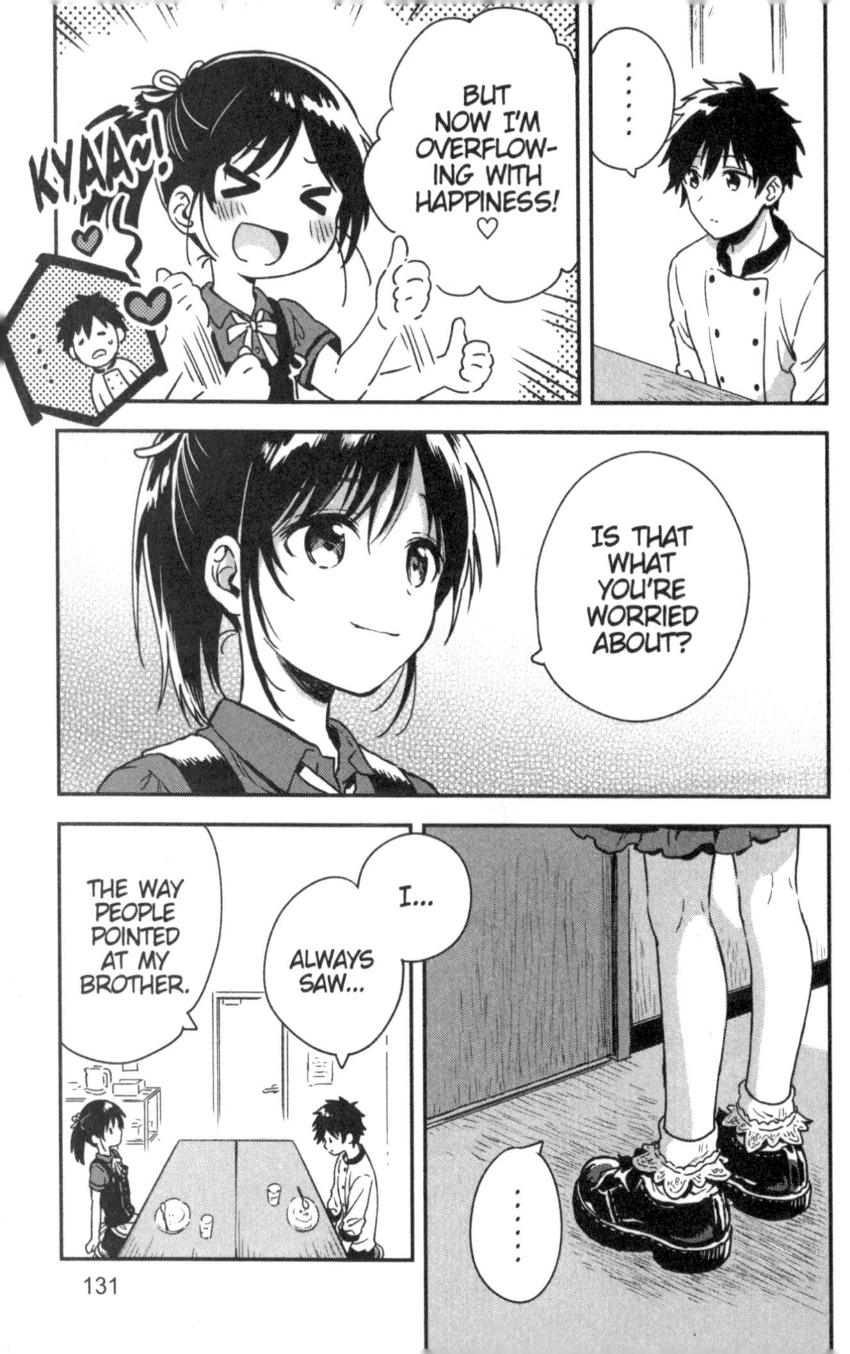
......
BUT NOW I'M OVERFLOWING WITH HAPPINESS! ♡
KYAA~!
IS THAT WHAT YOU'RE WORRIED ABOUT?
......
I...
ALWAYS SAW...
THE WAY PEOPLE POINTED AT MY BROTHER.

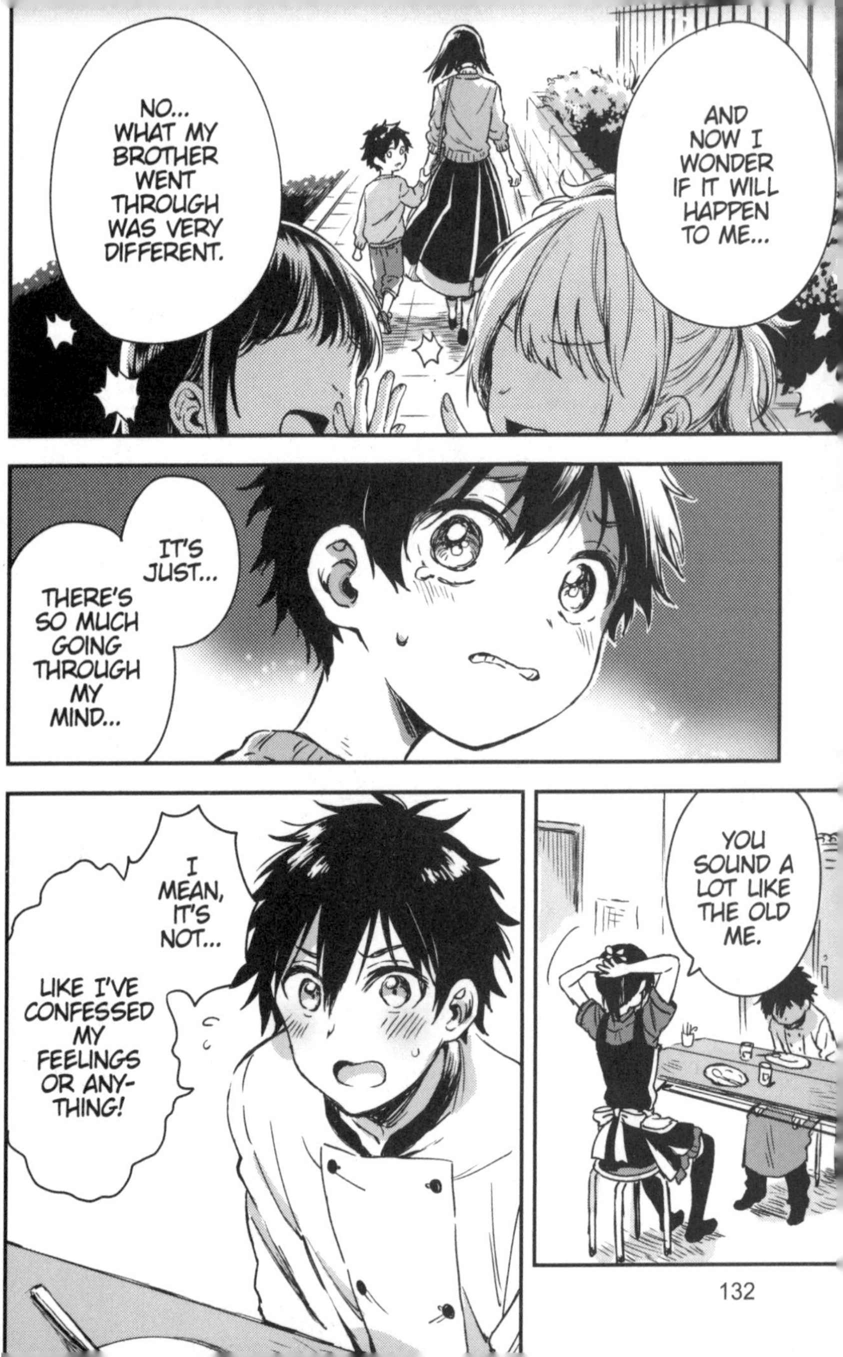
AND NOW I WONDER IF IT WILL HAPPEN TO ME...
NO... WHAT MY BROTHER WENT THROUGH WAS VERY DIFFERENT.
IT'S JUST... THERE'S SO MUCH GOING THROUGH MY MIND...
YOU SOUND A LOT LIKE THE OLD ME.
I MEAN, IT'S NOT...
LIKE I'VE CONFESSED MY FEELINGS OR ANY-THING!

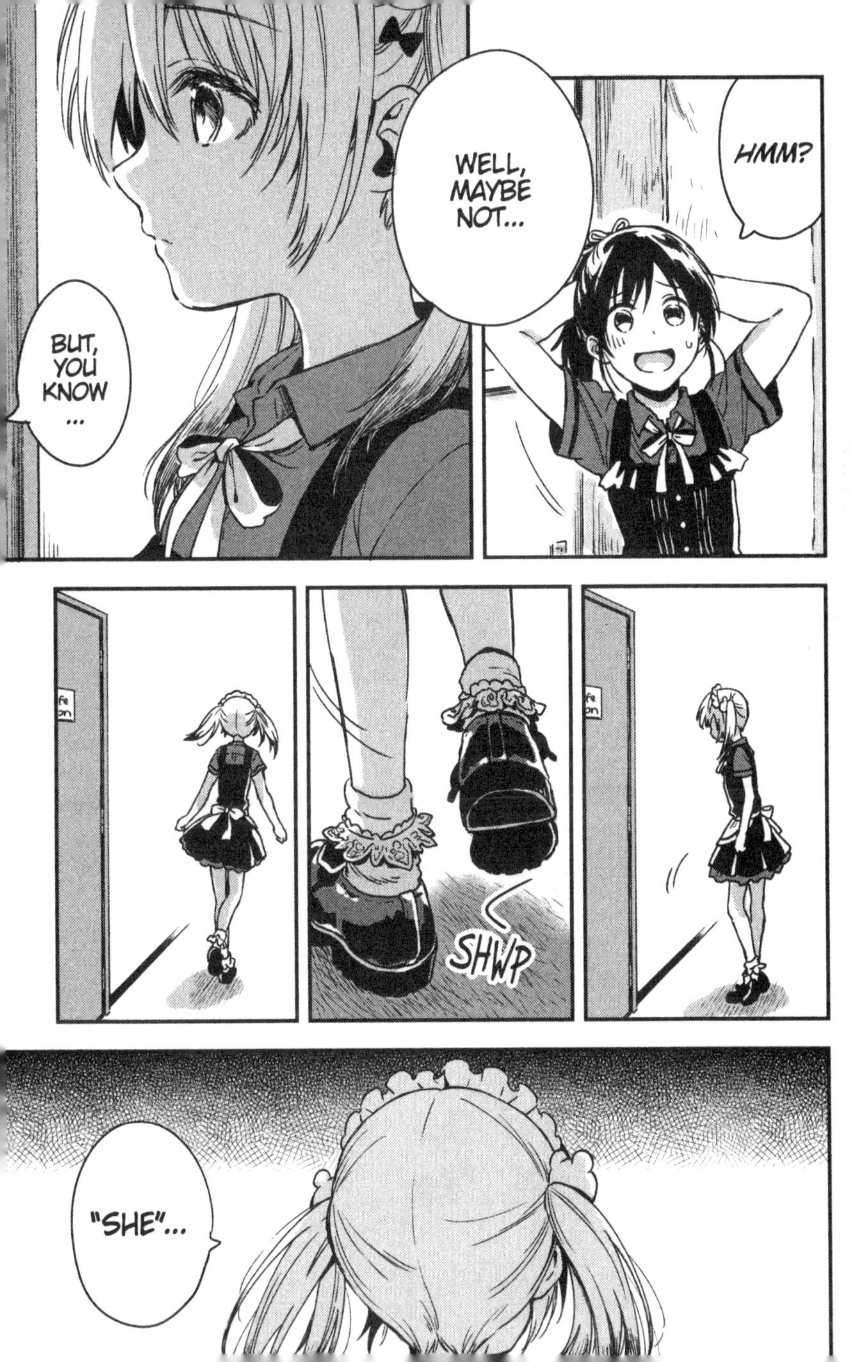
HMM?
WELL, MAYBE NOT...
BUT, YOU KNOW ...
SHWP
"SHE"...

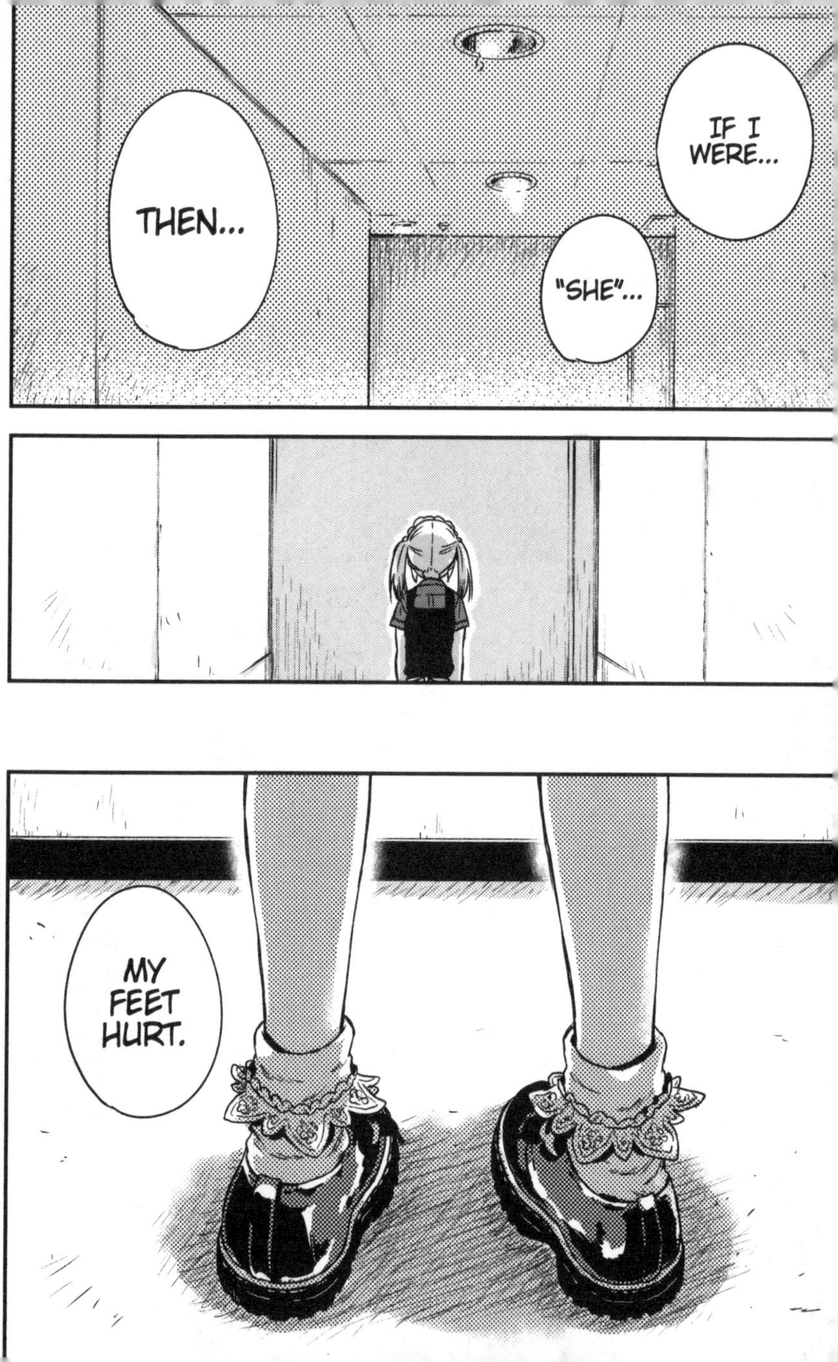
IF I WERE...
"SHE"...
THEN...
MY FEET HURT.

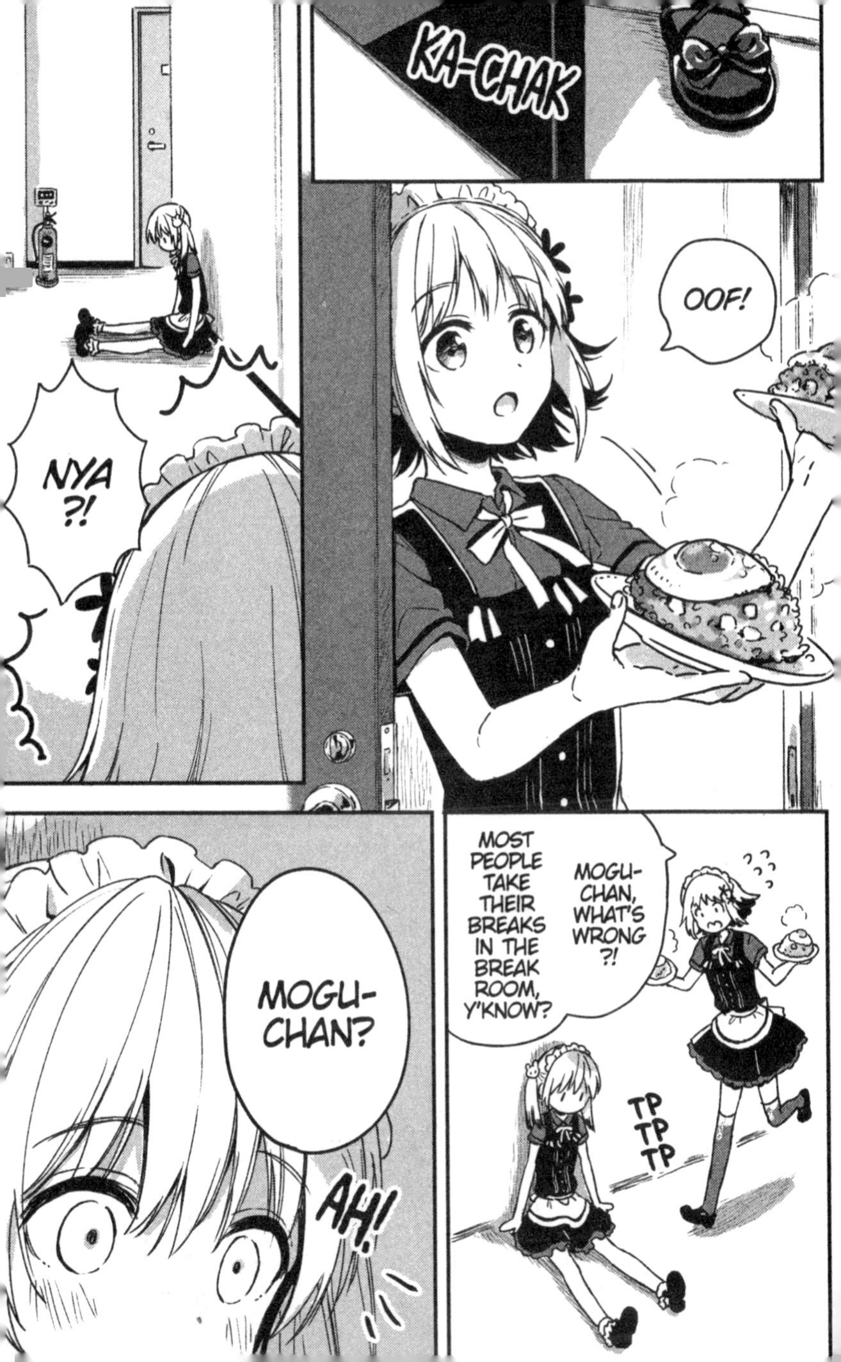
KA-CHAK
OOF!
NYA ?!
MOGU-CHAN, WHAT'S WRONG ?!
MOST PEOPLE TAKE THEIR BREAKS IN THE BREAK ROOM, Y'KNOW?
TP TP TP
MOGU-CHAN?
AH!

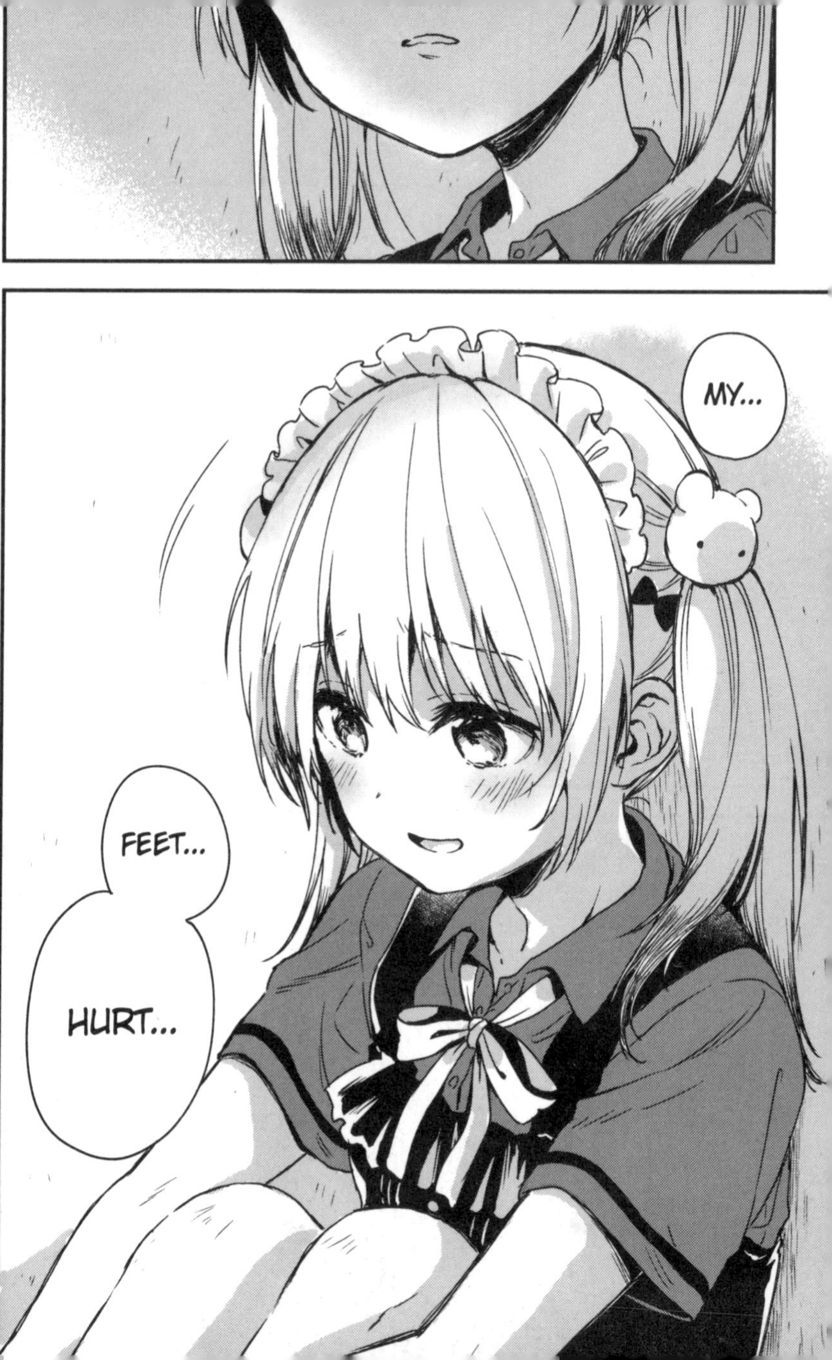
MY...
FEET...
HURT...

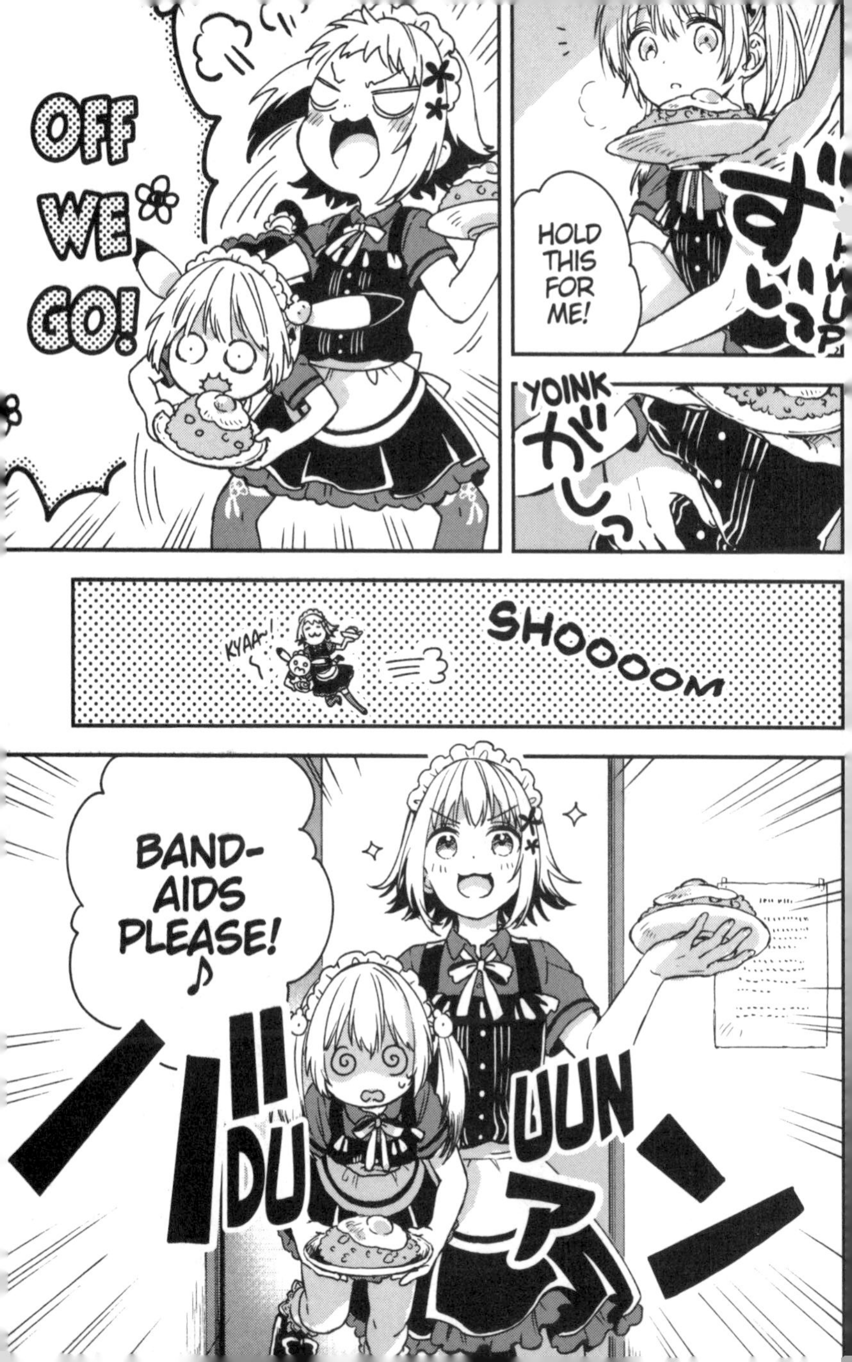
HOLD THIS FOR ME!
ずいっ
UP
YOINK
がしっ
OFF WE GO!
KYAA~!
SHOOOOOM
BAND-AIDS PLEASE! ♪
DUUN

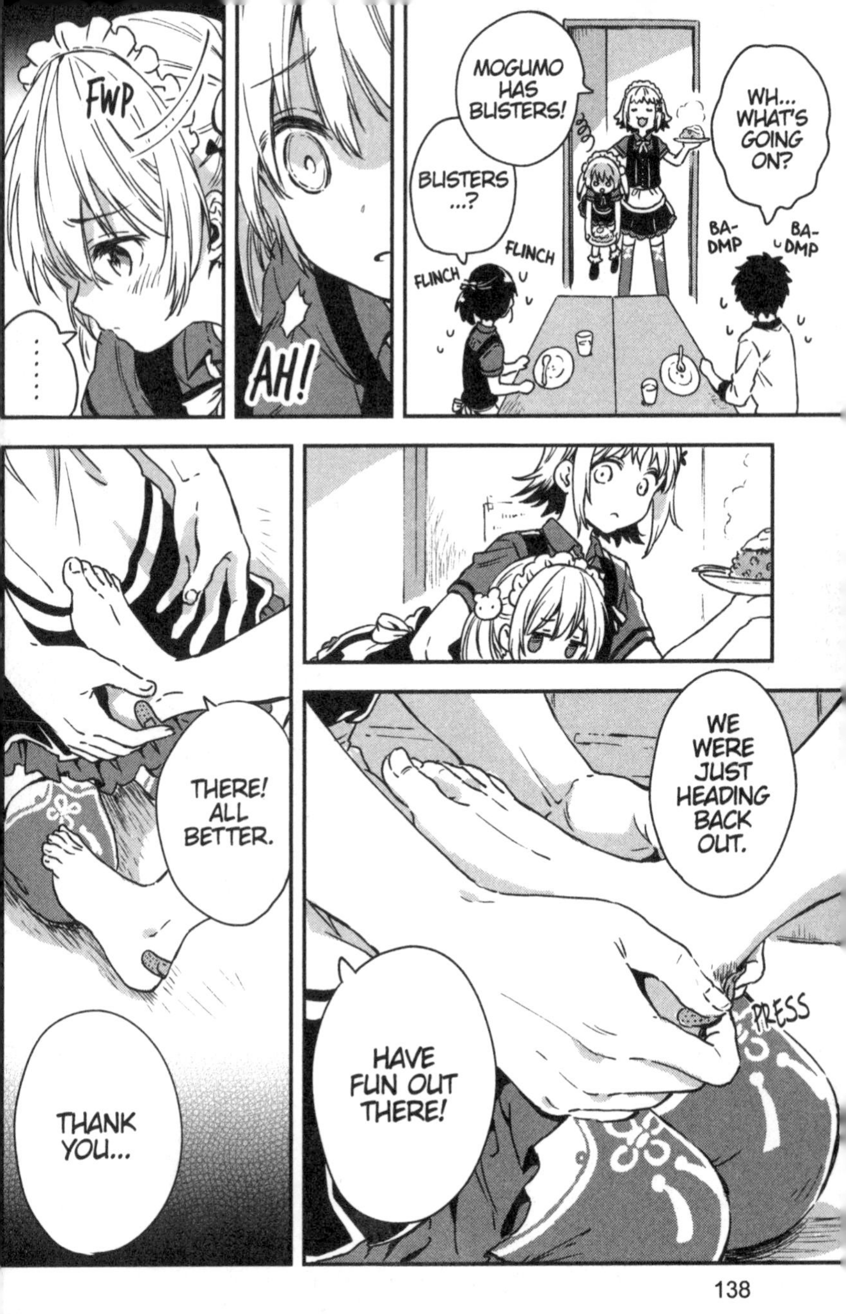
WH... WHAT'S GOING ON?
MOGUMO HAS BLISTERS!
BLISTERS ...?
BA-DMP BA-DMP
FLINCH
FLINCH
AH!
FWP
......
WE WERE JUST HEADING BACK OUT.
PRESS
HAVE FUN OUT THERE!
THERE! ALL BETTER.
THANK YOU...

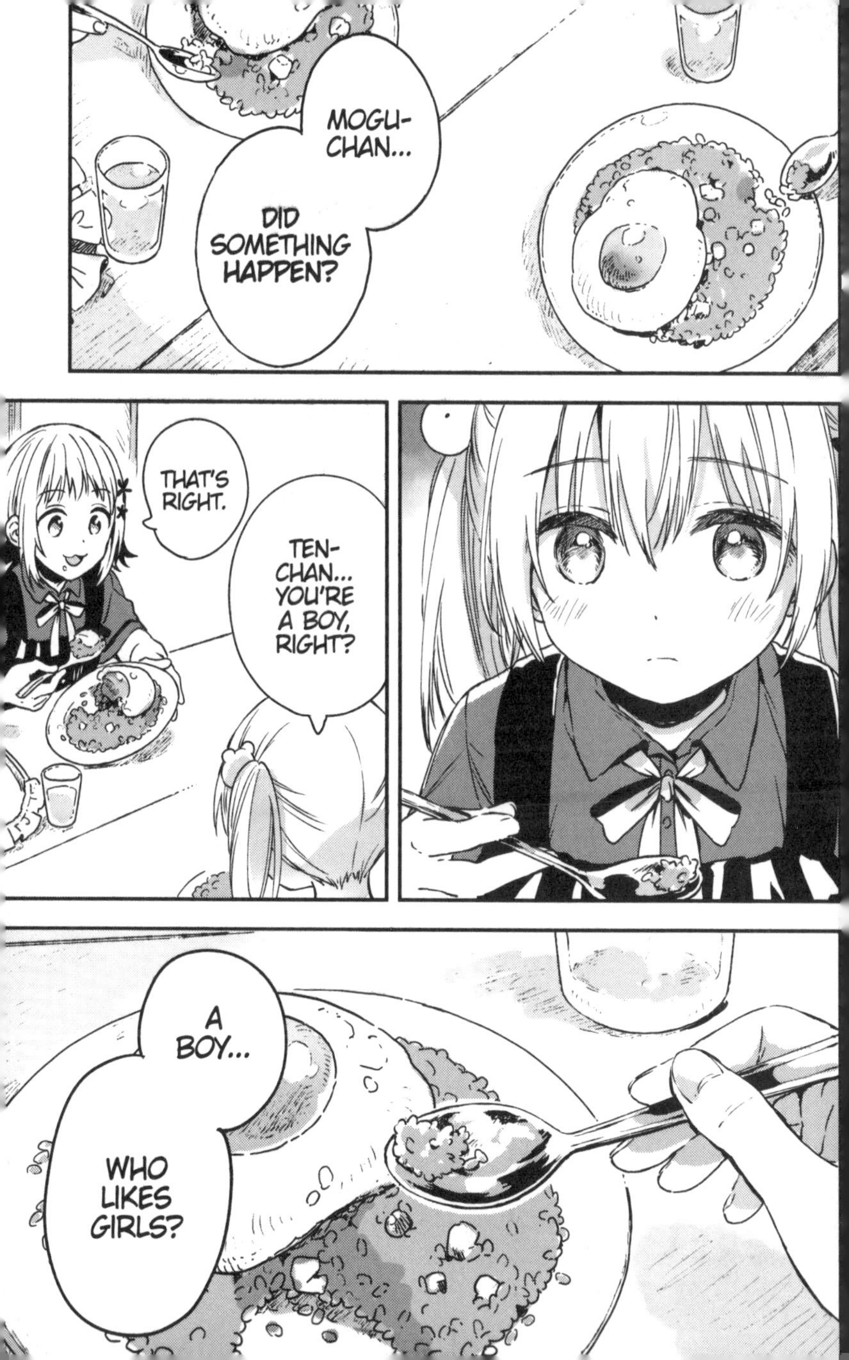
MOGU-CHAN...
DID SOMETHING HAPPEN?
TEN-CHAN... YOU'RE A BOY, RIGHT?
THAT'S RIGHT.
A BOY...
WHO LIKES GIRLS?

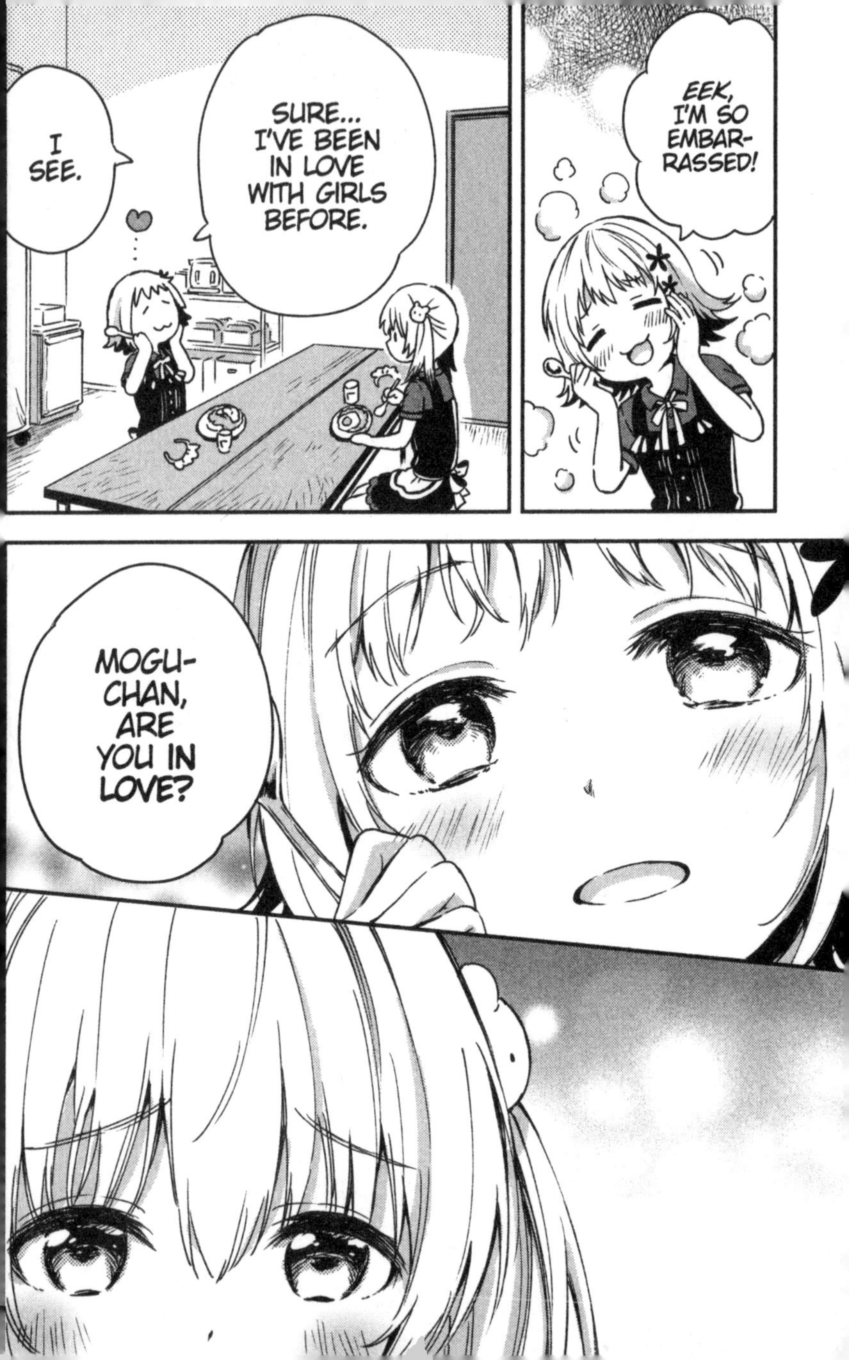
EEK, I'M SO EMBAR-RASSED!
SURE... I'VE BEEN IN LOVE WITH GIRLS BEFORE.
I SEE.
MOGU-CHAN, ARE YOU IN LOVE?

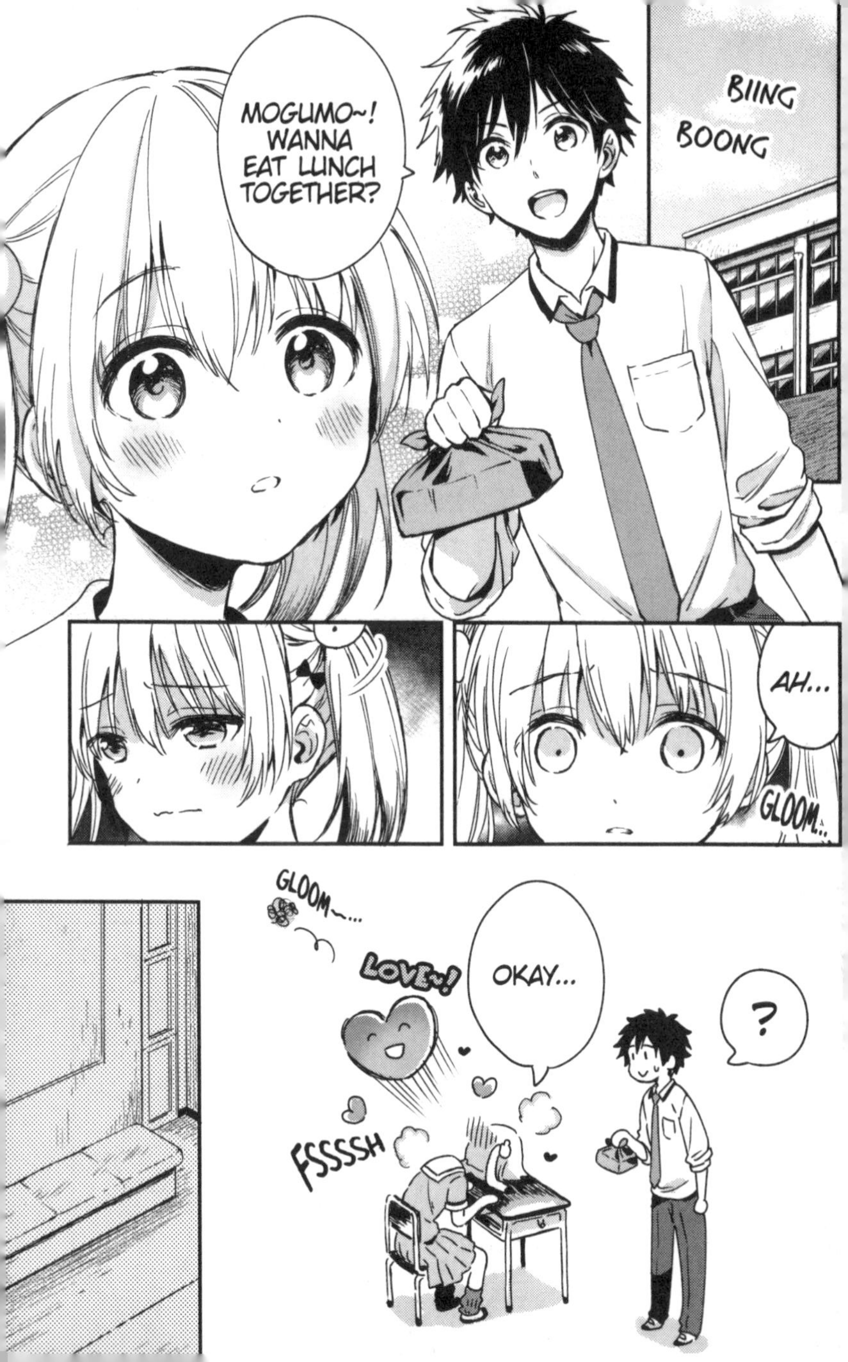
BIING
BOONG
MOGUMO~! WANNA EAT LUNCH TOGETHER?
AH...
GLOOM...
?
OKAY...
GLOOM~...
LOVE~!
FSSSSH

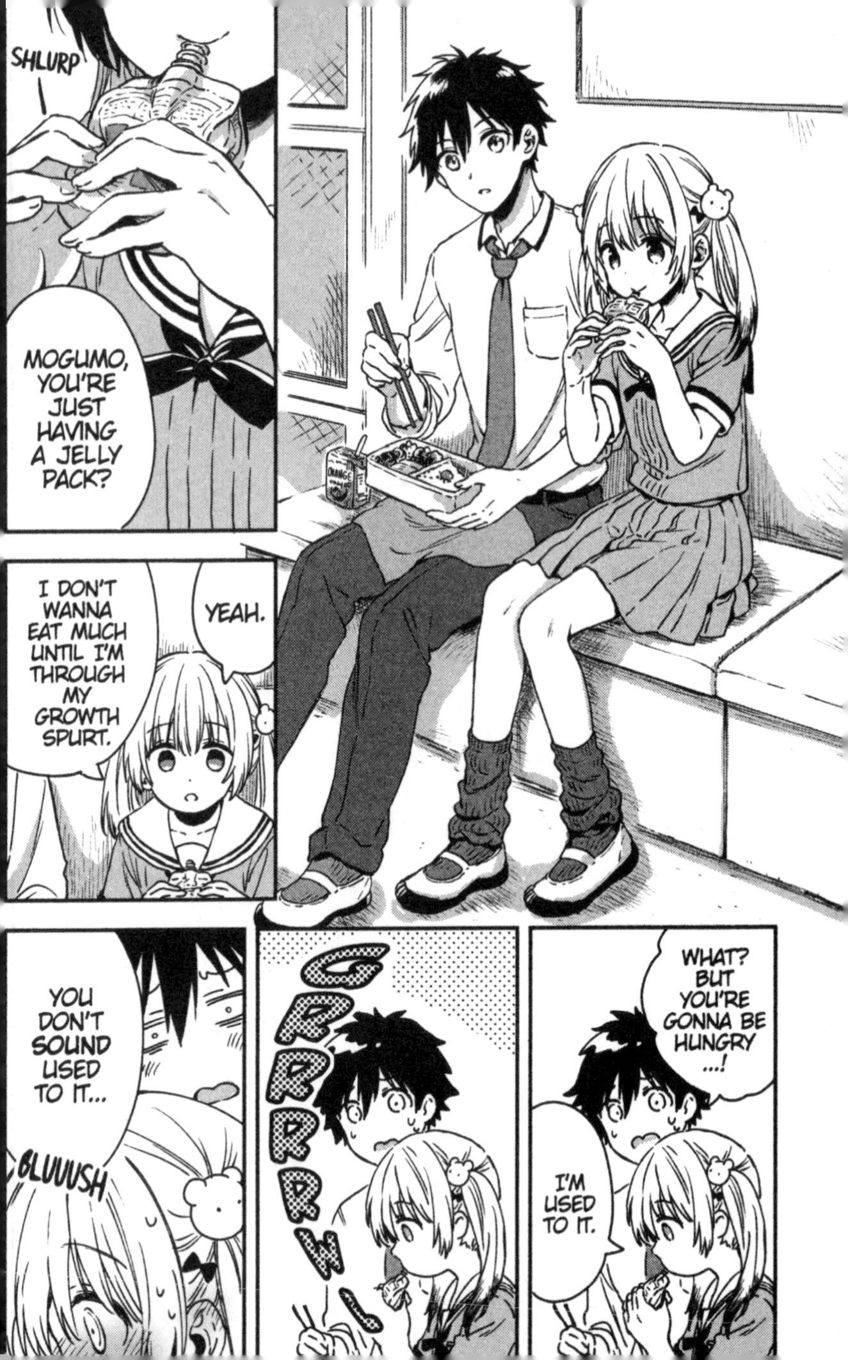
SHLURP
MOGUMO, YOU'RE JUST HAVING A JELLY PACK?
YEAH.
I DON'T WANNA EAT MUCH UNTIL I'M THROUGH MY GROWTH SPURT.
WHAT? BUT YOU'RE GONNA BE HUNGRY ...!
I'M USED TO IT.
GRRRRW!
YOU DON'T SOUND USED TO IT...
BLUUUSH

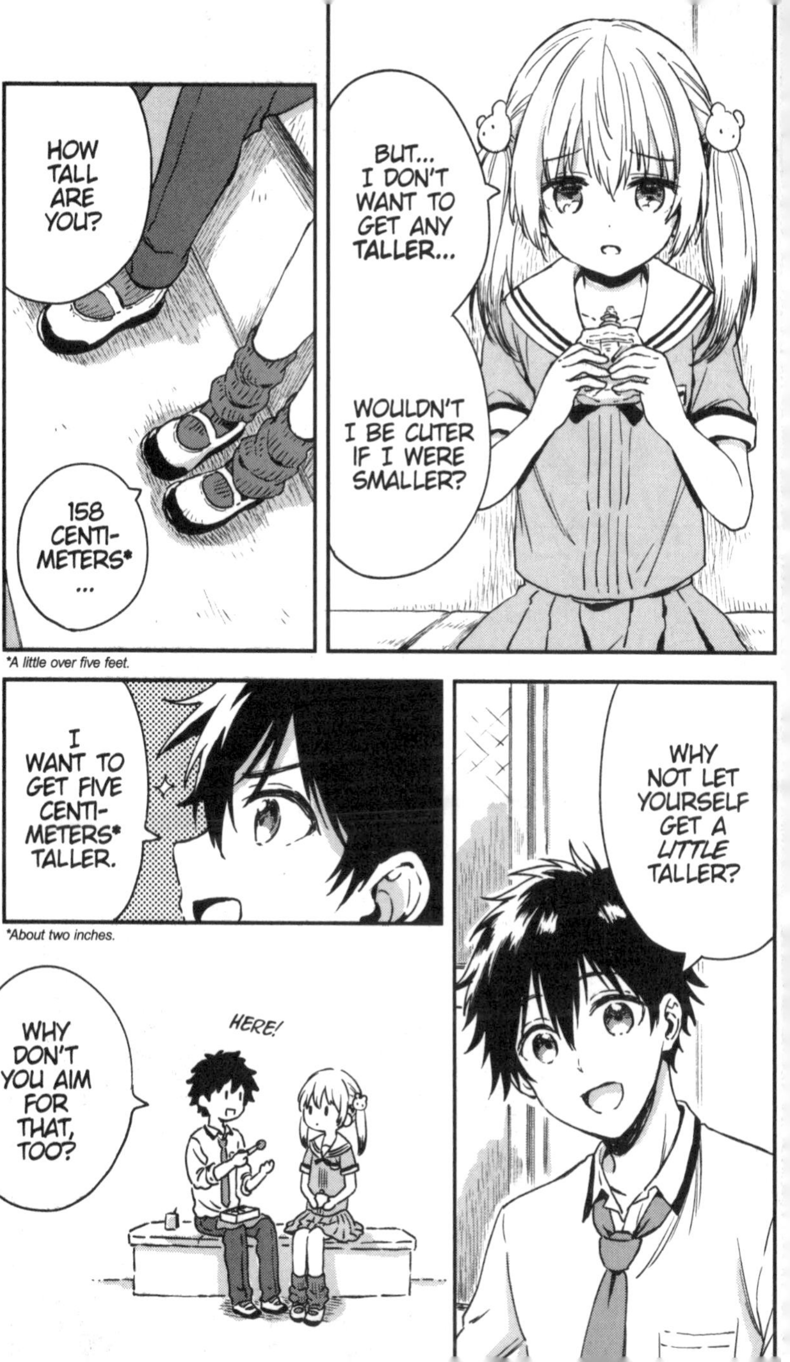
BUT... I DON'T WANT TO GET ANY TALLER...
WOULDN'T I BE CUTER IF I WERE SMALLER?
HOW TALL ARE YOU?
158 CENTIMETERS* ...
WHY NOT LET YOURSELF GET A *LITTLE* TALLER?
I WANT TO GET FIVE CENTIMETERS* TALLER.
HERE!
WHY DON'T YOU AIM FOR THAT, TOO?

*A little over five feet.

*About two inches.

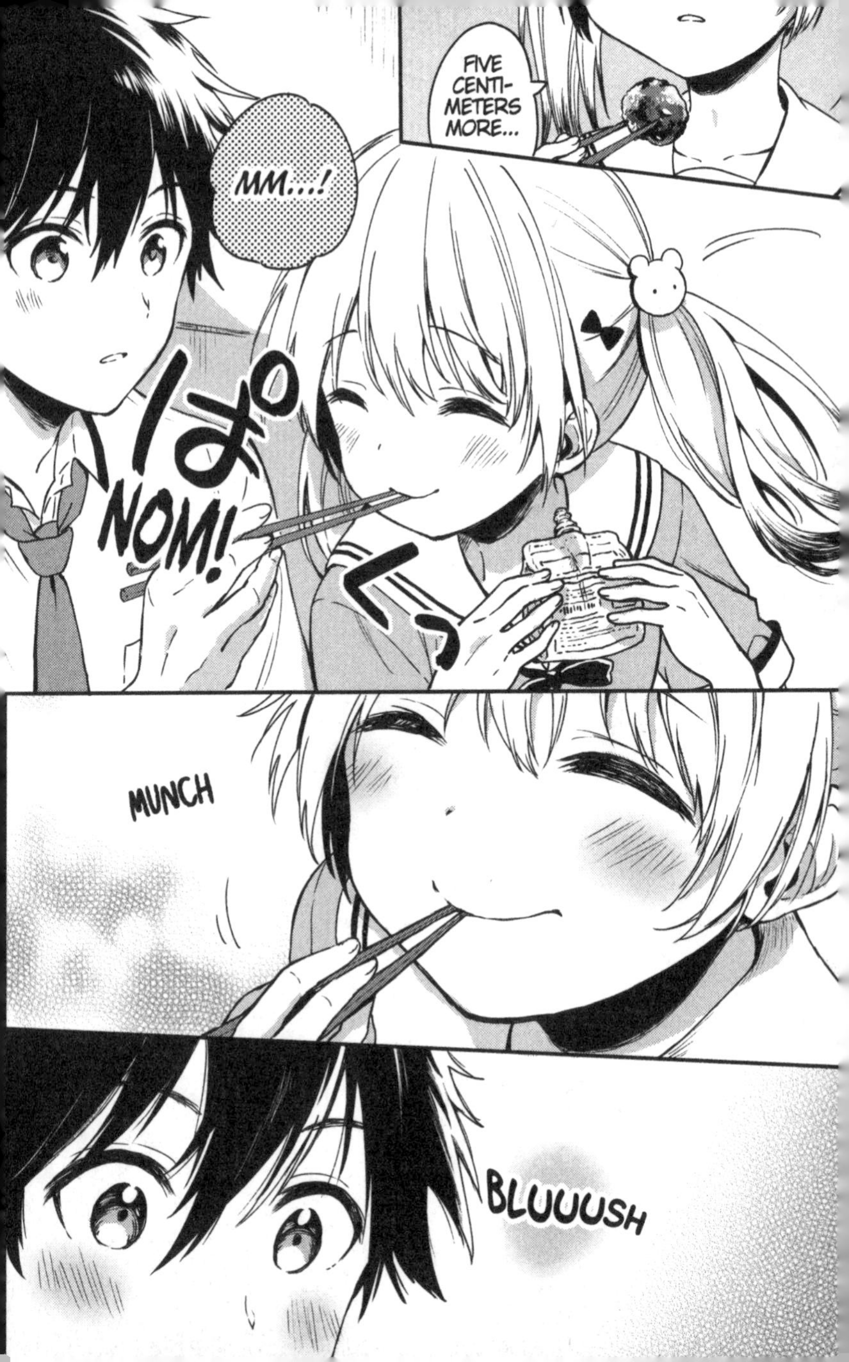
FIVE CENTIMETERS MORE...
MM...!
NOM!
MUNCH
BLUUUSH

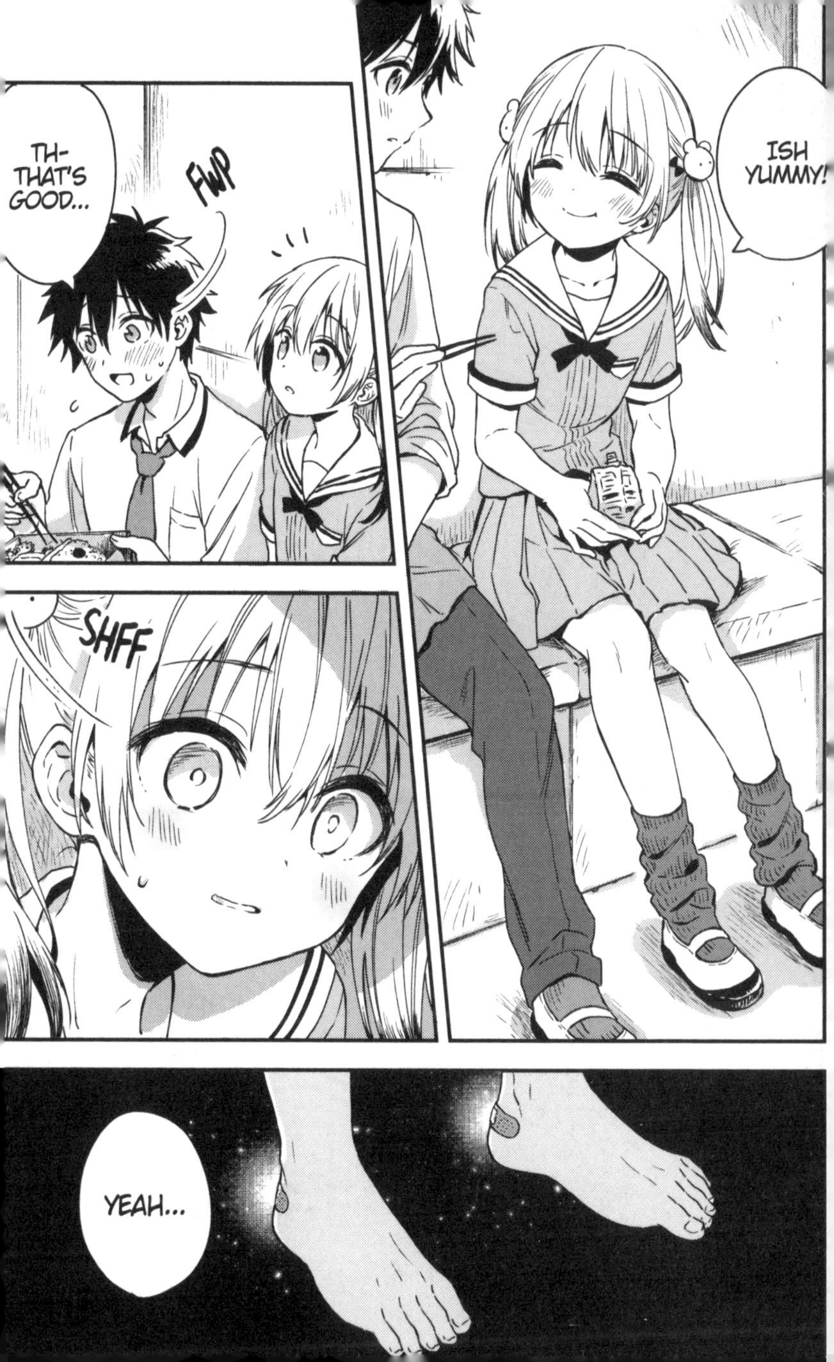
ISH YUMMY!
TH-THAT'S GOOD...
FWP
SHFF
YEAH...

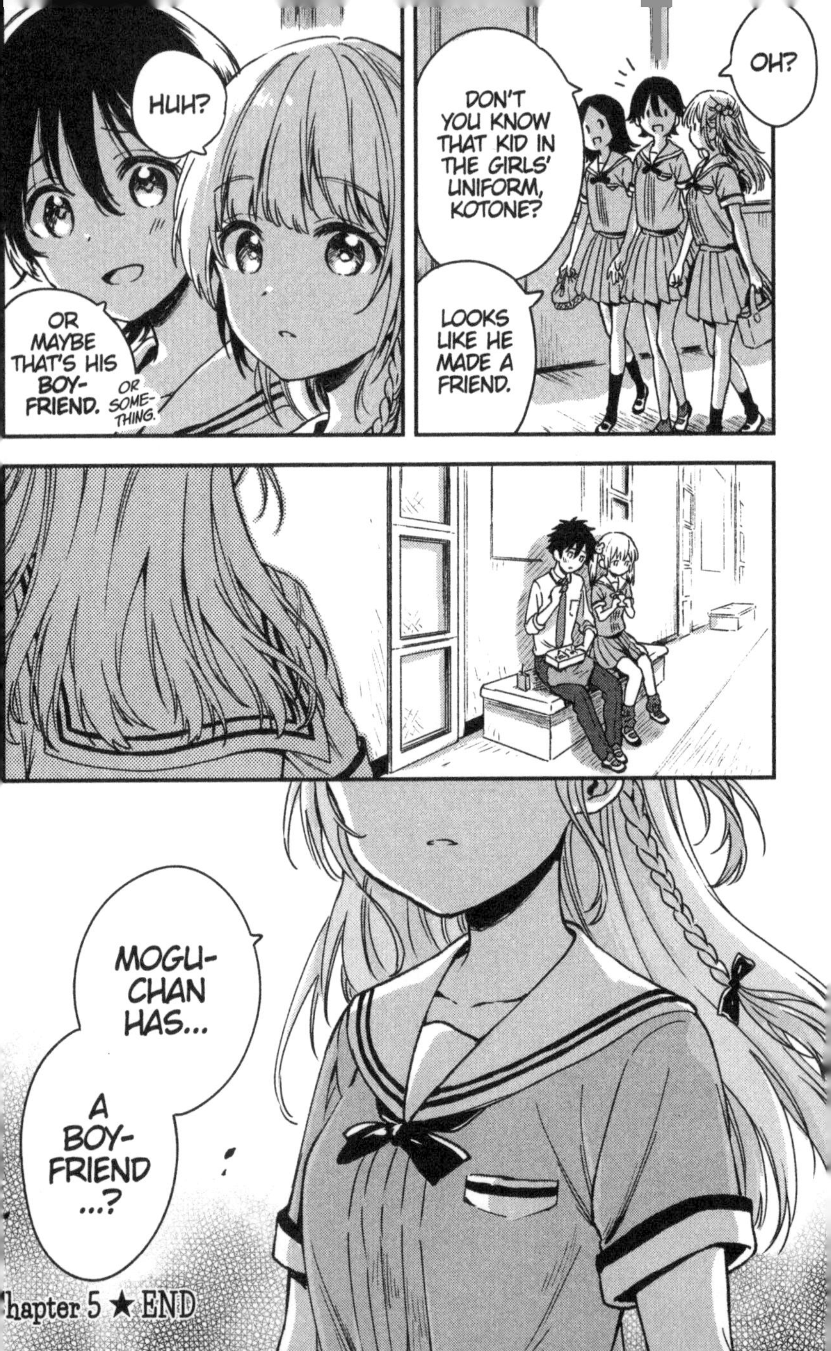
OH?
DON'T YOU KNOW THAT KID IN THE GIRLS' UNIFORM, KOTONE?
LOOKS LIKE HE MADE A FRIEND.
HUH?
OR MAYBE THAT'S HIS BOY-FRIEND.
OR SOME-THING.
MOGU-CHAN HAS...
A BOY-FRIEND ...?
hapter 5 ★ END

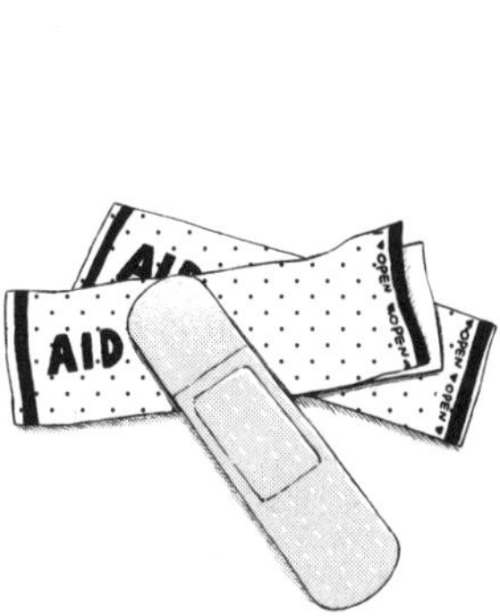
AID
AID
OPEN
OPEN

Love me for
who I am

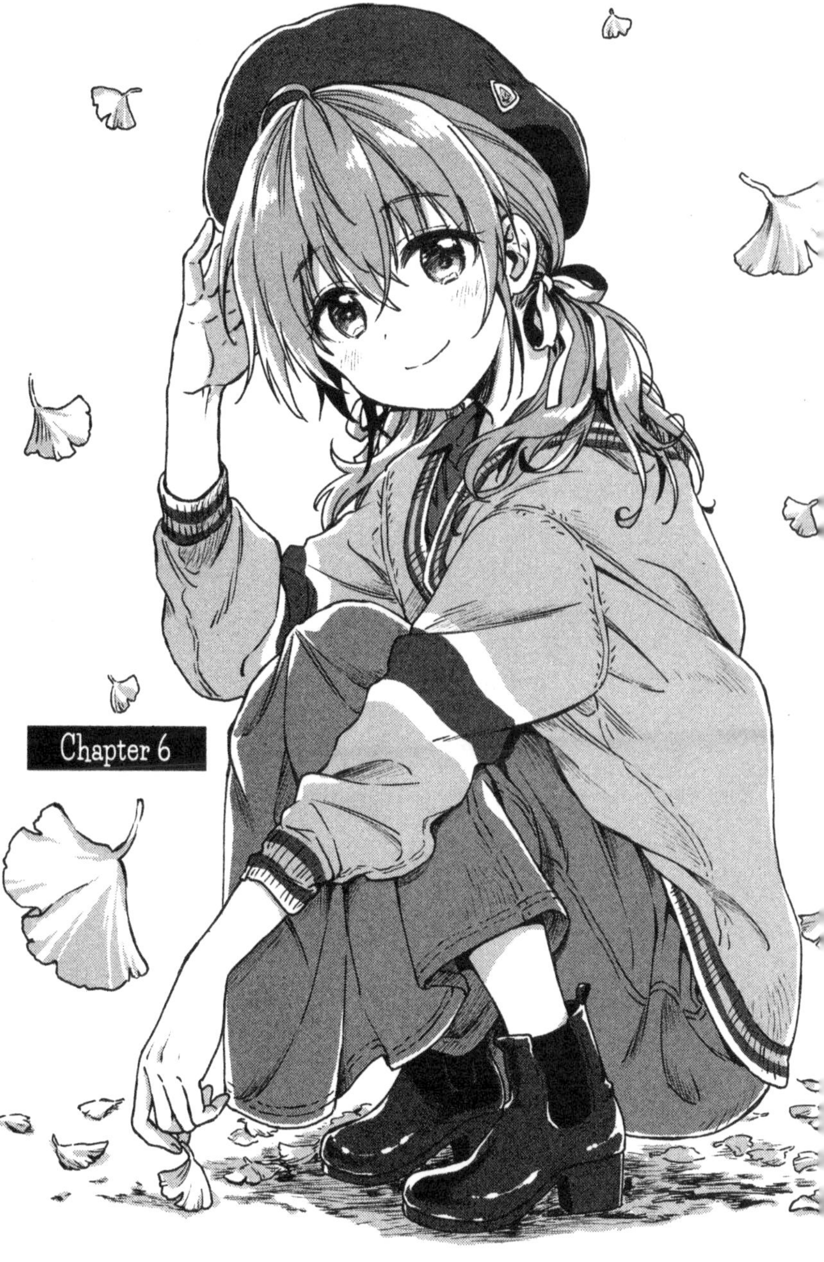
Chapter 6

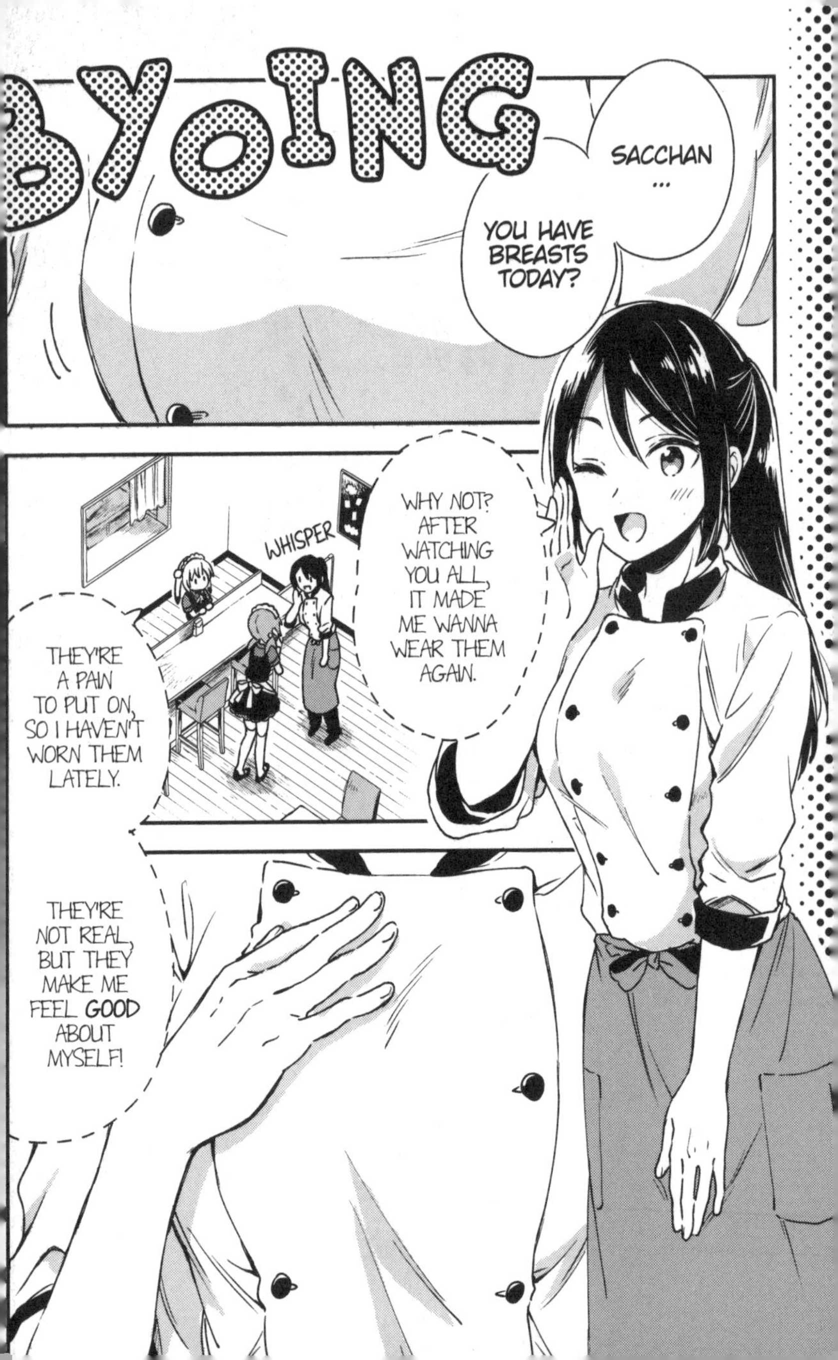
BYOING
SACCHAN ...
YOU HAVE BREASTS TODAY?
WHY NOT? AFTER WATCHING YOU ALL, IT MADE ME WANNA WEAR THEM AGAIN.
WHISPER
THEY'RE A PAIN TO PUT ON, SO I HAVEN'T WORN THEM LATELY.
THEY'RE NOT REAL, BUT THEY MAKE ME FEEL **GOOD** ABOUT MYSELF!

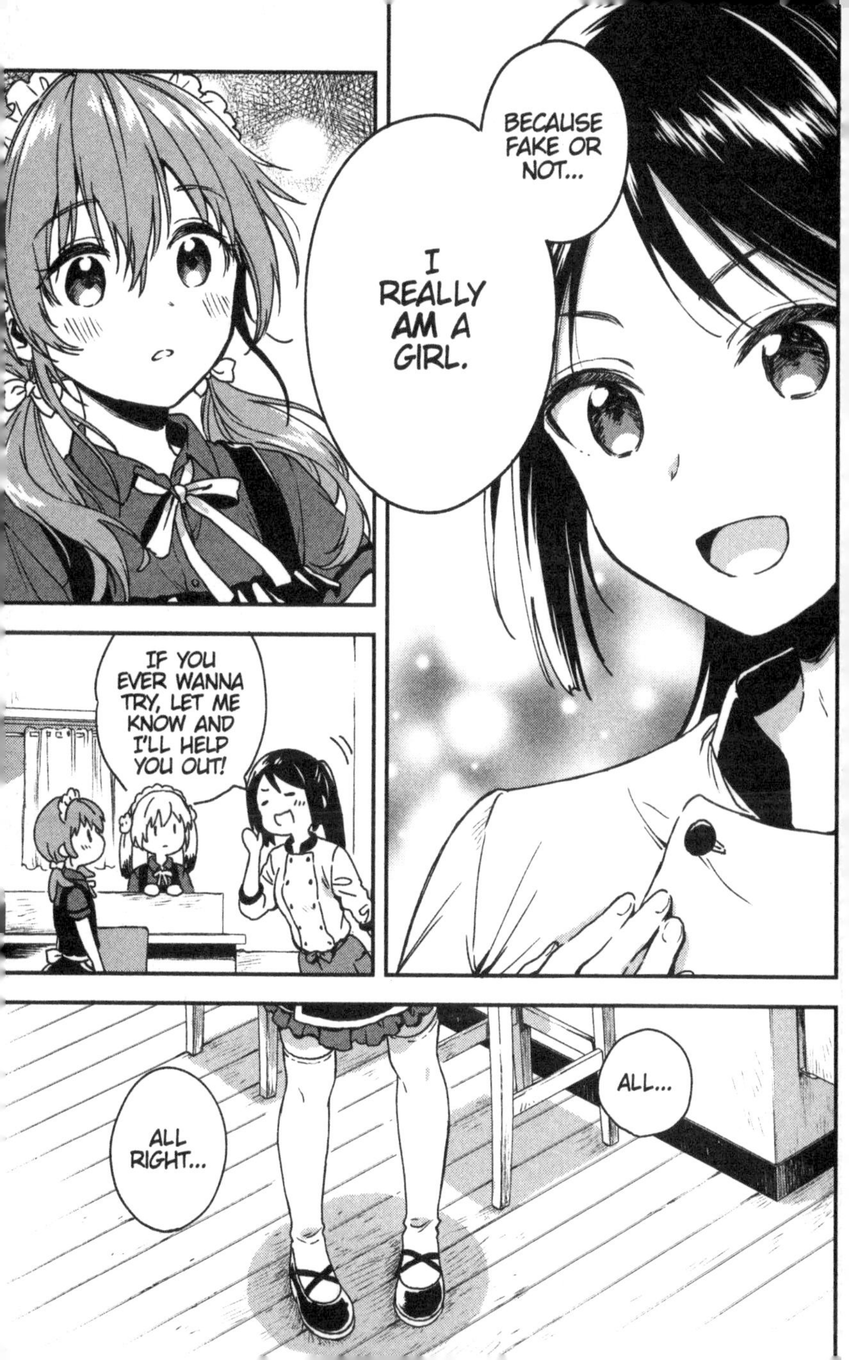
BECAUSE FAKE OR NOT...
I REALLY AM A GIRL.
IF YOU EVER WANNA TRY, LET ME KNOW AND I'LL HELP YOU OUT!
ALL...
ALL RIGHT...

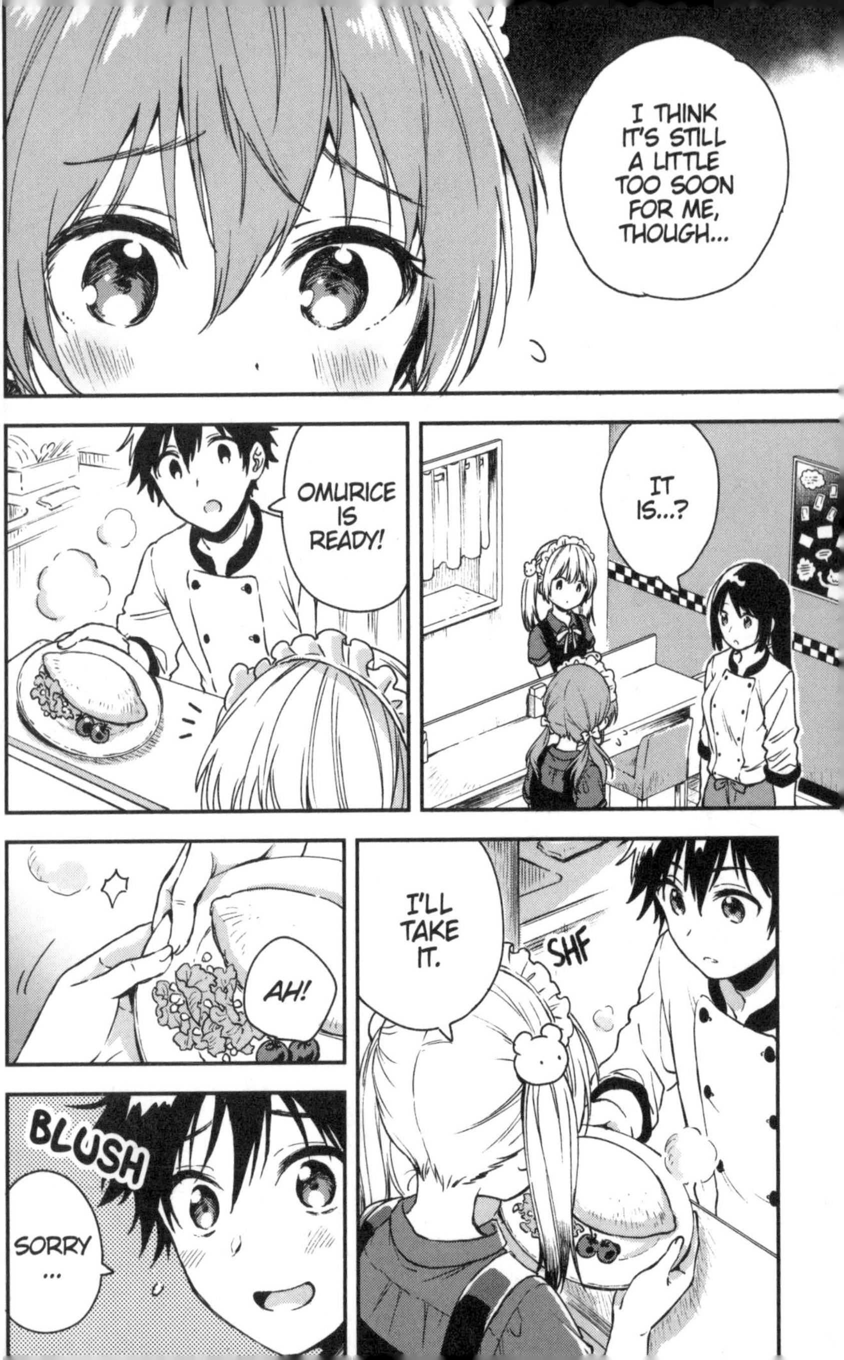
I THINK IT'S STILL A LITTLE TOO SOON FOR ME, THOUGH...
IT IS...?
OMURICE IS READY!
I'LL TAKE IT.
SHF
AH!
BLUSH
SORRY ...

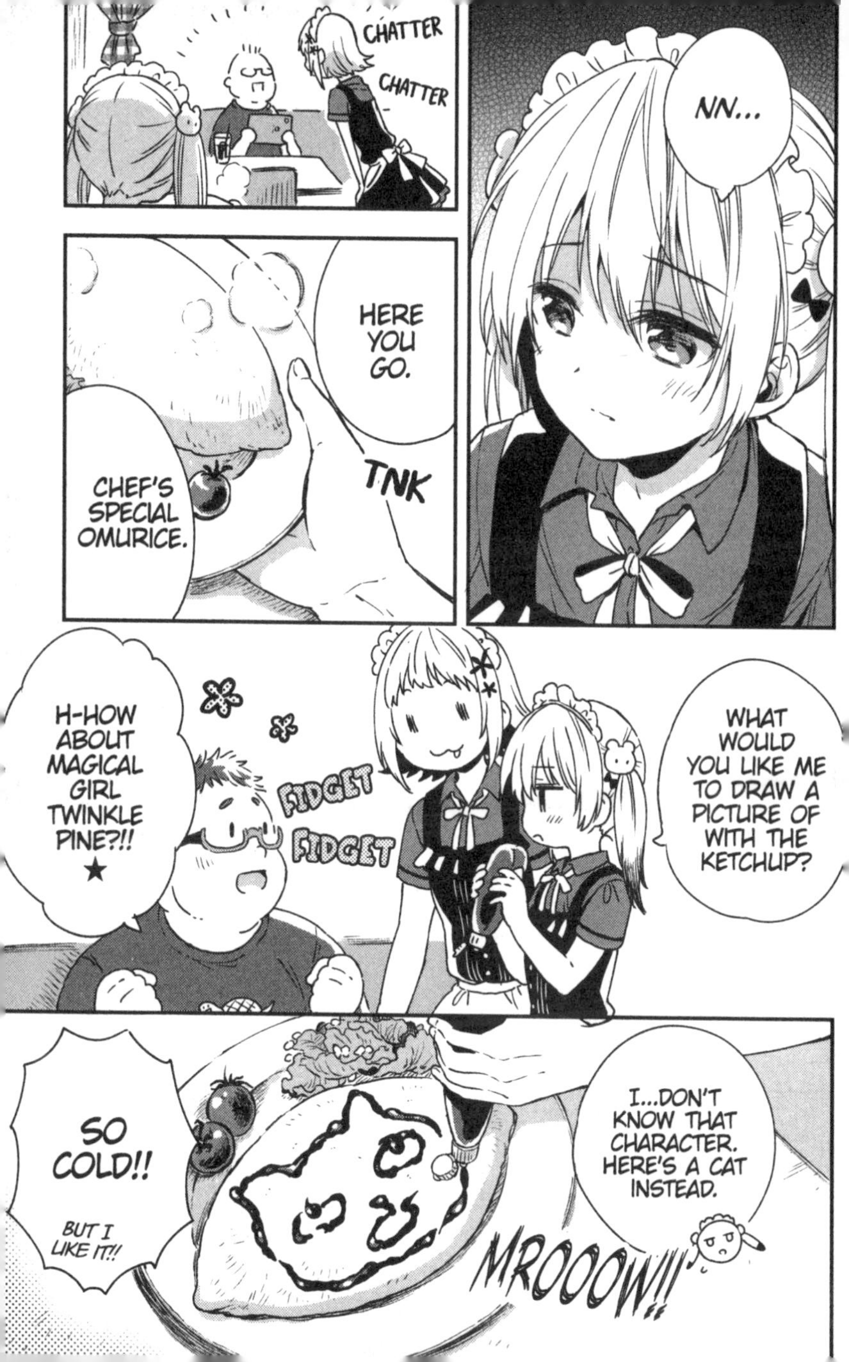
NN...
CHATTER
CHATTER
HERE YOU GO.
TNK
CHEF'S SPECIAL OMURICE.
WHAT WOULD YOU LIKE ME TO DRAW A PICTURE OF WITH THE KETCHUP?
FIDGET
FIDGET
H-HOW ABOUT MAGICAL GIRL TWINKLE PINE?!! ★
I...DON'T KNOW THAT CHARACTER. HERE'S A CAT INSTEAD.
MROOOW!!
SO COLD!!
BUT I LIKE IT!!

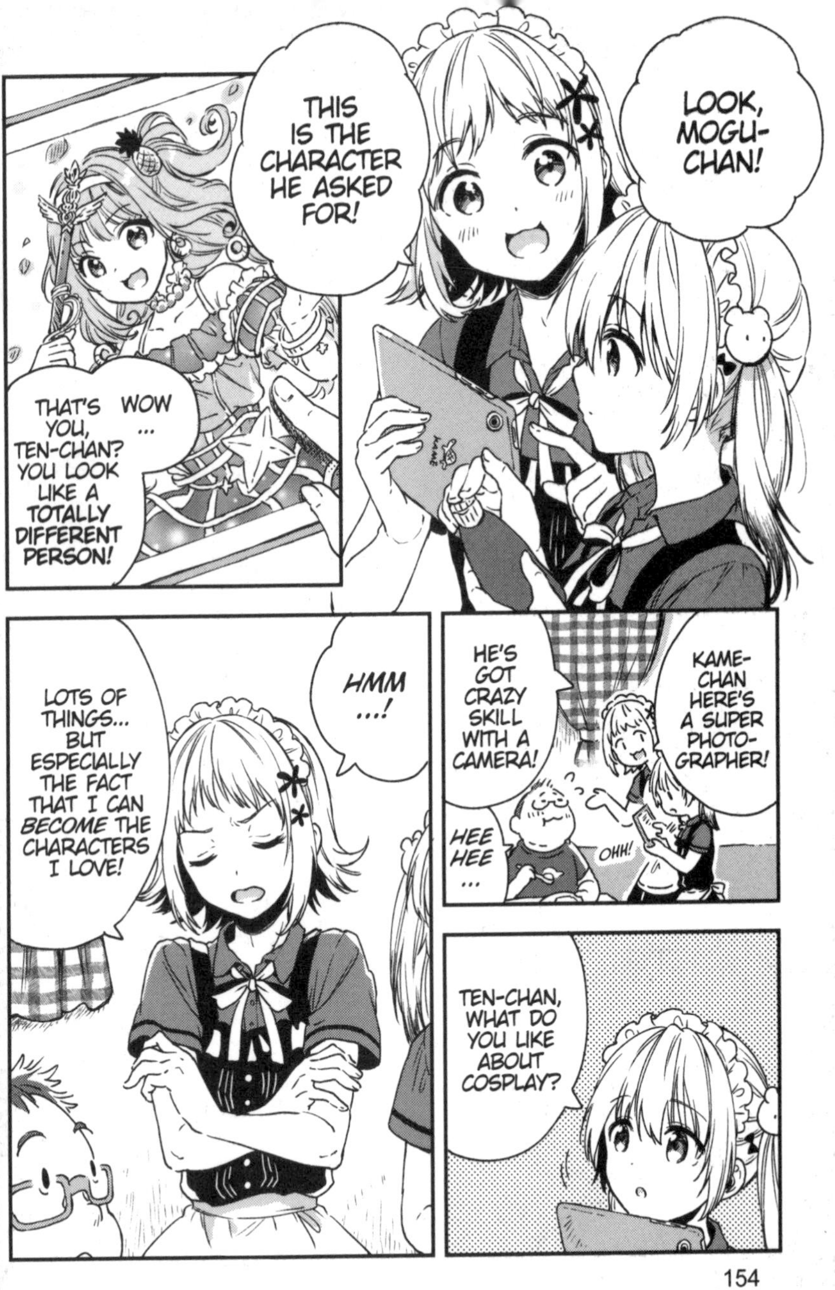

LOOK, MOGU-CHAN!
THIS IS THE CHARACTER HE ASKED FOR!
WOW ...
THAT'S YOU, TEN-CHAN? YOU LOOK LIKE A TOTALLY DIFFERENT PERSON!
KAME-CHAN HERE'S A SUPER PHOTOGRAPHER!
HE'S GOT CRAZY SKILL WITH A CAMERA!
OHH!
HEE HEE ...
TEN-CHAN, WHAT DO YOU LIKE ABOUT COSPLAY?
HMM ...!
LOTS OF THINGS... BUT ESPECIALLY THE FACT THAT I CAN *BECOME* THE CHARACTERS I LOVE!

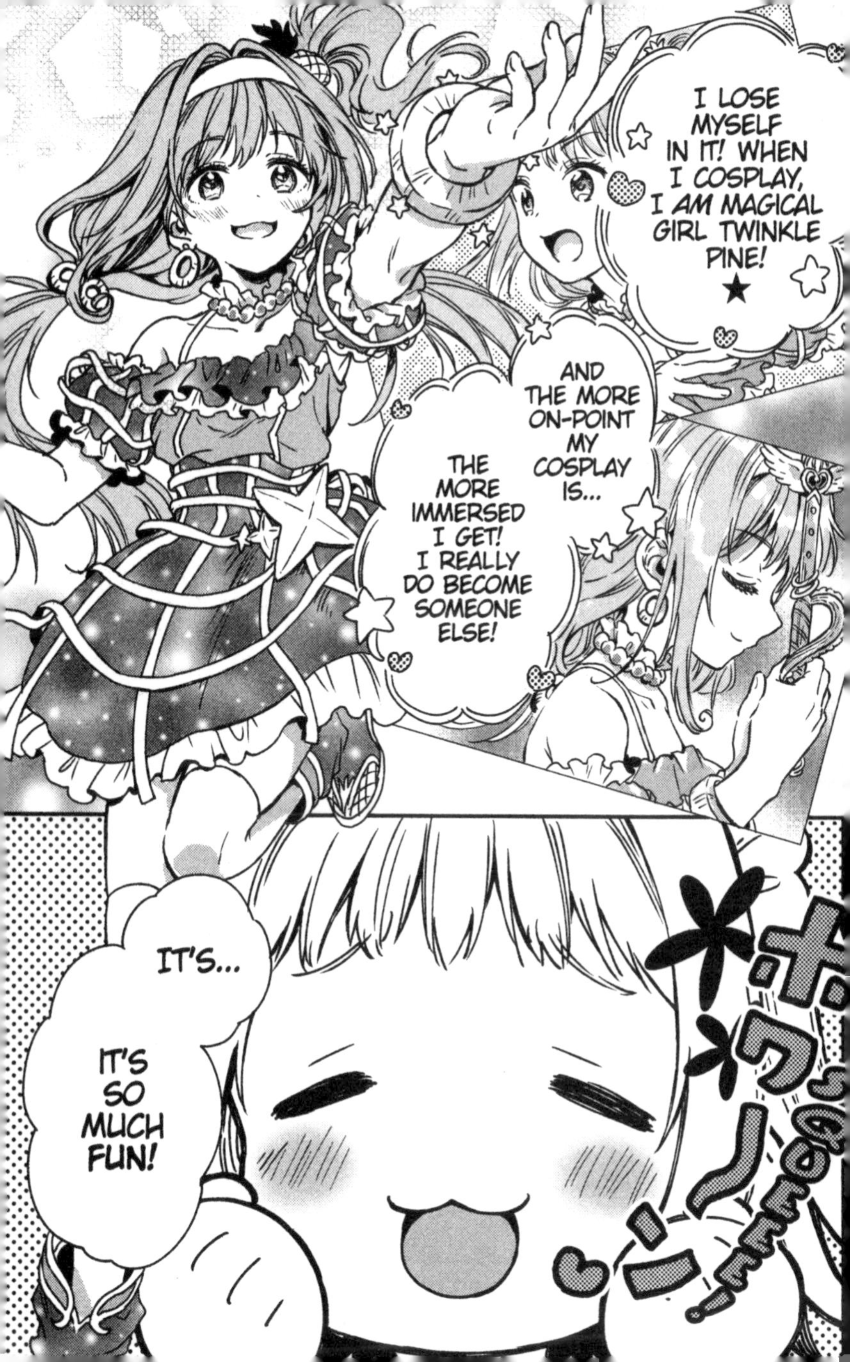
I LOSE MYSELF IN IT! WHEN I COSPLAY, I *AM* MAGICAL GIRL TWINKLE PINE! ★
AND THE MORE ON-POINT MY COSPLAY IS...
THE MORE IMMERSED I GET! I REALLY DO BECOME SOMEONE ELSE!
ホワン
IT'S...
IT'S SO MUCH FUN!

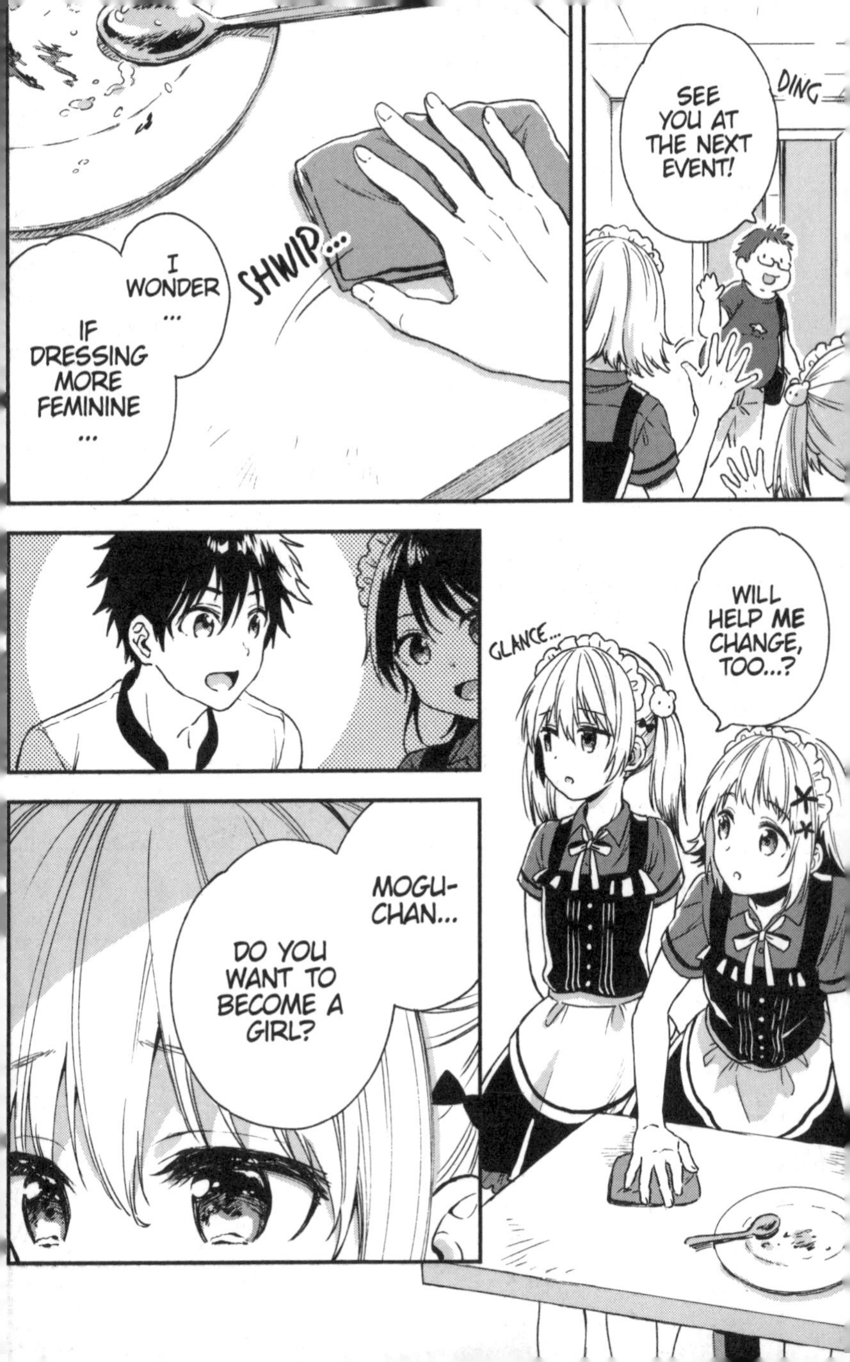
DING
SEE YOU AT THE NEXT EVENT!
SHWIP...
I WONDER...
IF DRESSING MORE FEMININE...
GLANCE...
WILL HELP ME CHANGE, TOO...?
MOGU-CHAN...
DO YOU WANT TO BECOME A GIRL?

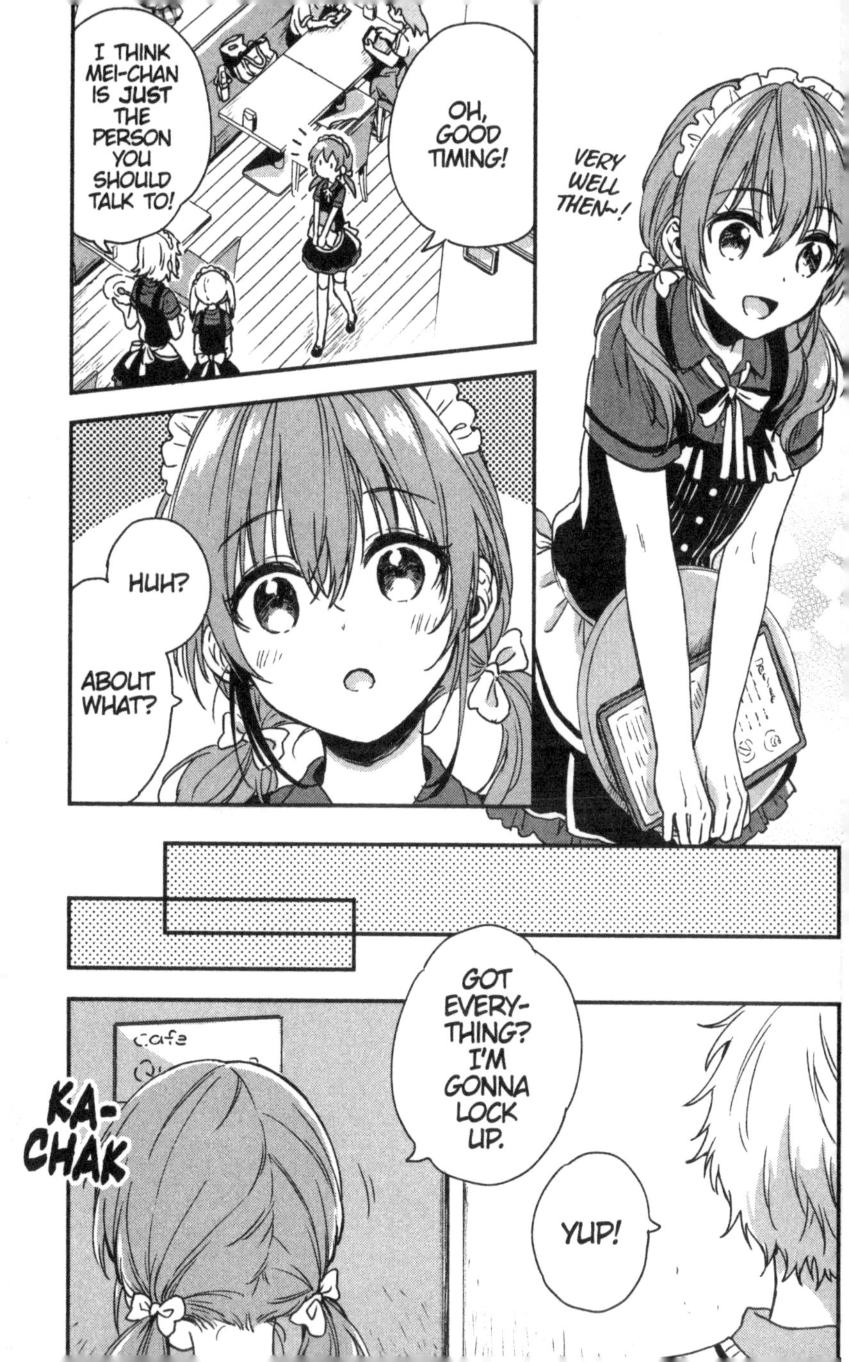
VERY WELL THEN~!
OH, GOOD TIMING!
I THINK MEI-CHAN IS JUST THE PERSON YOU SHOULD TALK TO!
HUH?
ABOUT WHAT?
GOT EVERYTHING? I'M GONNA LOCK UP.
YUP!
KA-CHAK
Cafe

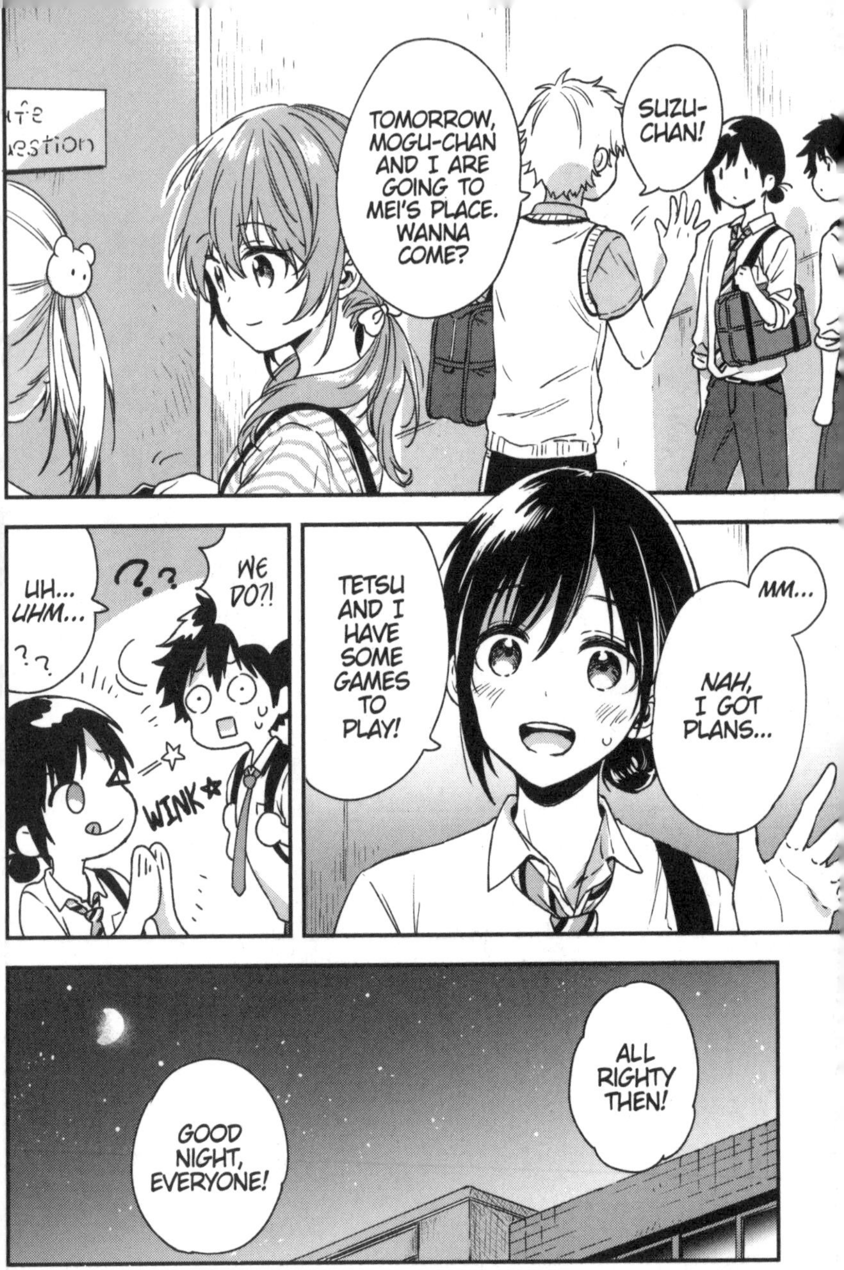
SUZU-CHAN!
TOMORROW, MOGU-CHAN AND I ARE GOING TO MEI'S PLACE. WANNA COME?
MM...
NAH, I GOT PLANS...
TETSU AND I HAVE SOME GAMES TO PLAY!
WE DO?!
UH... UHM...
WINK☆
ALL RIGHTY THEN!
GOOD NIGHT, EVERYONE!

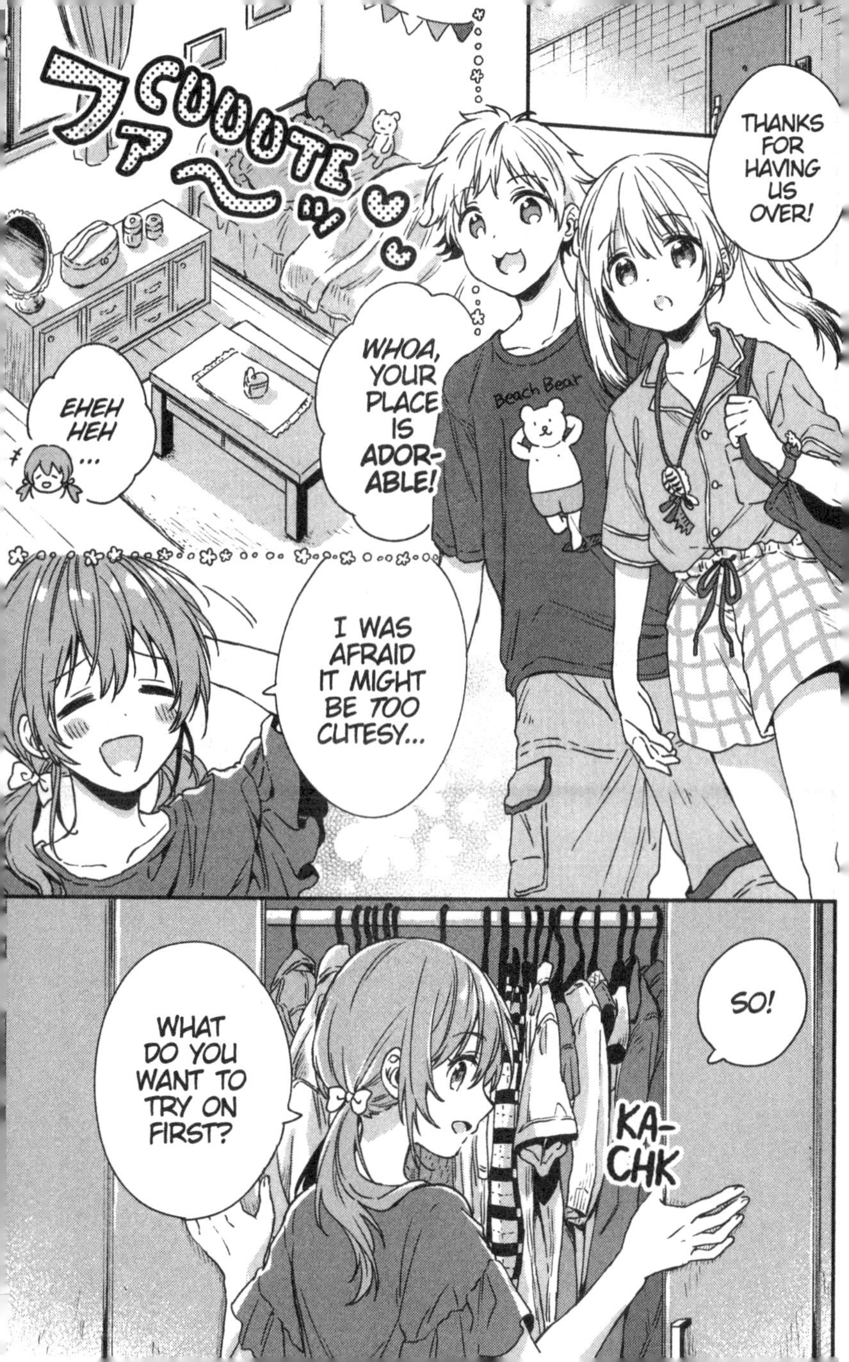
THANKS FOR HAVING US OVER!
WHOA, YOUR PLACE IS ADORABLE!
ファ～
CUUUTE
BOY
EHEH HEH...
I WAS AFRAID IT MIGHT BE *TOO* CUTESY...
SO!
KA-CHK
WHAT DO YOU WANT TO TRY ON FIRST?

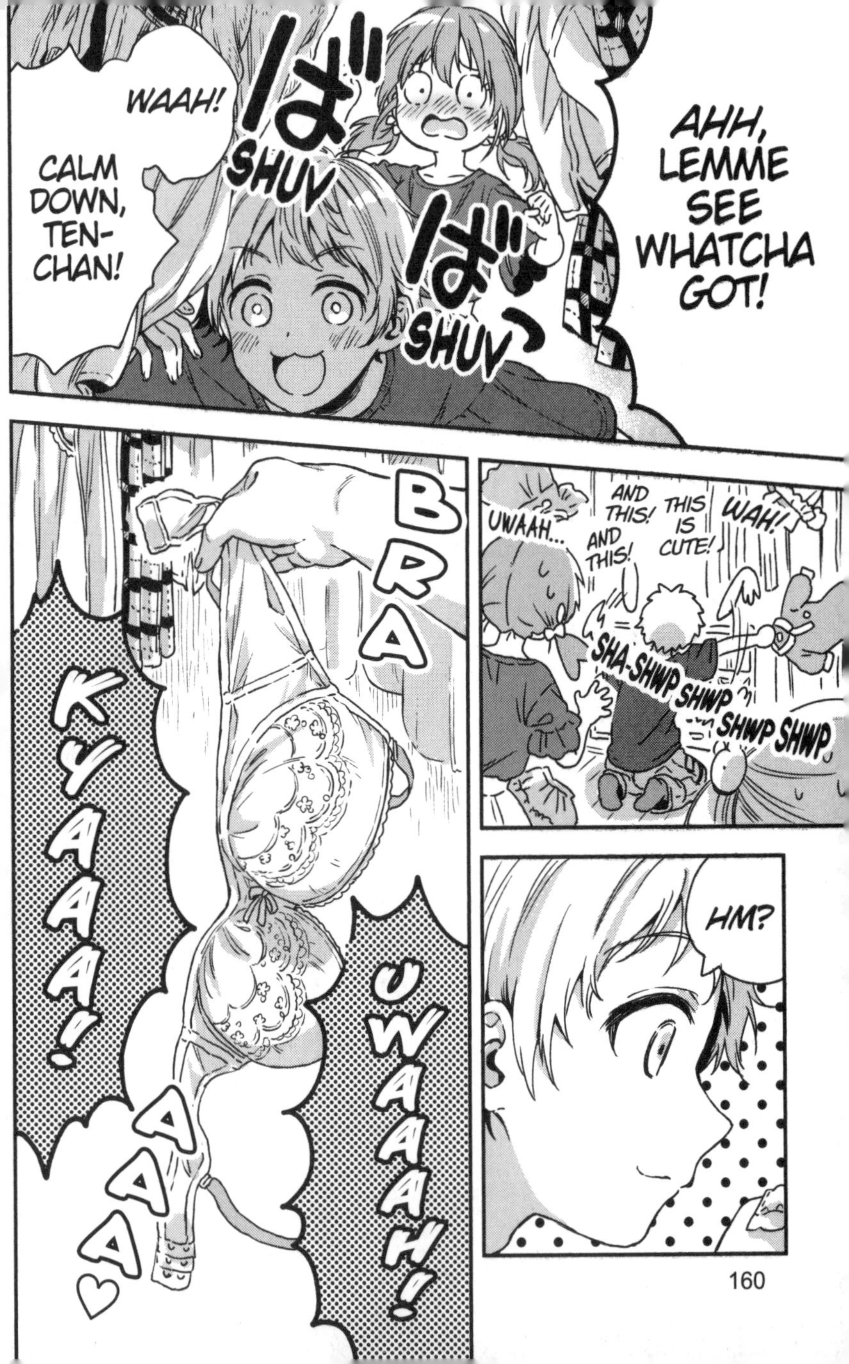
AHH, LEMME SEE WHATCHA GOT!
ば SHUV
WAAH!
ば SHUV
CALM DOWN, TEN-CHAN!
WAH!
THIS IS CUTE!
AND THIS!
AND THIS!
UWAAH...
SHA-SHWP SHWP SHWP SHWP
HM?
BRA
UWAAAAH!
KYAAAAA! AAA♥

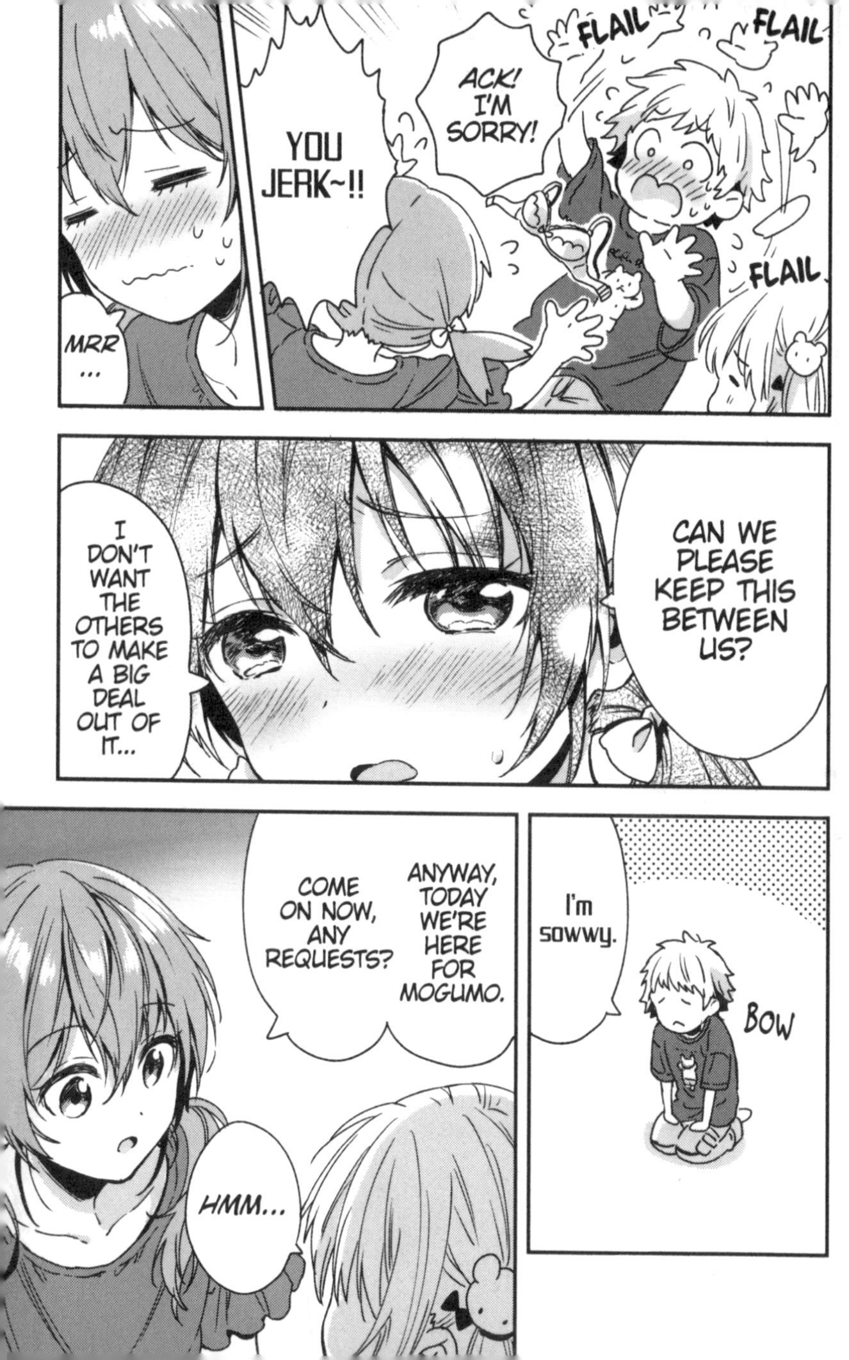
FLAIL
FLAIL
ACK! I'M SORRY!
YOU JERK~!!
FLAIL
MRR...
CAN WE PLEASE KEEP THIS BETWEEN US?
I DON'T WANT THE OTHERS TO MAKE A BIG DEAL OUT OF IT...
I'm sowwy.
BOW
ANYWAY, TODAY WE'RE HERE FOR MOGUMO.
COME ON NOW, ANY REQUESTS?
HMM...

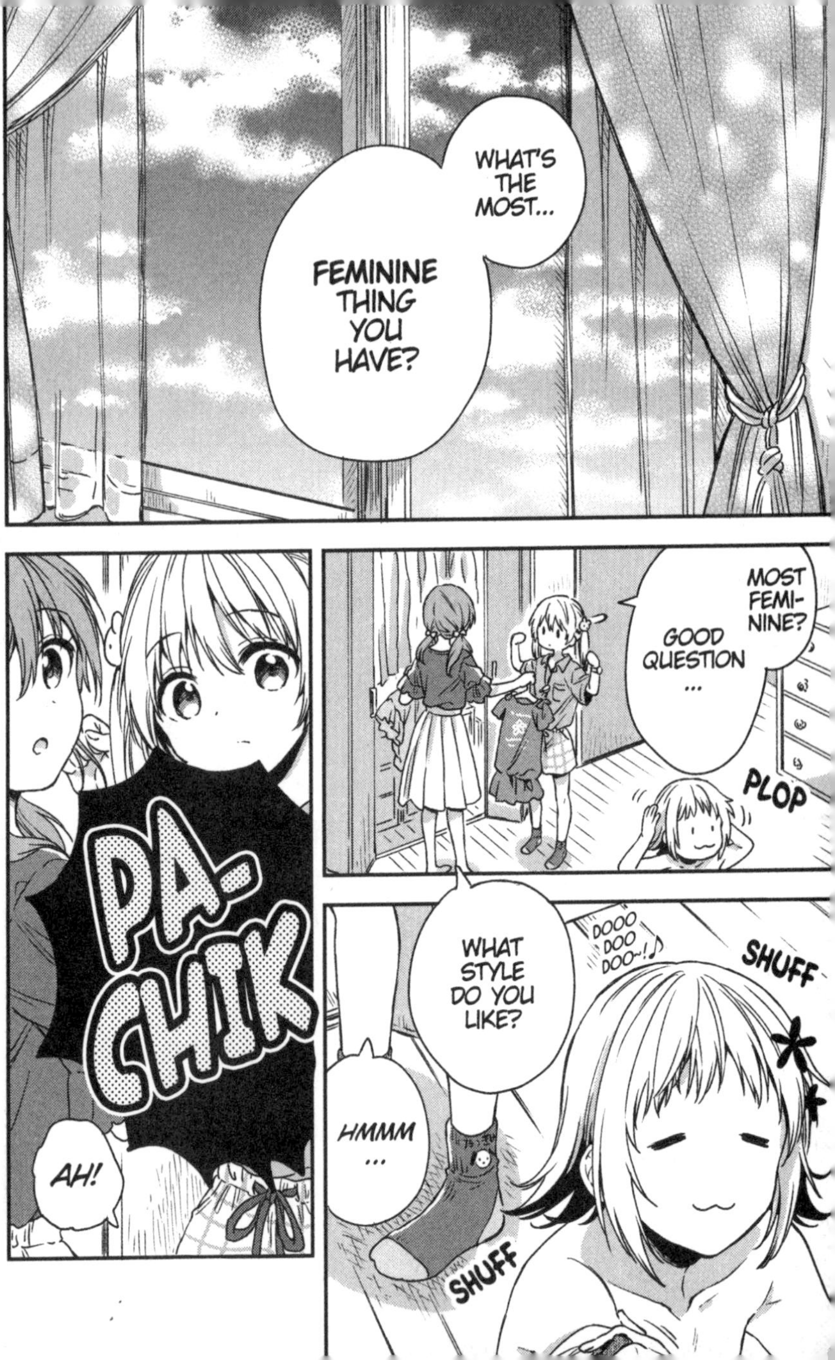
WHAT'S THE MOST...
FEMININE THING YOU HAVE?
MOST FEMI-NINE?
GOOD QUESTION ...
PLOP
DOOO DOO DOO~!♪
SHUFF
WHAT STYLE DO YOU LIKE?
HMMM ...
SHUFF
PA-CHIK
AH!

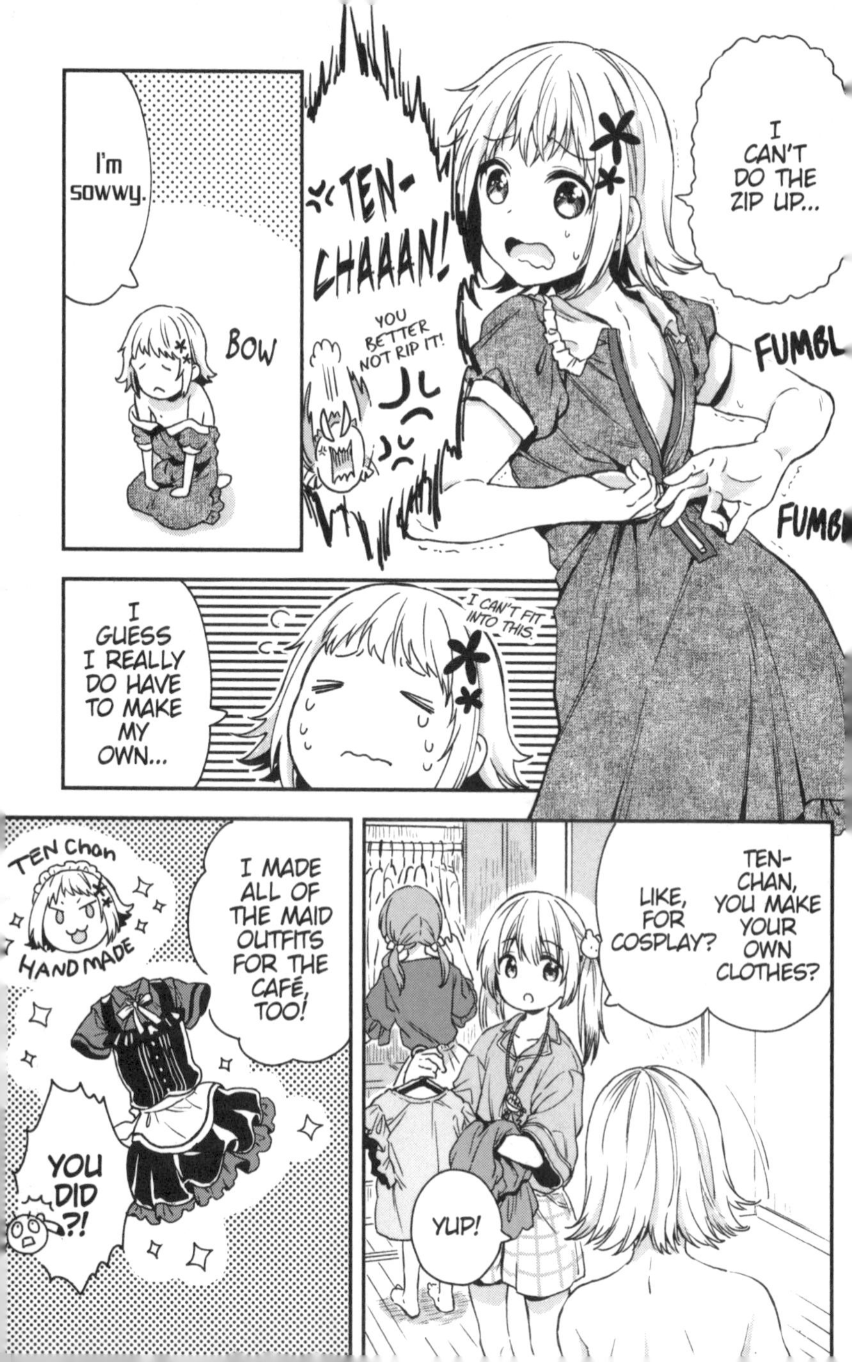
I CAN'T DO THE ZIP UP...
FUMBL
FUMBL
TEN-CHAAAN!
YOU BETTER NOT RIP IT!
I'm sowwy.
BOW
I CAN'T FIT INTO THIS.
I GUESS I REALLY DO HAVE TO MAKE MY OWN...
TEN-CHAN, YOU MAKE YOUR OWN CLOTHES?
LIKE, FOR COSPLAY?
YUP!
I MADE ALL OF THE MAID OUTFITS FOR THE CAFÉ, TOO!
TEN Chan
HAND MADE
YOU DID?!

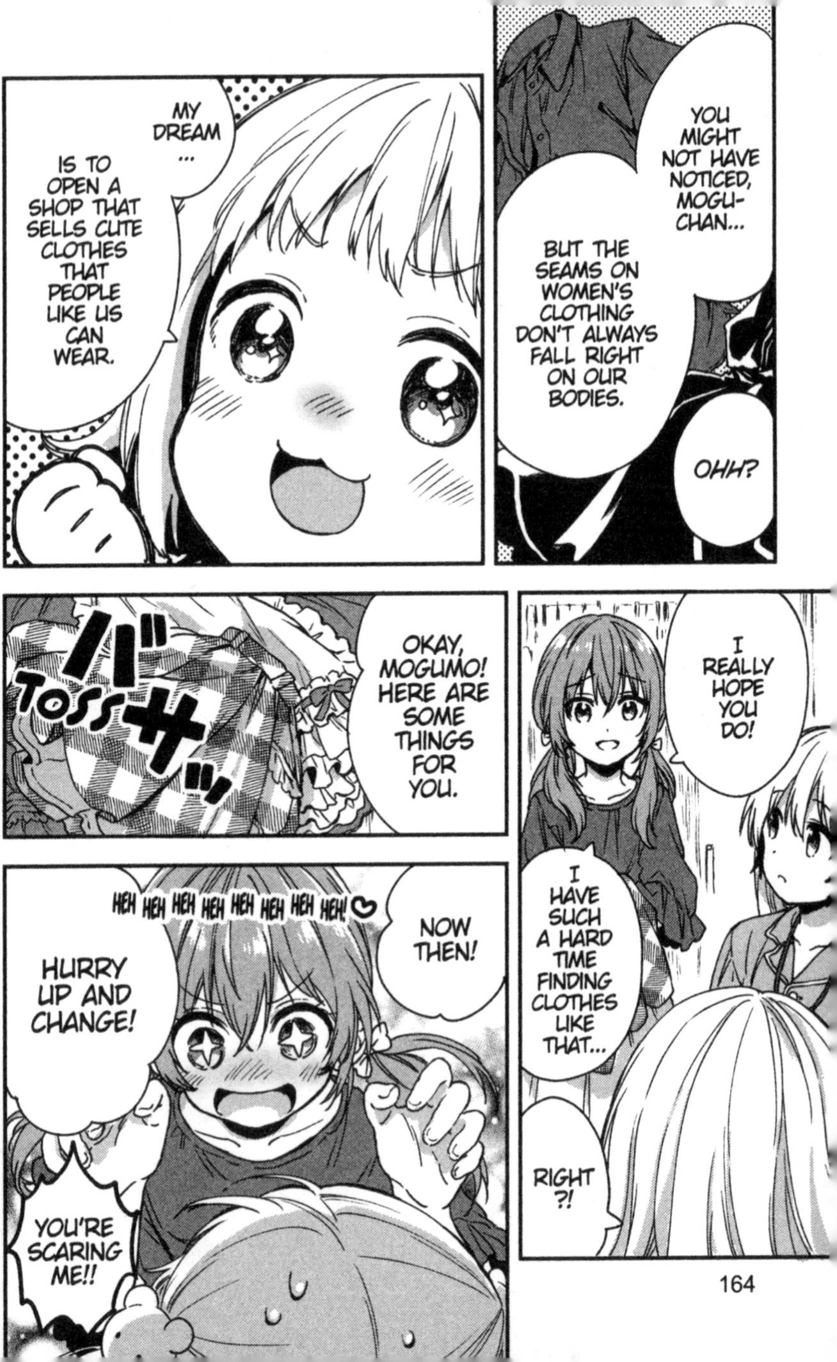
YOU MIGHT NOT HAVE NOTICED, MOGU-CHAN...
BUT THE SEAMS ON WOMEN'S CLOTHING DON'T ALWAYS FALL RIGHT ON OUR BODIES.
OHH?
MY DREAM ...
IS TO OPEN A SHOP THAT SELLS CUTE CLOTHES THAT PEOPLE LIKE US CAN WEAR.
I REALLY HOPE YOU DO!
I HAVE SUCH A HARD TIME FINDING CLOTHES LIKE THAT...
RIGHT ?!
バ
TOSS
サッ
OKAY, MOGUMO! HERE ARE SOME THINGS FOR YOU.
NOW THEN!
HEH HEH HEH HEH HEH HEH HEH HEH!
HURRY UP AND CHANGE!
YOU'RE SCARING ME!!

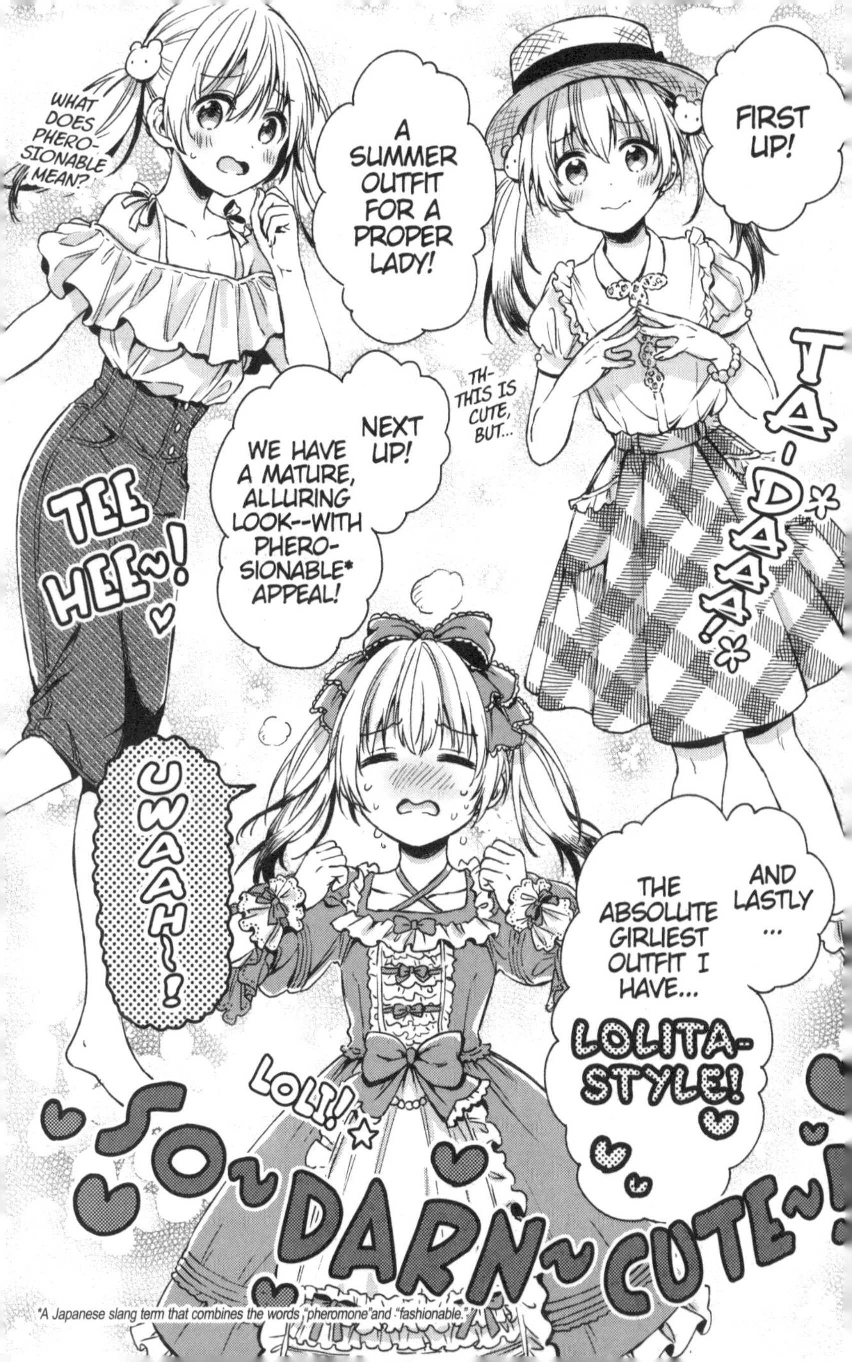
FIRST UP!
A SUMMER OUTFIT FOR A PROPER LADY!
TA-DAAA!
TH-THIS IS CUTE, BUT...
NEXT UP!
WE HAVE A MATURE, ALLURING LOOK--WITH PHERO-SIONABLE* APPEAL!
TEE HEE~!
WHAT DOES PHERO-SIONABLE MEAN?
AND LASTLY...
THE ABSOLUTE GIRLIEST OUTFIT I HAVE...
LOLITA-STYLE!
LOLI!
UWAAAH~!
SO~ DARN~ CUTE~!

*A Japanese slang term that combines the words "pheromone" and "fashionable."

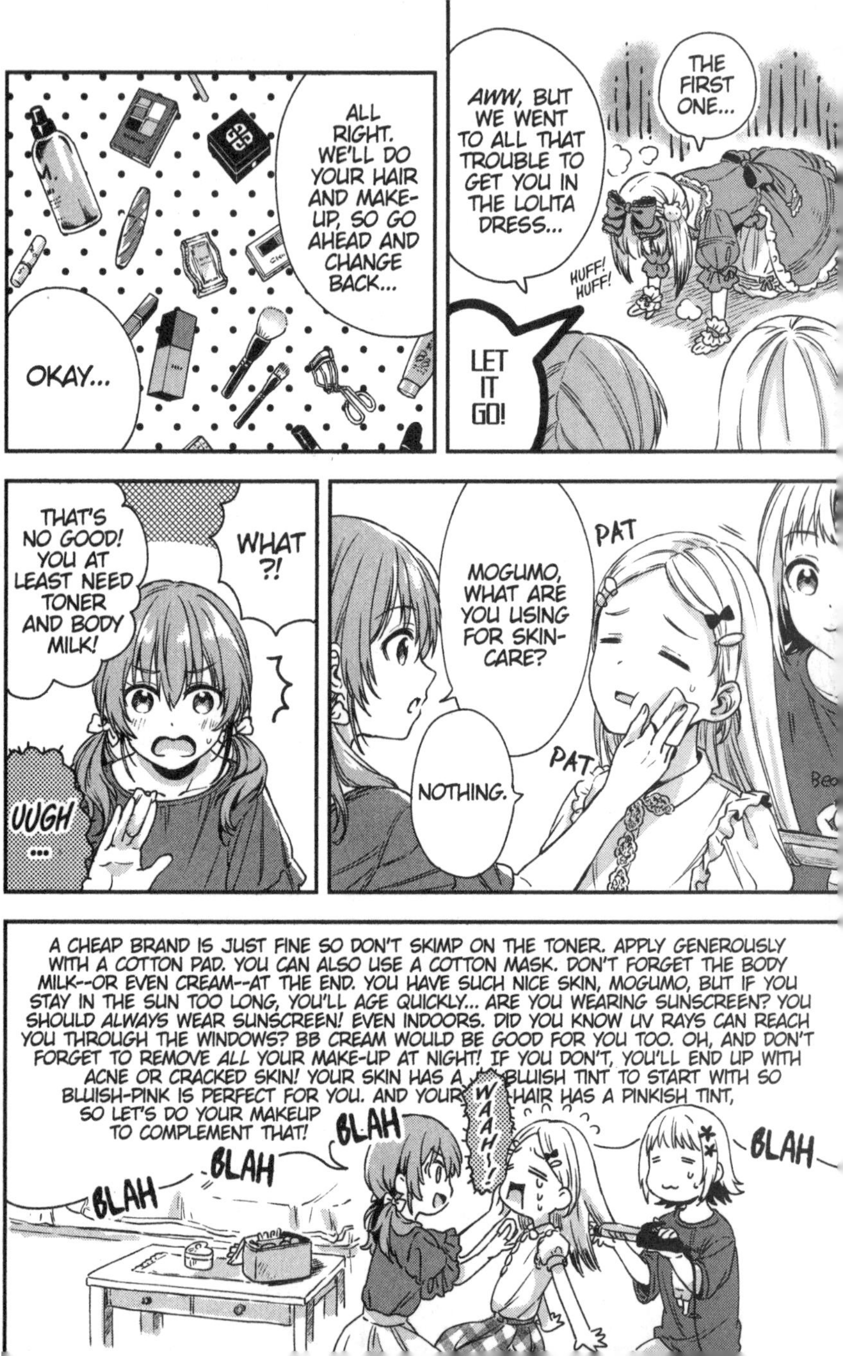
THE FIRST ONE...
AWW, BUT WE WENT TO ALL THAT TROUBLE TO GET YOU IN THE LOLITA DRESS...
HUFF! HUFF!
LET IT GO!
ALL RIGHT. WE'LL DO YOUR HAIR AND MAKE-UP, SO GO AHEAD AND CHANGE BACK...
OKAY...
PAT
MOGUMO, WHAT ARE YOU USING FOR SKIN-CARE?
PAT
NOTHING.
WHAT ?!
THAT'S NO GOOD! YOU AT LEAST NEED TONER AND BODY MILK!
UUGH ...
A CHEAP BRAND IS JUST FINE SO DON'T SKIMP ON THE TONER. APPLY GENEROUSLY WITH A COTTON PAD. YOU CAN ALSO USE A COTTON MASK. DON'T FORGET THE BODY MILK--OR EVEN CREAM--AT THE END. YOU HAVE SUCH NICE SKIN, MOGUMO, BUT IF YOU STAY IN THE SUN TOO LONG, YOU'LL AGE QUICKLY... ARE YOU WEARING SUNSCREEN? YOU SHOULD ALWAYS WEAR SUNSCREEN! EVEN INDOORS. DID YOU KNOW UV RAYS CAN REACH YOU THROUGH THE WINDOWS? BB CREAM WOULD BE GOOD FOR YOU TOO. OH, AND DON'T FORGET TO REMOVE ALL YOUR MAKE-UP AT NIGHT! IF YOU DON'T, YOU'LL END UP WITH ACNE OR CRACKED SKIN! YOUR SKIN HAS A BLUISH TINT TO START WITH SO BLUISH-PINK IS PERFECT FOR YOU. AND YOUR HAIR HAS A PINKISH TINT, SO LET'S DO YOUR MAKEUP TO COMPLEMENT THAT!
WAAAH—!
BLAH
BLAH
BLAH
BLAH
BLAH

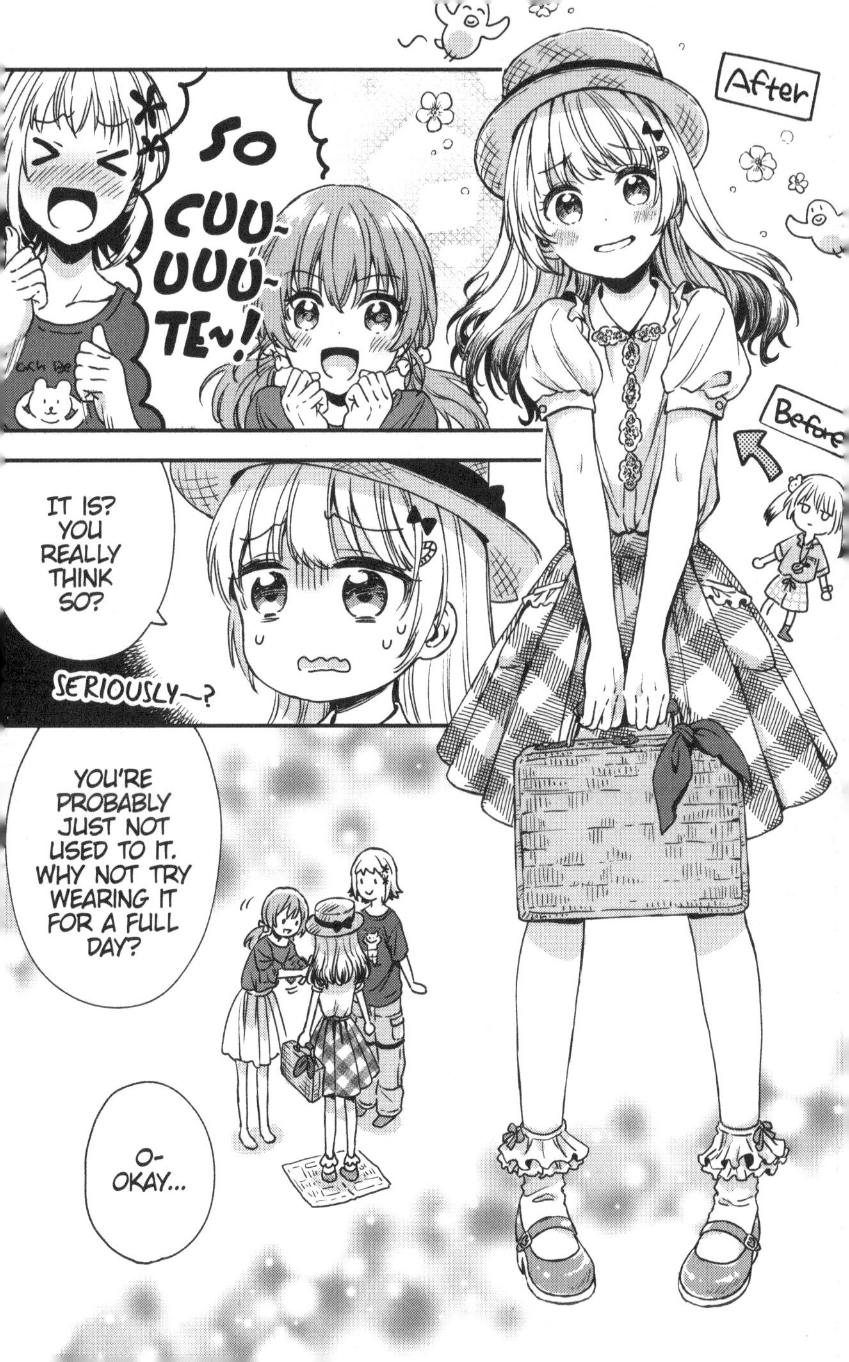
After
Before
SO CUUU-UUU-TE~!
IT IS? YOU REALLY THINK SO?
SERIOUSLY~?
YOU'RE PROBABLY JUST NOT USED TO IT. WHY NOT TRY WEARING IT FOR A FULL DAY?
O-OKAY...

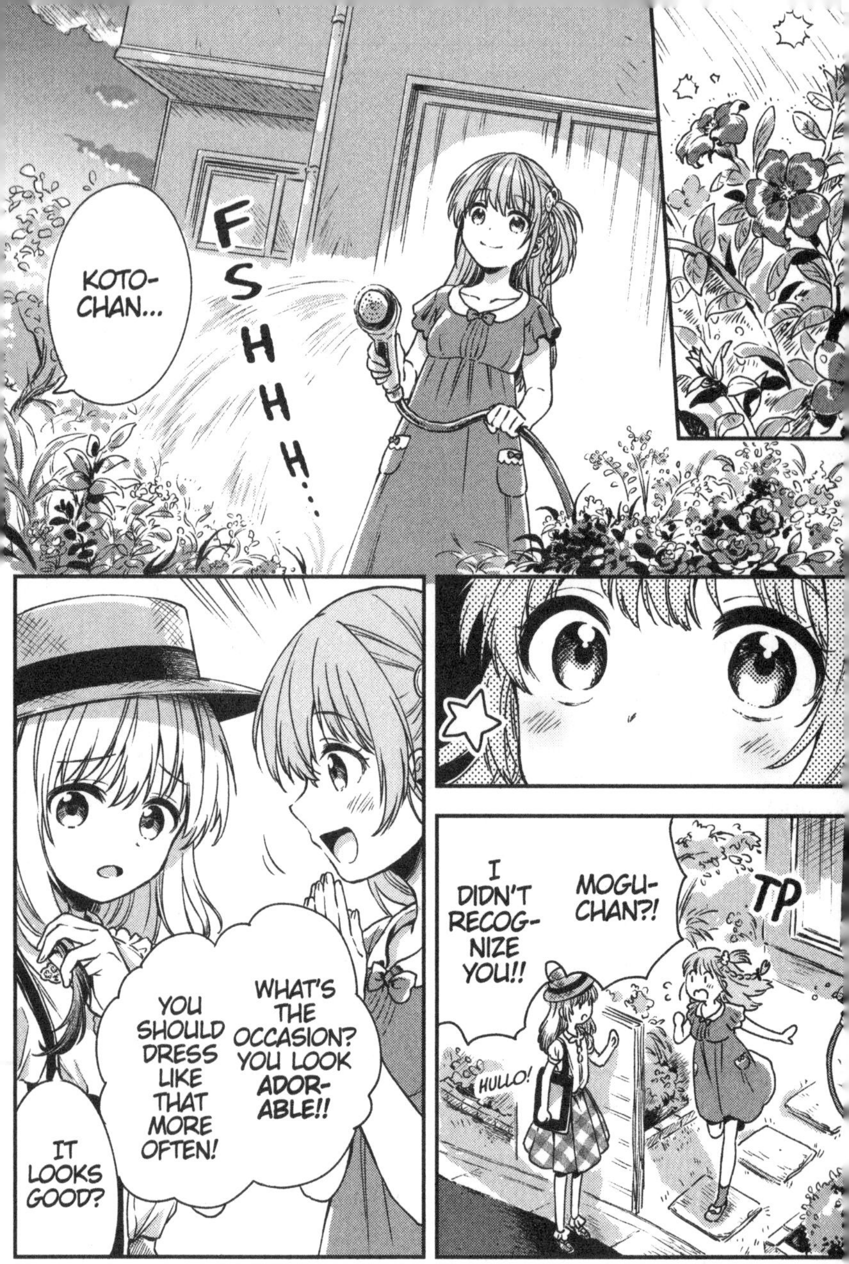
FSHHH...
KOTO-CHAN...
TP
MOGU-CHAN?!
I DIDN'T RECOGNIZE YOU!!
HULLO!
WHAT'S THE OCCASION? YOU LOOK ADORABLE!!
YOU SHOULD DRESS LIKE THAT MORE OFTEN!
IT LOOKS GOOD?

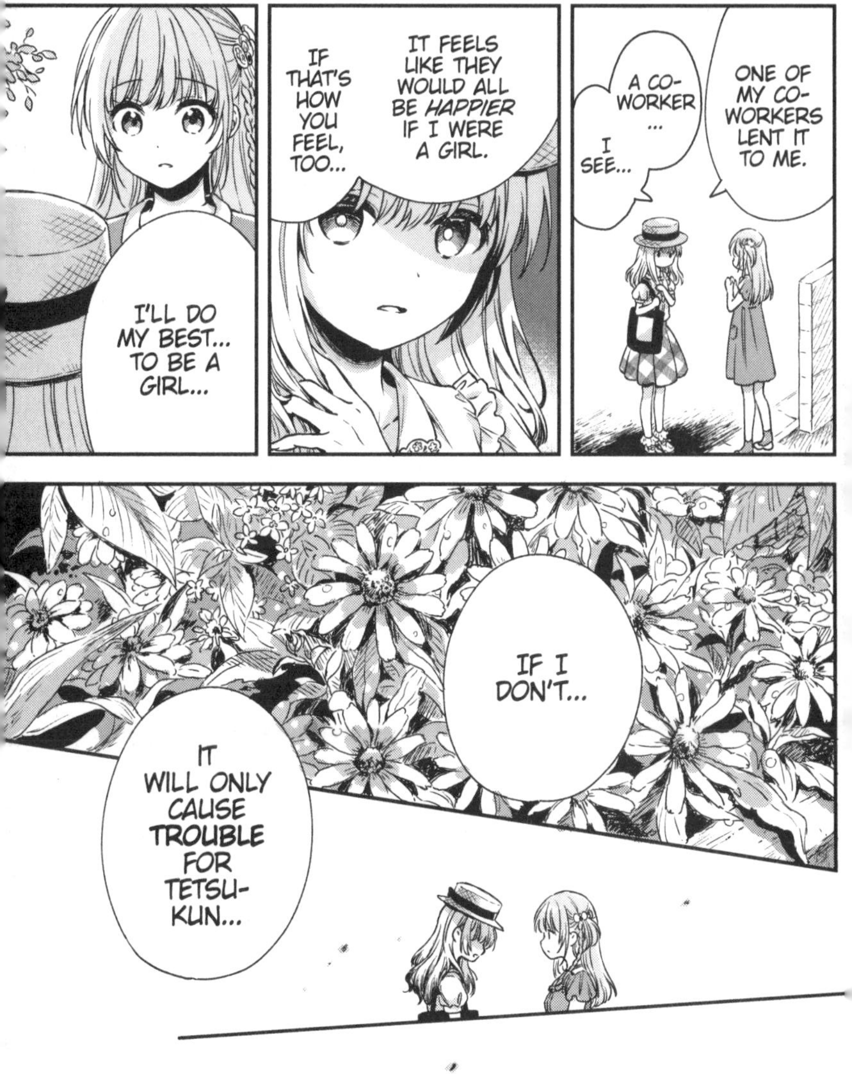
ONE OF MY CO-WORKERS LENT IT TO ME.
A CO-WORKER... I SEE...
IT FEELS LIKE THEY WOULD ALL BE *HAPPIER* IF I WERE A GIRL.
IF THAT'S HOW YOU FEEL, TOO...
I'LL DO MY BEST... TO BE A GIRL...
IF I DON'T...
IT WILL ONLY CAUSE TROUBLE FOR TETSU-KUN...

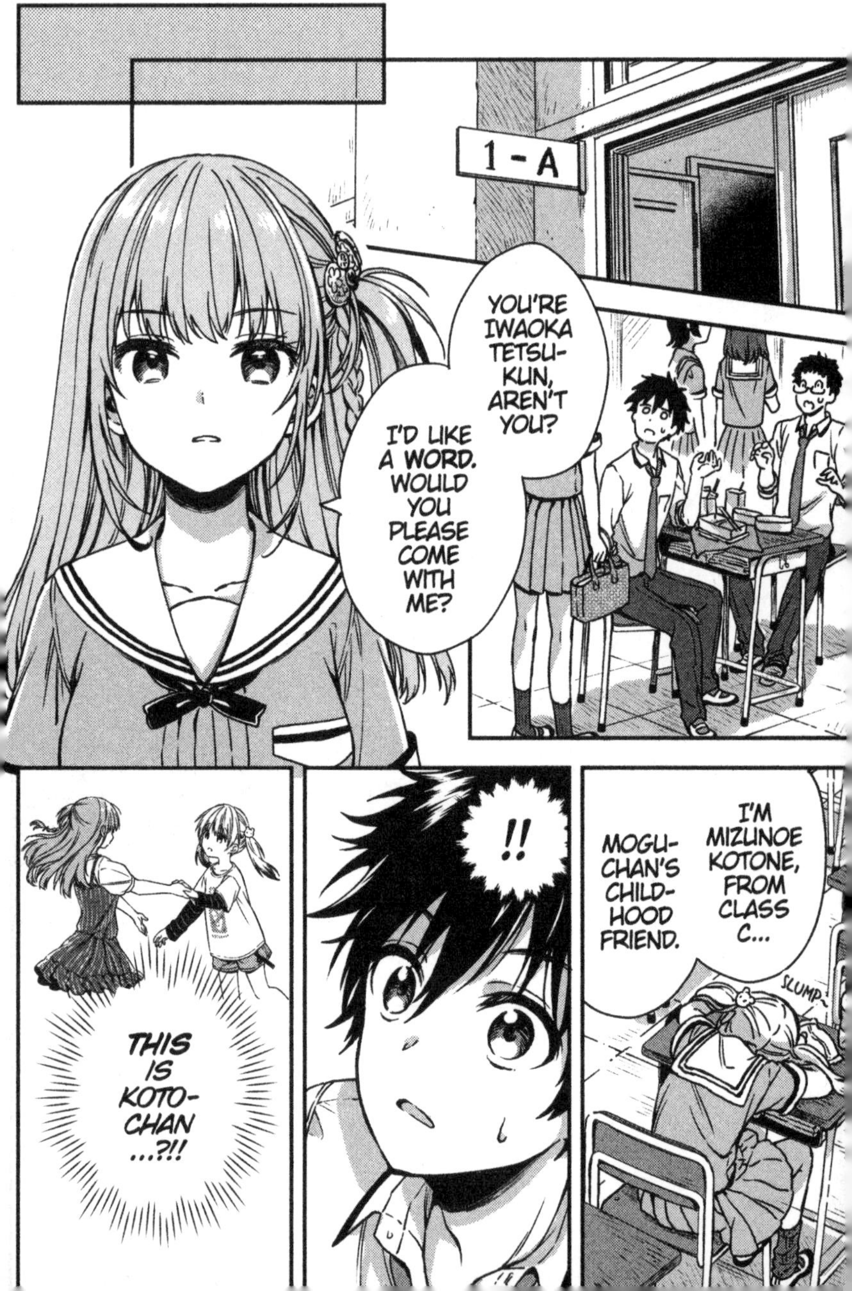

1 - A
YOU'RE IWAOKA TETSU-KUN, AREN'T YOU?
I'D LIKE A WORD. WOULD YOU PLEASE COME WITH ME?
I'M MIZUNOE KOTONE, FROM CLASS C...
MOGU-CHAN'S CHILDHOOD FRIEND.
SLUMP~
!!
THIS IS KOTO-CHAN...?!!

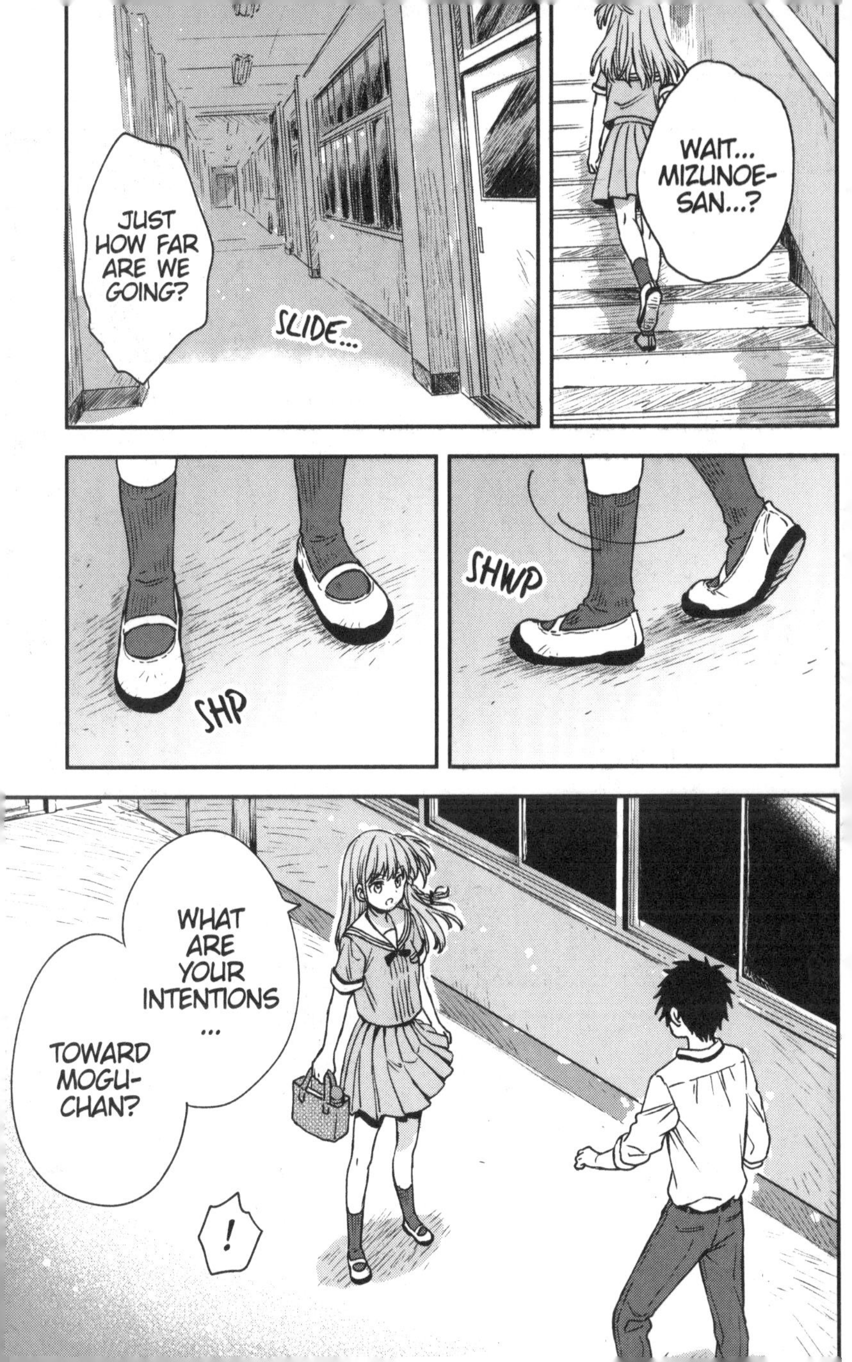
WAIT... MIZUNOE-SAN...?
JUST HOW FAR ARE WE GOING?
SLIDE...
SHWP
SHP
WHAT ARE YOUR INTENTIONS ... TOWARD MOGU-CHAN?
!

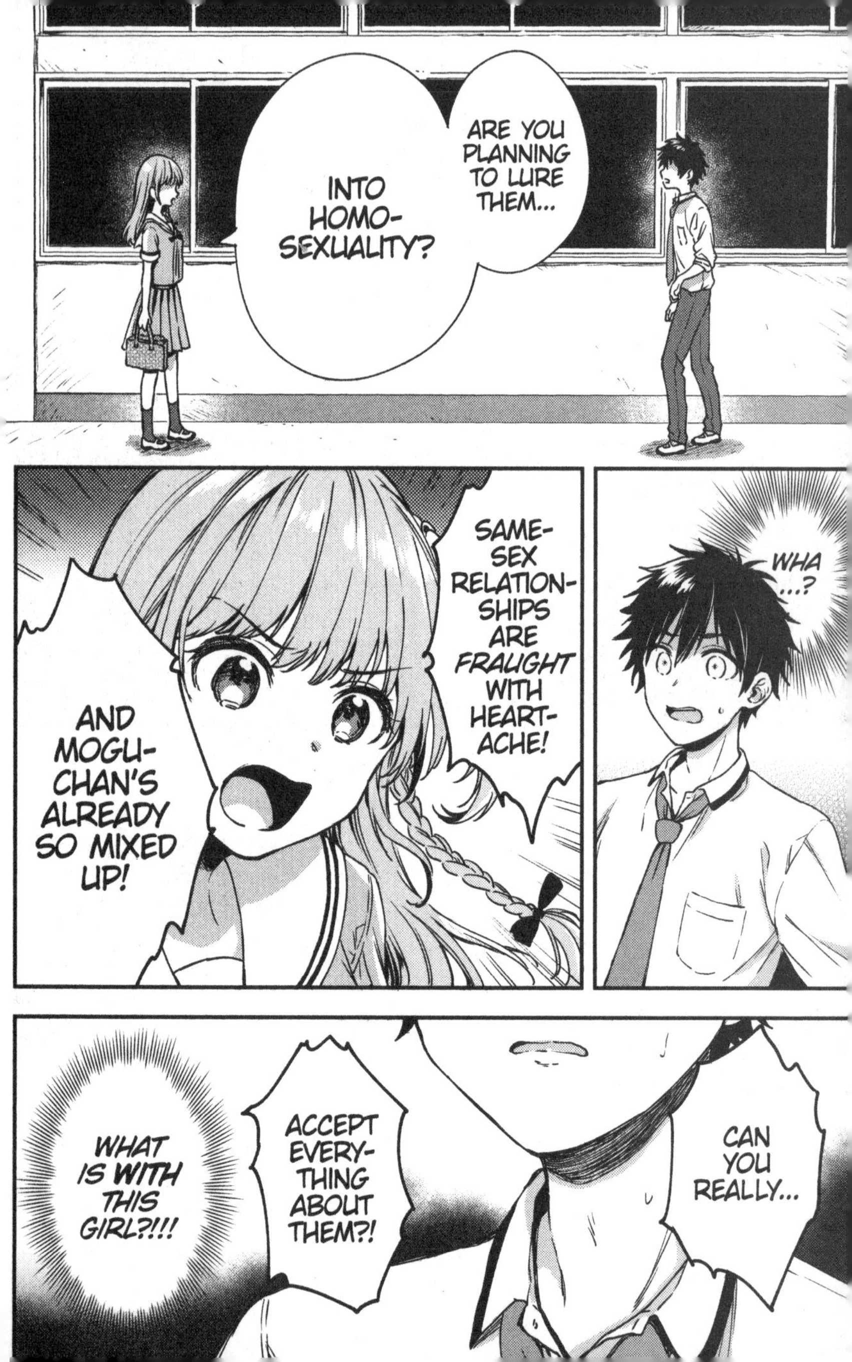
ARE YOU PLANNING TO LURE THEM...
INTO HOMOSEXUALITY?
WHA...?
SAME-SEX RELATIONSHIPS ARE FRAUGHT WITH HEARTACHE!
AND MOGU-CHAN'S ALREADY SO MIXED UP!
CAN YOU REALLY...
ACCEPT EVERYTHING ABOUT THEM?!
WHAT IS WITH THIS GIRL?!!!

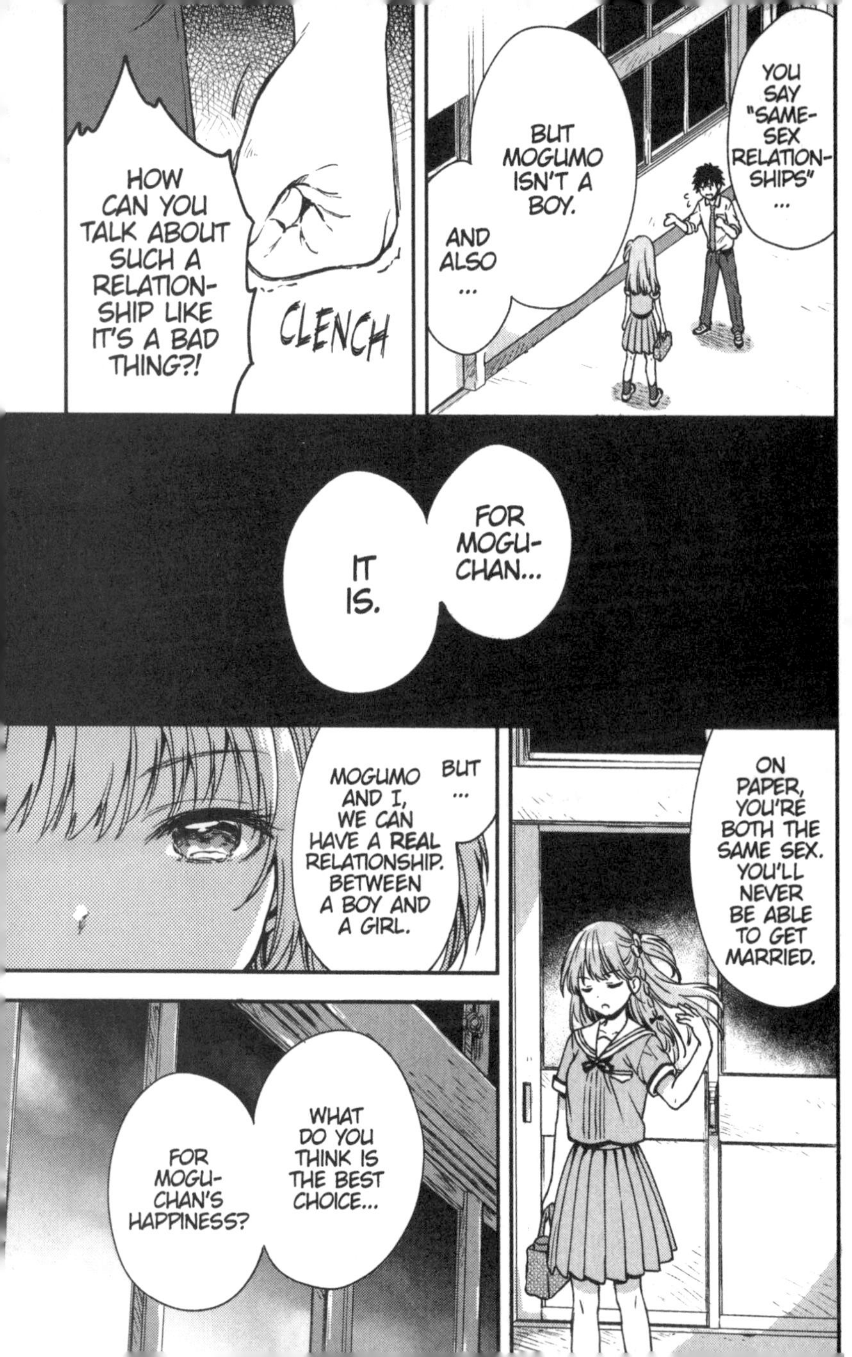
YOU SAY "SAME-SEX RELATIONSHIPS" ...
BUT MOGUMO ISN'T A BOY.
AND ALSO ...
HOW CAN YOU TALK ABOUT SUCH A RELATIONSHIP LIKE IT'S A BAD THING?!
CLENCH
FOR MOGU-CHAN...
IT IS.
ON PAPER, YOU'RE BOTH THE SAME SEX. YOU'LL NEVER BE ABLE TO GET MARRIED.
BUT ...
MOGUMO AND I, WE CAN HAVE A REAL RELATIONSHIP. BETWEEN A BOY AND A GIRL.
WHAT DO YOU THINK IS THE BEST CHOICE...
FOR MOGU-CHAN'S HAPPINESS?

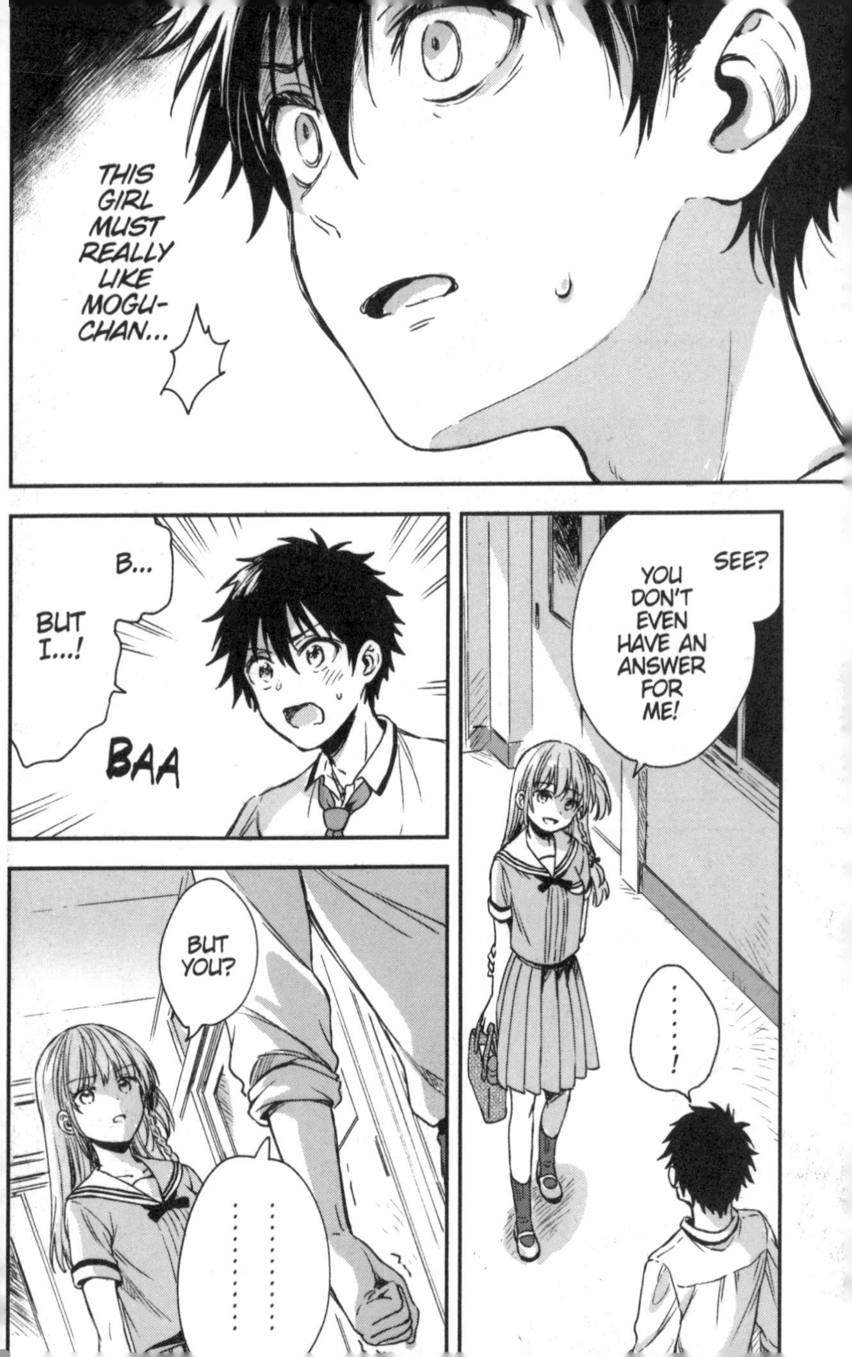
THIS GIRL MUST REALLY LIKE MOGU-CHAN...
SEE?
YOU DON'T EVEN HAVE AN ANSWER FOR ME!
......!
B...
BUT I...!
BAA
BUT YOU?
......

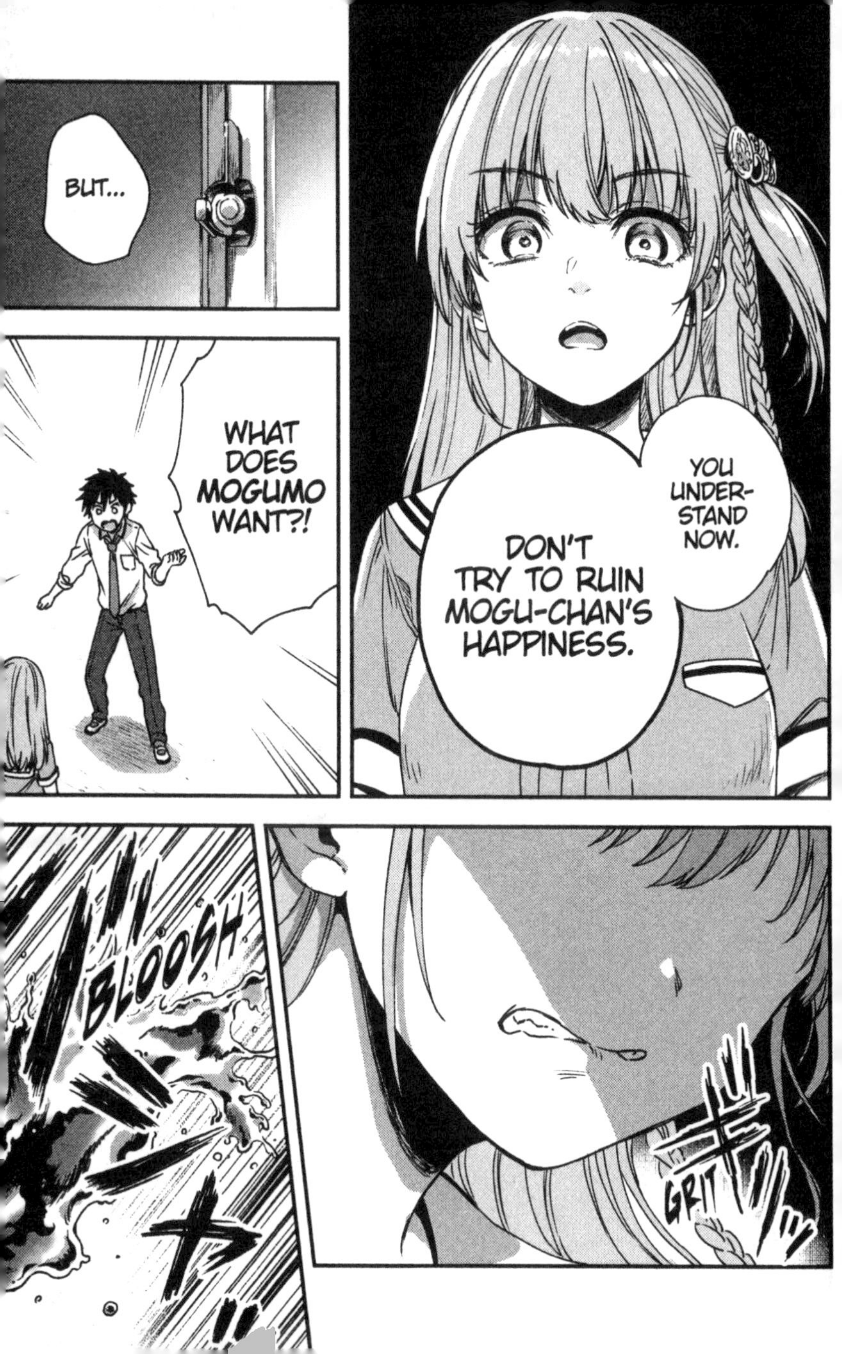
YOU UNDER-STAND NOW.
DON'T TRY TO RUIN MOGU-CHAN'S HAPPINESS.
BUT...
WHAT DOES MOGUMO WANT?!
GRIT
BLOOSH

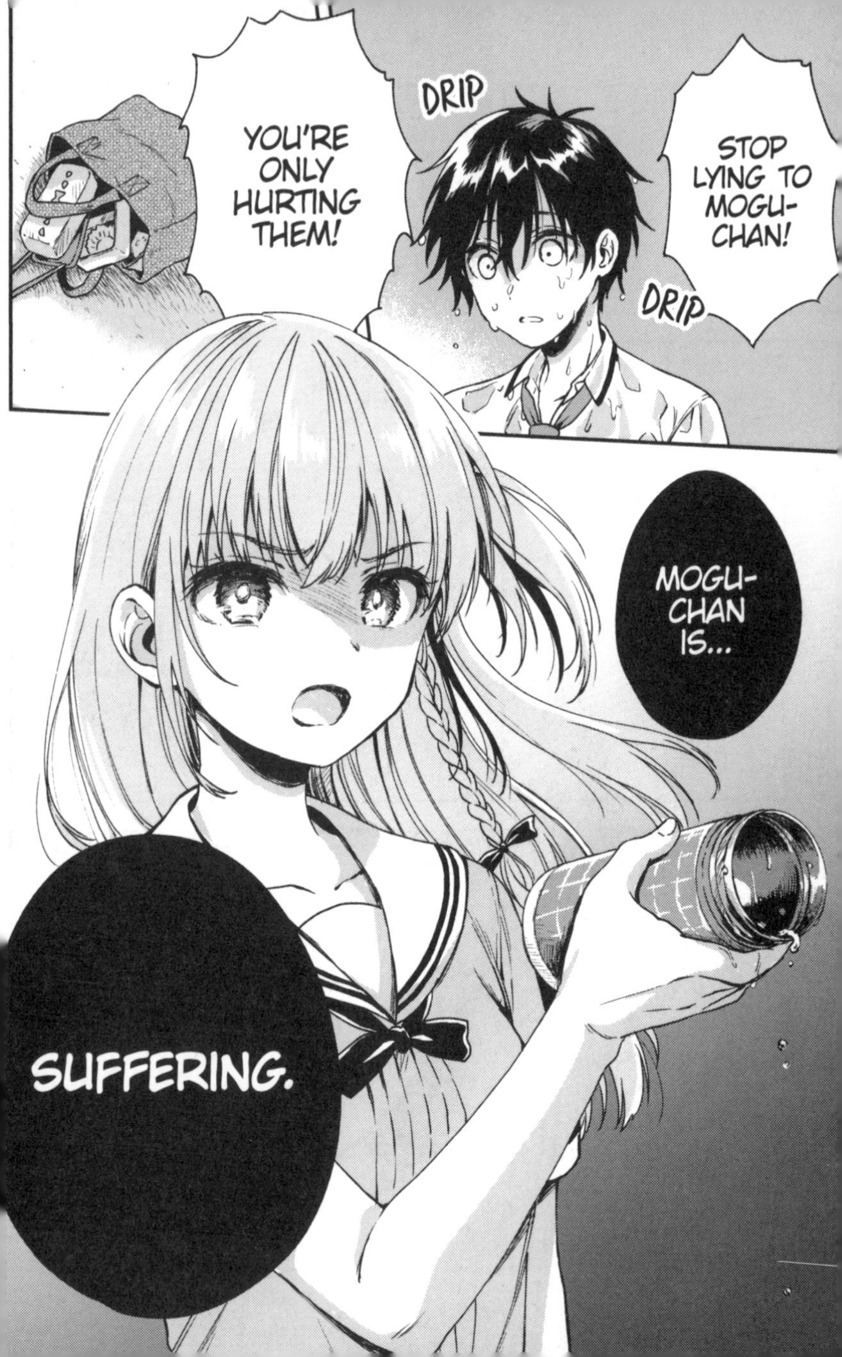
STOP LYING TO MOGU-CHAN!
DRIP
DRIP
YOU'RE ONLY HURTING THEM!
MOGU-CHAN IS...
SUFFERING.

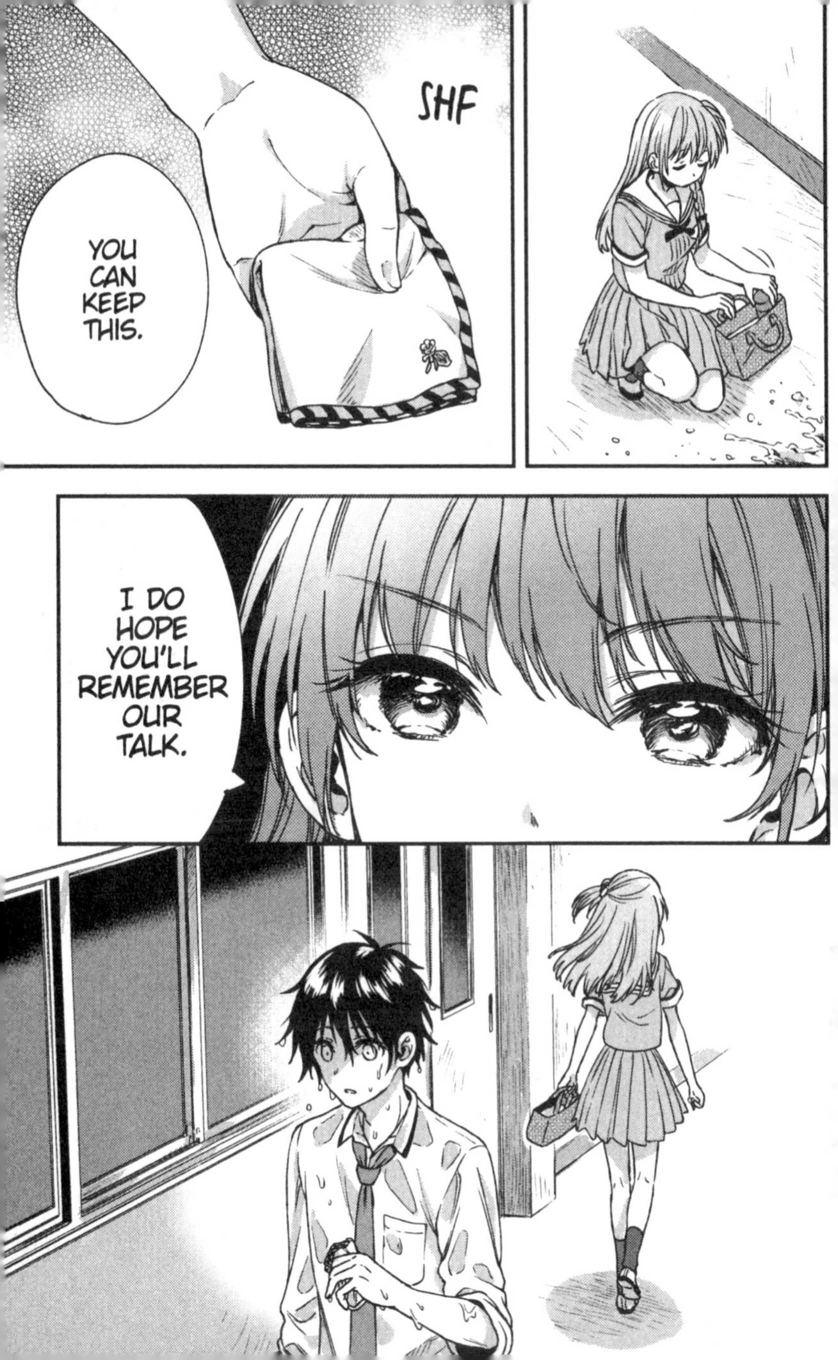
SHF
YOU CAN KEEP THIS.
I DO HOPE YOU'LL REMEMBER OUR TALK.

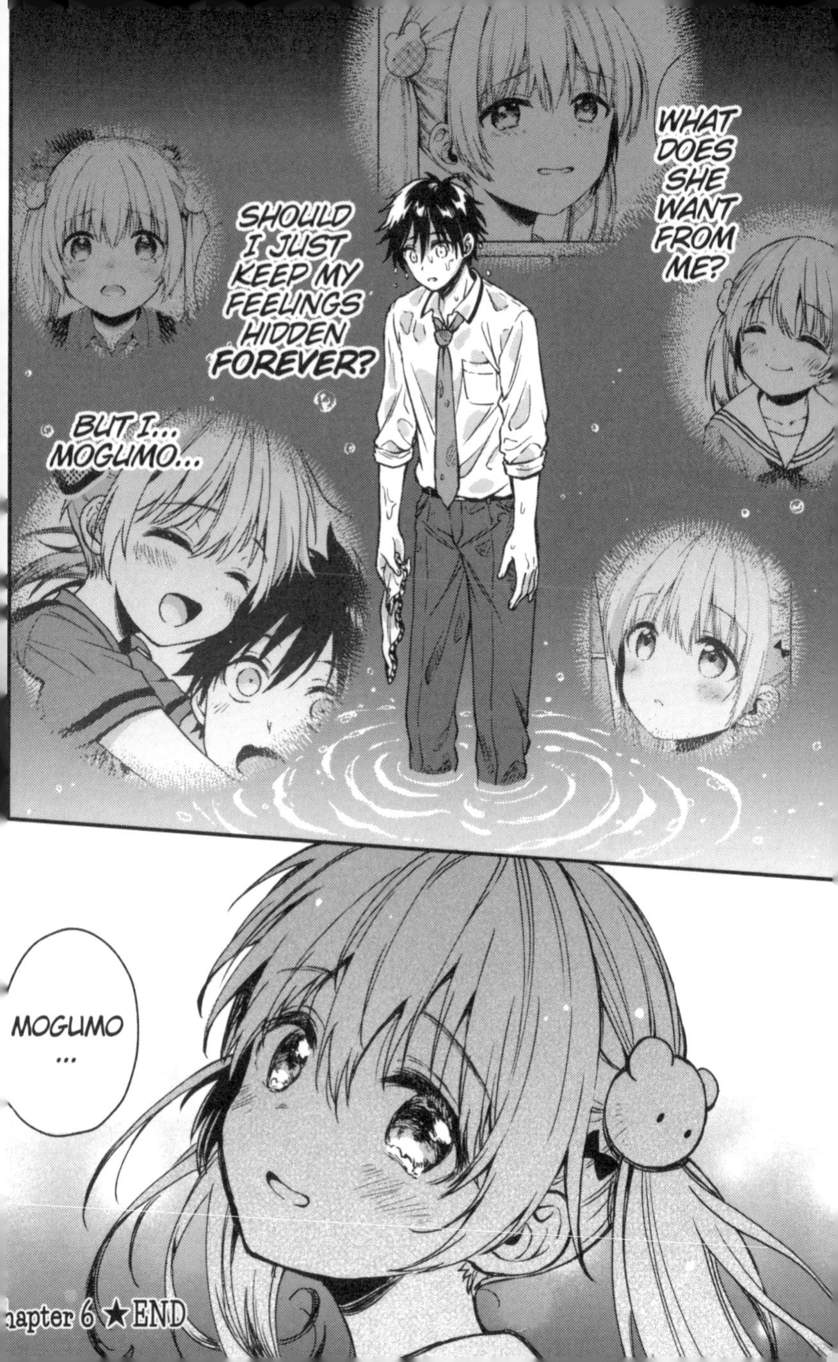
WHAT DOES SHE WANT FROM ME?
SHOULD I JUST KEEP MY FEELINGS HIDDEN FOREVER?
BUT I... MOGUMO...
MOGUMO ...
hapter 6 ★END

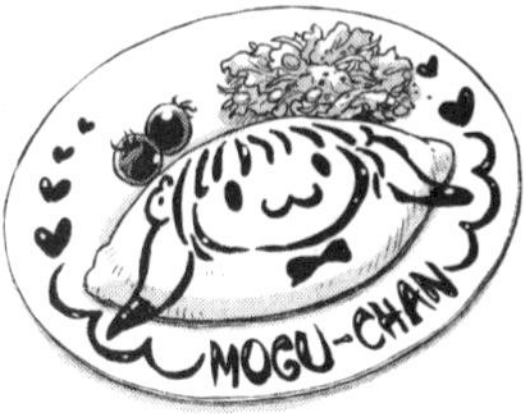
MOGU-CHAN

• BY TEN-CHAN

MEI

BIRTH NAME:	TATEBAYASHI AKIRA
BIRTHDAY:	MAY 9th
HEIGHT:	165cm
FAVORITE FOOD:	CREAM PUFFS, SOY MILK
FAMILY:	FATHER, MOTHER
HOBBIES:	REARRANGING HER HOME, MAKEUP
SPECIAL TRAIT:	FIXATING ON CERTAIN IDEAS

MOGUMO

BIRTH NAME:	MOGUMO RYUUNOSUKE
BIRTHDAY:	MARCH 14th
HEIGHT:	158cm
FAVORITE FOOD:	POTATO CHIPS
FAMILY:	FATHER, MOTHER, YOUNGER SISTER
HOBBIES:	VIDEO GAMES
SPECIAL TRAIT:	QUICKLY TAKES TO OTHER PEOPLE

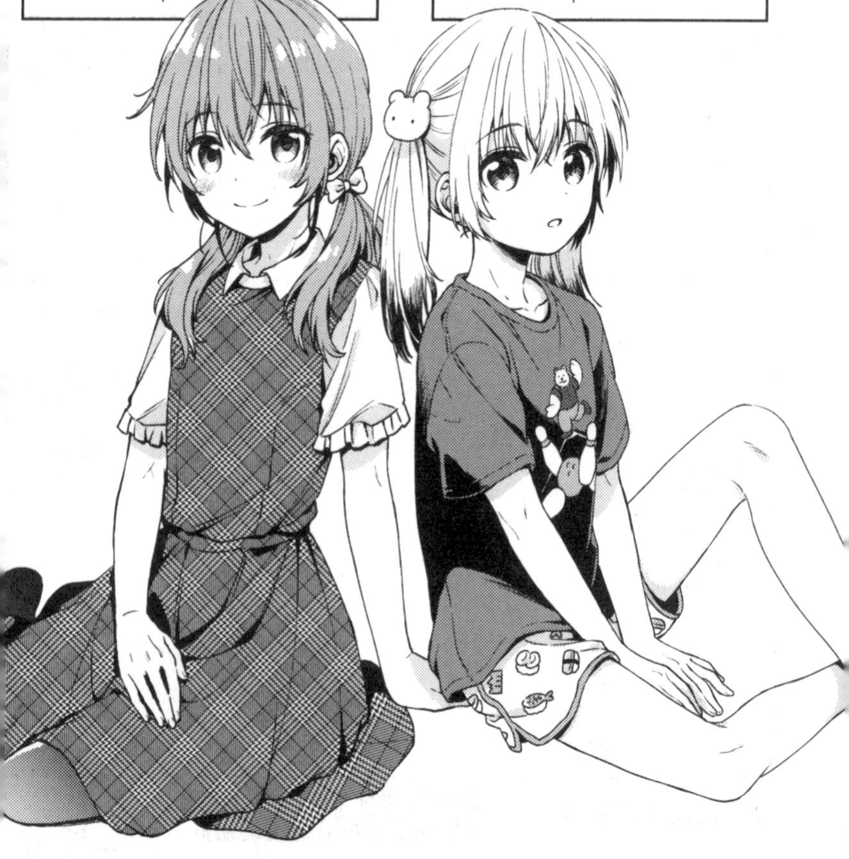

AFTERWORD

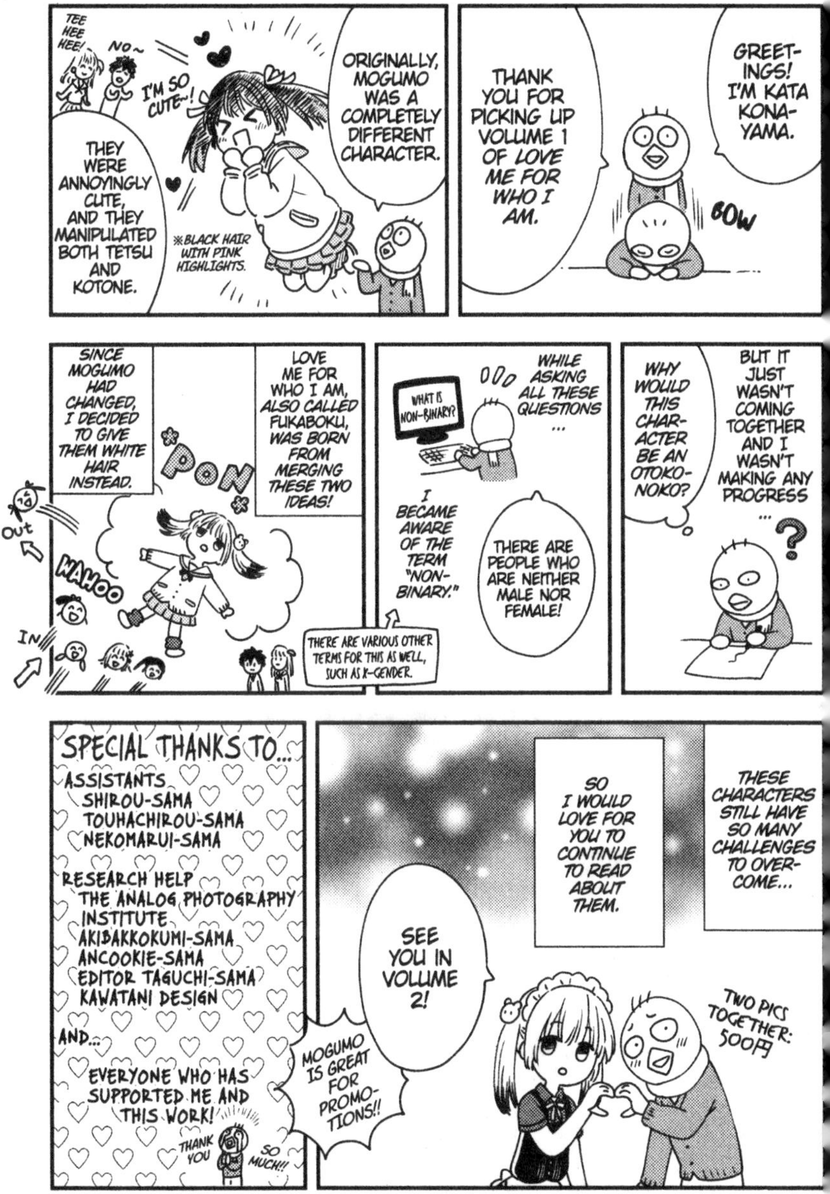
GREETINGS! I'M KATA KONAYAMA.
BOW
THANK YOU FOR PICKING UP VOLUME 1 OF LOVE ME FOR WHO I AM.
ORIGINALLY, MOGUMO WAS A COMPLETELY DIFFERENT CHARACTER.
I'M SO CUTE~!
NO~
TEE HEE HEE!
THEY WERE ANNOYINGLY CUTE, AND THEY MANIPULATED BOTH TETSU AND KOTONE.
※BLACK HAIR WITH PINK HIGHLIGHTS.
BUT IT JUST WASN'T COMING TOGETHER AND I WASN'T MAKING ANY PROGRESS...
WHY WOULD THIS CHARACTER BE AN OTOKO-NOKO?
?
WHILE ASKING ALL THESE QUESTIONS...
WHAT IS NON-BINARY?
I BECAME AWARE OF THE TERM "NON-BINARY."
THERE ARE PEOPLE WHO ARE NEITHER MALE NOR FEMALE!
THERE ARE VARIOUS OTHER TERMS FOR THIS AS WELL, SUCH AS X-GENDER.
LOVE ME FOR WHO I AM, ALSO CALLED FUKABOKU, WAS BORN FROM MERGING THESE TWO IDEAS!
SINCE MOGUMO HAD CHANGED, I DECIDED TO GIVE THEM WHITE HAIR INSTEAD.
PON
OUT
WAHOO
IN
THESE CHARACTERS STILL HAVE SO MANY CHALLENGES TO OVERCOME...
SO I WOULD LOVE FOR YOU TO CONTINUE TO READ ABOUT THEM.
SEE YOU IN VOLUME 2!
TWO PICS TOGETHER: 500円
MOGUMO IS GREAT FOR PROMOTIONS!!
SPECIAL THANKS TO...
ASSISTANTS
SHIROU-SAMA
TOUHACHIROU-SAMA
NEKOMARUI-SAMA
RESEARCH HELP
THE ANALOG PHOTOGRAPHY INSTITUTE
AKIBAKKOKUMI-SAMA
ANCOOKIE-SAMA
EDITOR TAGUCHI-SAMA
KAWATANI DESIGN
AND...
EVERYONE WHO HAS SUPPORTED ME AND THIS WORK!
THANK YOU
SO MUCH!!

OFFICIAL TWITTER @FUKA_BOKU FOLLOW US!!

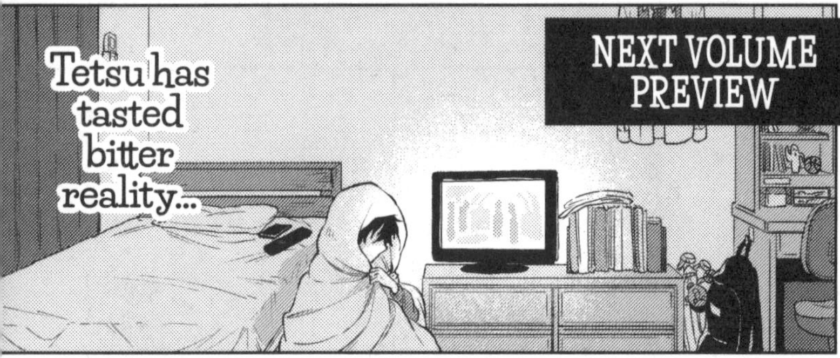
NEXT VOLUME PREVIEW
Tetsu has tasted bitter reality...

Mogumo is trying to change...

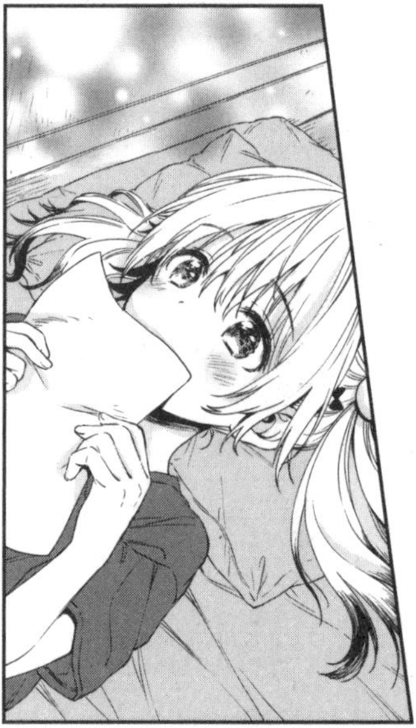

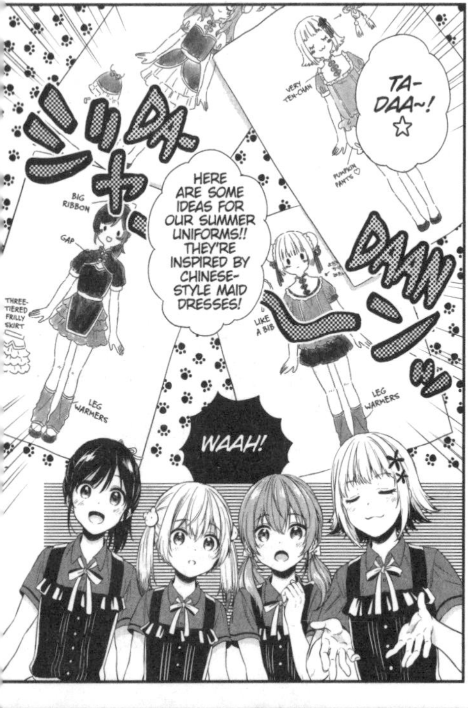
TA-DAA~! ☆
VERY TEN-CHAN
PUMPKIN PANTS ♡
DAAN
HERE ARE SOME IDEAS FOR OUR SUMMER UNIFORMS!! THEY'RE INSPIRED BY CHINESE-STYLE MAID DRESSES!
DA
BIG RIBBON
GAP
LIKE A BIB
THREE-TIERED FRILLY SKIRT
LEG WARMERS
LEG WARMERS
WAAH!

As Café Question's summer event approaches...

Volume 2 Coming soon!!

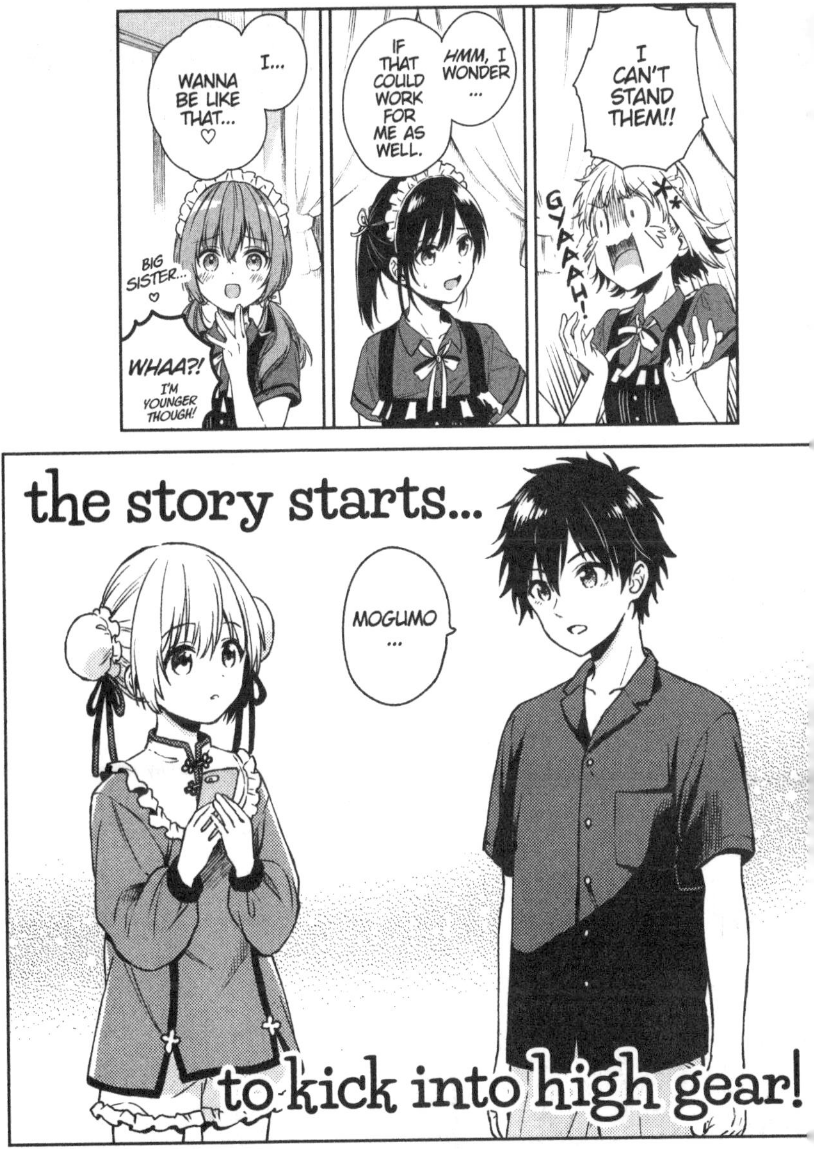
I CAN'T STAND THEM!!
GYAAAH!
HMM, I WONDER ...
IF THAT COULD WORK FOR ME AS WELL.
I...
WANNA BE LIKE THAT... ♡
BIG SISTER... ♡
WHAA?!
I'M YOUNGER THOUGH!
the story starts...
MOGUMO ...
to kick into high gear!

Love me for who I am

SEVEN SEAS ENTERTAINMENT PRESENTS

Love me for who I am

story and art by KATA KONAYAMA

VOL. 1

TRANSLATION
Amber Tamosaitis

ADAPTATION
Cae Hawksmoor

LETTERING AND RETOUCH
Ray Steeves

COVER DESIGN
Nicky Lim
(LOGO) **George Panella**

PROOFREADER
Danielle King

EDITOR
Jenn Grunigen

PREPRESS TECHNICIAN
Rhiannon Rasmussen-Silverstein

PRODUCTION MANAGER
Lissa Pattillo

MANAGING EDITOR
Julie Davis

ASSOCIATE PUBLISHER
Adam Arnold

PUBLISHER
Jason DeAngelis

LOVE ME FOR WHO I AM VOL. 1
© Kata Konayama 2019
Original Japanese edition published in 2019 by GOT Corporation.
English translation rights arranged worldwide with GOT Corporation through
Digital Catapult Inc., Tokyo.

Seven Seas press and purchase enquiries can be sent to Marketing Manager
Lianne Sentar at press@gomanga.com. Information regarding the distribution
and purchase of digital editions is available from Digital Manager CK Russell
at digital@gomanga.com.

Seven Seas and the Seven Seas logo are trademarks of
Seven Seas Entertainment. All rights reserved.

ISBN: 978-1-64505-467-2

Printed in Canada

First Printing: June 2020

10 9 8 7 6 5 4 3 2 1

FOLLOW US ONLINE: www.sevenseasentertainment.com

READING DIRECTIONS

This book reads from **right to left**, Japanese style.
If this is your first time reading manga, you start
reading from the top right panel on each page and
take it from there. If you get lost, just follow the
numbered diagram here. It may seem backwards at
first, but you'll get the hang of it! Have fun!!

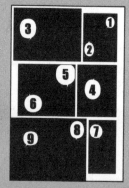